Generation
X

AMERICANS
BORN 1965 to 1976

Generation X

X

AMERICANS
BORN 1965 to 1976

5th EDITION

BY THE NEW STRATEGIST EDITORS

New Strategist Publications, Inc.
Ithaca, New York

New Strategist Publications, Inc.
P.O. Box 242, Ithaca, New York 14851
800/848-0842; 607/273-0913
www.newstrategist.com

Copyright 2006. NEW STRATEGIST PUBLICATIONS, INC.

ISBN 1-885070-89-6

Printed in the United States of America

Table of Contents

Chapter 5. Labor Force

Chapter 6. Living Arrangements

Chapter 7. Population

Tables

Chapter 3. Housing

Chapter 4. Income

Chapter 5. Labor Force

Chapter 8. Spending

Chapter 9. Time Use

Chapter 10. Wealth

Illustrations

Chapter 5. Lab or Force

Chapter 6. Living Arrangements

Chapter 7. Population

Chapter 8. Spending

Chapter 9. Time Use

Chapter 10. Wealth

Introduction

Generation X gained fame simply for following the Baby-Boom generation onto the stage of youth, a stage Boomers created and made the center of the nation's attention. Generation X was everything Boomers were not—small in number, cynical rather than idealistic, they were expected to make their way easily through life because of the swath Boomers had carved. But it did not turn out that way. Generation Xers have struggled to compete with the masses of Boomers ahead of them and the large Millennial generation that follows at their heels. They have found jobs scarce, promotions hard to come by, and housing expensive. The fifth edition of *Generation X: Americans Born 1965 to 1976* tells the story of the small generation spanning the ages of 30 to 41 in 2006.

Although their numbers are small, lifestage dictates that Generation X is a vital part of the nation's commerce and culture. People in their thirties are having children and buying homes. They are moving up in their careers, their incomes are growing, and their spending is too. *Generation X: Americans Born 1965 to 1976* shows how Gen Xers are changing and what to expect from them in the future.

Generation Xers are a diverse segment of the population, with minorities accounting for a large share of the whole. One issue binds together this diverse generation: cutthroat competition in the job market. While other generations are facing the same issue, getting ahead is proving more difficult for Generation X because they lack the power of numbers. Only 17 percent of Americans are Gen Xers, while 26 percent are Boomers, and 25 percent are Millennials (see the Population chapter). In the 2004 presidential election, Gen Xers accounted for only 19 percent of voters versus the 40 percent share accounted for by Boomers (see the Time Use chapter). Perhaps because they are overshadowed by others, Gen Xers are suffering economically. The percentage of men aged 35 to 44 who have worked for their current employer for ten or more years has plummeted (see the Labor Force chapter). The median income of men aged 35 to 44 is lower today than it was in 1990, after adjusting for inflation (see the Income chapter). And the net worth of householders aged 35 to 44 has fallen sharply during the past few years—the only age group to lose ground (see the Wealth chapter).

It is not easy to study Generation Xers. Few government surveys focus on the generation, and the ages spanned by the members of the generation make it difficult to tease them out of the government's traditional five- or ten-year age categories. To analyze Gen X lifestyles, then, most of the tables in *Generation X: Americans Born 1965 to 1976* approximate the generation. Single-year-of-age data are shown whenever they are available, but five-year age groups are more common. When five-year age categories are shown, Gen Xers can be included in the 25-to-29, 30-to-34, 35-to-39, and 40-to-44 age groups, depending on the year for which data are presented. In a few tables, data are available only for much broader age groups, forcing a more general analysis of trends among Gen Xers.

Whether Generation X age groups are exact or approximate, however, the results are clear. Generation Xers are entering the prime of life. They account for a growing share of households with incomes of $100,000 or more. Their spending is on the rise, their families are expanding, and they are moving into larger homes. One of the more distinct features of the generation is its diversity, with blacks, Hispanics, and Asians all accounting for a significant proportion of the whole. Gen Xers are searching for success, and *Generation X: Americans Born 1965 to 1976* is your guide to how well they are doing.

How to use this book

Generation X: Americans Born 1965 to 1976 is designed for easy use. It is divided into ten chapters, organized alphabetically: Education, Health, Housing, Income, Labor Force, Living Arrangements, Population, Spending, Time Use, and Wealth.

The fifth edition of *Generation X* includes the latest statistics on the labor force participation, living arrangements, incomes, health, spending, and wealth of this rising generation. The socioeconomic estimates presented here are the all-important mid-decade demographics, offering enough of a trend line into the 21st century to guide researchers in their business plans or government policies. *Generation X* presents labor force data for 2005, including the government's updated labor force projections. It contains new data on the health of the population, including updated estimates of the overweight and obese. The Census Bureau's latest population projections are also included in the book, showing how the aging of Generation X will reduce the number of Americans in their forties in the decade ahead. *Generation X* also presents the latest estimates of household wealth from the recently released Federal Reserve Board's 2004 Survey of Consumer Finances. New to this edition is the Time Use chapter, with many tables based on the Bureau of Labor Statistics' new American Time Use Survey. The results show Gen Xers moving into the lifestage with the least amount of leisure time as they manage busy households and devote long hours to their career.

Most of the tables in *Generation X* are based on data collected by the federal government, in particular the Census Bureau, the Bureau of Labor Statistics, the National Center for Education Statistics, the National Center for Health Statistics, and the Federal Reserve Board. The federal government is the best source of up-to-date, reliable information on the changing characteristics of Americans.

Generation X includes the demographic and lifestyle data most important to researchers. Most of the tables are based on data collected by the federal government, but they are not simply reprints of government spreadsheets—as is the case in many reference books. Instead, each table is individually compiled and created by New Strategist's editors, with calculations designed to reveal the trends. The task of extracting and processing raw data from the government's web sites at times requires hours of effort to create a single table. The effort is worthwhile, however, because each table tells a story about Gen Xers, a story explained by the accompanying text and chart, which analyze the data and highlight future trends. If you need more information than the tables and text provide, you can plumb the original source listed at the bottom of each table.

The book contains a comprehensive table list to help you locate the information you need. For a more detailed search, see the index at the back of the book. Also at the back of the book is the bibliography and the glossary, which defines the terms and describes the many surveys referenced in the tables and text.

With *Generation X: Americans Born 1965 to 1976* on your bookshelf, an in-depth understanding of this struggling and influential generation is at hand.

1

Education

■ In 1950, barely half of young adults had graduated from high school. Today, nearly 90 percent have a high school diploma.

■ The women of Generation X are better educated than their male counterparts. They are, in fact, the best-educated women in the nation. Thirty-three percent have at least a bachelor's degree. Among Generation X men, only 30 percent are college graduates.

■ Among Generation Xers, Asians are by far the best educated, while Hispanics have the least education. The 59 percent majority of Asian men aged 28 to 39 are college graduates. In contrast, only 59 percent of Hispanic men in the age group have even graduated from high school.

■ People aged 25 to 39 account for only 20 percent of the nation's college undergraduates. But they are fully 52 percent of graduate students.

■ More than 40 percent of people aged 25 to 39 took work-related courses in 2003, and more than two-thirds participated in less-formal work-related learning activities.

Big Gains in Educational Attainment

Young women have closed the educational attainment gap with men.

Of all the social revolutions that have occurred over the past half-century, one of the most dramatic is the rise in the educational attainment of the nation's population. In 1950, barely half of young adults aged 25 to 34 had graduated from high school. Today, nearly 90 percent have a high school diploma.

Young adult women are now better educated than their male counterparts. Thirty-two percent of women aged 25 to 34 are college graduates versus a smaller 28 percent of men. In 1960, men aged 25 to 34 were almost twice as likely as their female counterparts to be college graduates.

■ Family life changed dramatically as Baby Boomer and Generation X women went to college and entered the workforce.

The educational attainment of young adults has grown sharply

(percent of people aged 25 to 34 who are high school graduates, by sex, 1950 and 2004)

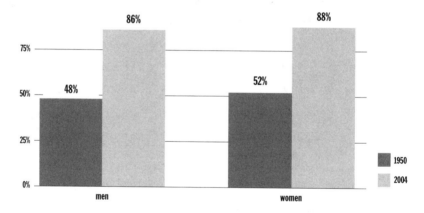

Table 1.1 Educational Attainment of People Aged 25 to 34, 1950 to 2004

(percent distribution of people aged 25 to 34 by sex and educational attainment, 1950 to 2004)

	total	not a high school graduate	high school graduate or more	some college or more	college, four years or more
Men aged 25 to 34					
2004	100.0%	14.3%	85.7%	55.0%	28.0%
2000	100.0	12.8	87.1	54.9	28.6
1990	100.0	14.9	85.1	44.8	24.3
1980	100.0	14.0	86.0	50.5	27.5
1970	100.0	25.7	74.3	34.8	19.7
1960	100.0	43.7	56.3	26.3	14.5
1950	100.0	51.6	48.4	19.3	9.3
Women aged 25 to 34					
2004	100.0	11.6	88.4	61.8	32.4
2000	100.0	10.9	89.2	60.2	29.9
1990	100.0	12.6	87.4	46.1	23.5
1980	100.0	15.2	84.8	41.2	20.9
1970	100.0	26.7	73.3	25.0	12.0
1960	100.0	40.3	59.6	18.3	7.5
1950	100.0	48.1	51.9	15.0	6.0

Source: Bureau of the Census, Educational Attainment, Historical Tables; Internet site http://www.census.gov/population/www/socdemo/educ-attn.html; calculations by New Strategist

Generation X Is the Best Educated

Boomers rank second in education.

The percentage of Americans with a college degree peaks in middle age. One reason for the middle-aged peak is that it takes many people more than four years to complete their bachelor's degree. Thirty-one percent of Generation Xers have a college degree, the highest level of education among the generations. Baby Boomers are not far behind, at 30 percent. Twenty-six percent of Millennials are college graduates, a figure that is certain to rise as they get older. Among older Americans (aged 59 or older), only 21 percent are college graduates.

Although Generation X is the best-educated generation overall, the oldest Baby Boomer men are better educated than any other Americans. Thirty-four percent of men aged 55 to 59 have a college degree, thanks to draft deferments offered to college students during the Vietnam War. Among the men of Generation X, only 30 percent have a college degree.

■ The women of Generation X are better educated than Baby Boomer women, pushing the percentage of Generation Xers with a college degree above that of Boomers.

Generation X is better educated than Baby Boomers

(percent of people aged 25 or older with a bachelor's degree, by generation, 2004)

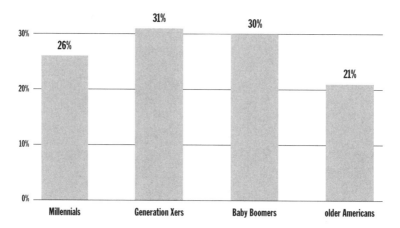

Table 1.2 Educational Attainment by Generation, 2004

(number and percent distribution of people aged 25 or older by highest level of education, 2004; numbers in thousands)

	total 25 or older	Millennials (25 to 27)	Generation Xers (28 to 39)	Boomers (40 to 58)	older Americans (59 or older)
Total people	**186,877**	**11,424**	**48,569**	**77,313**	**49,571**
Not a high school graduate	27,744	1,590	5,961	8,612	11,589
High school graduate	59,810	3,438	14,276	24,281	17,814
Some college, no degree	31,808	2,448	8,657	13,525	7,177
Associate's degree	15,764	932	4,496	7,658	2,675
Bachelor's degree	33,766	2,533	10,651	14,585	5,998
Master's degree	12,609	357	3,266	6,166	2,819
Professional degree	2,952	93	773	1,334	753
Doctoral degree	2,422	36	487	1,150	749
High school graduate or more	159,131	9,837	42,606	68,699	37,985
Some college or more	99,321	6,399	28,330	44,418	20,171
Bachelor's degree or more	51,749	3,019	15,177	23,235	10,319
Total people	**100.0%**	**100.0%**	**100.0%**	**100.0%**	**100.0%**
Not a high school graduate	14.8	13.9	12.3	11.1	23.4
High school graduate	32.0	30.1	29.4	31.4	35.9
Some college, no degree	17.0	21.4	17.8	17.5	14.5
Associate's degree	8.4	8.2	9.3	9.9	5.4
Bachelor's degree	18.1	22.2	21.9	18.9	12.1
Master's degree	6.7	3.1	6.7	8.0	5.7
Professional degree	1.6	0.8	1.6	1.7	1.5
Doctoral degree	1.3	0.3	1.0	1.5	1.5
High school graduate or more	85.2	86.1	87.7	88.9	76.6
Some college or more	53.1	56.0	58.3	57.5	40.7
Bachelor's degree or more	27.7	26.4	31.2	30.1	20.8

Source: Bureau of the Census, Educational Attainment in the United States: 2004, detailed tables; Internet site http://www .census.gov/population/www/socdemo/education/cps2004.html; calculations by New Strategist

Most Generation Xers Have Been to College

More than three out of ten are college graduates.

Generation X followed the Baby-Boom generation onto the nation's college campuses. Overall, the 58 percent majority of Gen Xers have been to college—18 percent have college experience but no degree, 9 percent have an associate's degree, 22 percent have a bachelor's degree, and 9 percent have a graduate degree.

Although Generation X is the best-educated generation overall, the oldest Boomer men are better educated than any other Americans. Thirty-four percent of men aged 55 to 59 have a college degree, thanks to draft deferments offered to college students during the Vietnam War. Among the men of Generation X, a smaller 30 percent have a college degree. Gen X women are better educated than Boomer women. Thirty-three percent of Gen X women are college graduates versus 28 percent of Baby-Boom women.

■ Because most Gen Xers have college experience, they will be eager to see their children go to college as well.

Among Generation Xers, nearly one in ten has a graduate degree

(percent distribution of people aged 28 to 39 by educational attainment, 2004)

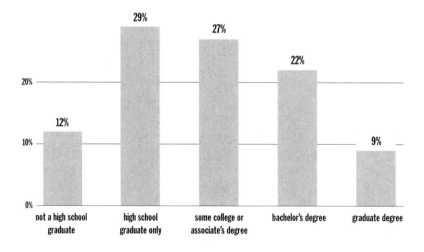

12%	29%	27%	22%	9%
not a high school graduate	high school graduate only	some college or associate's degree	bachelor's degree	graduate degree

Table 1.3 Educational Attainment of Generation Xers, 2004

(number and percent distribution of people aged 25 or older, aged 28 to 39, and aged 25 to 39 in five-year age groups, by highest level of education 2004; numbers in thousands)

			five-year age groups		
	total 25 or older	28 to 39	25 to 29	30 to 34	35 to 39
Total people	**186,877**	**48,569**	**19,008**	**20,193**	**20,791**
Not a high school graduate	27,744	5,961	2,554	2,518	2,477
High school graduate only	59,810	14,276	5,557	5,687	6,470
Some college, no degree	31,808	8,657	3,891	3,692	3,524
Associate's degree	15,764	4,496	1,549	1,913	1,967
Bachelor's degree	33,766	10,651	4,358	4,400	4,428
Master's degree	12,609	3,266	785	1,449	1,388
Professional degree	2,952	773	218	338	309
Doctoral degree	2,422	487	96	198	228
High school graduate or more	159,131	42,606	16,454	17,677	18,314
Some college or more	99,321	28,330	10,897	11,990	11,844
Bachelor's degree or more	51,749	15,177	5,457	6,385	6,353
Total people	**100.0%**	**100.0%**	**100.0%**	**100.0%**	**100.0%**
Not a high school graduate	14.8	12.3	13.4	12.5	11.9
High school graduate only	32.0	29.4	29.2	28.2	31.1
Some college, no degree	17.0	17.8	20.5	18.3	16.9
Associate's degree	8.4	9.3	8.1	9.5	9.5
Bachelor's degree	18.1	21.9	22.9	21.8	21.3
Master's degree	6.7	6.7	4.1	7.2	6.7
Professional degree	1.6	1.6	1.1	1.7	1.5
Doctoral degree	1.3	1.0	0.5	1.0	1.1
High school graduate or more	85.2	87.7	86.6	87.5	88.1
Some college or more	53.1	58.3	57.3	59.4	57.0
Bachelor's degree or more	27.7	31.2	28.7	31.6	30.6

Source: Bureau of the Census, Educational Attainment in the United States: 2004, detailed tables; Internet site http://www .census.gov/population/www/socdemo/education/cps2004.html; calculations by New Strategist

Nearly 30 Percent of Generation X Men Are College Graduates

Many of those without a college degree will get one later in life.

The men of Generation X are well educated, although not as highly educated as Baby-Boom men. Eighty-six percent of men aged 28 to 39 are high school graduates. That leaves a substantial 14 percent who do not have a high school diploma. These men will have a difficult time making ends meet in an economy that rewards the well educated.

Fifty-five percent of men aged 28 to 39 have attended college. Nearly 30 percent are college graduates—meaning many men who start college drop out before getting their degree. Some are likely to return to school as older students to complete their education.

■ Most men are aware of the importance of education for their career. Even if they do not obtain a college degree, attending college for a year or two should boost their earnings significantly.

Most men aged 28 to 39 have at least some college experience

(percent distribution of men aged 28 to 39 by educational attainment, 2004)

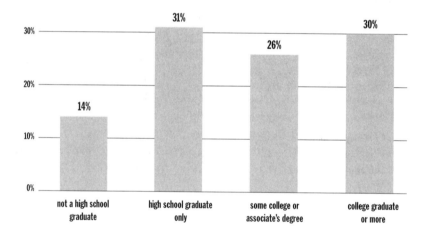

Table 1.4 Educational Attainment of Generation X Men, 2004

(number and percent distribution of men aged 25 or older, aged 28 to 39, and aged 25 to 39 in five-year age groups, by highest level of education 2004; numbers in thousands)

			five-year age groups		
	total 25 or older	28 to 39	25 to 29	30 to 34	35 to 39
Total men	**89,558**	**24,146**	**9,543**	**10,056**	**10,309**
Not a high school graduate	13,569	3,254	1,413	1,385	1,333
High school graduate only	27,889	7,504	3,032	2,988	3,354
Some college, no degree	15,012	4,141	1,919	1,762	1,696
Associate's degree	6,751	2,040	692	913	846
Bachelor's degree	16,632	4,987	2,015	2,057	2,077
Master's degree	6,158	1,511	318	652	696
Professional degree	1,925	435	113	178	184
Doctoral degree	1,621	268	41	121	122
High school graduate or more	75,988	20,886	8,130	8,671	8,975
Some college or more	48,099	13,382	5,098	5,683	5,621
Bachelor's degree or more	26,336	7,201	2,487	3,008	3,079
Total men	**100.0%**	**100.0%**	**100.0%**	**100.0%**	**100.0%**
Not a high school graduate	15.2	13.5	14.8	13.8	12.9
High school graduate only	31.1	31.1	31.8	29.7	32.5
Some college, no degree	16.8	17.1	20.1	17.5	16.5
Associate's degree	7.5	8.4	7.3	9.1	8.2
Bachelor's degree	18.6	20.7	21.1	20.5	20.1
Master's degree	6.9	6.3	3.3	6.5	6.8
Professional degree	2.1	1.8	1.2	1.8	1.8
Doctoral degree	1.8	1.1	0.4	1.2	1.2
High school graduate or more	84.8	86.5	85.2	86.2	87.1
Some college or more	53.7	55.4	53.4	56.5	54.5
Bachelor's degree or more	29.4	29.8	26.1	29.9	29.9

Source: Bureau of the Census, Educational Attainment in the United States: 2004, detailed tables; Internet site http://www .census.gov/population/www/socdemo/education/cps2004.html; calculations by New Strategist

Gen X Women Are Better Educated than Gen X Men

They are more likely to have attended and completed college.

As educational opportunities for women broadened over the years, increasing numbers of women took advantage of them. Women aged 28 to 39 are better educated than their male counterparts.

The women of Generation X, in fact, are the best-educated women in the nation. Thirty-three percent have at least a bachelor's degree, and 61 percent have at least some college experience. Among men aged 28 to 39, a smaller 30 percent have at least a bachelor's degree, while 55 percent have at least some college experience.

The higher educational attainment of Baby-Boom and younger women is the driving factor behind the changing roles of women in society. With greater education, women expect to work and are eager to advance in their careers.

■ Among high school graduates, girls are more likely than boys to go to college. Consequently, among Generation Xers, women are more likely than men to have a college degree.

Most women aged 28 to 39 have at least some college experience

(percent distribution of women aged 28 to 39 by educational attainment, 2004)

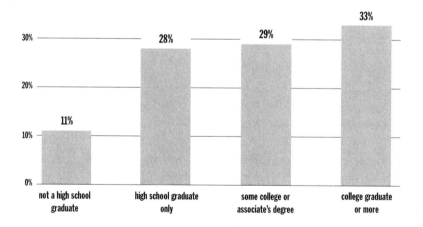

Table 1.5 Educational Attainment of Generation X Women, 2004

(number and percent distribution of women aged 25 or older, aged 28 to 39, and aged 25 to 39 in five-year age groups, by highest level of education 2004; numbers in thousands)

			five-year age groups		
	total 25 or older	28 to 39	25 to 29	30 to 34	35 to 39
Total women	**97,319**	**24,423**	**9,465**	**10,138**	**10,483**
Not a high school graduate	14,175	2,707	1,140	1,133	1,144
High school graduate only	31,921	6,770	2,525	2,699	3,116
Some college, no degree	16,796	4,518	1,972	1,929	1,828
Associate's degree	9,013	2,456	856	999	1,122
Bachelor's degree	17,134	5,663	2,343	2,343	2,351
Master's degree	6,451	1,755	468	797	692
Professional degree	1,027	339	106	160	125
Doctoral degree	801	219	55	77	106
High school graduate or more	83,143	21,720	8,325	9,004	9,340
Some college or more	51,222	14,950	5,800	6,305	6,224
Bachelor's degree or more	25,413	7,976	2,972	3,377	3,274
Total women	**100.0%**	**100.0%**	**100.0%**	**100.0%**	**100.0%**
Not a high school graduate	14.6	11.1	12.0	11.2	10.9
High school graduate only	32.8	27.7	26.7	26.6	29.7
Some college, no degree	17.3	18.5	20.8	19.0	17.4
Associate's degree	9.3	10.1	9.0	9.9	10.7
Bachelor's degree	17.6	23.2	24.8	23.1	22.4
Master's degree	6.6	7.2	4.9	7.9	6.6
Professional degree	1.1	1.4	1.1	1.6	1.2
Doctoral degree	0.8	0.9	0.6	0.8	1.0
High school graduate or more	85.4	88.9	88.0	88.8	89.1
Some college or more	52.6	61.2	61.3	62.2	59.4
Bachelor's degree or more	26.1	32.7	31.4	33.3	31.2

Source: Bureau of the Census, Educational Attainment in the United States: 2004, detailed tables; Internet site http://www .census.gov/population/www/socdemo/education/cps2004.html; calculations by New Strategist

Among Gen Xers, Asian Men Have the Highest Educational Attainment

Hispanics are least likely to have completed high school.

There are substantial socioeconomic differences between Americans of different racial and ethnic backgrounds. Differences in educational attainment are the primary reason for the disparity.

Among Gen X men, Asians are by far the best educated. Fully 76 percent of Asian men aged 28 to 39 have college experience and the 59 percent majority are college graduates. Among non-Hispanic white men in the age group, 62 percent have college experience and 35 percent have a college degree.

Hispanics are the least educated. Only 59 percent of Hispanic men aged 28 to 39 have even graduated from high school. Just 11 percent have a college degree. Black Gen X men are much better educated than Hispanics. Forty-nine percent have college experience, and 19 percent are college graduates.

■ The educational attainment of Hispanics is low because many are recent immigrants from countries with little educational opportunity.

Education gaps point to continued socioeconomic differences

(percent of men aged 28 to 39 with a bachelor's degree or more, by race and Hispanic origin, 2004)

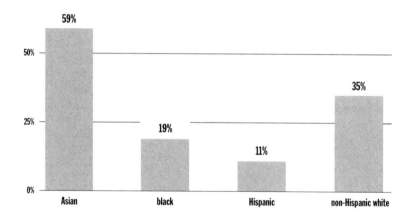

Table 1.6 Educational Attainment of Generation X Men by Race and Hispanic Origin, 2004

(number and percent distribution of men aged 28 to 39 by educational attainment, race, and Hispanic origin, 2004; numbers in thousands)

	total	Asian	black	Hispanic	non-Hispanic white
Total men aged 28 to 39	**24,146**	**1,401**	**2,808**	**4,414**	**15,277**
Not a high school graduate	3,254	108	305	1,803	1,036
High school graduate only	7,504	230	1,139	1,301	4,767
Some college, no degree	4,141	146	600	600	2,735
Associate's degree	2,040	98	220	235	1,452
Bachelor's degree	4,987	437	410	362	3,717
Master's degree	1,511	271	92	77	1,060
Professional degree	435	57	29	18	329
Doctoral degree	268	55	11	11	187
High school graduate or more	20,886	1,294	2,501	2,604	14,247
Some college or more	13,382	1,064	1,362	1,303	9,480
Bachelor's degree or more	7,201	820	542	468	5,293
Total men aged 28 to 39	**100.0%**	**100.0%**	**100.0%**	**100.0%**	**100.0%**
Not a high school graduate	13.5	7.7	10.9	40.8	6.8
High school graduate only	31.1	16.4	40.6	29.5	31.2
Some college, no degree	17.1	10.4	21.4	13.6	17.9
Associate's degree	8.4	7.0	7.8	5.3	9.5
Bachelor's degree	20.7	31.2	14.6	8.2	24.3
Master's degree	6.3	19.3	3.3	1.7	6.9
Professional degree	1.8	4.1	1.0	0.4	2.2
Doctoral degree	1.1	3.9	0.4	0.2	1.2
High school graduate or more	86.5	92.4	89.1	59.0	93.3
Some college or more	55.4	75.9	48.5	29.5	62.1
Bachelor's degree or more	29.8	58.5	19.3	10.6	34.6

Note: Asians and blacks are those identifying themselves as being of the race alone and those identifying themselves as being of the race in combination with other races; non-Hispanic whites are those identifying themselves as being white alone and not Hispanic. Numbers will not add to total because not all races are shown and Hispanics may be of any race.
Source: Bureau of the Census, Educational Attainment in the United States: 2004, detailed tables; Internet site http://www .census.gov/population/www/socdemo/education/cps2004.html; calculations by New Strategist

Hispanic Women Are Least Likely to Be High School Graduates

Asians are most likely to be college graduates.

Although the educational attainment of women has been rising for decades, substantial gaps persist among Gen Xers by race and Hispanic origin. From 89 to 95 percent of Asian, black, and non-Hispanic white women aged 28 to 39 have graduated from high school versus only 62 percent of Hispanic women in the age group. The majority of Asian, black, and non-Hispanic white women have college experience compared with only 33 percent of their Hispanic counterparts.

Asians are the best-educated Gen X women. Fully 56 percent have a college degree. Among non-Hispanic white women in the age group, the proportion is 38 percent. Twenty-two percent of black women aged 28 to 39 have a college diploma, while the figure is just 13 percent for Hispanics.

■ The educational attainment of Hispanics will remain low as long as immigrants are a large share of the Hispanic population.

Young Asian women have the highest educational attainment

(percent of women aged 28 to 39 with a bachelor's degree or more, by race and Hispanic origin, 2004)

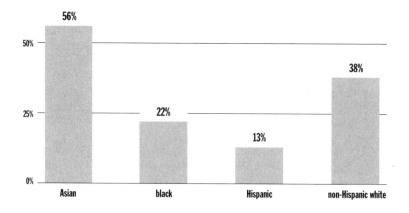

Table 1.7 Educational Attainment of Generation X Women by Race and Hispanic Origin, 2004

(number and percent distribution of women aged 28 to 39 by educational attainment, race, and Hispanic origin, 2004; numbers in thousands)

	total	Asian	black	Hispanic	non-Hispanic white
Total women aged 28 to 39	**24,423**	**1,481**	**3,472**	**3,861**	**15,444**
Not a high school graduate	2,707	117	380	1,457	747
High school graduate only	6,770	246	1,191	1,108	4,157
Some college, no degree	4,518	162	817	531	2,965
Associate's degree	2,456	117	319	247	1,720
Bachelor's degree	5,663	529	573	383	4,165
Master's degree	1,755	208	155	95	1,304
Professional degree	339	52	31	29	226
Doctoral degree	219	44	8	6	163
High school graduate or more	21,720	1,358	3,094	2,399	14,700
Some college or more	14,950	1,112	1,903	1,291	10,543
Bachelor's degree or more	7,976	833	767	513	5,858
Total women aged 28 to 39	**100.0%**	**100.0%**	**100.0%**	**100.0%**	**100.0%**
Not a high school graduate	11.1	7.9	10.9	37.7	4.8
High school graduate only	27.7	16.6	34.3	28.7	26.9
Some college, no degree	18.5	10.9	23.5	13.8	19.2
Associate's degree	10.1	7.9	9.2	6.4	11.1
Bachelor's degree	23.2	35.7	16.5	9.9	27.0
Master's degree	7.2	14.0	4.5	2.5	8.4
Professional degree	1.4	3.5	0.9	0.8	1.5
Doctoral degree	0.9	3.0	0.2	0.2	1.1
High school graduate or more	88.9	91.7	89.1	62.1	95.2
Some college or more	61.2	75.1	54.8	33.4	68.3
Bachelor's degree or more	32.7	56.2	22.1	13.3	37.9

Note: Asians and blacks are those identifying themselves as being of the race alone and those identifying themselves as being of the race in combination with other races; non-Hispanic whites are those identifying themselves as being white alone and not Hispanic. Numbers will not add to total because not all races are shown and Hispanics may be of any race.
Source: Bureau of the Census, Educational Attainment in the United States: 2004, detailed tables; Internet site http://www .census.gov/population/www/socdemo/education/cps2004.html; calculations by New Strategist

Many Gen Xers Are Still in School

Among people aged 25 to 39, nearly one in twelve is a student.

School is a major part of life for many people in their twenties and thirties. Among 25-to-29-year-olds, a substantial 13 percent are in school. The proportion drops to 7 percent among 30-to-34-year-olds and falls to 5 percent among 35-to-39-year-olds. Among people aged 40 or older, fewer than 2 percent are enrolled in school.

Women are more likely to go to college than men. This is why a larger proportion of 25-to-39-year-old women than men are enrolled in school. Nine percent of women in the age group are students versus 7 percent of men.

■ Among students in the 25-to-39 age group, women outnumber men by more than 700,000.

Among students, women outnumber men

(number of people aged 25 to 39 enrolled in school, by sex, 2004)

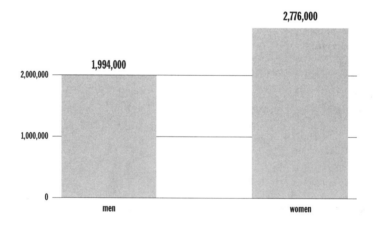

Table 1.8 School Enrollment by Sex and Age, 2004

(total number of people aged 3 or older, and number and percent enrolled in school by sex and age, 2004; numbers in thousands)

		enrolled	
	total	number	percent
Total people	**277,467**	**75,461**	**27.2%**
Under age 25	89,779	68,620	76.4
Aged 25 to 39	59,502	4,760	8.0
Aged 25 to 29	19,125	2,479	13.0
Aged 30 to 34	19,864	1,321	6.7
Aged 35 to 39	20,513	960	4.7
Aged 40 or older	128,186	2,083	1.6
Total females	**141,957**	**38,012**	**26.8**
Under age 25	44,015	33,922	77.1
Aged 25 to 39	30,000	2,766	9.2
Aged 25 to 29	9,570	1,381	14.4
Aged 30 to 34	10,028	769	7.7
Aged 35 to 39	10,402	616	5.9
Aged 40 or older	67,942	1,322	1.9
Total males	**135,510**	**37,449**	**27.6**
Under age 25	45,762	34,694	75.8
Aged 25 to 39	29,502	1,994	6.8
Aged 25 to 29	9,555	1,098	11.5
Aged 30 to 34	9,836	552	5.6
Aged 35 to 39	10,111	344	3.4
Aged 40 or older	60,244	759	1.3

Source: Bureau of the Census, School Enrollment—Social and Economic Characteristics of Students: October 2004, detailed tables; Internet site http://www.census.gov/population/www/socdemo/school/cps2004.html; calculations by New Strategist

Gen Xers Dominate Graduate Schools

They account for a smaller share of undergraduates.

Although the college enrollment of older people has grown over the years, young adults still dominate the nation's college campuses. In 2004, fully 62 percent of college students were under age 25. People aged 25 to 39 (Gen Xers were aged 28 to 39 in that year) account for only 27 percent of college students, while people aged 40 or older were another 11 percent.

Students aged 25 to 39 account for 20 percent of all undergraduates—13 percent of those attending school full-time and 41 percent of part-timers. The majority of graduate students are in the 25-to-39 age group.

■ Although Generation X is small, its presence on college campuses is substantial.

Most graduate students are aged 25 to 39

(percent distribution of graduate students by age, 2004)

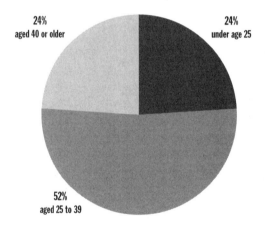

24%
aged 40 or older

24%
under age 25

52%
aged 25 to 39

Table 1.9 College Students by Age and Attendance Status, 2004

(number and percent distribution of people aged 15 or older enrolled in institutions of higher education, by age and full- or part-time attendance status, 2004; numbers in thousands)

| | total | undergraduate | | | graduate | | |
		total	full-time	part-time	total	full-time	part-time
Total enrolled	**17,383**	**14,005**	**10,418**	**3,587**	**3,378**	**1,572**	**1,806**
Under age 25	10,811	9,993	8,619	1,374	813	644	169
Aged 25 to 39	4,611	2,842	1,372	1,470	1,771	766	1,005
Aged 25 to 29	2,403	1,487	807	680	917	471	446
Aged 30 to 34	1,287	770	344	426	517	205	312
Aged 35 to 39	921	585	221	364	337	90	247
Aged 40 or older	1,964	1,169	428	741	794	161	633

PERCENT DISTRIBUTION BY ATTENDANCE STATUS

| | total | undergraduate | | | graduate | | |
		total	full-time	part-time	total	full-time	part-time
Total enrolled	–	**100.0%**	**74.4%**	**25.6%**	**100.0%**	**46.5%**	**53.5%**
Under age 25	–	100.0	86.3	13.7	100.0	79.2	20.8
Aged 25 to 39	–	100.0	48.3	51.7	100.0	43.3	56.7
Aged 25 to 29	–	100.0	54.3	45.7	100.0	51.4	48.6
Aged 30 to 34	–	100.0	44.7	55.3	100.0	39.7	60.3
Aged 35 to 39	–	100.0	37.8	62.2	100.0	26.7	73.3
Aged 40 or older	–	100.0	36.6	63.4	100.0	20.3	79.7

PERCENT DISTRIBUTION BY AGE

| | total | undergraduate | | | graduate | | |
		total	full-time	part-time	total	full-time	part-time
Total enrolled	**100.0%**	**100.0%**	**100.0%**	**100.0%**	**100.0%**	**100.0%**	**100.0%**
Under age 25	62.2	71.4	82.7	38.3	24.1	41.0	9.4
Aged 25 to 39	26.5	20.3	13.2	41.0	52.4	48.7	55.6
Aged 25 to 29	13.8	10.6	7.7	19.0	27.1	30.0	24.7
Aged 30 to 34	7.4	5.5	3.3	11.9	15.3	13.0	17.3
Aged 35 to 39	5.3	4.2	2.1	10.1	10.0	5.7	13.7
Aged 40 or older	11.3	8.3	4.1	20.7	23.5	10.2	35.0

Note: "–" means not applicable.
Source: Bureau of the Census, School Enrollment—Social and Economic Characteristics of Students: October 2004, detailed tables; Internet site http://www.census.gov/population/www/socdemo/school/cps2004.html; calculations by New Strategist

Many Participate in Adult Education for Job-Related Reasons

Life-long learning is becoming a necessity for job security.

As job security dwindles, many workers are turning to the educational system to try to stay on track. Overall, 33 percent of Americans aged 17 or older participated in work-related adult education during the past 12 months. An even larger 58 percent participated in less-formal work-related learning activities, such as seminars offered by employers.

The percentage of Americans involved in work-related adult education does not vary much by age. Between 41 and 44 percent of people spanning the ages from 25 to 54 took part in work-related courses in 2003. The percentage participating in less-formal work-related learning activities ranges from 65 to 75 percent.

■ Many Americans who participate in work-related education are retraining themselves to compete in the increasingly global economy.

More than 40 percent of people aged 25 to 39 took a work-related course

(percent of people aged 17 or older participating in job- or career-related courses, by age, 2003)

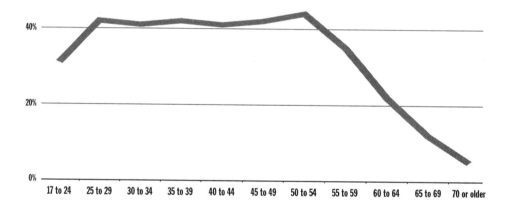

Table 1.10 Participation in Adult Education for Work-Related Reasons, 2003

(percent of people aged 17 or older participating in work-related adult education during the past 12 months, by age and type, 2003; numbers in thousands)

	career- or job-related courses	less formal work-related learning activities
Total people	**33.2%**	**58.3%**
Aged 17 to 24	30.9	73.4
Aged 25 to 29	42.4	75.4
Aged 30 to 34	40.7	68.4
Aged 35 to 39	41.6	67.5
Aged 40 to 44	40.7	70.4
Aged 45 to 49	42.2	65.3
Aged 50 to 54	43.6	65.7
Aged 55 to 59	34.9	56.3
Aged 60 to 64	21.7	39.4
Aged 65 to 69	11.9	27.0
Aged 70 or older	4.7	12.9

Note: Adult education is defined as all education activities except full-time enrollment in higher education credential programs. Examples include part-time college attendance and classes or seminars given by employers.
Source: National Center for Education Statistics, Digest of Education Statistics, 2004, list of tables, Internet site http:// nces.ed.gov/programs/digest/d04/list_tables3.asp#c3b_1; calculations by New Strategist

2

Health

■ The 54 percent majority of Americans aged 18 or older say their health is excellent or very good. The figure peaks at 64 percent in the 25-to-34 age group.

■ Americans have a weight problem, and younger adults are no exception. The average man aged 30 to 39 has gained 19 pounds over the past four decades. The average woman in the age group has gained 24 pounds.

■ Men aged 15 to 44 have had a median of 5.6 opposite-sex partners in their lifetime. Women in the age group have had a median of 3.3 partners.

■ The average woman aged 30 to 34 has borne 1.58 children. She expects to have an additional 0.69 children for a total of 2.27 children in her lifetime.

■ Many younger adults do not have health insurance, including 26 percent of those aged 25 to 34. Cost is the number-one reason for the lack of health insurance coverage.

■ Twenty-four percent of Americans aged 18 to 44 have experienced lower back pain for at least one full day in the past three months, making it the most common health condition in the age group.

■ Thirty-six percent of people aged 25 to 44 have taken at least one prescription drug in the past month, and 8 percent have taken three or more.

■ Accidents, the most important cause of death among 25-to-44-year-olds, account for 30 percent of deaths among 25-to-34-year-olds and 18 percent of deaths among 35-to-44-year-olds.

Most Young Adults Say Their Health Is Excellent or Very Good

The proportion of people in very good or excellent health declines with age.

Overall, the 54 percent majority of Americans aged 18 or older say their health is excellent or very good. The figure peaks at 64 percent in the 25-to-34 age group. Young adults are more likely than their elders to report being in tip-top shape for good reason. Although many of the conditions and diseases associated with aging have diminished in severity thanks to healthier lifestyles and better medical care, health deteriorates with age as chronic conditions become common.

Older Americans are less likely than younger adults to report excellent or very good health. Nevertheless, the proportion of people who report poor health remains below 10 percent, regardless of age.

■ Basic biology dictates that young adults will always feel fitter than their elders.

People aged 25 to 34 are most likely to report excellent or very good health

(percent of people aged 18 or older who say their health is excellent or very good, by age, 2004)

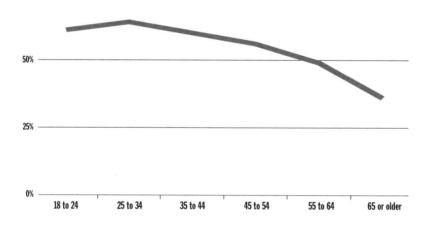

Table 2.1 Health Status by Age, 2004

(percent distribution of people aged 18 or older by self-reported health status, 2004)

	excellent	very good	good	fair	poor
Total people	**20.8%**	**33.6%**	**29.8%**	**10.8%**	**3.9%**
Aged 18 to 24	24.6	36.5	30.3	6.7	0.8
Aged 25 to 34	26.5	37.6	27.9	6.2	1.0
Aged 35 to 44	24.4	35.8	28.6	8.1	2.3
Aged 45 to 54	21.4	34.2	28.6	10.0	4.3
Aged 55 to 64	18.5	30.5	30.5	12.3	6.5
Aged 65 or older	10.6	25.7	34.5	19.8	8.6

Source: Centers for Disease Control and Prevention, Behavioral Risk Factor Surveillance System Prevalence Data, 2004, Internet site http://apps.nccd.cdc.gov/brfss/

Weight Problems Are the Norm, Even among Younger Adults

The majority of young adults are overweight and many are trying to shed pounds.

Americans have a weight problem, and younger adults are no exception. The average man aged 30 to 39 has gained 19 pounds over the past four decades. The average woman in the age group has gained 24 pounds. Among men and women aged 20 to 34, fully 53 to 57 percent are overweight. The problems only increase with age. Among those aged 35 to 44, an even larger 61 to 71 percent are overweight.

Not surprisingly, many Americans are trying to lose weight. Among 25-to-34-year-olds, 38 percent are trying to shed pounds. Only 12 percent say they are eating fewer calories to lose or maintain their weight. More than two out of three say they are exercising to lose or maintain their weight.

Although many people claim to exercise, only 35 percent of adults aged 25 to 44 participate regularly in leisure-time physical activity, according to government data. The proportion engaging in regular physical activity falls with age.

■ Many young adults lack the willpower to eat less or exercise more, and their weight problems are likely to increase as they get older.

Younger adults weigh more

(average weight in pounds of people aged 30 to 39, by sex, 1960–62 and 1999–02)

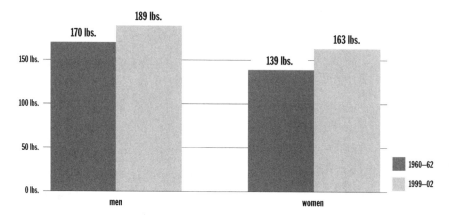

Table 2.2 Average Measured Weight by Sex and Age, 1960–62 and 1999–02

(average weight in pounds of people aged 20 to 74, by sex and age, 1960–62 and 1999–02; change in pounds 1960–62 to 1999–02)

	1999–02	1960–62	change in pounds
Men aged 20 to 74	**191.0 lbs.**	**166.3 lbs.**	**24.7 lbs.**
Aged 20 to 29	183.4	163.9	19.5
Aged 30 to 39	189.1	169.9	19.2
Aged 40 to 49	196.0	169.1	26.9
Aged 50 to 59	195.4	167.7	27.7
Aged 60 to 74	191.5	158.9	32.6
Women aged 20 to 74	**164.3**	**140.2**	**24.1**
Aged 20 to 29	156.5	127.7	28.8
Aged 30 to 39	163.0	138.8	24.2
Aged 40 to 49	168.2	142.8	25.4
Aged 50 to 59	169.2	146.5	22.7
Aged 60 to 74	164.7	147.3	17.4

Note: Data are based on measured weight of a sample of the civilian noninstitutionalized population.
Source: National Center for Health Statistics, Mean Body Weight, Height, and Body Mass Index, United States 1960–2002, Advance Data, No. 347, 2004, Internet site http://www.cdc.gov/nchs/pressroom/04news/americans.htm; calculations by New Strategist

Table 2.3 Weight Status by Sex and Age, 1999–02

(percent distribution of people aged 20 or older by weight status, sex, and age, 1999–02)

	healthy weight	overweight total	obese
Total people	**32.9%**	**65.2%**	**30.5%**
Total men	**30.4**	**68.6**	**27.5**
Aged 20 to 34	40.3	57.4	21.7
Aged 35 to 44	29.0	70.5	28.5
Aged 45 to 54	24.0	75.7	30.6
Aged 55 to 64	23.8	75.4	35.5
Aged 65 to 74	22.8	76.2	31.9
Aged 75 or older	32.0	67.4	18.0
Total women	**35.4**	**62.0**	**33.4**
Aged 20 to 34	42.6	52.8	28.4
Aged 35 to 44	37.1	60.6	32.1
Aged 45 to 54	33.1	65.1	36.9
Aged 55 to 64	27.6	72.2	42.1
Aged 65 to 74	26.4	70.9	39.3
Aged 75 or older	36.9	59.9	23.6

Note: Data are based on measured height and weight of a sample of the civilian noninstitutionalized population. Being overweight is defined as having a body mass index of 25 or higher. Obesity is defined as a body mass index of 30 or higher. Body mass index is calculated by dividing weight in kilograms by height in meters squared.
Source: National Center for Health Statistics, Health United States, 2005, Internet site http://www.cdc.gov/nchs/hus.htm

Table 2.4 Weight Loss Behavior by Age, 2000

(percent of people aged 18 or older engaging in selected weight loss behaviors, by age, 2000)

	total	18 to 24	25 to 34	35 to 44	45 to 54	55 to 64	65 or older
Trying to lose weight	38.0%	30.2%	38.0%	40.4%	44.7%	42.6%	30.6%
Trying to maintain weight	58.9	51.9	56.9	59.8	63.1	60.8	58.4
Eating fewer calories to lose/maintain weight*	13.5	11.4	12.1	13.9	15.2	13.2	12.0
Eating less fat to lose/maintain weight*	27.4	25.3	25.8	27.7	28.3	29.1	29.4
Eating fewer calories and less fat to lose/maintain weight*	29.6	25.5	27.0	30.1	32.6	33.0	29.0
Using physical activity or exercise to lose/maintain weight*	60.7	74.7	67.7	64.0	60.5	55.4	43.3
Advised by health professional to lose weight	11.7	4.0	8.4	11.3	16.0	17.7	11.2

* Among those trying to lose or maintain weight.
Source: Centers for Disease Control and Prevention, Behavioral Risk Factor Surveillance System Prevalence Data, 2000, Internet site http://apps.nccd.cdc.gov/brfss/index.asp

Table 2.5 Leisure-Time Physical Activity Level by Sex and Age, 2003

(percent distribution of people aged 18 or older by leisure-time physical activity level, by sex and age, 2003)

	total	physically inactive	at least some physical activity	regular physical activity
Total people	**100.0%**	**37.6%**	**29.6%**	**32.8%**
Aged 18 to 24	100.0	29.6	28.2	42.3
Aged 25 to 44	100.0	34.0	31.0	34.9
Aged 45 to 54	100.0	36.5	30.8	32.8
Aged 55 to 64	100.0	40.8	30.1	29.2
Aged 65 to 74	100.0	45.8	25.8	28.4
Aged 75 or older	100.0	57.5	24.8	17.7
Total men	**100.0**	**35.4**	**29.2**	**35.4**
Aged 18 to 44	100.0	30.9	29.5	39.6
Aged 45 to 54	100.0	36.4	30.5	33.2
Aged 55 to 64	100.0	39.5	29.7	30.8
Aged 65 to 74	100.0	43.0	24.9	32.1
Aged 75 or older	100.0	48.1	28.9	23.0
Total women	**100.0**	**39.5**	**29.9**	**30.6**
Aged 18 to 44	100.0	34.9	31.1	34.0
Aged 45 to 54	100.0	36.5	31.1	32.4
Aged 55 to 64	100.0	41.9	30.4	27.6
Aged 65 to 74	100.0	48.0	26.6	25.4
Aged 75 or older	100.0	63.7	22.0	14.3

Note: "Physically inactive" are those with no sessions of light/moderate or vigorous leisure-time physical activity of at least 10 minutes duration during past week. "At least some physical activity" includes those who performed at least one light/moderate or vigorous leisure-time physical activity of at least 10 minutes duration during past week, but did not meet the definition for regular leisure-time activity. "Regular physical activity" includes those with three or more sessions per week of vigorous activity lasting at least 20 minutes or five or more sessions per week of light/moderate activity lasting at least 30 minutes.
Source: National Center for Health Statistics, Health, United States, 2005, Internet site http://www.cdc.gov/nchs/hus.htm

Americans Report on Their Sexual Behavior

For most, sexual activity is limited to one partner.

Every few years the federal government fields the National Survey of Family Growth (NSFG), which examines the sexual behavior, contraceptive use, and childbearing patterns of Americans aged 15 to 44. Results from the latest survey, taken in 2002, are now being released by the National Center for Health Statistics.

Overall 90 percent of men and 91 percent of women aged 15 to 44 have had at least one opposite-sex partner in their lifetime. Even among 15-to-19-year-olds, 57 percent of men and 62 percent of women are sexually experienced. Men aged 15 to 44 have had a median of 5.6 opposite-sex partners in their lifetime, with the figure peaking at 8.2 among men aged 40 to 44. Women have had a median of 3.3 partners in their lifetime, with a peak of 3.8 to 3.9 partners among women aged 30 or older. Among those with an opposite-sex partner in the past year, most had only one.

Ninety percent of men and women aged 15 to 44 identify themselves as heterosexual. Only 2 percent of men and 1 percent of women say they are homosexual. But 6 percent of men and 11 percent of women say they have had sexual activity with a same-sex partner in their lifetime (the 2002 NSFG questions regarding same-sex activity were worded differently for men and women, a factor that may explain the different percentages reporting same-sex activity).

■ Twenty-three percent of men and 9 percent of women report having had 15 or more opposite-sex partners in their lifetime.

Most Americans aged 18 or older are sexually active

(percent of people aged 15 to 44 who have had at least one opposite-sex partner during the past 12 months, by sex and age, 2002)

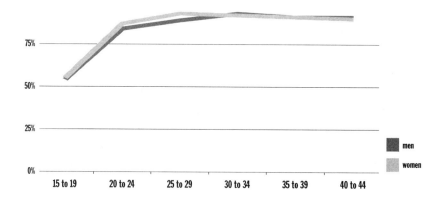

Table 2.6 Lifetime Sexual Activity of 15-to-44-Year-Olds by Sex, 2002

(number of people aged 15 to 44 and percent distribution by sexual experience with opposite-sex partners during lifetime, by sex and age, 2002; numbers in thousands)

	total		number of opposite-sex partners in lifetime							
	number	percent	none	1 or more	1	2	3 to 6	7 to 14	15 or more	median
Total men aged 15 to 44	**61,147**	**100.0%**	**9.6%**	**90.4%**	**12.5%**	**8.0%**	**27.2%**	**19.5%**	**23.2%**	**5.6**
Aged 15 to 19	10,208	100.0	43.5	56.6	23.4	9.0	17.0	4.9	2.3	1.6
Aged 20 to 24	9,883	100.0	9.9	90.1	15.7	11.6	33.1	13.9	15.8	3.8
Aged 25 to 29	9,226	100.0	5.0	94.9	10.0	8.7	29.3	23.1	23.8	5.9
Aged 30 to 34	10,138	100.0	3.0	97.0	10.7	6.9	28.4	21.9	29.1	6.4
Aged 35 to 39	10,557	100.0	2.1	97.9	8.9	7.0	27.9	25.4	28.7	6.9
Aged 40 to 44	11,135	100.0	1.9	98.2	8.8	5.4	25.6	24.2	34.2	8.2
Total women aged 15 to 44	**61,561**	**100.0**	**8.6**	**91.4**	**22.5**	**10.8**	**32.6**	**16.3**	**9.2**	**3.3**
Aged 15 to 19	9,834	100.0	37.8	62.2	27.2	9.0	19.1	5.0	1.9	1.4
Aged 20 to 24	9,840	100.0	8.9	91.1	24.6	13.0	32.2	14.4	6.9	2.8
Aged 25 to 29	9,249	100.0	2.5	97.5	22.5	11.7	31.3	20.1	11.9	3.5
Aged 30 to 34	10,272	100.0	1.9	98.0	20.5	9.4	38.8	18.0	11.3	3.8
Aged 35 to 39	10,853	100.0	1.1	98.9	20.2	11.2	35.8	20.5	11.2	3.9
Aged 40 to 44	11,512	100.0	1.4	98.6	20.4	10.5	37.4	19.1	11.2	3.8

Source: National Center for Health Statistics, Sexual Behavior and Selected Health Measures: Men and Women 15–44 Years of Age, United States, 2002, Advance Data, No. 362, 2005, Internet site http://www.cdc.gov/nchs/nsfg.htm

Table 2.7 Past Year Sexual Activity of 15-to-44-Year-Olds by Sex, 2002

(percent distribution of people aged 15 to 44 by sexual experience with opposite-sex partners during the past 12 months, and percent distribution by number of opposite-sex partners in past 12 months, by sex and age, 2002; numbers in thousands)

	total	no opposite-sex partners in past year	one or more opposite-sex partners in past year
Sexual activity in past year			
Total men	**100.0%**	**16.4%**	**83.6%**
Aged 15 to 19	100.0	46.2	53.8
Aged 20 to 24	100.0	15.6	84.4
Aged 25 to 29	100.0	11.4	88.6
Aged 30 to 34	100.0	7.4	92.7
Aged 35 to 39	100.0	9.3	90.8
Aged 40 to 44	100.0	9.0	91.1
Total women	**100.0**	**15.3**	**84.7**
Aged 15 to 19	100.0	44.8	55.3
Aged 20 to 24	100.0	13.4	86.7
Aged 25 to 29	100.0	6.9	93.0
Aged 30 to 34	100.0	7.9	92.1
Aged 35 to 39	100.0	9.2	90.8
Aged 40 to 44	100.0	10.5	89.5

	total with one or more	one	two	three or more	not reported
Number of sex partners in past year					
Total men	**100.0%**	**75.0%**	**9.6%**	**12.4%**	**3.0%**
Aged 15 to 19	100.0	56.3	21.9	19.9	1.9
Aged 20 to 24	100.0	58.4	15.0	22.9	3.7
Aged 25 to 29	100.0	75.7	7.4	14.1	2.7
Aged 30 to 34	100.0	80.7	7.3	9.4	2.6
Aged 35 to 39	100.0	84.6	5.5	7.5	2.4
Aged 40 to 44	100.0	83.9	6.0	5.8	4.3
Total women	**100.0**	**80.5**	**9.0**	**8.0**	**2.5**
Aged 15 to 19	100.0	58.2	17.5	20.4	3.8
Aged 20 to 24	100.0	70.2	14.5	13.3	2.0
Aged 25 to 29	100.0	81.6	10.1	6.1	2.2
Aged 30 to 34	100.0	86.5	6.1	5.4	2.0
Aged 35 to 39	100.0	86.2	6.7	4.8	2.2
Aged 40 to 44	100.0	88.7	3.8	4.1	3.4

Source: National Center for Health Statistics, Sexual Behavior and Selected Health Measures: Men and Women 15–44 Years of Age, United States, 2002, Advance Data, No. 362, 2005, Internet site http://www.cdc.gov/nchs/nsfg.htm; calculations by New Strategist

Table 2.8 Sexual Orientation of 18-to-44-Year-Olds, 2002

(number of people aged 18 to 44 and percent distribution by sexual orientation, by sex and age, 2002; numbers in thousands)

	total		sexual orientation				
	number	percent	heterosexual	homosexual	bisexual	something else	did not report
Total men aged 18 to 44	**55,399**	**100.0%**	**90.2%**	**2.3%**	**1.8%**	**3.9%**	**1.8%**
Aged 18 to 19	4,460	100.0	91.3	1.7	1.4	3.5	2.1
Aged 20 to 24	9,883	100.0	91.0	2.3	2.0	3.5	1.3
Aged 25 to 29	9,226	100.0	87.3	2.8	0.9	5.7	3.3
Aged 30 to 34	10,138	100.0	91.1	2.0	1.7	4.0	1.2
Aged 35 to 44	21,692	100.0	90.3	2.4	2.2	3.5	1.6
Total women aged 18 to 44	**55,742**	**100.0**	**90.3**	**1.3**	**2.8**	**3.8**	**1.8**
Aged 18 to 19	4,015	100.0	84.2	0.9	7.4	5.7	1.9
Aged 20 to 24	9,840	100.0	90.0	0.8	3.5	4.4	1.3
Aged 25 to 29	9,249	100.0	89.9	1.5	2.8	2.8	3.1
Aged 30 to 34	10,272	100.0	91.2	1.3	2.1	3.8	1.6
Aged 35 to 44	22,365	100.0	91.4	1.5	2.0	3.5	1.6

Source: National Center for Health Statistics, Sexual Behavior and Selected Health Measures: Men and Women 15–44 Years of Age, United States, 2002, Advance Data, No. 362, 2005, Internet site http://www.cdc.gov/nchs/nsfg.htm

Table 2.9 Lifetime Same-Sex Sexual Activity of 15-to-44-Year-Olds, 2002

(percent of people aged 15 to 44 reporting any sexual activity with same-sex partners in their lifetime, by age and sex, 2002)

	men	women
Total aged 15 to 44	**6.0%**	**11.2%**
Aged 15 to 19	4.5	10.6
Aged 20 to 24	5.5	14.2
Aged 25 to 29	5.7	14.1
Aged 30 to 34	6.2	9.1
Aged 35 to 39	8.0	12.3
Aged 40 to 44	6.0	7.8

Note: The question about same-sex sexual contact was worded differently for men and women. Women were asked whether they had ever had a sexual experience of any kind with another female. Men were asked whether they had performed any of four specific sexual acts with another male. The question asked of women may have elicited more "yes" answers than the questions asked of men.
Source: National Center for Health Statistics, Sexual Behavior and Selected Health Measures: Men and Women 15–44 Years of Age, United States, 2002, Advance Data, No. 362, 2005, Internet site http://www.cdc.gov/nchs/nsfg.htm

Birth Rate Is Falling among Women under Age 30

Rate is rising among women aged 30 or older.

The birth rate fell between 1990 and 2004 for women under age 30. The biggest decline has been among teenagers, with the number of births per 1,000 women aged 15 to 19 falling from 59.9 in 1990 to 41.2 in 2004. The birth rate among 20-to-24-year-olds fell 13 percent during those years, while the rate for women aged 25 to 29 fell 4 percent. Interestingly, the birth rate among 25-to-29-year-old women bottomed out in 1997 and has been rising since then.

The birth rate climbed among women aged 30 or older between 1990 and 2004, increasing the most for the oldest women, those aged 45 to 49—up 200 percent. But the birth rate is so tiny at that age that even a significant rise makes little difference to overall childbearing patterns.

■ Because the majority of today's young women go to college and then enter the workforce, they are delaying childbearing until their later twenties and catching up in their thirties.

Birth rate is highest in the 25-to-29 age group

(births per 1,000 women in age group, 2004)

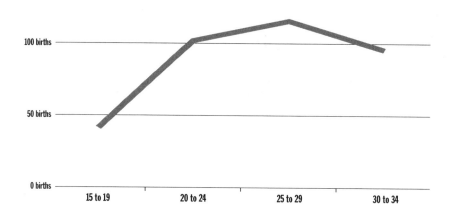

Table 2.10   Birth Rate by Age, 1990 to 2004

(number of live births per 1,000 women in age group, 1990 to 2004; percent change in rate, 1990–2004)

	15 to 19	20 to 24	25 to 29	30 to 34	35 to 39	40 to 44	45 to 49
2004	41.2	101.8	115.5	95.5	45.4	9.0	0.6
2003	41.6	102.6	115.6	95.1	43.8	8.7	0.5
2002	43.0	103.6	113.6	91.5	41.4	8.3	0.5
2001	45.3	106.2	113.4	91.9	40.6	8.1	0.5
2000	47.7	109.7	113.5	91.2	39.7	8.0	0.5
1999	48.8	107.9	111.2	87.1	37.8	7.4	0.4
1998	50.3	108.4	110.2	85.2	36.9	7.4	0.4
1997	51.3	107.3	108.3	83.0	35.7	7.1	0.4
1996	53.5	107.8	108.6	82.1	34.9	6.8	0.3
1995	56.0	107.5	108.8	81.1	34.0	6.6	0.3
1994	58.2	109.2	111.0	80.4	33.4	6.4	0.3
1993	59.0	111.3	113.2	79.9	32.7	6.1	0.3
1992	60.3	113.7	115.7	79.6	32.3	5.9	0.3
1991	61.8	115.3	117.2	79.2	31.9	5.5	0.2
1990	59.9	116.5	120.2	80.8	31.7	5.5	0.2

Percent change

| 1990 to 2004 | −31.2% | −12.6% | −3.9% | 18.2% | 43.2% | 63.6% | 200.0% |

Source: National Center for Health Statistics, Revised Birth and Fertility Rates for the 1990s and New Rates for the Hispanic Populations 2000 and 2001: United States, National Vital Statistics Report, Vol. 51, No. 12, 2003; and Births: Final Data for 2003, National Vital Statistics Report Vol. 54, No. 2, 2005, Internet site http://www.cdc.gov/nchs/births.htm; and Preliminary Births for 2004, Internet site http://www.cdc.gov/nchs/products/pubs/pubd/hestats/prelim_births/prelim_births04.htm; calculations by New Strategist

Most Women Aged 25 to 29 Have Borne Children

Women in the age group expect to have at least one more child.

The proportion of women who have never had a child falls from 93 percent among 15-to-19-year-olds to a much smaller (but still substantial) 19 percent among women aged 40 to 44. The average woman aged 30 to 34 has had 1.58 children. She expects to have an additional 0.69 children for a total of 2.27 children in her lifetime.

Six percent of women aged 15 to 44 gave birth in the past year, and 2 percent had their first child. Women aged 25 to 29 were most likely to have given birth in the past year, with 9.9 percent doing so. By race and Hispanic origin, Hispanics are most likely to have given birth in the past year, at 8.5 percent. While 5.7 percent of native-born women aged 15 to 44 had a child in the past year, the figure is a larger 8.4 percent among foreign-born women in the age group.

■ The two-child family is the norm in the United States, but some women find they cannot have as many children as they like, while others have more than they expected.

Most women expect to have at least two children

(average number of children ever born and additional births expected by women aged 15 to 44, by age, 2002)

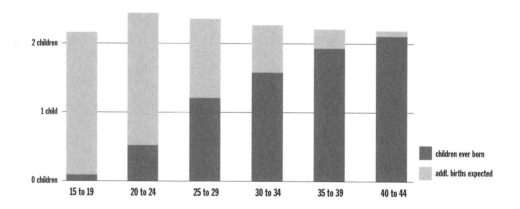

children ever born

addl. births expected

Table 2.11 Number of Children Born to Women Aged 15 to 44, 2004

(total number of women aged 15 to 44, and percent distribution by number of children ever borne, by age, 2004; numbers in thousands)

	total		number of children							
	number	percent	none	one or more	one	two	three	four	five or six	seven+
Total aged 15 to 44	**61,588**	**100.0%**	**44.6%**	**55.3%**	**17.2%**	**21.9%**	**10.8%**	**3.6%**	**1.5%**	**0.3%**
Aged 15 to 19	9,964	100.0	93.3	6.6	4.6	1.4	0.6	0.0	0.0	0.0
Aged 20 to 24	10,068	100.0	68.9	31.1	18.3	9.2	2.6	0.8	0.1	0.1
Aged 25 to 29	9,498	100.0	44.2	55.9	23.5	20.7	8.1	2.5	0.9	0.2
Aged 30 to 34	10,082	100.0	27.6	72.4	20.9	28.9	15.8	4.5	2.1	0.2
Aged 35 to 39	10,442	100.0	19.6	80.5	18.8	34.3	18.3	5.8	2.6	0.7
Aged 40 to 44	11,535	100.0	19.3	80.8	17.4	34.5	18.1	7.4	2.9	0.5

Source: Bureau of the Census, Fertility of American Women, Current Population Survey—June 2004, Detailed Tables, Internet site http://www.census.gov/population/www/socdemo/fertility/cps2004.html; calculations by New Strategist

Table 2.12 Average Number of Children Borne and Expected, 2002

(average number of children ever borne among women aged 15 to 44, average number of additional births expected, and average number of total births expected, by age, 2002)

	average number of children ever borne	average number of additional births expected	average number of total births expected
Total women aged 15 to 44	**1.28**	**0.99**	**2.27**
Aged 15 to 19	0.09	2.07	2.15
Aged 20 to 24	0.52	1.92	2.44
Aged 25 to 29	1.21	1.15	2.36
Aged 30 to 34	1.58	0.69	2.27
Aged 35 to 39	1.93	0.28	2.21
Aged 40 to 44	2.11	0.08	2.19

Source: National Center for Health Statistics, Fertility, Family Planning, and Reproductive Health of U.S. Women: Data from the 2002 National Survey of Family Growth, Vital and Health Statistics, Series 23, No. 25, December 2005, Internet site http://www.cdc.gov/nchs/nsfg.htm

Table 2.13 Women Giving Birth in the Past Year, 2004

(total number of women aged 15 to 44, number and percent who gave birth in the past year, and number and percent who had a first birth in past year, by age, 2004; numbers in thousands)

	total	gave birth in past year		first birth in past year	
		number	percent	number	percent
Total aged 15 to 44	**61,588**	**3,746**	**6.1%**	**1,474**	**2.4%**
Age					
Aged 15 to 19	9,964	385	3.9	221	2.2
Aged 20 to 24	10,068	882	8.8	433	4.3
Aged 25 to 29	9,498	938	9.9	382	4.0
Aged 30 to 34	10,082	946	9.4	286	2.8
Aged 35 to 39	10,442	443	4.2	120	1.1
Aged 40 to 44	11,535	153	1.3	33	0.3
Race and Hispanic origin					
Asian	3,262	243	7.4	121	3.7
Black	9,065	537	5.9	199	2.2
Hispanic	9,618	817	8.5	269	2.8
Non-Hispanic white	39,120	2,114	5.4	875	2.2
Nativity status					
Native born	52,107	2,953	5.7	1,181	2.3
Foreign born	9,481	794	8.4	293	3.1
Region					
Northeast	11,412	656	5.7	254	2.2
Midwest	13,703	898	6.6	339	2.5
South	22,182	1,338	6.0	530	2.4
West	14,291	854	6.0	352	2.5

Source: Bureau of the Census, Fertility of American Women, Current Population Survey—June 2004, Detailed Tables, Internet site http://www.census.gov/population/www/socdemo/fertility/cps2004.html

Generation X Dominates Births

More than 60 percent of babies are born to women aged 25 to 39.

Despite an increase in the number of older mothers during the past few decades, the great majority of women giving birth are in their twenties and thirties. Women spanning the ages from 25 to 39 accounted for 62 percent of the nation's births in 2004 (Generation X was aged 28 to 39 in that year). Only 3 percent of newborns had a mother aged 40 or older, while a substantial 35 percent were born to a mother under age 25.

Generation X's dominance of births varies by the race and Hispanic origin of the woman giving birth. Women aged 25 to 39 accounted for 79 percent of babies born to Asian women in 2004 and for 67 of babies born to non-Hispanic whites. But the age group accounts for only 48 percent of births to blacks.

Among women aged 25 to 39 who gave birth in 2004, 31 percent were having their first child. This figure was surpassed by the 34 percent having their second child and the 35 percent having their third or subsequent child.

■ Generation Xers account for most births today, but Millennials will soon replace them as the dominant generation entering parenthood.

The women of Generation X account for most births

(percent distribution of births by age of mother, 2004)

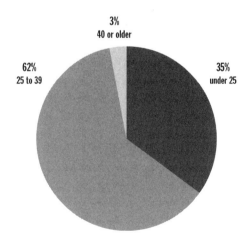

3%
40 or older

62%
25 to 39

35%
under 25

Table 2.14 Births by Age, Race, and Hispanic Origin, 2004

(number and percent distribution of births by age, race, and Hispanic origin of mother, 2004)

	total	American Indian	Asian	non-Hispanic black	Hispanic	non-Hispanic white
Total births	**4,115,590**	**43,931**	**229,532**	**576,105**	**944,993**	**2,304,181**
Under age 25	1,457,031	22,968	38,559	287,223	414,913	689,617
Aged 25 to 39	2,548,428	20,216	182,454	276,588	512,075	1,544,762
Aged 25 to 29	1,105,297	10,726	65,052	137,445	253,980	633,588
Aged 30 to 34	967,008	6,506	79,726	92,338	177,330	606,165
Aged 35 to 39	476,123	2,984	37,676	46,805	80,765	305,009
Aged 40 or older	110,131	748	8,339	12,295	18,005	69,801
PERCENT DISTRIBUTION BY AGE						
Total births	**100.0%**	**100.0%**	**100.0%**	**100.0%**	**100.0%**	**100.0%**
Under age 25	35.4	52.3	16.8	49.9	43.9	29.9
Aged 25 to 39	61.9	46.0	79.5	48.0	54.2	67.0
Aged 25 to 29	26.9	24.4	28.3	23.9	26.9	27.5
Aged 30 to 34	23.5	14.8	34.7	16.0	18.8	26.3
Aged 35 to 39	11.6	6.8	16.4	8.1	8.5	13.2
Aged 40 or older	2.7	1.7	3.6	2.1	1.9	3.0
PERCENT DISTRIBUTION BY RACE AND HISPANIC ORIGIN						
Total births	**100.0%**	**1.1%**	**5.6%**	**14.0%**	**23.0%**	**56.0%**
Under age 25	100.0	1.6	2.6	19.7	28.5	47.3
Aged 25 to 39	100.0	0.8	7.2	10.9	20.1	60.6
Aged 25 to 29	100.0	1.0	5.9	12.4	23.0	57.3
Aged 30 to 34	100.0	0.7	8.2	9.5	18.3	62.7
Aged 35 to 39	100.0	0.6	7.9	9.8	17.0	64.1
Aged 40 or older	100.0	0.7	7.6	11.2	16.3	63.4

Note: Numbers will not add to total because Hispanics may be of any race.
Source: National Center for Health Statistics, Preliminary Births for 2004, Internet site http://www.cdc.gov/nchs/products/pubs/pubd/hestats/prelim_births/prelim_births04.htm; calculations by New Strategist

Table 2.15 Births by Age and Birth Order, 2004

(number and percent distribution of births by age and birth order, 2004)

	total	first child	second child	third child	fourth or later child
Total births	**4,115,590**	**1,632,543**	**1,320,853**	**694,584**	**449,049**
Under age 25	1,457,031	820,848	421,389	153,032	55,187
Aged 25 to 39	2,548,428	787,311	868,749	518,658	362,413
Aged 25 to 29	1,105,297	396,349	370,771	208,216	125,228
Aged 30 to 34	967,008	280,348	342,181	200,365	139,856
Aged 35 to 39	476,123	110,614	155,797	110,077	97,329
Aged 40 or older	110,131	24,385	30,715	22,893	31,449
PERCENT DISTRIBUTION BY BIRTH ORDER					
Total births	**100.0%**	**39.7%**	**32.1%**	**16.9%**	**10.9%**
Under age 25	100.0	56..	28.9	10.5	3.8
Aged 25 to 39	100.0	30.9	34.1	20.4	14.2
Aged 25 to 29	100.0	35.9	33.5	18.8	11.3
Aged 30 to 34	100.0	29.0	35.4	20.7	14.5
Aged 35 to 39	100.0	23.2	32.7	23.1	20.4
Aged 40 or older	100.0	22.1	27.9	20.8	28.6
PERCENT DISTRIBUTION BY AGE					
Total births	**100.0%**	**100.0%**	**100.0%**	**100.0%**	**100.0%**
Under age 25	35.4	50.3	31.9	22.0	12.3
Aged 25 to 39	61.9	48.2	65.8	74.7	80.7
Aged 25 to 29	26.9	24.3	28.1	30.0	27.9
Aged 30 to 34	23.5	17.2	25.9	28.8	31.1
Aged 35 to 39	11.6	6.8	11.8	15.8	21.7
Aged 40 or older	2.7	1.5	2.3	3.3	7.0

Note: Numbers will not add to total because "not stated" is not shown.
Source: National Center for Health Statistics, Births: Preliminary Data for 2004, National Vital Statistics Report, Vol. 54, No. 8, 2005, Internet site http://www.cdc.gov/nchs/products/pubs/pubd/nvsr/54/54-pre.htm; calculations by New Strategist

Many Generation X Mothers Are Not Married

Out-of-wedlock births fall with age.

Slightly more than one-third of babies born in 2003 had a mother who was not married. There are sharp differences by age in the percentage of new mothers who are not married, however. The younger the woman, the more likely she is to give birth out of wedlock.

Among babies born to women under age 25 in 2003, the 61 percent majority was born to single mothers. The figure stood at a much smaller 20 percent among babies born to women aged 25 to 39. Among those born to women aged 40 or older, 18 percent had an unmarried mother.

Black women are most likely to be single mothers. Fully 50 percent of babies born to black women aged 25 to 39 in 2003 were out-of-wedlock. Among Hispanics, the share is 32 percent. Among non-Hispanic whites, it is a much smaller 12 percent, and Asians have the smallest proportion at 9 percent.

■ The differences in out-of-wedlock childbearing by race and Hispanic origin result in different lifestyles among adults in their twenties and thirties.

Half of babies born to black women aged 25 to 39 have a single mother

(percent of babies born to unmarried women aged 25 to 39, by race and Hispanic origin, 2003)

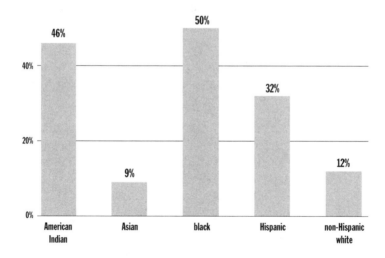

Table 2.16 Births to Unmarried Women by Age, Race, and Hispanic Origin, 2003

(total number of births and number and percent to unmarried women, by age, race, and Hispanic origin of mother, 2003)

	total	American Indian	Asian	black	Hispanic	non-Hispanic white
Total births	**4,089,950**	**43,052**	**221,203**	**599,847**	**912,329**	**2,321,904**
Under age 25	1,453,546	22,489	38,178	299,945	404,191	696,294
Aged 25 to 39	2,529,554	19,853	175,165	287,365	491,216	1,557,106
Aged 25 to 29	1,086,366	10,524	64,399	139,947	246,361	627,437
Aged 30 to 34	975,546	6,423	75,692	97,529	169,054	626,315
Aged 35 to 39	467,642	2,906	35,074	49,889	75,801	303,354
Aged 40 or older	106,850	710	7,860	12,537	16,922	68,504
BIRTHS TO UNMARRIED WOMEN						
Total births to unmarried women	**1,415,995**	**26,401**	**33,249**	**409,333**	**410,620**	**546,991**
Under age 25	893,023	16,932	16,762	260,027	246,878	358,776
Aged 25 to 39	503,831	9,154	15,704	144,373	158,797	179,973
Aged 25 to 29	287,205	5,293	7,886	83,421	91,644	101,454
Aged 30 to 34	147,555	2,668	5,238	41,692	46,995	52,167
Aged 35 to 39	69,071	1,193	2,580	19,260	20,158	26,352
Aged 40 or older	19,141	315	783	4,933	4,945	8,242
PERCENT OF BIRTHS TO UNMARRIED WOMEN						
Total births	**34.6%**	**61.3%**	**15.0%**	**68.2%**	**45.0%**	**23.6%**
Under age 25	61.4	75.3	43.9	86.7	61.1	51.5
Aged 25 to 39	19.9	46.1	9.0	50.2	32.3	11.6
Aged 25 to 29	26.4	50.3	12.2	59.6	37.2	16.2
Aged 30 to 34	15.1	41.5	6.9	42.7	27.8	8.3
Aged 35 to 39	14.8	41.1	7.4	38.6	26.6	8.7
Aged 40 or older	17.9	44.4	10.0	39.3	29.2	12.0

Note: Births by race and Hispanic origin will not add to total because Hispanics may be of any race and "not stated" is not shown.
Source: National Center for Health Statistics, Births: Final Data for 2003, National Vital Statistics Reports, Vol. 54, No. 2, 2005, Internet site http://www.cdc.gov/nchs/products/pubs/pubd/nvsr/54/54-pre.htm; calculations by New Strategist

Caesarean Deliveries Are Common among Women of All Ages

The rate is highest among older women, however.

Delayed childbearing can have an unanticipated cost. The older a woman is when she has a child, the greater the likelihood of complications that necessitate Caesarean delivery.

Among babies born in 2003, more than one in four (27 percent) were Caesarean deliveries. Only 22 percent of babies born to women under age 25 were delivered by Caesarean section, but the share stood at 30 percent among women aged 25 to 39, and topped 42 percent among women aged 40 or older.

Many women whose first child is delivered by Caesarean hope that subsequent children can be delivered vaginally. Age influences the likelihood of a subsequent Caesarean delivery, however. Repeat Caesareans are more common among older women.

■ As women delay childbearing, the rate of Caesarean delivery increases. With new fertility technologies enabling more women to have children later in life, the rate is likely to rise further.

Young women are least likely to require Caesarean deliveries

(percent of births delivered by Caesarean section, by age of mother, 2003)

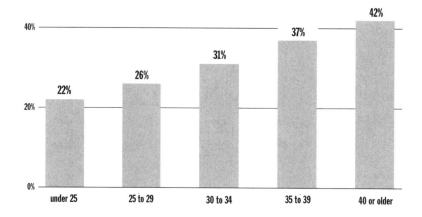

Table 2.17 Births by Age and Method of Delivery, 2003

(number and percent distribution of births by age and method of delivery, 2003)

		vaginal		Caesarean		
	total births	total	after previous Caesarean	total	primary	repeat
Total births	**4,089,950**	**2,949,853**	**51,602**	**1,119,388**	**684,484**	**434,699**
Under age 25	1,453,546	1,134,471	10,174	312,761	224,557	88,187
Aged 25 to 39	2,529,554	1,754,404	39,321	761,475	434,258	327,052
Aged 25 to 29	1,086,366	795,736	14,123	285,231	172,845	112,353
Aged 30 to 34	975,546	665,025	16,004	305,102	170,728	134,296
Aged 35 to 39	467,642	293,643	9,194	171,142	90,685	80,403
Aged 40 or older	106,850	60,978	2,107	45,152	25,669	19,460
PERCENT DISTRIBUTION BY METHOD OF DELIVERY						
Total births	**100.0%**	**72.1%**	**1.3%**	**27.4%**	**16.7%**	**10.6%**
Under age 25	100.0	78.0	0.7	21.5	15.4	6.1
Aged 25 to 39	100.0	69.4	1.6	30.1	17.2	12.9
Aged 25 to 29	100.0	73.2	1.3	26.3	15.9	10.3
Aged 30 to 34	100.0	68.2	1.6	31.3	17.5	13.8
Aged 35 to 39	100.0	62.8	2.0	36.6	19.4	17.2
Aged 40 or older	100.0	57.1	2.0	42.3	24.0	18.2
PERCENT DISTRIBUTION BY AGE						
Total births	**100.0%**	**100.0%**	**100.0%**	**100.0%**	**100.0%**	**100.0%**
Under age 25	35.5	38.5	19.7	27.9	32.8	20.3
Aged 25 to 39	61.8	59.5	76.2	68.0	63.4	75.2
Aged 25 to 29	26.6	27.0	27.4	25.5	25.3	25.8
Aged 30 to 34	23.9	22.5	31.0	27.3	24.9	30.9
Aged 35 to 39	11.4	10.0	17.8	15.3	13.2	18.5
Aged 40 or older	2.6	2.1	4.1	4.0	3.8	4.5

Note: Numbers will not add to total because "not stated" is not shown.
Source: National Center for Health Statistics, Births: Final Data for 2003, National Vital Statistics Reports, Vol. 54, No. 2, 2005, Internet site http://www.cdc.gov/nchs/products/pubs/pubd/nvsr/54/54-pre.htm; calculations by New Strategist

Many Younger Adults Smoke Cigarettes

Former smokers do not outnumber current smokers until the 45-to-54 age group.

The percentage of Americans who smoke cigarettes is sharply lower than what it was a few decades ago. Nevertheless, a substantial 21 percent of people aged 18 or older were current smokers in 2004. The figure peaks among 18-to-24-year-olds at 27 percent. In the 25-to-34 age group, a slightly smaller 25 percent smoke. The figure declines to 24 percent in the 35-to-44 age group.

Drinking is much more popular than smoking. Overall, 57 percent of people aged 18 or older have had an alcoholic beverage in the past month. The proportion of people who have had a drink in the past month peaks in the 25-to-34 age group at 63 percent, then declines with age. A minority of people aged 65 or older have had a drink in the past month.

■ Generation X is exiting the risk-taking age groups. The percentage of Gen Xers who smoke and drink will decline as they get older.

Some Generation Xers have quit smoking

(percent distribution of people aged 25 to 34 by cigarette smoking status, 2004)

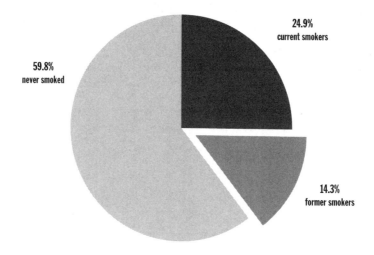

24.9%
current smokers

59.8%
never smoked

14.3%
former smokers

Table 2.18 Cigarette Smoking Status by Age, 2004

(percent distribution of people aged 18 or older by age and cigarette smoking status, 2004)

	total	current smokers			former smoker	never smoked
		total	smoke every day	smoke some days		
Total people	**100.0%**	**20.9%**	**15.6%**	**5.3%**	**23.9%**	**54.9%**
Aged 18 to 24	100.0	26.9	18.5	8.4	8.0	64.1
Aged 25 to 34	100.0	24.9	17.4	7.5	14.3	59.8
Aged 35 to 44	100.0	23.7	18.4	5.3	17.2	58.0
Aged 45 to 54	100.0	22.4	17.4	5.0	25.6	50.9
Aged 55 to 64	100.0	18.2	14.6	3.6	36.3	45.5
Aged 65 or older	100.0	9.0	6.9	2.1	39.5	51.0

Source: Centers for Disease Control and Prevention, Behavioral Risk Factor Surveillance System Prevalence Data, 2004, Internet site http://apps.nccd.cdc.gov/brfss/index.asp; calculations by New Strategist

Table 2.19 Alcohol Use by Age, 2004

(percent distribution of people aged 18 or older by whether they have had at least one drink of alcohol within the past 30 days, by age, 2004)

	yes	no
Total people	**56.8%**	**43.1%**
Aged 18 to 24	58.4	40.8
Aged 25 to 34	62.9	37.0
Aged 35 to 44	60.6	39.3
Aged 45 to 54	58.5	41.4
Aged 55 to 64	53.3	46.6
Aged 65 or older	39.9	60.0

Source: Centers for Disease Control and Prevention, Behavioral Risk Factor Surveillance System Prevalence Data, 2004, Internet site http://apps.nccd.cdc.gov/brfss/index.asp

Most Generation Xers Have Used Illicit Drugs

Generation X is much less likely to have used illicit drugs in the past month than 18-to-25-year-olds, however.

People aged 18 to 25 are most likely to be current drug users. Nineteen percent have used illicit drugs in the past month. The percentage of current users falls to 13 percent among 26-to-29-year-olds and to just 9 percent among 30-to-34-year-olds.

More than half of Generation Xers have used illicit drugs at some time during their life, with the percentage standing at 55 to 60 percent in the 26-to-39 age group. The figure peaks at 65 percent among the youngest Baby Boomers, aged 40 to 44.

■ Although drug use among young adults is a serious concern, chronic use drops sharply as people age into their late twenties, establish careers, and start families.

Generation Xers are less likely than Baby Boomers to have used illicit drugs

(percent of people aged 12 or older who have ever used any illicit drug, by age, 2004)

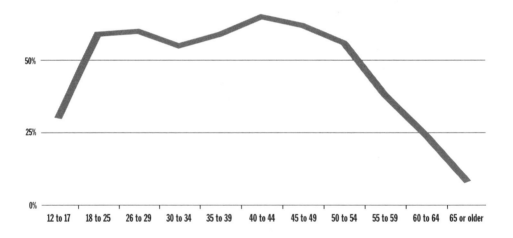

Table 2.20 Illicit Drug Use by Age, 2004

(percent of people aged 12 or older who ever used any illicit drug, who used an illicit drug in the past year, and who used an illicit drug in the past month, by age, 2004)

	ever used	used in past year	used in past month
Total people	**45.8%**	**14.5%**	**7.9%**
Aged 12 to 17	30.0	21.0	10.6
Aged 18 to 25	59.2	33.9	19.4
Aged 26 to 29	60.0	23.5	13.2
Aged 30 to 34	54.5	15.7	9.4
Aged 35 to 39	59.4	14.1	7.2
Aged 40 to 44	64.9	14.4	7.5
Aged 45 to 49	61.8	11.8	6.8
Aged 50 to 54	56.3	9.0	4.8
Aged 55 to 59	38.2	5.1	2.6
Aged 60 to 64	24.2	2.0	1.1
Aged 65 or older	8.3	0.9	0.4

Note: Illicit drugs include marijuana/hashish, cocaine (including crack), heroin, hallucinogens, inhalants, or any prescription-type psychotherapeutic used nonmedically.
Source: SAMHSA, Office of Applied Studies, National Survey on Drug Use and Health, 2004, Internet site http://oas.samhsa .gov/nsduh/2k4nsduh/2k4Results/apph.htm

One in Four Generation Xers Has No Health Insurance

The figure is even higher among 18-to-24-year-olds.

People aged 18 to 34 are more likely than middle-aged or older adults to be without health insurance. Entering the workforce at the age of 18, or graduating from college at the age of 21, usually means health insurance coverage is no longer available through a parent's plan. This partly explains why a substantial 31 percent of the nation's 18-to-24-year-olds and 26 percent of 25-to-34-year-olds have no health insurance. The figure stands at 19 percent among 35-to-44-year-olds.

Most Americans obtain health insurance coverage through their employer, but among 25-to-34-year-olds only 61 percent had employment-based coverage in 2004 and an even smaller 46 percent had their own employment-based coverage. Among 18-to-44-year-olds without health insurance in 2003, the biggest reason for not having coverage was the high cost (cited by 54 percent), followed by losing employment (26 percent). In third place, 18 percent said their employer did not offer health insurance. Because so many young adults lack health insurance, the government's Medicaid program picks up a good portion of their health care tab. In 2003, Medicaid paid for 11 to 15 percent of the health care expenses of people aged 25 to 39.

■ The health insurance needs of young adults are a problem without an easy solution since few can afford to buy private insurance.

Many Americans do not have health insurance coverage

(percent of people aged 18 or older without health insurance, by age, 2004)

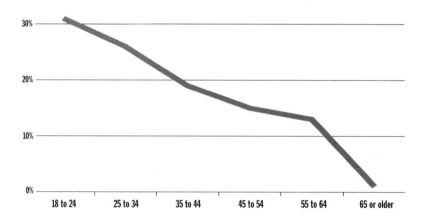

Table 2.21 Health Insurance Coverage by Age, 2004

(number and percent distribution of people by age and health insurance coverage status, 2004; numbers in thousands)

	total	with health insurance coverage during year			not covered at any time during the year
		total	private	government	
Total people	**291,155**	**245,335**	**198,262**	**79,086**	**45,820**
Under age 18	73,821	65,553	48,462	21,922	8,269
Aged 18 to 24	27,972	19,200	16,229	4,022	8,772
Aged 25 to 34	39,307	29,130	25,765	4,578	10,177
Aged 35 to 44	43,350	35,240	31,883	4,680	8,110
Aged 45 to 54	41,960	35,700	32,414	4,847	6,260
Aged 55 to 64	29,532	25,596	22,174	5,442	3,936
Aged 65 or older	35,213	34,916	21,336	33,595	297

PERCENT DISTRIBUTION BY COVERAGE STATUS

	total	total	private	government	not covered
Total people	**100.0%**	**84.3%**	**68.1%**	**27.2%**	**15.7%**
Under age 18	100.0	88.8	65.6	29.7	11.2
Aged 18 to 24	100.0	68.6	58.0	14.4	31.4
Aged 25 to 34	100.0	74.1	65.5	11.6	25.9
Aged 35 to 44	100.0	81.3	73.5	10.8	18.7
Aged 45 to 54	100.0	85.1	77.2	11.6	14.9
Aged 55 to 64	100.0	86.7	75.1	18.4	13.3
Aged 65 or older	100.0	99.2	60.6	95.4	0.8

PERCENT DISTRIBUTION BY AGE

	total	total	private	government	not covered
Total people	**100.0%**	**100.0%**	**100.0%**	**100.0%**	**100.0%**
Under age 18	25.4	26.7	24.4	27.7	18.0
Aged 18 to 24	9.6	7.8	8.2	5.1	19.1
Aged 25 to 34	13.5	11.9	13.0	5.8	22.2
Aged 35 to 44	14.9	14.4	16.1	5.9	17.7
Aged 45 to 54	14.4	14.6	16.3	6.1	13.7
Aged 55 to 64	10.1	10.4	11.2	6.9	8.6
Aged 65 or older	12.1	14.2	10.8	42.5	0.6

Note: Numbers may not add to total because some people have more than one type of health insurance coverage.
Source: Bureau of the Census, 2005 Current Population Survey, Internet site http://pubdb3.census.gov/macro/032005/health/h01_000.htm; calculations by New Strategist

Table 2.22 Private Health Insurance Coverage by Age, 2004

(number and percent distribution of people by age and private health insurance coverage status, 2004; numbers in thousands)

| | | with private health insurance | | | |
| | | | employment based | | |
	total	total	total	own	direct purchase
Total people	**291,155**	**198,262**	**174,174**	**91,709**	**26,961**
Under age 18	73,821	48,462	44,892	237	4,166
Aged 18 to 24	27,972	16,229	12,966	5,122	1,495
Aged 25 to 34	39,307	25,765	24,027	18,151	2,266
Aged 35 to 44	43,350	31,883	29,824	21,335	2,773
Aged 45 to 54	41,960	32,414	30,088	22,141	3,215
Aged 55 to 64	29,532	22,174	19,872	14,907	3,066
Aged 65 or older	35,213	21,336	12,505	9,817	9,979
PERCENT DISTRIBUTION BY COVERAGE STATUS					
Total people	**100.0%**	**68.1%**	**59.8%**	**31.5%**	**9.3%**
Under age 18	100.0	65.6	60.8	0.3	5.6
Aged 18 to 24	100.0	58.0	46.4	18.3	5.3
Aged 25 to 34	100.0	65.5	61.1	46.2	5.8
Aged 35 to 44	100.0	73.5	68.8	49.2	6.4
Aged 45 to 54	100.0	77.2	71.7	52.8	7.7
Aged 55 to 64	100.0	75.1	67.3	50.5	10.4
Aged 65 or older	100.0	60.6	35.5	27.9	28.3
PERCENT DISTRIBUTION BY AGE					
Total people	**100.0%**	**100.0%**	**100.0%**	**100.0%**	**100.0%**
Under age 18	25.4	24.4	25.8	0.3	15.5
Aged 18 to 24	9.6	8.2	7.4	5.6	5.5
Aged 25 to 34	13.5	13.0	13.8	19.8	8.4
Aged 35 to 44	14.9	16.1	17.1	23.3	10.3
Aged 45 to 54	14.4	16.3	17.3	24.1	11.9
Aged 55 to 64	10.1	11.2	11.4	16.3	11.4
Aged 65 or older	12.1	10.8	7.2	10.7	37.0

Note: Numbers may not add to total because some people have more than one type of health insurance coverage.
Source: Bureau of the Census, 2005 Current Population Survey, Internet site http://pubdb3.census.gov/macro/032005/health/ h01_000.htm; calculations by New Strategist

Table 2.23 Government Health Insurance Coverage by Age, 2004

(number and percent distribution of people by age and government health insurance coverage status, 2004; numbers in thousands)

| | total | with government health insurance | | | |
		total	Medicaid	Medicare	military
Total people	**291,155**	**79,086**	**37,514**	**39,745**	**10,680**
Under age 18	73,821	21,922	19,847	500	2,045
Aged 18 to 24	27,972	4,022	3,196	212	804
Aged 25 to 34	39,307	4,578	3,408	482	982
Aged 35 to 44	43,350	4,680	3,135	900	1,129
Aged 45 to 54	41,960	4,847	2,595	1,548	1,425
Aged 55 to 64	29,532	5,442	2,036	2,651	1,785
Aged 65 or older	35,213	33,595	3,297	33,452	2,509

PERCENT DISTRIBUTION BY COVERAGE STATUS

Total people	**100.0%**	**27.2%**	**12.9%**	**13.7%**	**3.7%**
Under age 18	100.0	29.7	26.9	0.7	2.8
Aged 18 to 24	100.0	14.4	11.4	0.8	2.9
Aged 25 to 34	100.0	11.6	8.7	1.2	2.5
Aged 35 to 44	100.0	10.8	7.2	2.1	2.6
Aged 45 to 54	100.0	11.6	6.2	3.7	3.4
Aged 55 to 64	100.0	18.4	6.9	9.0	6.0
Aged 65 or older	100.0	95.4	9.4	95.0	7.1

PERCENT DISTRIBUTION BY AGE

Total people	**100.0%**	**100.0%**	**100.0%**	**100.0%**	**100.0%**
Under age 18	25.4	27.7	52.9	1.3	19.1
Aged 18 to 24	9.6	5.1	8.5	0.5	7.5
Aged 25 to 34	13.5	5.8	9.1	1.2	9.2
Aged 35 to 44	14.9	5.9	8.4	2.3	10.6
Aged 45 to 54	14.4	6.1	6.9	3.9	13.3
Aged 55 to 64	10.1	6.9	5.4	6.7	16.7
Aged 65 or older	12.1	42.5	8.8	84.2	23.5

Note: Numbers may not add to total because some people have more than one type of health insurance coverage.
Source: Bureau of the Census, 2005 Current Population Survey, Internet site http://pubdb3.census.gov/macro/032005/health/ h01_000.htm; calculations by New Strategist

Table 2.24 **People Aged 18 to 44 by Health Insurance Coverage Status and Reason for No Coverage, 2003**

(number and percent distribution of people aged 18 to 44 by health insurance coverage status and reasons for no coverage, 2003)

	number	percent
HEALTH INSURANCE STATUS		
Total people aged 18 to 44	**110,537**	**100.0%**
With health insurance	84,958	76.9
Without health insurance	25,579	23.1
REASON FOR NO HEALTH INSURANCE		
People aged 18 to 44 without health insurance	**25,579**	**100.0**
Cost	12,749	54.1
Lost job or change in employment	6,150	26.1
Employer didn't offer insurance/company refused	4,266	18.1
Ineligible due to age/left school	2,818	12.0
Medicaid stopped	2,019	8.6
Change in marital status or death of parent	511	2.2
Other reason	1,420	6.0

Note: Numbers will not sum to total because unknowns are not shown and people could report more than one reason.
Source: National Center for Health Statistics, Summary Health Statistics for the U.S. Population: National Health Interview Survey, 2003, Vital and Health Statistics, Series 10, No. 224, 2005, Internet site http://www.cdc.gov/nchs/nhis.htm

Table 2.25 Spending on Health Care by Age, 2003

(percent of people with health care expense, median expense per person, total expenses, and percent distribution of total expenses by source of payment, by age, 2003)

	total (thousands)	percent with expense	median expense per person	total expenses amount (millions)	total expenses percent distribution
Total people	**290,604**	**85.6%**	**$1,021**	**$895,527**	**100.0%**
Under age 18	72,996	86.4	425	80,187	9.0
Aged 18 to 24	27,156	74.6	561	39,654	4.4
Aged 25 to 29	20,425	76.3	703	37,357	4.2
Aged 30 to 39	40,068	80.2	823	76,237	8.5
Aged 40 to 49	44,703	85.8	1,161	131,343	14.7
Aged 50 to 59	35,265	89.6	1,995	166,300	18.6
Aged 60 to 64	13,293	93.4	2,646	74,167	8.3
Aged 65 or older	36,699	96.3	3,649	290,283	32.4

PERCENT DISTRIBUTION BY SOURCE OF PAYMENT

	total	out of pocket	private insurance	Medicare	Medicaid	other
Total people	**100.0%**	**19.6%**	**42.4%**	**19.9%**	**9.2%**	**8.9%**
Under age 18	100.0	20.5	50.3	–	22.6	6.3
Aged 18 to 24	100.0	20.0	52.0	–	20.9	6.9
Aged 25 to 29	100.0	19.2	56.2	–	14.5	9.0
Aged 30 to 39	100.0	20.3	59.3	–	11.0	6.4
Aged 40 to 49	100.0	19.8	48.3	–	9.5	–
Aged 50 to 59	100.0	19.0	59.2	–	7.0	8.0
Aged 60 to 64	100.0	22.4	56.3	–	7.0	6.4
Aged 65 or older	100.0	18.8	16.7	53.0	4.3	7.2

Note: "Other" insurance includes Department of Veterans Affairs (except Tricare), American Indian Health Service, state and local clinics, worker's compensation, homeowner's and automobile insurance, etc. "–" means not applicable or sample is too small to make a reliable estimate.
Source: Agency for Healthcare Research and Quality, Medical Expenditure Panel Survey, 2003, Internet site http://www.meps .ahrq.gov/CompendiumTables/TC_TOC.htm; calculations by New Strategist

Health Problems Are Few in the 18-to-44 Age Group

Lower back pain is by far the most common health condition in the age group.

Twenty-four percent of Americans aged 18 to 44 have experienced lower back pain for at least one full day in the past three months, making it the most common health condition in the age group. Migraines or severe headaches are second, with 18 percent having the problem. Chronic joint symptoms are third, with 16 percent reporting this problem. Sinusitis is mentioned by 13 percent. The 18-to-44 age group accounts for more than half of those ever experiencing asthma.

Few adults aged 18 to 44 have hearing or vision problems. But they are just as likely as older adults to have emotional problems. The proportion of people saying they feel sad, hopeless, or worthless at least some of the time does not vary much by age.

While 10 percent of people aged 16 to 64 have a health problem that prevents them from working or limits the kind of work they can do, the proportion is a smaller 6 percent among 25-to-34-year-olds, rising to 9 percent in the 35-to-44 age group. But the less educated the young adult, the more likely he or she is to have a work disability.

People with AIDS are sometimes counted among the nation's disabled. As of 2003, more than 900,000 people had been diagnosed with AIDS, most of them aged 25 to 44. People aged 25 to 44 account for 73 percent of those diagnosed with AIDS.

■ As Generation X ages into its forties, the number of Xers with chronic conditions such as heart disease, arthritis, and hearing problems will rise.

The top five health conditions among people aged 18 to 44

(percent of people aged 18 to 44 with selected health conditions, 2004)

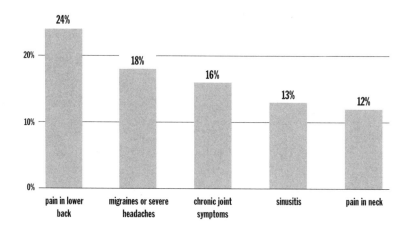

Table 2.26 Health Conditions among People Aged 18 or Older by Age, 2004

(number of people aged 18 or older with selected health conditions, by type of condition and age, 2004; numbers in thousands)

	total	18 to 44	45 to 64	65 to 74	75 or older
NUMBER					
Total people	**215,191**	**110,417**	**70,182**	**18,360**	**16,232**
Selected circulatory diseases					
Heart disease, all types	24,666	4,953	8,636	4,994	6,082
Coronary	13,621	1,184	4,858	3,358	4,221
Hypertension	47,493	8,133	21,303	9,089	8,968
Stroke	5,519	510	1,750	1,257	2,002
Selected respiratory conditions					
Emphysema	3,576	309	1,393	904	970
Asthma					
Ever	21,300	10,959	6,973	1,893	1,474
Still	14,358	7,058	4,871	1,368	1,061
Hay fever	18,629	8,777	7,252	1,475	1,126
Sinusitis	30,789	13,976	11,769	2,780	2,265
Chronic bronchitis	9,047	3,483	3,413	1,126	1,026
Cancer, any	**15,024**	**2,046**	**5,551**	**3,428**	**3,999**
Breast cancer (men and women)	2,581	160	1,089	555	778
Cervical cancer	1,108	506	430	79	93
Prostate cancer	1,688	–	379	488	815
Other selected diseases and conditions					
Diabetes	15,126	2,173	6,963	3,393	2,598
Ulcers	14,828	4,956	5,722	2,002	2,148
Kidney disease	3,652	972	1,250	629	801
Liver disease	2,860	878	1,449	263	270
Arthritic diagnosis	46,515	8,841	20,169	8,496	9,008
Chronic joint symptoms	58,005	17,349	24,439	8,181	8,036
Migraines or severe headaches	32,923	20,279	10,523	1,292	830
Pain in neck	31,742	13,721	13,050	2,540	2,430
Pain in lower back	58,394	26,382	21,543	5,225	5,243
Pain in face or jaw	9,215	4,939	3,272	598	406
Selected sensory problems					
Hearing trouble	35,135	8,459	12,960	5,800	7,917
Vision trouble	19,086	5,624	7,641	2,591	3,230
Absence of all natural teeth	16,814	2,016	5,927	3,909	4,962

(continued)

	total	18 to 44	45 to 64	65 to 74	75 or older
Selected mental health problems					
Sadness	24,232	11,215	8,984	1,948	2,085
Hopelessness	13,259	6,570	5,006	741	942
Worthlessness	10,400	5,033	3,816	603	947
Everything is an effort	29,686	15,395	9,783	2,133	2,375
Nervousness	33,450	17,899	10,996	2,311	2,244
Restlessness	36,172	19,322	11,909	2,573	2,367

Note: The conditions shown are those that have ever been diagnosed by a doctor, except as noted. Hay fever, sinusitis, and chronic bronchitis have been diagnosed in the past twelve months. Kidney and liver disease have been diagnosed in the past twelve months and exclude kidney stones, bladder infections, and incontinence. Chronic joint symptoms are shown if the respondent had pain, aching, or stiffness in or around a joint (excluding back and neck) and the condition began more than three months ago. Migraines, pain in neck, lower back, face, or jaw are shown only if pain lasted a whole day or more. Hearing trouble is anyone saying they had at least "a little trouble." Vision trouble is anyone with "any trouble seeing" even when wearing glasses or contacts. Mental health problems are indicated if the person had the feeling during the past 30 days at least "some of the time." "–" means sample is too small to make a reliable estimate.

Source: National Center for Health Statistics, Summary Health Statistics for U.S. Adults: National Health Interview Survey, 2004, Series 10, No. 228, 2005, Internet site http://www.cdc.gov/nchs/nhis.htm; calculations by New Strategist

Table 2.27 Percent with Health Condition by Age, 2004

(percent of people aged 18 or older with selected health conditions, by type of condition and age, 2004)

	total	18 to 44	45 to 64	65 to 74	75 or older
PERCENT WITH CONDITION					
Total people	**100.0%**	**100.0%**	**100.0%**	**100.0%**	**100.0%**
Selected circulatory diseases					
Heart disease, all types	11.5	4.5	12.3	27.3	37.6
Coronary	6.3	1.1	6.9	18.4	26.1
Hypertension	22.1	7.4	30.5	49.8	55.4
Stroke	2.6	0.5	2.5	6.9	12.4
Selected respiratory conditions					
Emphysema	1.7	0.3	2.0	4.9	6.0
Asthma					
Ever	9.9	9.9	10.0	10.3	9.1
Still	6.7	6.4	7.0	7.5	6.6
Hay fever	8.7	8.0	10.4	8.0	7.0
Sinusitis	14.3	12.7	16.8	15.2	14.0
Chronic bronchitis	4.2	3.2	4.9	6.1	6.3
Cancer, any	**7.0**	**1.9**	**7.9**	**18.7**	**24.7**
Breast cancer (men and women)	1.2	0.1	1.6	3.0	4.8
Cervical cancer	1.0	0.9	1.2	0.8	0.9
Prostate cancer	1.6	–	1.1	5.8	13.0
Other selected diseases and conditions					
Diabetes	7.1	2.0	10.1	18.9	16.4
Ulcers	6.9	4.5	8.2	10.9	13.3
Kidney disease	1.7	0.9	1.8	3.4	4.9
Liver disease	1.3	0.8	2.1	1.4	1.7
Arthritic diagnosis	21.7	8.0	28.8	46.5	55.8
Chronic joint symptoms	27.0	15.7	35.0	44.7	49.8
Migraines or severe headaches	15.3	18.4	15.0	7.1	5.1
Pain in neck	14.8	12.4	18.7	13.9	15.0
Pain in lower back	27.2	23.9	30.8	28.5	32.5
Pain in face or jaw	4.3	4.5	4.7	3.3	2.5
Selected sensory problems					
Hearing trouble	16.3	7.7	18.5	31.7	48.9
Vision trouble	8.9	5.1	10.9	14.1	19.9
Absence of all natural teeth	7.8	1.8	8.5	21.3	30.7

(continued)

	total	18 to 44	45 to 64	65 to 74	75 or older
Selected mental health problems					
Sadness	11.4%	10.3%	13.0%	10.8%	13.3%
Hopelessness	6.3	6.1	7.3	4.1	6.1
Worthlessness	4.9	4.6	5.5	3.4	6.1
Everything is an effort	14.1	14.2	14.2	11.9	15.2
Nervousness	15.8	16.4	15.9	12.8	14.3
Restlessness	17.1	17.7	17.2	14.3	15.1

Note: The conditions shown are those that have ever been diagnosed by a doctor, except as noted. Hay fever, sinusitis, and chronic bronchitis have been diagnosed in the past twelve months. Kidney and liver disease have been diagnosed in the past twelve months and exclude kidney stones, bladder infections, and incontinence. Chronic joint symptoms are shown if the respondent had pain, aching, or stiffness in or around a joint (excluding back and neck) and the condition began more than three months ago. Migraines, pain in neck, lower back, face, or jaw are shown only if pain lasted a whole day or more. Hearing trouble is anyone saying they had at least "a little trouble." Vision trouble is anyone with "any trouble seeing" even when wearing glasses or contacts. Mental health problems are indicated if the person had the feeling during the past 30 days at least "some of the time." "–" means sample is too small to make a reliable estimate.

Source: National Center for Health Statistics, Summary Health Statistics for U.S. Adults: National Health Interview Survey, 2004, Series 10, No. 228, 2005, Internet site http://www.cdc.gov/nchs/nhis.htm; calculations by New Strategist

Table 2.28 Distribution of Health Conditions by Age, 2004

(percent distribution of people aged 18 or older with selected health conditions, by type of condition and age, 2004)

	total	18 to 44	45 to 64	65 to 74	75 or older
PERCENT DISTRIBUTION					
Total people	**100.0%**	**51.3%**	**32.6%**	**8.5%**	**7.5%**
Selected circulatory diseases					
Heart disease, all types	100.0	20.1	35.0	20.2	24.7
Coronary	100.0	8.7	35.7	24.7	31.0
Hypertension	100.0	17.1	44.9	19.1	18.9
Stroke	100.0	9.2	31.7	22.8	36.3
Selected respiratory conditions					
Emphysema	100.0	8.6	39.0	25.3	27.1
Asthma					
Ever	100.0	51.5	32.7	8.9	6.9
Still	100.0	49.2	33.9	9.5	7.4
Hay fever	100.0	47.1	38.9	7.9	6.0
Sinusitis	100.0	45.4	38.2	9.0	7.4
Chronic bronchitis	100.0	38.5	37.7	12.4	11.3
Cancer, any	**100.0**	**13.6**	**36.9**	**22.8**	**26.6**
Breast cancer (men and women)	100.0	6.2	42.2	21.5	30.1
Cervical cancer	100.0	45.7	38.8	7.1	8.4
Prostate cancer	100.0	–	22.5	28.9	48.3
Other selected diseases and conditions					
Diabetes	100.0	14.4	46.0	22.4	17.2
Ulcers	100.0	33.4	38.6	13.5	14.5
Kidney disease	100.0	26.6	34.2	17.2	21.9
Liver disease	100.0	30.7	50.7	9.2	9.4
Arthritic diagnosis	100.0	19.0	43.4	18.3	19.4
Chronic joint symptoms	100.0	29.9	42.1	14.1	13.9
Migraines or severe headaches	100.0	61.6	32.0	3.9	2.5
Pain in neck	100.0	43.2	41.1	8.0	7.7
Pain in lower back	100.0	45.2	36.9	8.9	9.0
Pain in face or jaw	100.0	53.6	35.5	6.5	4.4
Selected sensory problems					
Hearing trouble	100.0	24.1	36.9	16.5	22.5
Vision trouble	100.0	29.5	40.0	13.6	16.9
Absence of all natural teeth	100.0	12.0	35.3	23.2	29.5

(continued)

	total	18 to 44	45 to 64	65 to 74	75 or older
Selected mental health problems					
Sadness	100.0%	46.3%	37.1%	8.0%	8.6%
Hopelessness	100.0	49.6	37.8	5.6	7.1
Worthlessness	100.0	48.4	36.7	5.8	9.1
Everything is an effort	100.0	51.9	33.0	7.2	8.0
Nervousness	100.0	53.5	32.9	6.9	6.7
Restlessness	100.0	53.4	32.9	7.1	6.5

Note: The conditions shown are those that have ever been diagnosed by a doctor, except as noted. Hay fever, sinusitis, and chronic bronchitis have been diagnosed in the past twelve months. Kidney and liver disease have been diagnosed in the past twelve months and exclude kidney stones, bladder infections, and incontinence. Chronic joint symptoms are shown if the respondent had pain, aching, or stiffness in or around a joint (excluding back and neck) and the condition began more than three months ago. Migraines, pain in neck, lower back, face, or jaw are shown only if pain lasted a whole day or more. Hearing trouble is anyone saying they had at least "a little trouble." Vision trouble is anyone with "any trouble seeing" even when wearing glasses or contacts. Mental health problems are indicated if the person had the feeling during the past 30 days at least "some of the time." "–" means sample is too small to make a reliable estimate.

Source: National Center for Health Statistics, Summary Health Statistics for U.S. Adults: National Health Interview Survey, 2004, Series 10, No. 228, 2005, Internet site http://www.cdc.gov/nchs/nhis.htm; calculations by New Strategist

Table 2.29 People Aged 25 to 44 with a Work Disability, 2005

(number and percent of people aged 16 or older with a work disability, by selected age group, education, and severity of disability, 2005; numbers in thousands)

| | | with a work disability | | | | | |
| | | total | | not severe | | severe | |
	total	number	percent	number	percent	number	percent
Total aged 16 to 64	**190,023**	**19,656**	**10.3%**	**5,414**	**2.8%**	**14,243**	**7.5%**
Not a high school graduate	33,536	5,226	15.6	821	2.4	4,406	13.1
High school graduate	56,398	7,413	13.1	1,797	3.2	5,615	10.0
Associate's degree or some college	52,347	4,647	8.9	1,706	3.3	2,942	5.6
Bachelor's degree or more	47,743	2,370	5.0	1,090	2.3	1,280	2.7
Total aged 25 to 34	**38,990**	**2,475**	**6.3**	**739**	**1.9**	**1,736**	**4.5**
Not a high school graduate	5,211	558	10.7	93	1.8	463	8.9
High school graduate	11,203	1,030	9.2	254	2.3	776	6.9
Associate's degree or some college	10,769	654	6.1	291	2.7	363	3.4
Bachelor's degree or more	11,806	233	2.0	100	0.8	134	1.1
Total aged 35 to 44	**43,057**	**3,764**	**8.7**	**1,067**	**2.5**	**2,697**	**6.3**
Not a high school graduate	5,039	852	16.9	121	2.4	731	14.5
High school graduate	13,681	1,509	11.0	343	2.5	1,166	8.5
Associate's degree or some college	11,489	906	7.9	332	2.9	574	5.0
Bachelor's degree or more	12,848	497	3.9	271	2.1	226	1.8

A person is considered to have a work disability if any of the following conditions are met:
1. Identified by the March supplement question "Does anyone in this household have a health problem or disability which prevents them from working or which limits the kind or amount of work they can do?"
2. Identified by the March supplement question "Is there anyone in this household who ever retired or left a job for health reasons?"
3. Identified by the core questionnaire as currently not in the labor force because of a disability.
4. Identified by the March supplement as a person who did not work at all in the previous year because of illness or disability.
5. Under 65 years old and covered by Medicare in previous year.
6. Under 65 years old and received Supplemental Security Income (SSI) in previous year.
7. Received VA disability income in previous year.
If one or more of conditions 3, 4, 5, or 6 are met, the person is considered to have a severe work disability.
Source: Bureau of the Census, 2005 Current Population Survey Annual Social and Economic Supplement, Internet site http://www.census.gov/hhes/www/disability/disabcps.html

Table 2.30 **AIDS Cases by Age, through 2003**

(cumulative number and percent distribution of AIDS cases by age at diagnosis through 2003)

	number	percent of total cases
Total cases	**929,985**	**100.0%**
Under age 13	9,419	1.0
Aged 13 to 14	891	0.1
Aged 15 to 24	37,599	4.0
Aged 25 to 34	311,137	33.5
Aged 35 to 44	365,432	39.3
Aged 45 to 54	148,347	16.0
Aged 55 to 64	43,451	4.7
Aged 65 or older	13,711	1.5

Source: National Center for Health Statistics, Health, United States, 2005, Internet site http://www.cdc.gov/nchs/hus.htm

Prescription Drug Use Is Increasing

More Americans use a growing number of prescriptions.

The use of prescription drugs to treat a variety of illnesses, particularly chronic conditions, increased substantially between 1988–94 and 1999–02. The percentage of people taking at least one drug in the past month rose from 38 to 45 percent during those years. The percentage using three or more prescription drugs in the past month climbed from 11 to 18 percent. Thirty-six percent of people aged 18 to 44 have taken at least one prescription drug in the past month, and 8 percent have taken three or more.

Regardless of age, most people have incurred a prescription drug expense during the past year, with the proportion rising from a low of 51 percent among 18-to-24-year-olds to a high of 91 percent among people aged 65 or older, according to the federal government's Medical Expenditure Panel Survey. Expenses for prescription drugs rise with age, to more than $1,200 per year for people aged 65 or older. The largest share of prescription drug expenses (45 percent) are paid for out-of-pocket.

■ Behind the increase in the use of prescriptions is the introduction and marketing of new drugs to treat chronic health problems.

Most people have prescription drug expenses

(percent of people with prescription drug expenses, by age, 2003)

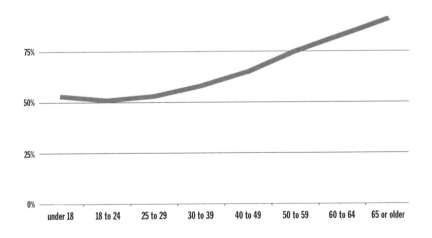

Table 2.31 Prescription Drug Use by Sex and Age, 1988–94 and 1999–02

(percent of people aged 18 or older taking at least one or three or more prescription drugs in the past month, by sex and age, 1988–94 and 1999–02; percentage point change, 1988–94 to 1999–02)

	at least one			three or more		
	1999–02	1988–94	percentage point change	1999–02	1988–94	percentage point change
Total people	**45.1%**	**37.8%**	**7.3**	**17.6%**	**11.0%**	**6.6**
Under age 18	24.2	20.5	3.7	4.1	2.4	1.7
Aged 18 to 44	35.9	31.3	4.6	8.4	5.7	2.7
Aged 45 to 64	64.1	54.8	9.3	30.8	20.0	10.8
Aged 65 or older	84.7	73.6	11.1	51.6	35.3	16.3
Total females	**51.2**	**44.6**	**6.6**	**21.1**	**13.6**	**7.5**
Under age 18	22.0	20.6	1.4	3.9	2.3	1.6
Aged 18 to 44	44.6	40.7	3.9	10.2	7.6	2.6
Aged 45 to 64	72.0	62.0	10.0	37.4	24.7	12.7
Aged 65 or older	88.1	78.3	9.8	55.7	38.2	17.5
Total males	**38.7**	**30.6**	**8.1**	**13.9**	**8.3**	**5.6**
Under age 18	26.2	20.4	5.8	4.3	2.6	1.7
Aged 18 to 44	27.1	21.5	5.6	6.7	3.6	3.1
Aged 45 to 64	55.6	47.2	8.4	23.5	15.1	8.4
Aged 65 or older	80.1	67.2	12.9	46.0	31.3	14.7

Source: National Center for Health Statistics, Health, United States, 2005, Internet site http://www.cdc.gov/nchs/hus.htm; calculations by New Strategist

Table 2.32 Spending on Prescription Medications by Age, 2003

(percent of people with prescription medication expense, median expense per person, total expenses, and percent-distribution of total expenses by source of payment, by age, 2003)

	total (thousands)	percent with expense	median expense per person	total expenses amount (millions)	total expenses percent distribution
Total people	**290,604**	**64.4%**	**$306**	**$177,653**	**100.0%**
Under age 18	72,996	53.2	72	10,464	5.9
Aged 18 to 24	27,156	51.4	117	5,294	3.0
Aged 25 to 29	20,425	53.4	135	4,571	2.6
Aged 30 to 39	40,068	58.0	198	14,985	8.4
Aged 40 to 49	44,703	65.2	344	26,663	15.0
Aged 50 to 59	35,265	75.2	679	38,017	21.4
Aged 60 to 64	13,293	82.9	983	18,022	10.1
Aged 65 or older	36,699	91.0	1,219	59,637	33.6

PERCENT DISTRIBUTION BY SOURCE OF PAYMENT

	total	out of pocket	private insurance	Medicare	Medicaid	other
Total people	**100.0%**	**44.9%**	**35.1%**	**3.3%**	**12.4%**	**4.3%**
Under age 18	100.0	38.3	37.4	–	24.2	–
Aged 18 to 24	100.0	45.1	35.2	–	18.8	–
Aged 25 to 29	100.0	46.9	39.8	–	11.4	–
Aged 30 to 39	100.0	37.3	41.8	–	19.7	–
Aged 40 to 49	100.0	40.9	39.6	–	14.7	–
Aged 50 to 59	100.0	39.0	45.1	–	11.2	4.1
Aged 60 to 64	100.0	44.5	42.4	–	9.5	2.2
Aged 65 or older	100.0	53.5	22.0	8.1	8.7	7.7

Note: "Other" insurance includes Department of Veterans Affairs (except Tricare), American Indian Health Service, state and local clinics, worker's compensation, homeowner's and automobile insurance, etc. "–" means sample is too small to make a reliable estimate or not applicable.
Source: Agency for Healthcare Research and Quality, Medical Expenditure Panel Survey, 2003, Internet site http://www.meps.ahrq.gov/CompendiumTables/TC_TOC.htm; calculations by New Strategist

Adults Aged 25 to 44 Account for More than One in Five Physician Visits

Among 25-to-44-year-olds, 67 percent of physician visits are made by women.

In 2003, Americans visited physicians a total of 906 million times. Twenty-two percent of visits were made by people aged 25 to 44. Women account for two-thirds of physician visits by those in the age group because of pregnancy and childbirth.

People aged 25 to 44 account for 26 percent of visits to hospital outpatient departments. Among outpatient visitors in the 25-to-44 age group, the largest share—44 percent—are there because of an acute problem.

People aged 25 to 44 account for the largest single share of visits to hospital emergency departments (29 percent) among age groups. This makes sense since so many people in the age group lack health insurance, and many people without health insurance end up in emergency rooms.

When people who visit a doctor or health care clinic are asked to rate the care they receive, fewer than half give it the highest rating (a 9 or 10 on a scale of 1 to 10). The proportion rating their experience a 9 or 10 rises with age to a peak of 58 percent among Medicare recipients. A much smaller 38 to 42 percent of people aged 25 to 39 give the health care they received the highest rating. A substantial 16 to 18 percent give the health care they received the lowest rating.

■ Without better health insurance coverage, more patients will be seen in emergency rooms rather than doctor's offices or health clinics.

People aged 25 to 44 see a doctor between two and three times a year

(average number of physician visits per person per year, by age, 2003)

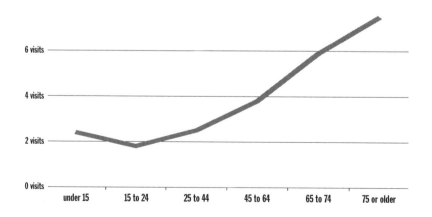

Table 2.33 Physician Office Visits by Sex and Age, 2003

(total number, percent distribution, and number of physician office visits per person per year, by sex and age, 2003; numbers in thousands)

	total	percent distribution	average visits per year
Total visits	**906,023**	**100.0%**	**3.2**
Under age 15	145,245	16.0	2.4
Aged 15 to 24	72,447	8.0	1.8
Aged 25 to 44	203,553	22.5	2.5
Aged 45 to 64	257,258	28.4	3.8
Aged 65 to 74	106,424	11.7	5.9
Aged 75 or older	121,096	13.4	7.5
Visits by females	**537,298**	**59.3**	**3.7**
Under age 15	67,442	7.4	2.3
Aged 15 to 24	46,705	5.2	2.3
Aged 25 to 44	136,881	15.1	3.3
Aged 45 to 64	153,417	16.9	4.4
Aged 65 to 74	60,449	6.7	6.1
Aged 75 or older	72,404	8.0	7.3
Visits by males	**368,724**	**40.7**	**2.6**
Under age 15	77,802	8.6	2.5
Aged 15 to 24	25,742	2.8	1.3
Aged 25 to 44	66,672	7.4	1.6
Aged 45 to 64	103,841	11.5	3.1
Aged 65 to 74	45,975	5.1	5.6
Aged 75 or older	48,692	5.4	7.8

Source: National Center for Health Statistics, National Ambulatory Medical Care Survey: 2003 Summary, Advance Data No. 365, 2005, Internet site http://www.cdc.gov/nchs/about/major/ahcd/adata.htm

Table 2.34 Hospital Outpatient Department Visits by Age and Reason, 2003

(number and percent distribution of visits to hospital outpatient departments by age and major reason for visit, 2003; numbers in thousands)

				major reason for visit			
	total	acute problem	chronic problem, routine	chronic problem, flare-up	pre- or post-surgery	preventive care	unknown
Total visits	**94,578**	**38,339**	**27,355**	**6,135**	**3,974**	**17,053**	**1,721**
Under age 15	21,822	10,354	4,762	1,273	581	4,423	427
Aged 15 to 24	11,521	4,847	2,007	436	280	3,783	168
Aged 25 to 44	24,784	10,812	5,839	1,332	1,003	5,449	348
Aged 45 to 64	23,307	8,123	8,894	2,053	1,394	2,388	454
Aged 65 to 74	7,077	2,070	3,236	588	412	598	173
Aged 75 or older	6,067	2,133	2,616	452	303	412	150
PERCENT DISTRIBUTION BY AGE							
Total visits	**100.0%**	**100.0%**	**100.0%**	**100.0%**	**100.0%**	**100.0%**	**100.0%**
Under age 15	23.1	27.0	17.4	20.7	14.6	25.9	24.8
Aged 15 to 24	12.2	12.6	7.3	7.1	7.0	22.2	9.8
Aged 25 to 44	26.2	28.2	21.3	21.7	25.2	32.0	20.2
Aged 45 to 64	24.6	21.2	32.5	33.5	35.1	14.0	26.4
Aged 65 to 74	7.5	5.4	11.8	9.6	10.4	3.5	10.1
Aged 75 or older	6.4	5.6	9.6	7.4	7.6	2.4	8.7
PERCENT DISTRIBUTION BY MAJOR REASON							
Total visits	**100.0%**	**40.5%**	**28.9%**	**6.5%**	**4.2%**	**18.0%**	**1.8%**
Under age 15	100.0	47.4	21.8	5.8	2.7	20.3	2.0
Aged 15 to 24	100.0	42.1	17.4	3.8	2.4	32.8	1.5
Aged 25 to 44	100.0	43.6	23.6	5.4	4.0	22.0	1.4
Aged 45 to 64	100.0	34.9	38.2	8.8	6.0	10.2	1.9
Aged 65 to 74	100.0	29.2	45.7	8.3	5.8	8.4	2.4
Aged 75 or older	100.0	35.2	43.1	7.5	5.0	6.8	2.5

Source: National Center for Health Statistics, National Hospital Ambulatory Medical Care Survey: 2003 Outpatient Department Summary, Advance Data No. 366, 2005, Internet site http://www.cdc.gov/nchs/about/major/ahcd/adata.htm; calculations by New Strategist

Table 2.35 Emergency Department Visits by Age and Urgency of Problem, 2003

(number of visits to emergency rooms and percent distribution by urgency of problem, by age, 2003; numbers in thousands)

| | number | percent distribution | percent distribution by urgency of problem | | | | | |
			total	emergent	urgent	semiurgent	nonurgent	unknown
Total visits	**113,903**	**100.0%**	**100.0%**	**15.2%**	**35.2%**	**20.0%**	**12.8%**	**16.7%**
Under age 15	24,733	21.7	100.0	10.8	33.7	22.3	15.5	17.7
Aged 15 to 24	17,731	15.6	100.0	11.9	34.6	22.0	15.1	16.5
Aged 25 to 44	32,906	28.9	100.0	13.3	35.8	20.9	13.8	16.2
Aged 45 to 64	20,992	18.4	100.0	17.7	35.7	18.3	11.5	16.9
Aged 65 to 74	7,153	6.3	100.0	24.5	36.3	15.3	7.2	16.6
Aged 75 or older	10,389	9.1	100.0	25.5	36.5	15.5	5.9	16.7

Note: Emergent is a status in which the patient should be seen in less than 15 minutes; urgent is a status in which the patient should be seen within 15 to 60 minutes; semiurgent is a status in which the patient should be seen within 61 to 120 minutes; nonurgent is a status in which the patient should be seen within 121 minutes to 24 hours; unknown denotes a visit with no mention of immediacy or triage or the patient was dead on arrival.
Source: National Center for Health Statistics, National Hospital Ambulatory Medical Care Survey: 2003 Emergency Department Summary, Advance Data No. 358, 2005, Internet site http://www.cdc.gov/nchs/about/major/ahcd/adata.htm

Table 2.36 Rating of Health Care Received from Doctor's Office or Clinic, 2003

(number of people aged 18 or older visiting a doctor or health care clinic in past 12 months, and percent distribution by rating for health care received on a scale from 0 (worst) to 10 (best), by age, 2003; people in thousands)

| | with health care visit | | rating | | |
	number	percent	9 to 10	7 to 8	6 or lower
Total people	**147,294**	**100.0%**	**47.2%**	**37.8%**	**14.2%**
Aged 18 to 24	14,088	100.0	42.2	37.8	19.2
Aged 25 to 29	11,589	100.0	38.1	43.1	18.4
Aged 30 to 39	24,952	100.0	42.1	41.6	15.6
Aged 40 to 49	29,918	100.0	44.2	40.1	14.9
Aged 50 to 59	26,402	100.0	48.6	37.5	13.1
Aged 60 to 64	10,615	100.0	51.0	35.9	12.7
Aged 65 or older	29,730	100.0	57.7	31.2	10.1

Source: Agency for Healthcare Research and Quality, Medical Expenditure Panel Survey, 2003, Internet site http://www.meps.ahrq.gov/CompendiumTables/TC_TOC.htm; calculations by New Strategist

Most Deaths of Younger Adults Are Preventable

Accidents are the leading killers of 25-to-44-year-olds.

When adults under age 45 die, it is often preventable. Accidents are the most important cause of death among 25-to-44-year-olds, accounting for 30 percent of deaths among 25-to-34-year-olds and 18 percent of deaths among 35-to-44-year-olds. Suicide ranks second among 25-to-34-year-olds, and homicide is third. Among 35-to-44-year-olds, cancer is the second most important cause of death, followed by heart disease. HIV infection ranks sixth as a cause of death among 25-to-34-year-olds and a higher fifth among 35-to-44-year-olds.

Although more could be done to reduce deaths among young adults, some progress has been made. The life expectancy of Americans continues to rise. At age 30, life expectancy is another 49 years. At age 35, another 44 years of life remain. Not until age 40 do years of life remaining fall below years of life already lived.

■ Young adults are not as safety conscious as middle-aged and older adults. Accidents will always rank as more important causes of death among young adults than among older Americans.

Cancer and heart disease are important causes of death among 35-to-44-year-olds

(percent of deaths among 35-to-44-year-olds from top three causes of death, 2002)

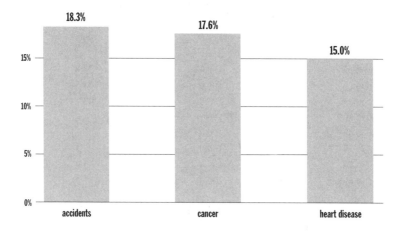

Table 2.37 Leading Causes of Death for People Aged 25 to 34, 2002

(number and percent distribution of deaths accounted for by the ten leading causes of death for people aged 25 to 34, 2002)

		number	percent distribution
All causes		**41,355**	**100.0%**
1.	Accidents (unintentional injuries) (5)	12,569	30.4
2.	Suicide (11)	5,046	12.2
3.	Homicide (14)	4,489	10.9
4.	Malignant neoplasms (cancer) (2)	3,872	9.4
5.	Diseases of the heart (1)	3,165	7.7
6.	Human immunodeficiency virus infection	1,839	4.4
7.	Diabetes mellitus (6)	642	1.6
8.	Cerebrovascular diseases (3)	567	1.4
9.	Congenital malformations, deformations	475	1.1
10.	Chronic liver disease and cirrhosis (12)	374	0.9
	All other causes	8,317	20.1

Note: Number in parentheses shows rank for all Americans if the cause of death is among the top fifteen.
Source: National Center for Health Statistics, Deaths: Final Data for 2002, National Vital Statistics Reports, Vol. 53, No. 5, 2004, Internet site http://www.cdc.gov/nchs/products/pubs/pubd/nvsr/53/53-21.htm; calculations by New Strategist

Table 2.38 Leading Causes of Death for People Aged 35 to 44, 2002

(number and percent distribution of deaths accounted for by the ten leading causes of death for people aged 35 to 44, 2002)

		number	percent distribution
All causes		**91,140**	**100.0%**
1.	Accidents (unintentional injuries) (5)	16,710	18.3
2.	Malignant neoplasms (cancer) (2)	16,085	17.6
3.	Diseases of the heart (1)	13,688	15.0
4.	Suicide (11)	6,851	7.5
5.	Human immunodeficiency virus infection	5,707	6.3
6.	Homicide (14)	3,239	3.6
7.	Chronic liver disease and cirrhosis (12)	3,154	3.5
8.	Cerebrovascular diseases (3)	2,425	2.7
9.	Diabetes mellitus (6)	2,164	2.4
10.	Chronic lower respiratory disease (4)	1,008	1.1
	All other causes	20,109	22.1

Note: Number in parentheses shows rank for all Americans if the cause of death is among the top fifteen.
Source: National Center for Health Statistics, Deaths: Final Data for 2002, National Vital Statistics Reports, Vol. 53, No. 5, 2004, Internet site http://www.cdc.gov/nchs/products/pubs/pubd/nvsr/53/53-21.htm; calculations by New Strategist

Table 2.39 Life Expectancy by Age and Sex, 2003

(years of life remaining at selected ages, by sex, 2003)

	total	females	males
At birth	**77.6**	**80.1**	**74.8**
Aged 1	77.1	79.6	74.4
Aged 5	73.2	75.7	70.5
Aged 10	68.2	70.8	65.6
Aged 15	63.3	65.8	60.7
Aged 20	58.5	60.9	55.9
Aged 25	53.8	56.1	51.3
Aged 30	49.0	51.2	46.6
Aged 35	44.3	46.4	41.9
Aged 40	39.6	41.7	37.3
Aged 45	35.0	37.0	32.8
Aged 50	30.6	32.5	28.5
Aged 55	26.4	28.0	24.4
Aged 60	22.3	23.8	20.5
Aged 65	18.5	19.8	16.8
Aged 70	15.0	16.1	13.5
Aged 75	11.8	12.7	10.6
Aged 80	9.1	9.7	8.1
Aged 85	6.9	7.2	6.1
Aged 90	5.1	5.3	4.5
Aged 95	3.8	4.0	3.4
Aged 100	2.9	3.0	2.7

Source: National Center for Health Statistics, Deaths: Preliminary Data for 2003, National Vital Statistics Report, Vol. 53, No. 15, 2005, Internet site http://www.cdc.gov/nchs/products/pubs/pubd/nvsr/53/53-21.htm; calculations by New Strategist

3

Housing

■ The nation's homeownership rate climbed substantially between 1990 and 2005, up 5 percentage points to 68.9 percent. The homeownership rate of householders aged 30 to 39 (Gen Xers were aged 29 to 40 in 2005) rose about an average amount during those years.

■ Most of Generation X has made the transition from renting to homeowning. Among householders aged 25 to 29, the 59 percent majority are renters. Among those aged 30 to 34, the 57 percent majority are homeowners.

■ Among married couples aged 25 to 29, the 59 percent majority are homeowners. The figure is a much higher 73 percent among couples aged 30 to 34 and rises to 82 percent in the 35-to-39 age group.

■ Sixty percent of householders under age 25 live in multi-unit buildings, as do 43 percent of those aged 25 to 29. The share drops to 30 percent in the 30-to-34 age group as the majority of people become homeowners.

■ Median monthly housing cost peaks among married-couple homeowners aged 30 to 34 at $1,100 and is an even higher $1,117 for couples aged 35 to 44.

■ Between March 2003 and March 2004, a substantial 28 percent of people aged 25 to 29 moved to a different home. Among those aged 30 to 34, nearly one in five moved during the year.

Homeownership Increased among Gen Xers

Most 30-to-39-year-olds own their home.

The nation's homeownership rate has climbed substantially since 1990, up by 5 percentage points to 68.9 percent in 2005. The homeownership rate of householders aged 30 to 39 (Gen Xers were aged 29 to 40 in 2005) rose about an average amount during those years. As Generation X aged into its thirties, the majority became homeowners. Fifty-seven percent of householders aged 30 to 34 owned their home in 2005, as did 67 percent of householders aged 35 to 39.

The majority of householders become homeowners in the 30-to-34 age group because that is when married life becomes the norm for men (most women marry during their twenties), and making a mortgage payment now requires two incomes. Homeownership will continue to rise for Gen Xers as they age into their forties.

■ The homeownership rate of people aged 30 to 39 grew more slowly than that of young adults. Householders under age 25 saw their homeownership rate rise by 10 percentage points between 1990 and 2005.

Between 1990 and 2005, homeownership increased the most among the young and the old

(percentage point change in homeownership rate for householders by age, 1990 to 2005)

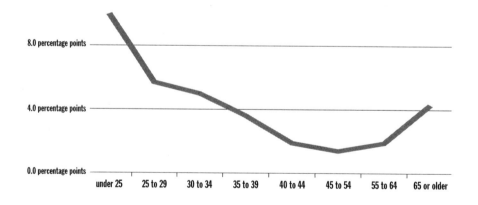

Table 3.1 Homeownership by Age of Householder, 1990 to 2005

(percentage of householders who own their home by age of householder, 1990 to 2005; percentage point change, 2000–05 and 1990–2005)

				percentage point change	
	2005	2000	1990	2000–05	1990–2005
Total households	**68.9%**	**67.4%**	**63.9%**	**1.5**	**5.0**
Under age 25	25.7	21.7	15.7	4.0	10.0
Aged 25 to 29	40.9	38.1	35.2	2.8	5.7
Aged 30 to 34	56.8	54.6	51.8	2.2	5.0
Aged 35 to 39	66.6	65.0	63.0	1.6	3.6
Aged 40 to 44	71.7	70.6	69.8	1.1	1.9
Aged 45 to 54	76.6	76.5	75.2	0.1	1.4
Aged 55 to 64	81.2	80.3	79.3	0.9	1.9
Aged 65 or older	80.6	80.4	76.3	0.2	4.3

Source: Bureau of the Census, Housing Vacancies and Homeownership Survey, Internet site http://www.census.gov/hhes/www/ housing/hvs/annual05/ann05t15.html; calculations by New Strategist

Homeownership Rises with Age

Most of the nation's renters are under age 40.

Most of Generation X has made the transition from renting to homeowning. The 59 percent majority of householders aged 25 to 29 were renters in 2005 (Gen Xers were aged 29 to 40 in that year). Among householders aged 30 to 34, the proportion of renters drops to the 43 percent minority. Only slightly more than one-third of householders aged 35 to 39 rent their home.

The homeownership rate climbs steeply as people enter their thirties and forties. During the past two decades, Boomers filled those age groups, fueling the real estate, construction, and home improvement industries. Now Generation X is shopping for homes. Because Gen X is small, it won't have as much of an impact as Boomers on the housing market. But it will add more fuel to the fire and help keep the housing industry vibrant.

■ As the large Millennial generation replaces Generation X in the young-adult age group, the rental market should get a boost.

Homeownership becomes the norm in the 30-to-34 age group

(percent distribution of householders aged 25 to 39 by homeownership status and age, 2005)

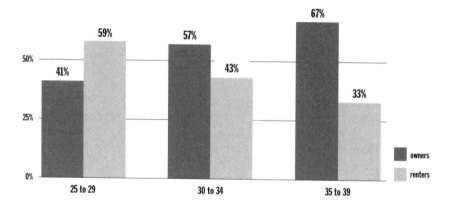

Table 3.2 Owners and Renters by Age of Householder, 2005

(number and percent distribution of householders by homeownership status, and owner and renter share of total, by age of householder, 2005; numbers in thousands)

	total	owners			renters		
		number	percent distribution	share of total	number	percent distribution	share of total
Total households	**108,231**	**74,553**	**100.0%**	**68.9%**	**33,678**	**100.0%**	**31.1%**
Under age 25	6,536	1,682	2.3	25.7	4,854	14.4	74.3
Aged 25 to 39	28,899	16,051	21.5	55.5	12,848	38.1	44.5
Aged 25 to 29	8,790	3,597	4.8	40.9	5,193	15.4	59.1
Aged 30 to 34	9,583	5,444	7.3	56.8	4,139	12.3	43.2
Aged 35 to 39	10,526	7,010	9.4	66.6	3,516	10.4	33.4
Aged 40 to 44	11,722	8,402	11.3	71.7	3,320	9.9	28.3
Aged 45 to 54	22,375	17,129	23.0	76.6	5,246	15.6	23.4
Aged 55 to 64	16,840	13,668	18.3	81.2	3,172	9.4	18.8
Aged 65 or older	21,859	17,622	23.6	80.6	4,237	12.6	19.4

Source: Bureau of the Census, Housing Vacancies and Homeownership Survey, Internet site http://www.census.gov/hhes/www/ housing/hvs/annual05/ann05t15.html; calculations by New Strategist

Married Couples Are Likely to Be Homeowners

Two incomes make homes more affordable.

The homeownership rate among all married couples was a lofty 84 percent in 2005, much higher than the 69 percent rate for all households. Couples in their twenties and thirties are less likely than average to own a home. Among couples aged 25 to 29, 59 percent were homeowners. The figure is a much higher 73 percent among couples aged 30 to 34, and rises to 82 percent in the 35-to-39 age group.

Homeownership is much lower for other types of households in the 25-to-39 age group. Among female-headed family householders in the age group, the homeownership rate ranges from 24 to 45 percent. The figures are similar for men and women who live alone. Homeownership rates are higher for male-headed family householders, ranging from 39 percent among those aged 25 to 29 to the 55 percent majority of those aged 35 to 39.

■ Among householders aged 45 or older, the majority owns a home, regardless of household type.

Most married couples aged 25 or older own their home

(percent of married-couple householders who own their home, by age, 2005)

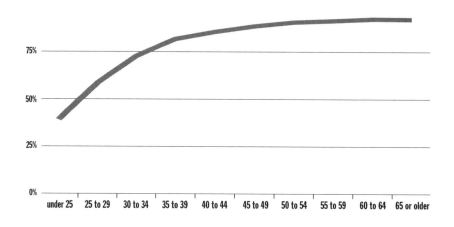

Table 3.3 Homeownership Rate by Age of Householder and Type of Household, 2005

(percent of households owning their home, by age of householder and type of household, 2005)

| | | family households | | | people living alone | |
	total	married couples	female hh, no spouse present	male hh, no spouse present	females	males
Total households	**68.9%**	**84.2%**	**51.0%**	**59.1%**	**59.6%**	**50.3%**
Under age 25	25.7	39.1	25.7	44.6	13.6	17.8
Aged 25 to 29	40.9	58.5	23.6	38.9	26.0	30.2
Aged 30 to 34	56.8	72.6	32.2	49.7	37.0	37.5
Aged 35 to 39	66.6	81.7	44.6	55.4	45.0	45.5
Aged 40 to 44	71.7	85.5	52.9	62.7	51.6	47.6
Aged 45 to 49	75.0	88.5	60.1	67.4	53.9	52.2
Aged 50 to 54	78.3	90.6	65.8	72.4	60.2	53.6
Aged 55 to 59	80.6	91.4	68.5	73.1	66.8	58.4
Aged 60 to 64	81.9	92.3	71.3	75.7	69.7	61.3
Aged 65 or older	80.6	92.2	82.0	83.4	70.2	68.1

Source: Bureau of the Census, Housing Vacancies and Homeownership Survey, Internet site http://www.census.gov/hhes/www/housing/hvs/annual05/ann05t15.html; calculations by New Strategist

Most Blacks and Hispanics Are Not Homeowners

The homeownership rate is below 50 percent for those in their twenties and thirties.

The homeownership rate of blacks and Hispanics is well below average. The overall homeownership rate stood at 68.3 percent for all households in 2003 (the latest data available by race, Hispanic origin, and age). Among blacks, the rate was a smaller 47.6 percent. The Hispanic rate was an even lower 46.3 percent.

Homeownership rises above 50 percent for black householders aged 45 or older. Among Hispanics, the rate reaches 50 percent in the 35-to-44 age group. Homeownership peaks in the 75-or-older age group for both blacks and Hispanics.

■ Blacks are less likely to be homeowners because a smaller share of their households are headed by married couples.

Among Hispanics, homeownership reaches 50 percent in the 35-to-44 age group

(homeownership rate of householders aged 30 to 54, by race and Hispanic origin, 2003)

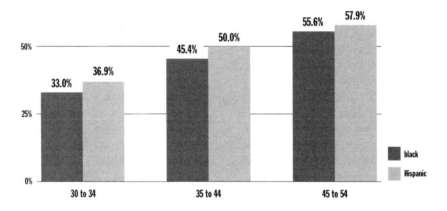

Table 3.4 Black and Hispanic Homeownership Rate by Age, 2003

(percent of total, black, and Hispanic households owning their home, by age of householder, 2003)

	total	black	Hispanic
Total households	**68.3%**	**47.6%**	**46.3%**
Under age 25	20.9	12.1	13.5
Aged 25 to 29	41.1	23.0	26.7
Aged 30 to 34	55.3	33.0	36.9
Aged 35 to 44	68.4	45.4	50.0
Aged 45 to 54	76.3	55.6	57.9
Aged 55 to 64	81.1	63.9	63.5
Aged 65 to 74	82.3	66.1	60.5
Aged 75 or older	78.1	66.6	64.6

Note: Blacks include only those identifying themselves as being black alone. Hispanics may be of any race.
Source: Bureau of the Census, American Housing Survey for the United States: 2003, Current Housing Reports, Internet site http://www.census.gov/hhes/www/ahs.html; calculations by New Strategist

Most Americans Live in Single-Family Homes

Many Gen Xers live in apartment buildings, however.

The majority of American households (64 percent) live in detached, single-family homes. The middle aged are most likely to live in this type of home, where the median age of householders is 49 years.

Sixty percent of householders under age 25 live in multi-unit buildings, as do 43 percent of those aged 25 to 29. The share drops to 30 percent in the 30-to-34 age group as the majority of people become homeowners. The median age of householders living in apartment buildings is 40 years.

Six percent of American households live in mobile homes, a figure that does not vary much by age. Householders aged 25 to 34 account for 17 percent of mobile home residents, a proportion higher than their 14 percent share of residents in single-family, detached homes.

■ The demand for apartments should rise as the large Millennial generation replaces small Generation X in the young-adult population.

Young adults are most likely to live in multi-unit buildings

(percent of households living in multi-unit buildings, by age of householder, 2003)

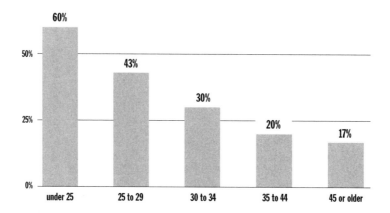

Table 3.5 Number of Units in Structure by Age of Householder, 2003

(number and percent distribution of households by age of householder and number of units in structure, 2003; numbers in thousands)

	total	one, detached	one, attached	multi-unit dwellings total	2 to 4	5 to 9	10 to 19	20 to 49	50 or more	mobile homes
Total households	**105,842**	**67,753**	**6,272**	**24,963**	**8,474**	**5,135**	**4,468**	**3,294**	**3,592**	**6,854**
Under age 25	6,087	1,618	447	3,681	1,165	891	858	470	297	341
Aged 25 to 29	7,805	3,282	615	3,384	1,191	755	664	478	295	524
Aged 30 to 34	10,575	5,980	803	3,135	1,030	710	624	440	331	656
Aged 35 to 44	22,516	15,192	1,291	4,561	1,655	956	868	554	528	1,472
Aged 45 or older	58,859	41,680	3,116	10,202	3,432	1,822	1,455	1,352	2,141	3,861
Median age (years)	47	49	44	40	40	37	36	39	51	48

PERCENT DISTRIBUTION BY AGE OF HOUSEHOLDER

	total	one, detached	one, attached	total	2 to 4	5 to 9	10 to 19	20 to 49	50 or more	mobile homes
Total households	**100.0%**	**100.0%**	**100.0%**	**100.0%**	**100.0%**	**100.0%**	**100.0%**	**100.0%**	**100.0%**	**100.0%**
Under age 25	5.8	2.4	7.1	14.7	13.7	17.4	19.2	14.3	8.3	5.0
Aged 25 to 29	7.4	4.8	9.8	13.6	14.1	14.7	14.9	14.5	8.2	7.6
Aged 30 to 34	10.0	8.8	12.8	12.6	12.2	13.8	14.0	13.4	9.2	9.6
Aged 35 to 44	21.3	22.4	20.6	18.3	19.5	18.6	19.4	16.8	14.7	21.5
Aged 45 or older	55.6	61.5	49.7	40.9	40.5	35.5	32.6	41.0	59.6	56.3

PERCENT DISTRIBUTION BY UNITS IN STRUCTURE

	total	one, detached	one, attached	total	2 to 4	5 to 9	10 to 19	20 to 49	50 or more	mobile homes
Total households	**100.0%**	**64.0%**	**5.9%**	**23.6%**	**8.0%**	**4.9%**	**4.2%**	**3.1%**	**3.4%**	**6.5%**
Under age 25	100.0	26.6	7.3	60.5	19.1	14.6	14.1	7.7	4.9	5.6
Aged 25 to 29	100.0	42.0	7.9	43.4	15.3	9.7	8.5	6.1	3.8	6.7
Aged 30 to 34	100.0	56.5	7.6	29.6	9.7	6.7	5.9	4.2	3.1	6.2
Aged 35 to 44	100.0	67.5	5.7	20.3	7.4	4.2	3.9	2.5	2.3	6.5
Aged 45 or older	100.0	70.8	5.3	17.3	5.8	3.1	2.5	2.3	3.6	6.6

Source: Bureau of the Census, American Housing Survey for the United States in 2003, Internet site http://www.census.gov/hhes/ www/housing/ahs/ahs03/ahs03.html; calculations by New Strategist

Generation Xers Are Most Likely to Live in New Homes

Older homeowners are least likely to live in recently built homes.

New homes are the province of the young. Overall, only 6 percent of homeowners live in a new home—meaning one built in the past four years. The share is much greater among younger homeowners, however. Among 25-to-29-year-olds, 16 percent live in a new home. The figure is 13 percent among those aged 30 to 34. Among homeowners aged 45 or older, only 4 percent live in new homes. Householders aged 25 to 34 account for a substantial 28 percent of homeowners living in newly built homes.

Overall, 3 percent of the nation's renters live in newly built housing units. The figure is a higher 5 percent among householders under age 25, then varies little by age.

■ The large Millennial generation is likely to boost sales of new homes as it replaces Generation X in the ages of first-home buying.

Many young homeowners live in new homes

(percent of homeowners living in homes built in the past four years, by age of householder, 2003)

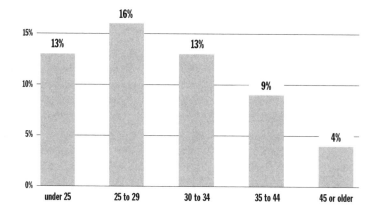

Table 3.6 Owners and Renters of New Homes by Age of Householder, 2003

(number of total occupied housing units, number and percent built in the past four years, and percent distribution of new units by housing tenure and age of householder, 2003; numbers in thousands)

	total	new homes number	new homes percent of total	new homes percent distribution
Total households	**105,842**	**5,691**	**5.4%**	**100.0%**
Under age 25	6,087	385	6.3	6.8
Aged 25 to 29	7,805	677	8.7	11.9
Aged 30 to 34	10,575	919	8.7	16.1
Aged 35 to 44	22,516	1,565	7.0	27.5
Aged 45 or older	58,859	2,144	3.6	37.7
Total owner households	**72,238**	**4,673**	**6.5**	**100.0**
Under age 25	1,272	159	12.5	3.4
Aged 25 to 29	3,207	515	16.1	11.0
Aged 30 to 34	5,845	784	13.4	16.8
Aged 35 to 44	15,406	1,381	9.0	29.6
Aged 45 or older	46,508	1,833	3.9	39.2
Total renter households	**33,604**	**1,018**	**3.0**	**100.0**
Under age 25	4,815	226	4.7	22.2
Aged 25 to 29	4,598	162	3.5	15.9
Aged 30 to 34	4,730	135	2.9	13.3
Aged 35 to 44	7,110	184	2.6	18.1
Aged 45 or older	12,350	310	2.5	30.5

Source: Bureau of the Census, American Housing Survey for the United States in 2003, Internet site http://www.census.gov/hhes/ www/housing/ahs/ahs03/ahs03.html; calculations by New Strategist

Housing Costs Are High for Generation Xers

Costs are lowest for homeowners aged 65 or older.

Monthly housing costs for the average household stood at a median of $684 in 2003, including mortgage interest and utilities. For homeowners, the median monthly housing cost was $717, and for renters the figure was a slightly smaller $651.

Among married-couple homeowners, housing costs are highest for those aged 30 to 44, not only because their homes are larger than average to accommodate children, but also because many are recent homeowners with hefty mortgage interest charges. The median monthly housing cost for married-couple homeowners aged 30 to 34 stood at $1,100 in 2003 and was a slightly higher $1,117 for those aged 35 to 44.

Housing costs are lowest for homeowning married couples aged 65 or older. For older renters, however, housing costs do not decline much with age. Among married householders aged 65 or older, homeowners paid a median of $398 for housing, while renters paid a median of $661.

■ The financial advantages of homeownership grow as householders age and pay off their mortgages.

Housing costs fall after age 45

(median monthly housing costs for married couples, by age of householder, 2003)

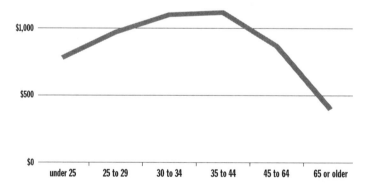

Table 3.7 Median Monthly Housing Costs by Household Type and Age of Householder, 2003

(median monthly housing costs and indexed costs by type of household, age of householder, and housing tenure, 2003)

	median monthly cost			indexed cost		
	total	owners	renters	total	owners	renters
Total households	**$684**	**$717**	**$651**	**100**	**105**	**95**
TWO-OR-MORE-PERSON HOUSEHOLDS	**761**	**806**	**704**	**111**	**118**	**103**
Married couples	**810**	**843**	**740**	**118**	**123**	**108**
Under age 25	688	779	653	101	114	95
Aged 25 to 29	825	969	700	121	142	102
Aged 30 to 34	954	1,100	756	139	161	111
Aged 35 to 44	1,023	1,117	792	150	163	116
Aged 45 to 64	852	869	763	125	127	112
Aged 65 or older	416	398	661	61	58	97
Other male householder	**740**	**752**	**734**	**108**	**110**	**107**
Aged 15 to 44	773	867	740	113	127	108
Aged 45 to 64	721	734	705	105	107	103
Aged 65 or older	479	416	714	70	61	104
Other female householder	**654**	**673**	**645**	**96**	**98**	**94**
Aged 15 to 44	679	778	642	99	114	94
Aged 45 to 64	693	742	656	101	108	96
Aged 65 or older	408	350	630	60	51	92
SINGLE-PERSON HOUSEHOLDS	**512**	**433**	**567**	**75**	**63**	**83**
Male householder	**557**	**517**	**574**	**81**	**76**	**84**
Aged 15 to 44	644	759	605	94	111	88
Aged 45 to 64	551	562	544	81	82	80
Aged 65 or older	354	307	478	52	45	70
Female householder	**474**	**391**	**559**	**69**	**57**	**82**
Aged 15 to 44	656	774	617	96	113	90
Aged 45 to 64	566	600	536	83	88	78
Aged 65 or older	329	294	470	48	43	69

Note: Housing costs include utilities, mortgages, real estate taxes, property insurance, and regime fees.
Source: Bureau of the Census, American Housing Survey for the United States in 2003, Internet site http://www.census.gov/hhes/www/housing/ahs/ahs03/ahs03.html; calculations by New Strategist

Many Young Adults Own High-Value Homes

Home values rise as young couples trade in their starter homes for more expensive models.

The median value of America's owned homes stood at $140,269 in 2003. Median home value is an even higher $157,610 among the nation's married couples. Home values peak among couples aged 35 to 44, with a median value of $170,314.

The value of the homes owned by married couples under age 30 is below average because many have small starter homes. Among couples aged 30 to 34, however, home values are higher as they trade in their starter homes for bigger models with more room for children. The median value of the homes owned by couples aged 30 to 34 is close to the married-couple average, at $155,125 in 2003. Seventeen percent own a home worth at least $300,000.

■ Home values have been rising steadily and are now significantly higher than the 2003 figures shown in this section.

Home values are highest for 35-to-44-year-old couples

(median value of homes owned by married couples, by age of householder, 2003)

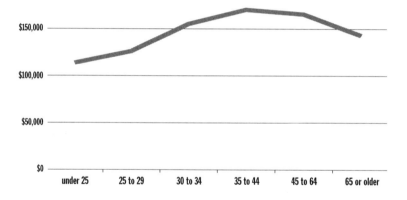

Table 3.8 Value of Owner-Occupied Homes by Type of Household and Age of Householder, 2003

(number of homeowners by value of home, median value of housing unit, and indexed median value, by type of household and age of householder, 2003)

	number (in 000s)	under $100,000	$100,000 to $149,999	$150,000 to $199,999	$200,000 to $249,999	$250,000 to $299,999	$300,000 or more	median value of home	indexed median value
Total homeowners	72,238	24,630	14,266	9,989	6,358	4,561	12,434	$140,269	100
TWO-OR-MORE-PERSON HOUSEHOLDS	56,783	17,689	11,119	8,104	5,287	3,869	10,715	148,124	106
Married couples	44,684	12,562	8,767	6,655	4,382	3,214	9,103	157,610	112
Under age 25	465	200	119	51	36	12	47	113,675	81
Aged 25 to 29	1,948	699	529	288	163	91	178	126,086	90
Aged 30 to 34	3,848	1,062	794	671	406	261	656	155,125	111
Aged 35 to 44	10,719	2,675	2,031	1,610	1,110	855	2,439	170,314	121
Aged 45 to 64	19,197	5,132	3,595	2,817	1,947	1,425	4,282	165,485	118
Aged 65 or older	8,506	2,796	1,701	1,218	720	570	1,501	142,851	102
Other male householder	4,363	1,730	862	517	351	242	660	126,163	90
Under age 45	2,220	923	492	248	142	96	319	119,009	85
Aged 45 to 64	1,594	580	289	195	136	106	288	137,391	98
Aged 65 or older	548	225	81	73	74	40	54	129,563	92
Other female householder	7,737	3,398	1,491	932	554	412	951	115,815	83
Under age 45	3,130	1,471	627	377	218	155	282	107,453	77
Aged 45 to 64	3,102	1,269	588	394	219	165	468	124,079	88
Aged 65 or older	1,506	657	276	161	117	92	202	117,197	84
SINGLE-PERSON HOUSEHOLDS	15,455	6,940	3,147	1,886	1,071	692	1,719	112,510	80
Male householder	6,078	2,732	1,189	674	443	239	800	112,898	80
Under age 45	2,074	907	449	253	130	56	279	114,450	82
Aged 45 to 64	2,340	1,038	437	255	202	99	309	115,075	82
Aged 65 or older	1,664	786	304	167	111	83	213	107,475	77
Female householder	9,376	4,208	1,957	1,211	627	454	919	112,274	80
Under age 45	1,325	487	357	198	95	48	140	124,647	89
Aged 45 to 64	2,925	1,206	629	374	218	179	319	120,388	86
Aged 65 or older	5,126	2,515	972	639	315	227	459	102,482	73

Source: Bureau of the Census, American Housing Survey for the United States in 2003, Internet site http://www.census.gov/hhes/ www/housing/ahs/ahs03/ahs03.html; calculations by New Strategist

Generation Xers Are on the Move

Young adults are more likely than older Americans to change houses.

Young adults are far more likely than their elders to move from one home to another. Only 7 percent of people aged 40 or older move in a typical year, but the proportion of adults in their twenties and thirties who change homes is much higher. Between March 2003 and March 2004, a substantial 28 percent of people aged 25 to 29 moved to a different home. Among those aged 30 to 34, nearly one in five moved during the year.

Most movers—even among Generation Xers— stay within the same county. Fifty-seven percent of movers aged 25 to 39 moved within the same county. Only 18 percent moved to a different state.

Most people move for housing-related reasons. Among 25-to-29-year-old movers, 51 percent moved for housing-related reasons, as did an even larger 55 percent of movers aged 30 to 44. Only 19 to 20 percent of 25-to-44-year-olds moved for job-related reasons.

■ Americans are moving less than they once did. Several factors are behind the lower mobility rate, including the aging of the population, greater homeownership, and more dual-income couples.

Mobility rate falls sharply with age

(percent of people who moved between March 2003 and March 2004, by age)

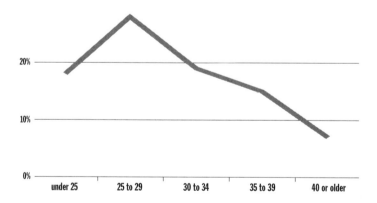

Table 3.9 Geographical Mobility by Age, 2003 to 2004

(total number and percent distribution of people aged 1 or older by mobility status between March 2003 and March 2004, by selected age groups; numbers in thousands)

		movers				
	total	total	same county	different county, same state	different state	abroad
Total, aged 1 or older	**284,367**	**38,995**	**22,551**	**7,842**	**7,330**	**1,272**
Under age 25	97,491	17,610	10,494	3,560	3,040	516
Aged 25 to 39	59,992	12,161	6,959	2,454	2,242	506
Aged 25 to 29	19,008	5,249	3,020	1,030	966	233
Aged 30 to 34	20,193	3,878	2,253	781	700	144
Aged 35 to 39	20,791	3,034	1,686	643	576	129
Aged 40 or older	126,885	9,222	5,097	1,828	2,046	251
PERCENT DISTRIBUTION BY MOBILITY STATUS						
Total, aged 1 or older	**100.0%**	**13.7%**	**7.9%**	**2.8%**	**2.6%**	**0.4%**
Under age 25	100.0	18.1	10.8	3.7	3.1	0.5
Aged 25 to 39	100.0	20.3	11.6	4.1	3.7	0.8
Aged 25 to 29	100.0	27.6	15.9	5.4	5.1	1.2
Aged 30 to 34	100.0	19.2	11.2	3.9	3.5	0.7
Aged 35 to 39	100.0	14.6	8.1	3.1	2.8	0.6
Aged 40 or older	100.0	7.3	4.0	1.4	1.6	0.2
PERCENT DISTRIBUTION OF MOVERS BY TYPE OF MOVE						
Total, aged 1 or older	–	**100.0%**	**57.8%**	**20.1%**	**18.8%**	**3.3%**
Under age 25	–	100.0	59.6	20.2	17.3	2.9
Aged 25 to 39	–	100.0	57.2	20.2	18.4	4.2
Aged 25 to 29	–	100.0	57.5	19.6	18.4	4.4
Aged 30 to 34	–	100.0	58.1	20.1	18.1	3.7
Aged 35 to 39	–	100.0	55.6	21.2	19.0	4.3
Aged 40 or older	–	100.0	55.3	19.8	22.2	2.7

Note: "–" means not applicable.
Source: Bureau of the Census, Geographical Mobility: 2004, Detailed Tables, Internet site http://www.census.gov/population/www/socdemo/migrate/cps2004.html; calculations by New Strategist

Table 3.10 Reason for Moving by Age, 2003 to 2004

(number and percent distribution of movers by primary reason for move between March 2003 and March 2004, by age; numbers in thousands)

	total	family reasons	employment reasons	housing reasons	other
Total movers	**38,995**	**9,475**	**6,624**	**20,577**	**2,319**
Under age 25	17,611	4,605	2,726	9,139	1,140
Aged 25 to 29	5,249	1,262	977	2,660	350
Aged 30 to 44	9,590	2,062	1,916	5,259	353
Aged 45 to 64	5,030	1,141	893	2,744	252
Aged 65 or older	1,516	404	113	776	223
Total movers	**100.0%**	**24.3%**	**17.0%**	**52.8%**	**5.9%**
Under age 25	100.0	26.1	15.5	51.9	6.5
Aged 25 to 29	100.0	24.0	18.6	50.7	6.7
Aged 30 to 44	100.0	21.5	20.0	54.8	3.7
Aged 45 to 64	100.0	22.7	17.8	54.6	5.0
Aged 65 or older	100.0	26.6	7.5	51.2	14.7

Note: "Other" includes to attend or leave college, change of climate, and health reasons.
Source: Bureau of the Census, Geographical Mobility: 2004, Detailed Tables, Internet site http://www.census.gov/population/ www/socdemo/migrate/cps2004.html; calculations by New Strategist

4

Income

■ Between 2000 and 2004, the median income of households headed by people aged 25 to 34 fell 7 percent, after adjusting for inflation. Despite the decline, their median income was higher in 2004 than in 1990.

■ The median income of householders aged 25 to 29, at $41,722 in 2004, was below the national median of $44,389. But householders aged 30 to 34 had a median income well above the national average, at $48,896.

■ Among households headed by people aged 25 to 39, married couples have the highest incomes—a median of $63,181 in 2004. Female-headed families have the lowest, a median of $25,364.

■ Between 1990 and 2004, the median income of men aged 35 to 44 fell 2.8 percent. In contrast, women's incomes rose substantially during that time period.

■ Generation Xers are slightly less likely to be poor than the average American. Overall, 12.7 percent of Americans lived in poverty in 2004. Among people aged 28 to 39, however, a smaller 11.5 percent are poor.

The Household Incomes of Generation Xers Have Declined

But incomes are higher than they were in 1990.

Between 2000 and 2004, the median income of households headed by people aged 25 to 34 fell 7 percent, after adjusting for inflation. (Generation Xers were aged 28 to 39 in 2004.) The median income of householders aged 35 to 44 fell 4 percent during those years. Behind the decline was the recession of 2001 and the lackluster recovery. Despite the decline since 2000, the median incomes of householders spanning the ages of 25 to 44 were higher in 2004 than they were in 1990.

The $45,485 median income of householders aged 25 to 34 was slightly higher than the national median of $44,389. The median income of householders aged 35 to 44, at $56,785, was well above the national median.

■ Householders in almost every age group have lost ground since 2000, with the biggest decline in median income occurring for those under age 35.

Household incomes have fallen since 2000

(median income of households headed by people aged 25 to 44, 2000 and 2004; in 2004 dollars)

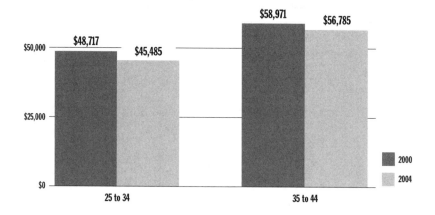

Table 4.1 Median Income of Households Headed by People Aged 25 to 44, 1990 to 2004

(median income of total households and households headed by people aged 25 to 44, 1990 to 2004; percent change for selected years; in 2004 dollars)

	total households	25 to 34	35 to 44
2004	$44,389	$45,485	$56,785
2003	44,482	45,982	56,523
2002	44,546	47,615	56,219
2001	45,062	48,105	56,898
2000	46,058	48,717	58,971
1999	46,129	47,709	57,592
1998	45,003	46,374	56,074
1997	43,430	44,802	54,409
1996	42,544	43,019	53,246
1995	41,943	42,713	53,500
1994	40,677	41,796	52,533
1993	40,217	40,269	52,602
1992	40,422	41,218	52,583
1991	40,746	41,714	53,220
1990	41,963	42,546	54,040
Percent change			
2000 to 2004	–3.6%	–6.6%	–3.7%
1990 to 2004	5.8	6.9	5.1

Source: Bureau of the Census, Current Population Survey Annual Social and Economic Supplements, Internet site http:// www.census.gov/hhes//www/income/histinc/inchhtoc.html; calculations by New Strategist

Household Income Rises with Age

Household income begins to exceed the average in the 30-to-34 age group.

The median income of householders aged 25 to 29, at $41,722 in 2004, was below the national median of $44,389. But householders aged 30 to 34 had a median income well above the national average, at $48,896. Behind the substantially higher incomes of the 30-to-34 age group is their lifestyle. At this age, most men and women are married, and most couples have two incomes.

In the nation as a whole, nearly 18 million households have incomes of $100,000 or more. More than 4 million of those householders are aged 25 to 39. Among all households, 16 percent have incomes of $100,000 or more. For householders aged 25 to 29, the figure is just 9 percent. It rises to 14 percent among 30-to-34-year-olds and surpasses the national average among 35-to-39-year-olds, at 19 percent.

■ The household incomes of Generation Xers are kept in check partly because they are competing for jobs with two much larger generations—the older Boomers and the younger Millennials.

Householders aged 25 to 29 have below-average incomes

(median income of total households and households headed by people aged 25 to 39, 2004)

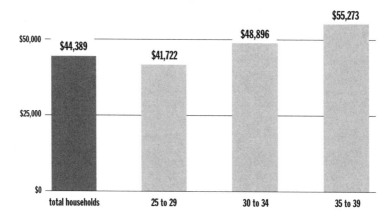

Table 4.2 Income of Households Headed by People Aged 25 to 39, 2004: Total Households

(number and percent distribution of total households and households headed by people aged 25 to 39 by income, 2004; households in thousands as of 2005)

	total	aged 25 to 39			
		total	25 to 29	30 to 34	aged 35 to 39
Total households	**113,146**	**30,272**	**9,145**	**10,110**	**11,017**
Under $10,000	9,805	2,007	703	633	671
$10,000 to $19,999	14,754	2,779	982	926	871
$20,000 to $29,999	14,263	3,550	1,241	1,189	1,120
$30,000 to $39,999	12,641	3,776	1,365	1,257	1,154
$40,000 to $49,999	10,743	3,434	1,172	1,164	1,098
$50,000 to $59,999	9,229	2,970	919	965	1,086
$60,000 to $69,999	8,078	2,600	794	853	953
$70,000 to $79,999	6,457	1,991	527	683	781
$80,000 to $89,999	5,294	1,650	418	573	659
$90,000 to $99,999	4,068	1,155	236	419	500
$100,000 or more	17,814	4,363	790	1,448	2,125
Median income	$44,389	$49,050	$41,722	$48,896	$55,273
Total households	**100.0%**	**100.0%**	**100.0%**	**100.0%**	**100.0%**
Under $10,000	8.7	6.6	7.7	6.3	6.1
$10,000 to $19,999	13.0	9.2	10.7	9.2	7.9
$20,000 to $29,999	12.6	11.7	13.6	11.8	10.2
$30,000 to $39,999	11.2	12.5	14.9	12.4	10.5
$40,000 to $49,999	9.5	11.3	12.8	11.5	10.0
$50,000 to $59,999	8.2	9.8	10.0	9.5	9.9
$60,000 to $69,999	7.1	8.6	8.7	8.4	8.7
$70,000 to $79,999	5.7	6.6	5.8	6.8	7.1
$80,000 to $89,999	4.7	5.5	4.6	5.7	6.0
$90,000 to $99,999	3.6	3.8	2.6	4.1	4.5
$100,000 or more	15.7	14.4	8.6	14.3	19.3

Source: Bureau of the Census, 2005 Current Population Survey Annual Social and Economic Supplement, Internet site http:// pubdb3.census.gov/macro/032003/hhinc/new02_000.htm; calculations by New Strategist

Incomes Are Highest for Asian Households

Among householders aged 25 to 39, the incomes of Asians are far higher than those of other racial or ethnic groups.

The median income of households headed by Asians aged 25 to 39 stood at $64,568 in 2004. (Generation Xers were aged 28 to 39 in that year.) Among Asian householders aged 35 to 39, median income was an even higher $75,092. The income of non-Hispanic whites aged 25 to 39 was lower than that of Asians, at $55,751. The incomes of Hispanics and blacks were much lower—$35,723 for Hispanic and $32,272 for black householders aged 25 to 39.

Behind the income differences by race and Hispanic origin is the number of earners per household. Because Asian and non-Hispanic white households are more likely than black or Hispanic households to be two-earner married couples, their incomes are considerably higher. Education also accounts for some of the gap. Asians are the best-educated Americans, followed by non-Hispanic whites. Hispanics are the least educated.

■ Black and Hispanic householders will not close the income gap until dual-earner couples make up a larger share of their households and college graduation rates approach those of Asians and non-Hispanic whites.

The incomes of young householders vary by race and Hispanic origin

(median income of housheolds headed by people aged 25 to 39, by race and Hispanic origin, 2004)

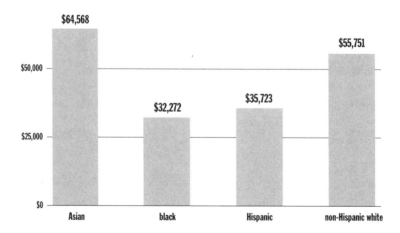

Table 4.3 Income of Households Headed by People Aged 25 to 39, 2004: Asian Households

(number and percent distribution of total Asians households and households headed by Asians aged 25 to 39 by income, 2004; households in thousands as of 2005)

	total	aged 25 to 39			
		total	25 to 29	30 to 34	35 to 39
Total Asian households	**4,360**	**1,661**	**427**	**591**	**643**
Under $10,000	331	94	27	23	44
$10,000 to $19,999	373	79	29	23	27
$20,000 to $29,999	405	138	45	47	46
$30,000 to $39,999	355	151	71	50	30
$40,000 to $49,999	420	160	32	85	43
$50,000 to $59,999	371	134	35	43	56
$60,000 to $69,999	315	150	34	68	48
$70,000 to $79,999	267	126	36	41	49
$80,000 to $89,999	236	121	30	39	52
$90,000 to $99,999	195	76	14	23	39
$100,000 or more	1,093	431	74	148	209
Median income	$57,475	$64,568	$52,055	$62,159	$75,092
Total Asian households	**100.0%**	**100.0%**	**100.0%**	**100.0%**	**100.0%**
Under $10,000	7.6	5.7	6.3	3.9	6.8
$10,000 to $19,999	8.6	4.8	6.8	3.9	4.2
$20,000 to $29,999	9.3	8.3	10.5	8.0	7.2
$30,000 to $39,999	8.1	9.1	16.6	8.5	4.7
$40,000 to $49,999	9.6	9.6	7.5	14.4	6.7
$50,000 to $59,999	8.5	8.1	8.2	7.3	8.7
$60,000 to $69,999	7.2	9.0	8.0	11.5	7.5
$70,000 to $79,999	6.1	7.6	8.4	6.9	7.6
$80,000 to $89,999	5.4	7.3	7.0	6.6	8.1
$90,000 to $99,999	4.5	4.6	3.3	3.9	6.1
$100,000 or more	25.1	25.9	17.3	25.0	32.5

Note: Asians include those identifying themselves as being Asian alone and those identifying themselves as being Asian in combination with one or more other races.
Source: Bureau of the Census, 2005 Current Population Survey Annual Social and Economic Supplement, Internet site http:// pubdb3.census.gov/macro/032003/hhinc/new02_000.htm; calculations by New Strategist

Table 4.4 Income of Households Headed by People Aged 25 to 39, 2004: Black Households

(number and percent distribution of total black households and households headed by blacks aged 25 to 39 by income, 2004; households in thousands as of 2005)

	total	aged 25 to 39 total	aged 25 to 39 25 to 29	aged 25 to 39 30 to 34	aged 25 to 39 35 to 39
Total black households	**14,127**	**4,312**	**1,338**	**1,489**	**1,485**
Under $10,000	2,496	657	258	199	200
$10,000 to $19,999	2,334	630	236	223	171
$20,000 to $29,999	2,167	709	227	255	227
$30,000 to $39,999	1,799	653	189	252	212
$40,000 to $49,999	1,290	425	110	144	171
$50,000 to $59,999	922	308	88	97	123
$60,000 to $69,999	842	304	87	104	113
$70,000 to $79,999	578	166	47	35	84
$80,000 to $89,999	416	126	17	56	53
$90,000 to $99,999	341	101	31	33	37
$100,000 or more	941	231	47	91	93
Median income	$30,268	$32,272	$27,816	$31,745	$36,816
Total black household	**100.0%**	**100.0%**	**100.0%**	**100.0%**	**100.0%**
Under $10,000	17.7	15.2	19.3	13.4	13.5
$10,000 to $19,999	16.5	14.6	17.6	15.0	11.5
$20,000 to $29,999	15.3	16.4	17.0	17.1	15.3
$30,000 to $39,999	12.7	15.1	14.1	16.9	14.3
$40,000 to $49,999	9.1	9.9	8.2	9.7	11.5
$50,000 to $59,999	6.5	7.1	6.6	6.5	8.3
$60,000 to $69,999	6.0	7.1	6.5	7.0	7.6
$70,000 to $79,999	4.1	3.8	3.5	2.4	5.7
$80,000 to $89,999	2.9	2.9	1.3	3.8	3.6
$90,000 to $99,999	2.4	2.3	2.3	2.2	2.5
$100,000 or more	6.7	5.4	3.5	6.1	6.3

Note: Blacks include those identifying themselves as being black alone and those identifying themselves as being black in combination with one or more other races.
Source: Bureau of the Census, 2005 Current Population Survey Annual Social and Economic Supplement, Internet site http:// pubdb3.census.gov/macro/032003/hhinc/new02_000.htm; calculations by New Strategist

Table 4.5 Income of Households Headed by People Aged 25 to 39, 2004: Hispanic Households

(number and percent distribution of total Hispanic households and households headed by Hispanics aged 25 to 39 by income, 2004; households in thousands as of 2005)

	total	aged 25 to 39			
		total	25 to 29	30 to 34	35 to 39
Total Hispanic households	**12,181**	**4,926**	**1,596**	**1,715**	**1,615**
Under $10,000	1,303	416	130	143	143
$10,000 to $19,999	1,957	731	258	245	228
$20,000 to $29,999	2,040	842	283	314	245
$30,000 to $39,999	1,631	748	268	248	232
$40,000 to $49,999	1,326	600	221	202	177
$50,000 to $59,999	1,018	439	130	141	168
$60,000 to $69,999	694	307	95	112	100
$70,000 to $79,999	562	227	71	81	75
$80,000 to $89,999	378	164	44	54	66
$90,000 to $99,999	293	109	23	48	38
$100,000 or more	980	342	73	125	144
Median income	$34,241	$35,723	$34,096	$35,622	$37,437
Total Hispanic households	**100.0%**	**100.0%**	**100.0%**	**100.0%**	**100.0%**
Under $10,000	10.7	8.4	8.1	8.3	8.9
$10,000 to $19,999	16.1	14.8	16.2	14.3	14.1
$20,000 to $29,999	16.7	17.1	17.7	18.3	15.2
$30,000 to $39,999	13.4	15.2	16.8	14.5	14.4
$40,000 to $49,999	10.9	12.2	13.8	11.8	11.0
$50,000 to $59,999	8.4	8.9	8.1	8.2	10.4
$60,000 to $69,999	5.7	6.2	6.0	6.5	6.2
$70,000 to $79,999	4.6	4.6	4.4	4.7	4.6
$80,000 to $89,999	3.1	3.3	2.8	3.1	4.1
$90,000 to $99,999	2.4	2.2	1.4	2.8	2.4
$100,000 or more	8.0	6.9	4.6	7.3	8.9

Source: Bureau of the Census, 2005 Current Population Survey Annual Social and Economic Supplement, Internet site http:// pubdb3.census.gov/macro/032003/hhinc/new02_000.htm; calculations by New Strategist

Table 4.6 Income of Households Headed by People Aged 25 to 39, 2004: Non-Hispanic White Households

(number and percent distribution of total non-Hispanic white households and households headed by non-Hispanic whites aged 25 to 39 by income, 2004; households in thousands as of 2005)

	total	aged 25 to 39			
		total	25 to 29	30 to 34	35 to 39
Total non-Hispanic white households	**81,445**	**19,149**	**5,710**	**6,233**	**7,206**
Under $10,000	5,593	842	283	270	289
$10,000 to $19,999	9,937	1,320	446	433	441
$20,000 to $29,999	9,578	1,843	671	576	596
$30,000 to $39,999	8,687	2,168	812	692	664
$40,000 to $49,999	7,623	2,228	798	727	703
$50,000 to $59,999	6,830	2,070	663	674	733
$60,000 to $69,999	6,131	1,814	576	562	676
$70,000 to $79,999	4,984	1,456	369	514	573
$80,000 to $89,999	4,203	1,221	327	418	476
$90,000 to $99,999	3,223	867	170	310	387
$100,000 and over	14,654	3,327	596	1,061	1,670
Median income	$48,977	$55,751	$47,929	$55,467	$62,196
Total non-Hispanic white households	**100.0%**	**100.0%**	**100.0%**	**100.0%**	**100.0%**
Under $10,000	6.9	4.4	5.0	4.3	4.0
$10,000 to $19,999	12.2	6.9	7.8	6.9	6.1
$20,000 to $29,999	11.8	9.6	11.8	9.2	8.3
$30,000 to $39,999	10.7	11.3	14.2	11.1	9.2
$40,000 to $49,999	9.4	11.6	14.0	11.7	9.8
$50,000 to $59,999	8.4	10.8	11.6	10.8	10.2
$60,000 to $69,999	7.5	9.5	10.1	9.0	9.4
$70,000 to $79,999	6.1	7.6	6.5	8.2	8.0
$80,000 to $89,999	5.2	6.4	5.7	6.7	6.6
$90,000 to $99,999	4.0	4.5	3.0	5.0	5.4
$100,000 and over	18.0	17.4	10.4	17.0	23.2

Note: Non-Hispanic whites are those identifying themselves as being white alone and not Hispanic.
Source: Bureau of the Census, 2005 Current Population Survey Annual Social and Economic Supplement, Internet site http://pubdb3.census.gov/macro/032003/hhinc/new02_000.htm; calculations by New Strategist

Couples Have the Highest Incomes

Female family heads have the lowest incomes.

The incomes of households headed by people aged 25 to 39 vary sharply by household type. Married couples have the highest incomes by far. Among households headed by people aged 25 to 39 (Generation Xers were aged 28 to 39 in 2004), married couples had a median income of $63,181 in 2004. In the 35-to-39 age group, the median income of married couples was a lofty $71,136. Behind the higher incomes is the fact that most couples are dual-earners.

Female-headed families in the 25-to-39 age group had a median income of only $25,364 in 2004. Most are single parents. The median income of male-headed families was nearly twice that of female-headed families ($45,871). The median income of women aged 25 to 39 who live alone was almost as high as that of their male counterparts, $31,083 versus $34,908.

■ Female-headed families have the lowest incomes because their households usually include only one earner and the presence of children makes them less flexible in their job choices.

The incomes of Generation X couples are above average

(median income of householders aged 25 to 39 by household type, 2004)

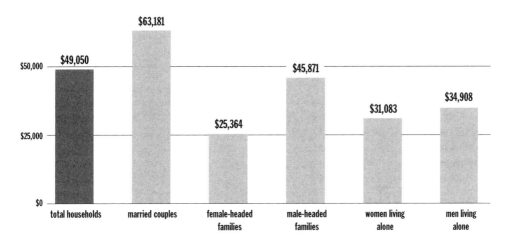

Table 4.7 Income of Households by Household Type, 2004: Aged 25 to 39

(number and percent distribution of households headed by people aged 25 to 39 by income and household type, 2004; households in thousands as of 2005)

| | family households | | | | nonfamily households | | | |
	total	married couples	female hh, no spouse present	male hh, no spouse present	female householder total	living alone	male householder total	living alone
Total households headed by 25-to-39-year-olds	**30,272**	**15,945**	**4,691**	**1,660**	**3,177**	**2,399**	**4,799**	**3,281**
Under $10,000	2,007	310	921	103	320	294	354	317
$10,000 to $19,999	2,779	812	910	134	404	360	518	445
$20,000 to $29,999	3,550	1,230	885	195	541	465	696	570
$30,000 to $39,999	3,776	1,561	676	255	556	474	729	565
$40,000 to $49,999	3,434	1,716	422	236	427	333	631	407
$50,000 to $59,999	2,970	1,853	263	173	201	125	478	308
$60,000 to $69,999	2,600	1,641	189	186	219	110	365	216
$70,000 to $79,999	1,991	1,399	142	84	121	60	241	125
$80,000 to $89,999	1,650	1,188	54	85	112	46	209	90
$90,000 to $99,999	1,155	896	59	42	48	26	110	49
$100,000 or more	4,363	3,335	163	171	225	102	469	189
Median income	$49,050	$63,181	$25,364	$45,871	$34,897	$31,083	$41,151	$34,908
Total households headed by 25-to-39-year-olds	**100.0%**	**100.0%**	**100.0%**	**100.0%**	**100.0%**	**100.0%**	**100.0%**	**100.0%**
Under $10,000	6.6	1.9	19.6	6.2	10.1	12.3	7.4	9.7
$10,000 to $19,999	9.2	5.1	19.4	8.1	12.7	15.0	10.8	13.6
$20,000 to $29,999	11.7	7.7	18.9	11.7	17.0	19.4	14.5	17.4
$30,000 to $39,999	12.5	9.8	14.4	15.4	17.5	19.8	15.2	17.2
$40,000 to $49,999	11.3	10.8	9.0	14.2	13.4	13.9	13.1	12.4
$50,000 to $59,999	9.8	11.6	5.6	10.4	6.3	5.2	10.0	9.4
$60,000 to $69,999	8.6	10.3	4.0	11.2	6.9	4.6	7.6	6.6
$70,000 to $79,999	6.6	8.8	3.0	5.1	3.8	2.5	5.0	3.8
$80,000 to $89,999	5.5	7.5	1.2	5.1	3.5	1.9	4.4	2.7
$90,000 to $99,999	3.8	5.6	1.3	2.5	1.5	1.1	2.3	1.5
$100,000 or more	14.4	20.9	3.5	10.3	7.1	4.3	9.8	5.8

Source: Bureau of the Census, 2005 Current Population Survey Annual Social and Economic Supplement, Internet site http:// pubdb3.census.gov/macro/032003/hhinc/new02_000.htm; calculations by New Strategist

Table 4.8 Income of Households by Household Type, 2004: Aged 25 to 29

(number and percent distribution of households headed by people aged 25 to 29, by income and household type, 2004; households in thousands as of 2005)

| | family households | | | | nonfamily households | | | |
| | | | female hh, no spouse present | male hh, no spouse present | female householder | | male householder | |
	total	married couples			total	living alone	total	living alone
Total households headed by 25-to-29-year-olds	**9,145**	**3,930**	**1,435**	**626**	**1,302**	**899**	**1,852**	**1,113**
Under $10,000	703	94	328	19	159	138	103	97
$10,000 to $19,999	982	262	298	60	165	147	196	164
$20,000 to $29,999	1,241	417	258	68	218	186	279	211
$30,000 to $39,999	1,365	532	202	111	225	179	296	216
$40,000 to $49,999	1,172	543	106	72	175	127	275	149
$50,000 to $59,999	919	505	82	71	74	27	187	108
$60,000 to $69,999	794	436	50	74	111	41	121	47
$70,000 to $79,999	527	318	28	33	50	15	97	41
$80,000 to $89,999	418	249	13	28	46	15	80	23
$90,000 to $99,999	236	138	22	15	17	2	46	15
$100,000 or more	790	438	44	75	60	21	173	44
Median income	$41,722	$51,858	$23,254	$47,601	$34,100	$28,897	$41,194	$33,244
Total households headed by 25-to-29-year-olds	**100.0%**	**100.0%**	**100.0%**	**100.0%**	**100.0%**	**100.0%**	**100.0%**	**100.0%**
Under $10,000	7.7	2.4	22.9	3.0	12.2	15.4	5.6	8.7
$10,000 to $19,999	10.7	6.7	20.8	9.6	12.7	16.4	10.6	14.7
$20,000 to $29,999	13.6	10.6	18.0	10.9	16.7	20.7	15.1	19.0
$30,000 to $39,999	14.9	13.5	14.1	17.7	17.3	19.9	16.0	19.4
$40,000 to $49,999	12.8	13.8	7.4	11.5	13.4	14.1	14.8	13.4
$50,000 to $59,999	10.0	12.8	5.7	11.3	5.7	3.0	10.1	9.7
$60,000 to $69,999	8.7	11.1	3.5	11.8	8.5	4.6	6.5	4.2
$70,000 to $79,999	5.8	8.1	2.0	5.3	3.8	1.7	5.2	3.7
$80,000 to $89,999	4.6	6.3	0.9	4.5	3.5	1.7	4.3	2.1
$90,000 to $99,999	2.6	3.5	1.5	2.4	1.3	0.2	2.5	1.3
$100,000 or more	8.6	11.1	3.1	12.0	4.6	2.3	9.3	4.0

Source: Bureau of the Census, 2005 Current Population Survey Annual Social and Economic Supplement, Internet site http://ferret. bls.census.gov/macro/032003/hhinc/new02_000.htm; calculations by New Strategist

Table 4.9 Income of Households by Household Type, 2004: Aged 30 to 34

(number and percent distribution of households headed by people aged 30 to 34, by income and household type, 2004; households in thousands as of 2005)

| | family households | | | | nonfamily households | | | |
| | | | female hh, no spouse present | male hh, no spouse present | female householder | | male householder | |
	total	married couples			total	living alone	total	living alone
Total households headed by 30-to-34-year-olds	**10,110**	**5,647**	**1,539**	**519**	**932**	**727**	**1,473**	**1,033**
Under $10,000	633	101	308	35	73	71	117	107
$10,000 to $19,999	926	300	303	43	125	110	154	128
$20,000 to $29,999	1,189	459	292	64	156	138	216	185
$30,000 to $39,999	1,257	562	227	81	168	154	219	172
$40,000 to $49,999	1,164	604	161	84	150	124	165	125
$50,000 to $59,999	965	643	78	40	55	38	148	90
$60,000 to $69,999	853	544	59	64	58	28	130	80
$70,000 to $79,999	683	505	39	29	34	18	76	41
$80,000 to $89,999	573	432	11	18	36	13	77	33
$90,000 to $99,999	419	359	8	8	7	3	35	15
$100,000 or more	1,448	1,134	53	54	70	27	137	56
Median income	$48,896	$62,090	$25,185	$43,529	$35,504	$31,841	$41,447	$35,269
Total households headed by 30-to-34-year-olds	**100.0%**	**100.0%**	**100.0%**	**100.0%**	**100.0%**	**100.0%**	**100.0%**	**100.0%**
Under $10,000	6.3	1.8	20.0	6.7	7.8	9.8	7.9	10.4
$10,000 to $19,999	9.2	5.3	19.7	8.3	13.4	15.1	10.5	12.4
$20,000 to $29,999	11.8	8.1	19.0	12.3	16.7	19.0	14.7	17.9
$30,000 to $39,999	12.4	10.0	14.7	15.6	18.0	21.2	14.9	16.7
$40,000 to $49,999	11.5	10.7	10.5	16.2	16.1	17.1	11.2	12.1
$50,000 to $59,999	9.5	11.4	5.1	7.7	5.9	5.2	10.0	8.7
$60,000 to $69,999	8.4	9.6	3.8	12.3	6.2	3.9	8.8	7.7
$70,000 to $79,999	6.8	8.9	2.5	5.6	3.6	2.5	5.2	4.0
$80,000 to $89,999	5.7	7.7	0.7	3.5	3.9	1.8	5.2	3.2
$90,000 to $99,999	4.1	6.4	0.5	1.5	0.8	0.4	2.4	1.5
$100,000 or more	14.3	20.1	3.4	10.4	7.5	3.7	9.3	5.4

Source: Bureau of the Census, 2005 Current Population Survey Annual Social and Economic Supplement, Internet site http://pubdb3.census.gov/macro/032003/hhinc/new02_000.htm; calculations by New Strategist

Table 4.10 Income of Households By Household Type, 2004: Aged 35 to 39

(number and percent distribution of households headed by people aged 35 to 39, by income and household type, 2004; households in thousands as of 2005)

| | family households | | | | nonfamily households | | | |
| | | | female hh, no spouse present | male hh, no spouse present | female householder | | male householder | |
	total	married couples			total	living alone	total	living alone
Total households headed by 35-to-39-year-olds	**11,017**	**6,368**	**1,717**	**515**	**943**	**773**	**1,474**	**1,135**
Under $10,000	671	115	285	49	88	85	134	113
$10,000 to $19,999	871	250	309	31	114	103	168	153
$20,000 to $29,999	1,120	354	335	63	167	141	201	174
$30,000 to $39,999	1,154	467	247	63	163	141	214	177
$40,000 to $49,999	1,098	569	155	80	102	82	191	133
$50,000 to $59,999	1,086	705	103	62	72	60	143	110
$60,000 to $69,999	953	661	80	48	50	41	114	89
$70,000 to $79,999	781	576	75	22	37	27	68	43
$80,000 to $89,999	659	507	30	39	30	18	52	34
$90,000 to $99,999	500	399	29	19	24	21	29	19
$100,000 or more	2,125	1,763	66	42	95	54	159	89
Median income	$55,273	$71,136	$27,288	$46,128	$35,396	$32,913	$40,801	$36,211
Total households headed by 35-to-39-year-olds	**100.0%**	**100.0%**	**100.0%**	**100.0%**	**100.0%**	**100.0%**	**100.0%**	**100.0%**
Under $10,000	6.1	1.8	16.6	9.5	9.3	11.0	9.1	10.0
$10,000 to $19,999	7.9	3.9	18.0	6.0	12.1	13.3	11.4	13.5
$20,000 to $29,999	10.2	5.6	19.5	12.2	17.7	18.2	13.6	15.3
$30,000 to $39,999	10.5	7.3	14.4	12.2	17.3	18.2	14.5	15.6
$40,000 to $49,999	10.0	8.9	9.0	15.5	10.8	10.6	13.0	11.7
$50,000 to $59,999	9.9	11.1	6.0	12.0	7.6	7.8	9.7	9.7
$60,000 to $69,999	8.7	10.4	4.7	9.3	5.3	5.3	7.7	7.8
$70,000 to $79,999	7.1	9.0	4.4	4.3	3.9	3.5	4.6	3.8
$80,000 to $89,999	6.0	8.0	1.7	7.6	3.2	2.3	3.5	3.0
$90,000 to $99,999	4.5	6.3	1.7	3.7	2.5	2.7	2.0	1.7
$100,000 or more	19.3	27.7	3.8	8.2	10.1	7.0	10.8	7.8

Source: Bureau of the Census, 2005 Current Population Survey Annual Social and Economic Supplement, Internet site http:// pubdb3.census.gov/macro/032003/hhinc/new02_000.htm; calculations by New Strategist

The Incomes of Men Aged 35 to 44 Are below 1990 Levels

Women's incomes have grown since 1990.

The incomes of men aged 25 to 44 fell between 2000 and 2004, after adjusting for inflation—down 7 percent for men aged 25 to 34 and down 2 percent for those aged 35 to 44 (Generation Xers were aged 28 to 39 in 2004). Women also experienced a decline, the median income of those aged 25 to 34 falling 5 percent. But women aged 35 to 44 saw their median income inch up by 0.5 percent between 2000 and 2004.

Behind the recent income decline is the recession of 2001 and the lackluster economic recovery. But for men the income decline began long before the recession. Between 1990 and 2004 the median income of men aged 35 to 44 fell 3 percent. In contrast, women's incomes soared during the 1990s. Women aged 25 to 34 saw their median income rise 25 percent between 1990 and 2004, while those aged 35 to 44 experienced a 20 percent gain, after adjusting for inflation.

■ Women's incomes have been rising rapidly because a growing share have joined the workforce.

Women have enjoyed big gains in income

(percent change in median income of people aged 25 to 44, by age and sex, 1990–2004; in 2004 dollars)

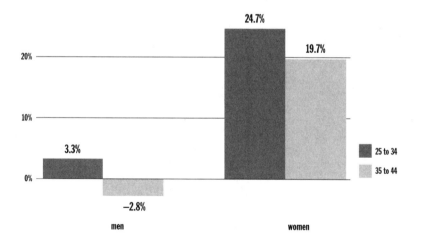

Table 4.11 Median Income of Men Aged 25 to 44, 1990 to 2004

(median income of men aged 15 or older and aged 25 to 44, 1990 to 2004; percent change for selected years; in 2004 dollars)

	total men	25 to 34	35 to 44
2004	$30,513	$30,984	$40,568
2003	30,735	31,383	40,248
2002	30,712	32,223	39,802
2001	31,054	32,557	40,913
2000	31,089	33,185	41,596
1999	30,937	33,299	41,256
1998	30,660	32,541	40,712
1997	29,590	30,510	38,555
1996	28,570	30,182	38,558
1995	27,771	29,060	38,674
1994	27,384	28,501	38,714
1993	27,165	28,227	39,060
1992	26,989	28,364	38,911
1991	27,684	29,207	39,630
1990	28,439	29,981	41,725
Percent change			
2000 to 2004	−1.9%	−6.6%	−2.5%
1990 to 2004	7.3	3.3	−2.8

Source: Bureau of the Census, data from the Current Population Survey Annual Demographic Supplements, Internet site http://www.census.gov/hhes/income/histinc/p08ar.html; calculations by New Strategist

Table 4.12 Median Income of Women Aged 25 to 44, 1990 to 2004

(median income of women aged 15 or older and aged 25 to 44, 1990 to 2004; percent change for selected years; in 2004 dollars)

	total women	25 to 34	35 to 44
2004	$17,629	$22,009	$24,332
2003	17,723	22,583	24,103
2002	17,659	22,740	23,447
2001	17,729	22,914	23,979
2000	17,619	23,088	24,216
1999	17,347	21,886	23,418
1998	16,700	21,130	23,477
1997	16,082	20,711	21,954
1996	15,361	19,639	22,112
1995	14,930	19,149	21,413
1994	14,456	18,765	20,411
1993	14,220	18,007	20,396
1992	14,136	17,985	20,342
1991	14,169	17,534	20,457
1990	14,112	17,643	20,326
Percent change			
2000 to 2004	0.1%	–4.7%	0.5%
1990 to 2004	24.9	24.7	19.7

Source: Bureau of the Census, data from the Current Population Survey Annual Demographic Supplements, Internet site http:// www.census.gov/hhes/income/histinc/p08ar.html; calculations by New Strategist

Men's Income Rises above Average in the 30-to-34 Age Group

Asian and Non-Hispanic white men have the highest incomes.

The incomes of men increase sharply during their twenties and thirties as they rise in their career. Among men aged 25 to 39, median income grows from a below-average $27,400 in the 25-to-29 age group to an above-average $39,941 among those aged 35 to 39 (Generation Xers were aged 28 to 39 in 2004). Income rises in part because a growing proportion of men work full-time. The figure rises from 68 percent in the 25-to-29 age group to 77 percent in the 35-to-39 age group.

Among men aged 25 to 39 working full-time, Asians have the highest median income, $46,903 in 2004. Non-Hispanic white men follow, with a median income of $43,663. Black and Hispanic men have the lowest incomes. Among black men aged 25 to 39 who work full-time, median income was $31,188 in 2004. Hispanic men who work full-time had an even lower income of $26,868.

■ Black and Hispanic men have lower incomes than Asian or non-Hispanic white men because they are much less educated.

Among men aged 25 to 39, Hispanics have the lowest incomes

(median income of men aged 25 to 39 who work full-time, by race and Hispanic origin, 2004)

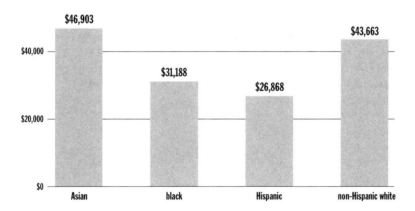

Table 4.13 Income of Men Aged 25 to 39, 2004: Total Men

(number and percent distribution of men aged 16 or older and aged 25 to 39 by income, 2004; median income by work status, and percent working year-round, full-time; men in thousands as of 2005)

		aged 25 to 39			
	total	total	25 to 29	30 to 34	35 to 39
TOTAL MEN	**111,686**	**29,940**	**9,825**	**9,851**	**10,264**
Without income	**9,909**	**1,367**	**551**	**401**	**415**
With income	**101,777**	**28,573**	**9,274**	**9,450**	**9,849**
Under $10,000	15,853	2,603	1,054	789	760
$10,000 to $19,999	18,096	4,441	1,833	1,375	1,233
$20,000 to $29,999	15,898	5,228	2,140	1,684	1,404
$30,000 to $39,999	13,391	4,751	1,629	1,591	1,531
$40,000 to $49,999	10,283	3,597	1,113	1,238	1,246
$50,000 to $59,999	7,376	2,498	613	886	999
$60,000 to $69,999	5,208	1,572	304	594	674
$70,000 to $79,999	3,767	1,121	240	402	479
$80,000 to $89,999	2,574	708	98	265	345
$90,000 to $99,999	1,881	504	57	163	284
$100,000 or more	7,452	1,547	193	462	892
Median income of men with income	$30,513	$34,259	$27,400	$35,179	$39,941
Median income of full-time workers	41,667	38,965	32,082	39,916	44,640
Percent working full-time	53.8%	73.6%	67.8%	75.6%	77.2%
TOTAL MEN	**100.0%**	**100.0%**	**100.0%**	**100.0%**	**100.0%**
Without income	**8.9**	**4.6**	**5.6**	**4.1**	**4.0**
With income	**91.1**	**95.4**	**94.4**	**95.9**	**96.0**
Under $10,000	14.2	8.7	10.7	8.0	7.4
$10,000 to $19,999	16.2	14.8	18.7	14.0	12.0
$20,000 to $29,999	14.2	17.5	21.8	17.1	13.7
$30,000 to $39,999	12.0	15.9	16.6	16.2	14.9
$40,000 to $49,999	9.2	12.0	11.3	12.6	12.1
$50,000 to $59,999	6.6	8.3	6.2	9.0	9.7
$60,000 to $69,999	4.7	5.3	3.1	6.0	6.6
$70,000 to $79,999	3.4	3.7	2.4	4.1	4.7
$80,000 to $89,999	2.3	2.4	1.0	2.7	3.4
$90,000 to $99,999	1.7	1.7	0.6	1.7	2.8
$100,000 or more	6.7	5.2	2.0	4.7	8.7

Source: Bureau of the Census, 2005 Current Population Survey Annual Social and Economic Supplement, Internet site http://pubdb3.census.gov/macro/032005/perinc/new01_000.htm; calculations by New Strategist

Table 4.14 Income of Men Aged 25 to 39, 2004: Asian Men

(number and percent distribution of Asian men aged 16 or older and aged 25 to 39 by income, 2004; median income by work status, and percent working year-round, full-time; men in thousands as of 2005)

	total	aged 25 to 39			
		total	25 to 29	30 to 34	35 to 39
TOTAL ASIAN MEN	**5,038**	**1,785**	**526**	**653**	**606**
Without income	**654**	**117**	**57**	**33**	**27**
With income	**4,384**	**1,668**	**469**	**620**	**579**
Under $10,000	695	158	70	42	46
$10,000 to $19,999	679	204	77	71	56
$20,000 to $29,999	607	264	96	103	65
$30,000 to $39,999	535	225	61	96	68
$40,000 to $49,999	388	176	44	68	64
$50,000 to $59,999	352	153	48	50	55
$60,000 to $69,999	205	98	11	51	36
$70,000 to $79,999	194	88	21	45	22
$80,000 to $89,999	154	71	14	28	29
$90,000 to $99,999	123	57	5	11	41
$100,000 or more	450	177	21	58	98
Median income of men with income	$32,419	$39,418	$28,951	$39,805	$48,085
Median income of full-time workers	46,429	46,903	38,311	46,612	54,673
Percent working full-time	57.1%	72.7%	59.7%	76.1%	80.2%
Total Asian men	**100.0%**	**100.0%**	**100.0%**	**100.0%**	**100.0%**
Without income	**13.0**	**6.6**	**10.8**	**5.1**	**4.5**
With income	**87.0**	**93.4**	**89.2**	**94.9**	**95.5**
Under $10,000	13.8	8.9	13.3	6.4	7.6
$10,000 to $19,999	13.5	11.4	14.6	10.9	9.2
$20,000 to $29,999	12.0	14.8	18.3	15.8	10.7
$30,000 to $39,999	10.6	12.6	11.6	14.7	11.2
$40,000 to $49,999	7.7	9.9	8.4	10.4	10.6
$50,000 to $59,999	7.0	8.6	9.1	7.7	9.1
$60,000 to $69,999	4.1	5.5	2.1	7.8	5.9
$70,000 to $79,999	3.9	4.9	4.0	6.9	3.6
$80,000 to $89,999	3.1	4.0	2.7	4.3	4.8
$90,000 to $99,999	2.4	3.2	1.0	1.7	6.8
$100,000 or more	8.9	9.9	4.0	8.9	16.2

Note: Asians are those identifying themselves as being Asian alone and those identifying themselves as being Asian in combination with one or more other races.
Source: Bureau of the Census, 2005 Current Population Survey Annual Social and Economic Supplement, Internet site http:// pubdb3.census.gov/macro/032005/perinc/new01_000.htm; calculations by New Strategist

Table 4.15 Income of Men Aged 25 to 39, 2004: Black Men

(number and percent distribution of black men aged 16 or older and aged 25 to 39 by income, 2004; median income by work status, and percent working year-round, full-time; men in thousands as of 2005)

| | total | aged 25 to 39 | | | |
		total	25 to 29	30 to 34	35 to 39
TOTAL BLACK MEN	**12,609**	**3,581**	**1,238**	**1,149**	**1,194**
Without income	**2,273**	**413**	**168**	**119**	**126**
With income	**10,336**	**3,168**	**1,070**	**1,030**	**1,068**
Under $10,000	2,363	472	184	160	128
$10,000 to $19,999	2,115	591	249	174	168
$20,000 to $29,999	1,889	716	288	230	198
$30,000 to $39,999	1,456	575	182	189	204
$40,000 to $49,999	896	323	76	109	138
$50,000 to $59,999	594	200	40	73	87
$60,000 to $69,999	314	96	9	29	58
$70,000 to $79,999	211	73	18	23	32
$80,000 to $89,999	99	24	5	14	5
$90,000 to $99,999	120	39	4	17	18
$100,000 or more	280	62	14	14	34
Median income of men with income	$22,740	$27,110	$23,163	$27,131	$31,183
Median income of full-time workers	31,724	31,188	26,597	31,304	35,838
Percent working full-time	46.2%	63.1%	56.5%	64.2%	68.8%
TOTAL BLACK MEN	**100.0%**	**100.0%**	**100.0%**	**100.0%**	**100.0%**
Without income	**18.0**	**11.5**	**13.6**	**10.4**	**10.6**
With income	**82.0**	**88.5**	**86.4**	**89.6**	**89.4**
Under $10,000	18.7	13.2	14.9	13.9	10.7
$10,000 to $19,999	16.8	16.5	20.1	15.1	14.1
$20,000 to $29,999	15.0	20.0	23.3	20.0	16.6
$30,000 to $39,999	11.5	16.1	14.7	16.4	17.1
$40,000 to $49,999	7.1	9.0	6.1	9.5	11.6
$50,000 to $59,999	4.7	5.6	3.2	6.4	7.3
$60,000 to $69,999	2.5	2.7	0.7	2.5	4.9
$70,000 to $79,999	1.7	2.0	1.5	2.0	2.7
$80,000 to $89,999	0.8	0.7	0.4	1.2	0.4
$90,000 to $99,999	1.0	1.1	0.3	1.5	1.5
$100,000 or more	2.2	1.7	1.1	1.2	2.8

Note: Blacks are those identifying themselves as being black alone and those identifying themselves as being black in combination with one or more other races.
Source: Bureau of the Census, 2005 Current Population Survey Annual Social and Economic Supplement, Internet site http:// pubdb3.census.gov/macro/032005/perinc/new01_000.htm; calculations by New Strategist

Table 4.16 Income of Men Aged 25 to 39, 2004: Hispanic Men

(number and percent distribution of Hispanic men aged 16 or older and aged 25 to 39 by income, 2004; median income by work status, and percent working year-round, full-time; men in thousands as of 2005)

	total	aged 25 to 39			
		total	25 to 29	30 to 34	35 to 39
TOTAL HISPANIC MEN	**15,223**	**5,870**	**2,177**	**1,956**	**1,737**
Without income	**1,968**	**269**	**131**	**74**	**64**
With income	**13,255**	**5,601**	**2,046**	**1,882**	**1,673**
Under $10,000	2,239	544	229	201	114
$10,000 to $19,999	3,700	1,572	613	519	440
$20,000 to $29,999	2,823	1,396	561	453	382
$30,000 to $39,999	1,725	825	306	260	259
$40,000 to $49,999	1,027	510	166	172	172
$50,000 to $59,999	616	311	75	119	117
$60,000 to $69,999	370	176	43	74	59
$70,000 to $79,999	198	80	21	23	36
$80,000 to $89,999	130	44	7	13	24
$90,000 to $99,999	88	34	4	16	14
$100,000 or more	336	113	22	33	58
Median income of men with income	$21,559	$23,811	$21,816	$23,581	$26,569
Median income of full-time workers	26,921	26,868	24,521	26,805	29,879
Percent working full-time	58.4%	74.4%	70.2%	75.7%	78.4%
TOTAL HISPANIC MEN	**100.0%**	**100.0%**	**100.0%**	**100.0%**	**100.0%**
Without income	**12.9**	**4.6**	**6.0**	**3.8**	**3.7**
With income	**87.1**	**95.4**	**94.0**	**96.2**	**96.3**
Under $10,000	14.7	9.3	10.5	10.3	6.6
$10,000 to $19,999	24.3	26.8	28.2	26.5	25.3
$20,000 to $29,999	18.5	23.8	25.8	23.2	22.0
$30,000 to $39,999	11.3	14.1	14.1	13.3	14.9
$40,000 to $49,999	6.7	8.7	7.6	8.8	9.9
$50,000 to $59,999	4.0	5.3	3.4	6.1	6.7
$60,000 to $69,999	2.4	3.0	2.0	3.8	3.4
$70,000 to $79,999	1.3	1.4	1.0	1.2	2.1
$80,000 to $89,999	0.9	0.7	0.3	0.7	1.4
$90,000 to $99,999	0.6	0.6	0.2	0.8	0.8
$100,000 or more	2.2	1.9	1.0	1.7	3.3

Source: Bureau of the Census, 2005 Current Population Survey Annual Social and Economic Supplement, Internet site http:// pubdb3.census.gov/macro/032005/perinc/new01_000.htm; calculations by New Strategist

Table 4.17 Income of Men Aged 25 to 39, 2004: Non-Hispanic White Men

(number and percent distribution of non-Hispanic white men aged 16 or older and aged 25 to 39 by income, 2004;
median income by work status, and percent working year-round, full-time; men in thousands as of 2005)

	total	aged 25 to 39 total	25 to 29	30 to 34	35 to 39
TOTAL NON-HISPANIC WHITE MEN	**77,680**	**18,435**	**5,800**	**5,995**	**6,640**
Without income	**4,912**	**541**	**185**	**164**	**192**
With income	**72,768**	**17,894**	**5,615**	**5,831**	**6,448**
Under $10,000	10,326	1,397	554	379	464
$10,000 to $19,999	11,441	2,044	877	601	566
$20,000 to $29,999	10,426	2,824	1,177	897	750
$30,000 to $39,999	9,557	3,092	1,071	1,024	997
$40,000 to $49,999	7,868	2,566	829	883	854
$50,000 to $59,999	5,717	1,802	443	627	732
$60,000 to $69,999	4,268	1,189	235	441	513
$70,000 to $79,999	3,137	874	180	308	386
$80,000 to $89,999	2,160	559	72	204	283
$90,000 to $99,999	1,535	361	44	115	202
$100,000 or more	6,334	1,188	136	350	702
Median income of men with income	$33,652	$38,893	$31,348	$40,086	$44,407
Median income of full-time workers	46,986	43,663	36,477	43,318	50,251
Percent working full-time	54.0%	75.7%	70.3%	78.0%	78.4%
TOTAL NON-HISPANIC WHITE MEN	**100.0%**	**100.0%**	**100.0%**	**100.0%**	**100.0%**
Without income	**6.3**	**2.9**	**3.2**	**2.7**	**2.9**
With income	**93.7**	**97.1**	**96.8**	**97.3**	**97.1**
Under $10,000	13.3	7.6	9.6	6.3	7.0
$10,000 to $19,999	14.7	11.1	15.1	10.0	8.5
$20,000 to $29,999	13.4	15.3	20.3	15.0	11.3
$30,000 to $39,999	12.3	16.8	18.5	17.1	15.0
$40,000 to $49,999	10.1	13.9	14.3	14.7	12.9
$50,000 to $59,999	7.4	9.8	7.6	10.5	11.0
$60,000 to $69,999	5.5	6.4	4.1	7.4	7.7
$70,000 to $79,999	4.0	4.7	3.1	5.1	5.8
$80,000 to $89,999	2.8	3.0	1.2	3.4	4.3
$90,000 to $99,999	2.0	2.0	0.8	1.9	3.0
$100,000 or more	8.2	6.4	2.3	5.8	10.6

Note: Non-Hispanic whites are those identifying themselves as being white alone and not Hispanic.
Source: Bureau of the Census, 2005 Current Population Survey Annual Social and Economic Supplement, Internet site http://
pubdb3.census.gov/macro/032005/perinc/new01_000.htm; calculations by New Strategist

Women's Incomes Do Not Rise Much with Age

Asian and non-Hispanic white women have the highest incomes.

The incomes of women do not change much as they age into their thirties. For Generation X women, median income ranges from a low of $21,349 among 25-to-29-year-olds to a high of $23,796 among 35-to-39-year-olds (Gen Xers were aged 28 to 39 in 2004). One reason for the relatively flat income trajectory is that only 46 to 50 percent of women aged 25 to 39 work full-time. Another reason is that many women choose lower-paying careers that allow them to spend more time with their children.

Among women aged 25 to 39 working full-time, Asians have the highest median income, $38,701 in 2004. Non-Hispanic white women follow, with a median income of $34,669. Black and Hispanic women have lower incomes. Among black women aged 25 to 39 who work full-time, median income was $29,463 in 2004. Their Hispanic counterparts had an even lower income of $24,511.

■ Black and Hispanic women have lower incomes than Asian or non-Hispanic white women because they are less educated.

Among women aged 25 to 39, Hispanics have the lowest incomes

(median income of women aged 25 to 39 who work full-time, by race and Hispanic origin, 2004)

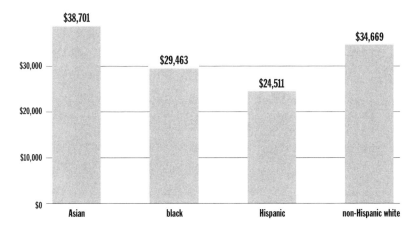

Table 4.18 Income of Women Aged 25 to 39, 2004: Total Women

(number and percent distribution of women aged 16 or older and aged 25 to 39 by income, 2004; median income by work status, and percent working year-round, full-time; women in thousands as of 2005)

	total	aged 25 to 39 total	25 to 29	30 to 34	35 to 39
TOTAL WOMEN	**118,739**	**30,018**	**9,674**	**9,957**	**10,387**
Without income	**15,370**	**3,731**	**1,406**	**1,202**	**1,123**
With income	**103,369**	**26,287**	**8,268**	**8,755**	**9,264**
Under $10,000	31,885	6,345	2,020	2,176	2,149
$10,000 to $19,999	23,868	5,093	1,789	1,597	1,707
$20,000 to $29,999	16,588	5,035	1,753	1,611	1,671
$30,000 to $39,999	11,583	4,055	1,297	1,395	1,363
$40,000 to $49,999	7,048	2,392	717	837	838
$50,000 to $59,999	4,128	1,217	286	461	470
$60,000 to $69,999	2,818	774	175	250	349
$70,000 to $79,999	1,737	448	73	131	244
$80,000 to $89,999	1,099	252	51	93	108
$90,000 to $99,999	675	199	39	53	107
$100,000 or more	1,939	476	69	151	256
Median income of women with income	$17,629	$22,735	$21,349	$22,975	$23,796
Median income of full-time workers	32,101	32,141	30,267	32,241	33,790
Percent working full-time	35.7%	48.0%	46.3%	47.8%	49.8%
TOTAL WOMEN	**100.0%**	**100.0%**	**100.0%**	**100.0%**	**100.0%**
Without income	**12.9**	**12.4**	**14.5**	**12.1**	**10.8**
With income	**87.1**	**87.6**	**85.5**	**87.9**	**89.2**
Under $10,000	26.9	21.1	20.9	21.9	20.7
$10,000 to $19,999	20.1	17.0	18.5	16.0	16.4
$20,000 to $29,999	14.0	16.8	18.1	16.2	16.1
$30,000 to $39,999	9.8	13.5	13.4	14.0	13.1
$40,000 to $49,999	5.9	8.0	7.4	8.4	8.1
$50,000 to $59,999	3.5	4.1	3.0	4.6	4.5
$60,000 to $69,999	2.4	2.6	1.8	2.5	3.4
$70,000 to $79,999	1.5	1.5	0.8	1.3	2.3
$80,000 to $89,999	0.9	0.8	0.5	0.9	1.0
$90,000 to $99,999	0.6	0.7	0.4	0.5	1.0
$100,000 or more	1.6	1.6	0.7	1.5	2.5

Source: Bureau of the Census, 2005 Current Population Survey Annual Social and Economic Supplement, Internet site http://pubdb3.census.gov/macro/032005/perinc/new01_000.htm; calculations by New Strategist

Table 4.19 Income of Women Aged 25 to 39, 2004: Asian Women

(number and percent distribution of Asian women aged 16 or older and aged 25 to 39 by income, 2004; median income by work status, and percent working year-round, full-time; women in thousands as of 2005)

	total	aged 25 to 39 total	25 to 29	30 to 34	35 to 39
TOTAL ASIAN WOMEN	**5,484**	**1,853**	**598**	**632**	**623**
Without income	**1,176**	**356**	**152**	**114**	**90**
With income	**4,308**	**1,497**	**446**	**518**	**533**
Under $10,000	1,338	382	127	128	127
$10,000 to $19,999	762	188	60	71	57
$20,000 to $29,999	610	222	72	73	77
$30,000 to $39,999	483	224	73	70	81
$40,000 to $49,999	338	144	32	59	53
$50,000 to $59,999	230	106	25	49	32
$60,000 to $69,999	168	70	16	19	35
$70,000 to $79,999	111	47	14	5	28
$80,000 to $89,999	79	28	6	15	7
$90,000 to $99,999	39	21	5	12	4
$100,000 or more	151	60	12	18	30
Median income of women with income	$20,618	$27,418	$24,581	$27,195	$30,368
Median income of full-time workers	36,491	38,701	35,661	39,448	40,860
Percent working full-time	37.5%	45.1%	38.8%	47.0%	49.3%
TOTAL ASIAN WOMEN	**100.0%**	**100.0%**	**100.0%**	**100.0%**	**100.0%**
Without income	**21.4**	**19.2**	**25.4**	**18.0**	**14.4**
With income	**78.6**	**80.8**	**74.6**	**82.0**	**85.6**
Under $10,000	24.4	20.6	21.2	20.3	20.4
$10,000 to $19,999	13.9	10.1	10.0	11.2	9.1
$20,000 to $29,999	11.1	12.0	12.0	11.6	12.4
$30,000 to $39,999	8.8	12.1	12.2	11.1	13.0
$40,000 to $49,999	6.2	7.8	5.4	9.3	8.5
$50,000 to $59,999	4.2	5.7	4.2	7.8	5.1
$60,000 to $69,999	3.1	3.8	2.7	3.0	5.6
$70,000 to $79,999	2.0	2.5	2.3	0.8	4.5
$80,000 to $89,999	1.4	1.5	1.0	2.4	1.1
$90,000 to $99,999	0.7	1.1	0.8	1.9	0.6
$100,000 or more	2.8	3.2	2.0	2.8	4.8

Note: Asians are those identifying themselves as being Asian alone and those identifying themselves as being Asian in combination with one or more other races.
Source: Bureau of the Census, 2005 Current Population Survey Annual Social and Economic Supplement, Internet site http://pubdb3.census.gov/macro/032005/perinc/new01_000.htm; calculations by New Strategist

Table 4.20 Income of Women Aged 25 to 39, 2004: Black Women

(number and percent distribution of black women aged 16 or older and aged 25 to 39 by income, 2004; median income by work status, and percent working year-round, full-time; women in thousands as of 2005)

	total	aged 25 to 39			
		total	25 to 29	30 to 34	35 to 39
TOTAL BLACK WOMEN	**15,365**	**4,354**	**1,459**	**1,449**	**1,446**
Without income	**2,380**	**412**	**160**	**105**	**147**
With income	**12,985**	**3,942**	**1,299**	**1,344**	**1,299**
Under $10,000	4,147	852	351	278	223
$10,000 to $19,999	2,946	855	303	285	267
$20,000 to $29,999	2,390	918	295	317	306
$30,000 to $39,999	1,571	657	183	239	235
$40,000 to $49,999	759	327	94	118	115
$50,000 to $59,999	415	123	25	47	51
$60,000 to $69,999	308	97	23	27	47
$70,000 to $79,999	176	46	12	10	24
$80,000 to $89,999	80	13	6	3	4
$90,000 to $99,999	55	16	4	3	9
$100,000 or more	137	37	6	15	16
Median income of women with income	$17,369	$22,162	$19,801	$22,425	$24,282
Median income of full-time workers	29,191	29,463	27,676	30,090	30,638
Percent working full-time	39.7%	54.2%	47.4%	54.9%	60.5%
TOTAL BLACK WOMEN	**100.0%**	**100.0%**	**100.0%**	**100.0%**	**100.0%**
Without income	**15.5**	**9.5**	**11.0**	**7.2**	**10.2**
With income	**84.5**	**90.5**	**89.0**	**92.8**	**89.8**
Under $10,000	27.0	19.6	24.1	19.2	15.4
$10,000 to $19,999	19.2	19.6	20.8	19.7	18.5
$20,000 to $29,999	15.6	21.1	20.2	21.9	21.2
$30,000 to $39,999	10.2	15.1	12.5	16.5	16.3
$40,000 to $49,999	4.9	7.5	6.4	8.1	8.0
$50,000 to $59,999	2.7	2.8	1.7	3.2	3.5
$60,000 to $69,999	2.0	2.2	1.6	1.9	3.3
$70,000 to $79,999	1.1	1.1	0.8	0.7	1.7
$80,000 to $89,999	0.5	0.3	0.4	0.2	0.3
$90,000 to $99,999	0.4	0.4	0.3	0.2	0.6
$100,000 or more	0.9	0.8	0.4	1.0	1.1

Note: Blacks are those identifying themselves as being black alone and those identifying themselves as being black in combination with one or more other races.
Source: Bureau of the Census, 2005 Current Population Survey Annual Social and Economic Supplement, Internet site http://pubdb3.census.gov/macro/032005/perinc/new01_000.htm; calculations by New Strategist

Table 4.21 Income of Women Aged 25 to 39, 2004: Hispanic Women

(number and percent distribution of Hispanic women aged 16 or older and aged 25 to 39 by income, 2004; median income by work status, and percent working year-round, full-time; women in thousands as of 2005)

	total	aged 25 to 39			
		total	25 to 29	30 to 34	35 to 39
TOTAL HISPANIC WOMEN	**14,381**	**5,064**	**1,771**	**1,732**	**1,561**
Without income	**3,992**	**1,370**	**495**	**470**	**405**
With income	**10,389**	**3,694**	**1,276**	**1,262**	**1,156**
Under $10,000	3,702	1,002	384	342	276
$10,000 to $19,999	2,880	1,050	365	334	351
$20,000 to $29,999	1,732	734	260	247	227
$30,000 to $39,999	944	469	149	174	146
$40,000 to $49,999	493	201	63	81	57
$50,000 to $59,999	232	88	23	32	33
$60,000 to $69,999	143	61	20	21	20
$70,000 to $79,999	101	36	5	8	23
$80,000 to $89,999	41	17	3	9	5
$90,000 to $99,999	29	8	1	4	3
$100,000 or more	95	26	3	8	15
Median income of women with income	$14,425	$17,330	$16,216	$18,181	$17,649
Median income of full-time workers	24,255	24,511	22,713	25,918	24,991
Percent working full-time	32.9%	40.9%	39.0%	41.3%	42.5%
TOTAL HISPANIC WOMEN	**100.0%**	**100.0%**	**100.0%**	**100.0%**	**100.0%**
Without income	**27.8**	**27.1**	**28.0**	**27.1**	**25.9**
With income	**72.2**	**72.9**	**72.0**	**72.9**	**74.1**
Under $10,000	25.7	19.8	21.7	19.7	17.7
$10,000 to $19,999	20.0	20.7	20.6	19.3	22.5
$20,000 to $29,999	12.0	14.5	14.7	14.3	14.5
$30,000 to $39,999	6.6	9.3	8.4	10.0	9.4
$40,000 to $49,999	3.4	4.0	3.6	4.7	3.7
$50,000 to $59,999	1.6	1.7	1.3	1.8	2.1
$60,000 to $69,999	1.0	1.2	1.1	1.2	1.3
$70,000 to $79,999	0.7	0.7	0.3	0.5	1.5
$80,000 to $89,999	0.3	0.3	0.2	0.5	0.3
$90,000 to $99,999	0.2	0.2	0.1	0.2	0.2
$100,000 or more	0.7	0.5	0.2	0.5	1.0

Source: Bureau of the Census, 2005 Current Population Survey Annual Social and Economic Supplement, Internet site http:// pubdb3.census.gov/macro/032005/perinc/new01_000.htm; calculations by New Strategist

Table 4.22 Income of Women Aged 25 to 39, 2004: Non-Hispanic White Women

(number and percent distribution of non-Hispanic white women aged 16 or older and aged 25 to 39 by income, 2004; median income by work status, and percent working year-round, full-time; women in thousands as of 2005)

	total	aged 25 to 39			
		total	25 to 29	30 to 34	35 to 39
TOTAL NON-HISPANIC WHITE WOMEN	**82,544**	**18,566**	**5,816**	**6,057**	**6,693**
Without income	**7,734**	**1,583**	**600**	**500**	**483**
With income	**74,810**	**16,983**	**5,216**	**5,557**	**6,210**
Under $10,000	22,391	4,062	1,157	1,393	1,512
$10,000 to $19,999	17,037	2,945	1,046	892	1,007
$20,000 to $29,999	11,753	3,121	1,111	968	1,042
$30,000 to $39,999	8,487	2,687	884	905	898
$40,000 to $49,999	5,402	1,716	532	576	608
$50,000 to $59,999	3,223	897	213	332	352
$60,000 to $69,999	2,180	543	116	180	247
$70,000 to $79,999	1,346	319	42	107	170
$80,000 to $89,999	895	193	39	64	90
$90,000 to $99,999	549	153	29	33	91
$100,000 or more	1,547	350	49	107	194
Median income of women with income	$18,379	$24,416	$23,014	$25,069	$25,043
Median income of full-time workers	34,878	34,669	31,695	35,485	36,516
Percent working full-time	35.3%	48.8%	48.8%	48.3%	49.2%
TOTAL NON-HISPANIC WHITE WOMEN	**100.0%**	**100.0%**	**100.0%**	**100.0%**	**100.0%**
Without income	**9.4**	**8.5**	**10.3**	**8.3**	**7.2**
With income	**90.6**	**91.5**	**89.7**	**91.7**	**92.8**
Under $10,000	27.1	21.9	19.9	23.0	22.6
$10,000 to $19,999	20.6	15.9	18.0	14.7	15.0
$20,000 to $29,999	14.2	16.8	19.1	16.0	15.6
$30,000 to $39,999	10.3	14.5	15.2	14.9	13.4
$40,000 to $49,999	6.5	9.2	9.1	9.5	9.1
$50,000 to $59,999	3.9	4.8	3.7	5.5	5.3
$60,000 to $69,999	2.6	2.9	2.0	3.0	3.7
$70,000 to $79,999	1.6	1.7	0.7	1.8	2.5
$80,000 to $89,999	1.1	1.0	0.7	1.1	1.3
$90,000 to $99,999	0.7	0.8	0.5	0.5	1.4
$100,000 or more	1.9	1.9	0.8	1.8	2.9

Note: Non-Hispanic whites are those identifying themselves as being white alone and not Hispanic.
Source: Bureau of the Census, 2005 Current Population Survey Annual Social and Economic Supplement, Internet site http://pubdb3.census.gov/macro/032005/perinc/new01_000.htm; calculations by New Strategist

Earnings Rise with Education

The highest earners are men with a professional degree.

For many years, a college degree has been well worth its cost. The higher the education, the greater the earnings. Among men aged 25 to 34 in 2004 (Generation Xers were aged 28 to 39 in that year), those with a professional degree (such as physicians and lawyers) who worked full-time earned a median of $67,422. Among men aged 35 to 44 working full-time, those with a professional degree had median earnings of $100,000 or more. Among women aged 25 to 34 who work full-time, median earnings also peak among those with a professional degree, at $71,046—higher than the median earnings of their male counterparts. Among women in the 35-to-44 age group who work full-time, those with a professional degree earned a median of $79,239.

Among men aged 25 to 44 who dropped out of high school, full-time workers earned less than $24,000 in 2004. For their counterparts with at least a college degree, earnings are above $50,000. The pattern is the same for women. Among women aged 25 to 34 who dropped out of high school, full-time workers earned less than $19,000 in 2004. Among the college graduates, earnings are above $40,000.

■ The steeply rising cost of a college degree combined with competition from well-educated but lower-paid workers in other countries may reduce the financial return of a college education in the years ahead.

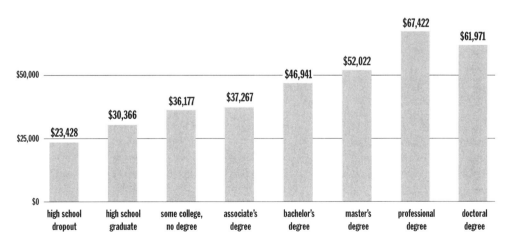

The college bonus is still big

(median earnings of men aged 25 to 34 who work full-time, by education, 2004)

high school dropout	high school graduate	some college, no degree	associate's degree	bachelor's degree	master's degree	professional degree	doctoral degree
$23,428	$30,366	$36,177	$37,267	$46,941	$52,022	$67,422	$61,971

Table 4.23 Earnings of Men by Education, 2004: Aged 25 to 34

(number and percent distribution of men aged 25 to 34 by earnings and education, 2004; men in thousands as of 2005)

	total	less than 9th grade	9th to 12th grade, no degree	high school graduate, including GED	some college, no degree	associate's degree	bachelor's degree or more				
							total	bachelor's degree	master's degree	professional degree	doctoral degree
TOTAL MEN AGED 25 TO 34	19,675	1,005	1,833	6,236	3,585	1,620	5,397	4,031	961	275	131
Without earnings	1,775	126	262	664	307	78	337	243	65	19	10
With earnings	17,900	878	1,570	5,572	3,277	1,542	5,060	3,788	896	255	121
Under $10,000	1,466	117	233	505	294	86	230	183	35	12	0
$10,000 to $19,999	3,059	386	486	1,157	495	194	340	268	50	13	10
$20,000 to $29,999	3,745	241	451	1,400	714	326	612	528	65	12	6
$30,000 to $39,999	3,194	79	222	1,113	665	321	794	668	93	16	14
$40,000 to $49,999	2,292	30	88	659	466	236	814	602	162	40	10
$50,000 to $59,999	1,496	16	54	355	259	172	642	437	151	35	19
$60,000 to $69,999	887	5	24	199	155	83	422	319	82	12	10
$70,000 to $79,999	594	0	5	80	111	47	350	259	64	15	11
$80,000 to $89,999	353	0	3	35	50	37	228	145	53	15	16
$90,000 to $99,999	203	4	0	13	16	11	157	101	43	11	3
$100,000 or more	612	0	4	54	52	29	471	278	97	75	21
Median earnings of men with earnings	$31,346	$17,400	$20,897	$27,073	$31,282	$34,405	$45,704	$42,110	$50,954	$58,360	$60,125
Median earnings of full-time workers	35,685	20,019	23,428	30,366	36,177	37,267	50,299	46,941	52,022	67,422	61,971
Percent working full-time	71.7%	66.0%	61.8%	69.6%	70.0%	77.9%	77.9%	78.6%	76.9%	72.4%	77.1%

(continued)

	total	less than 9th grade	9th to 12th grade, no degree	high school graduate, including GED	some college, no degree	associate's degree	bachelor's degree or more				
							total	bachelor's degree	master's degree	professional degree	doctoral degree
TOTAL MEN AGED 25 TO 34	100.0%	100.0%	100.0%	100.0%	100.0%	100.0%	100.0%	100.0%	100.0%	100.0%	100.0%
Without earnings	9.0	12.5	14.3	10.6	8.6	4.8	6.2	6.0	6.8	6.9	7.6
With earnings	91.0	87.4	85.7	89.4	91.4	95.2	93.8	94.0	93.2	92.7	92.4
Under $10,000	7.5	11.6	12.7	8.1	8.2	5.3	4.3	4.5	3.6	4.4	0.0
$10,000 to $19,999	15.5	38.4	26.5	18.6	13.8	12.0	6.3	6.6	5.2	4.7	7.6
$20,000 to $29,999	19.0	24.0	24.6	22.5	19.9	20.1	11.3	13.1	6.8	4.4	4.6
$30,000 to $39,999	16.2	7.9	12.1	17.8	18.5	19.8	14.7	16.6	9.7	5.8	10.7
$40,000 to $49,999	11.6	3.0	4.8	10.6	13.0	14.6	15.1	14.9	16.9	14.5	7.6
$50,000 to $59,999	7.6	1.6	2.9	5.7	7.2	10.6	11.9	10.8	15.7	12.7	14.5
$60,000 to $69,999	4.5	0.5	1.3	3.2	4.3	5.1	7.8	7.9	8.5	4.4	7.6
$70,000 to $79,999	3.0	0.0	0.3	1.3	3.1	2.9	6.5	6.4	6.7	5.5	8.4
$80,000 to $89,999	1.8	0.0	0.2	0.6	1.4	2.3	4.2	3.6	5.5	5.5	12.2
$90,000 to $99,999	1.0	0.4	0.0	0.2	0.4	0.7	2.9	2.5	4.5	4.0	2.3
$100,000 or more	3.1	0.0	0.2	0.9	1.5	1.8	8.7	6.9	10.1	27.3	16.0

Source: Bureau of the Census, 2005 Current Population Survey Annual Social and Economic Supplement, Internet site http://pubdb3.census.gov/macro/032005/perinc/new03_000.htm; calculations by New Strategist

Table 4.24 Earnings of Men by Education, 2004: Aged 35 to 44

(number and percent distribution of men aged 35 to 44 by earnings and education, 2004; men in thousands as of 2005)

	total	less than 9th grade	9th to 12th grade, no degree	high school graduate, including GED	some college, no degree	associate's degree	bachelor's degree or more total	bachelor's degree	master's degree	professional degree	doctoral degree
TOTAL MEN AGED 35 TO 44	21,468	1,080	1,691	7,284	3,349	1,841	6,223	4,117	1,397	423	286
Without earnings	1,917	178	323	847	254	86	228	158	47	19	4
With earnings	19,551	902	1,368	6,437	3,095	1,755	5,995	3,959	1,350	404	282
Under $10,000	1,126	94	146	525	146	66	149	97	33	6	15
$10,000 to $19,999	2,213	308	365	882	314	114	231	176	49	5	2
$20,000 to $29,999	2,870	266	368	1,163	445	245	384	313	45	18	6
$30,000 to $39,999	3,059	113	218	1,314	517	313	585	472	83	12	20
$40,000 to $49,999	2,573	62	105	1,011	497	294	602	444	122	18	17
$50,000 to $59,999	2,045	23	68	655	409	236	651	458	137	34	23
$60,000 to $69,999	1,466	27	50	377	266	200	547	385	107	10	44
$70,000 to $79,999	969	3	14	177	176	104	496	323	133	23	16
$80,000 to $89,999	702	0	10	109	84	62	437	261	126	27	24
$90,000 to $99,999	534	2	4	48	60	34	385	243	107	24	10
$100,000 or more	1,995	5	21	175	179	86	1,529	790	408	226	105
Median earnings of men with earnings	$41,029	$21,091	$23,733	$34,224	$41,288	$42,429	$66,028	$60,290	$76,478	$100,000+	$76,972
Median earnings of full-time workers	44,748	22,381	26,290	36,956	43,665	45,946	70,773	61,995	80,773	100,000+	81,360
Percent working full-time	77.1%	65.4%	61.6%	72.5%	78.5%	83.4%	86.0%	85.7%	86.3%	88.2%	86.4%

(continued)

	total	less than 9th grade	9th to 12th grade, no degree	high school graduate, including GED	some college, no degree	associate's degree	bachelor's degree or more				
							total	bachelor's degree	master's degree	professional degree	doctoral degree
TOTAL MEN AGED 35 TO 44	**100.0%**	**100.0%**	**100.0%**	**100.0%**	**100.0%**	**100.0%**	**100.0%**	**100.0%**	**100.0%**	**100.0%**	**100.0%**
Without earnings	**8.9**	**16.5**	**19.1**	**11.6**	**7.6**	**4.7**	**3.7**	**3.8**	**3.4**	**4.5**	**1.4**
With earnings	**91.1**	**83.5**	**80.9**	**88.4**	**92.4**	**95.3**	**96.3**	**96.2**	**96.6**	**95.5**	**98.6**
Under $10,000	5.2	8.7	8.6	7.2	4.4	3.6	2.4	2.4	2.4	1.4	5.2
$10,000 to $19,999	10.3	28.5	21.6	12.1	9.4	6.2	3.7	4.3	3.5	1.2	0.7
$20,000 to $29,999	13.4	24.6	21.8	16.0	13.3	13.3	6.2	7.6	3.2	4.3	2.1
$30,000 to $39,999	14.2	10.5	12.9	18.0	15.4	17.0	9.4	11.5	5.9	2.8	7.0
$40,000 to $49,999	12.0	5.7	6.2	13.9	14.8	16.0	9.7	10.8	8.7	4.3	5.9
$50,000 to $59,999	9.5	2.1	4.0	9.0	12.2	12.8	10.5	11.1	9.8	8.0	8.0
$60,000 to $69,999	6.8	2.5	3.0	5.2	7.9	10.9	8.8	9.4	7.7	2.4	15.4
$70,000 to $79,999	4.5	0.3	0.8	2.4	5.3	5.6	8.0	7.8	9.5	5.4	5.6
$80,000 to $89,999	3.3	0.0	0.6	1.5	2.5	3.4	7.0	6.3	9.0	6.4	8.4
$90,000 to $99,999	2.5	0.2	0.2	0.7	1.8	1.8	6.2	5.9	7.7	5.7	3.5
$100,000 or more	9.3	0.5	1.2	2.4	5.3	4.7	24.6	19.2	29.2	53.4	36.7

Source: Bureau of the Census, 2005 Current Population Survey Annual Social and Economic Supplement, Internet site http://pubdb3.census.gov/macro/032005/perinc/new03_000.htm; calculations by New Strategist

Table 4.25 Earnings of Women by Education, 2004: Aged 25 to 34

(number and percent distribution of women aged 25 to 34 by earnings and education, 2004; women in thousands as of 2005)

	total	less than 9th grade	9th to 12th grade, no degree	high school graduate, including GED	some college, no degree	associate's degree	bachelor's degree or more				
							total	bachelor's degree	master's degree	professional degree	doctoral degree
TOTAL WOMEN AGED 25 TO 34	**19,632**	**782**	**1,596**	**5,066**	**3,779**	**1,904**	**6,504**	**4,763**	**1,387**	**227**	**127**
Without earnings	**4,789**	**440**	**714**	**1,515**	**801**	**313**	**1,006**	**754**	**196**	**41**	**15**
With earnings	**14,843**	**342**	**882**	**3,551**	**2,978**	**1,591**	**5,498**	**4,009**	**1,191**	**186**	**112**
Under $10,000	2,816	146	330	857	647	256	580	432	131	16	1
$10,000 to $19,999	3,114	130	313	1,014	673	352	632	506	108	8	10
$20,000 to $29,999	3,169	50	159	948	741	397	875	709	135	22	10
$30,000 to $39,999	2,594	13	53	472	527	321	1,209	905	252	24	25
$40,000 to $49,999	1,453	0	10	157	220	143	923	624	248	30	18
$50,000 to $59,999	718	3	9	30	108	72	498	357	128	8	5
$60,000 to $69,999	383	0	2	31	21	22	305	209	77	9	9
$70,000 to $79,999	180	1	3	4	13	21	137	77	40	14	6
$80,000 to $89,999	143	0	1	10	21	3	108	67	26	9	6
$90,000 to $99,999	69	0	0	4	0	2	62	35	14	4	9
$100,000 or more	204	0	0	24	8	4	169	86	30	41	12
Median earnings of women with earnings	$24,165	$11,638	$12,847	$18,647	$21,552	$24,570	$35,236	$32,431	$38,281	$46,308	$46,673
Median earnings of full-time workers	30,777	15,873	18,613	24,166	27,639	30,326	40,238	37,702	42,574	71,046	52,393
Percent working full-time	47.0%	22.6%	28.4%	42.9%	46.4%	50.7%	57.1%	56.9%	56.3%	57.3%	70.1%

(continued)

TOTAL WOMEN AGED 25 TO 34	total	less than 9th grade	9th to 12th grade, no degree	high school graduate, including GED	some college, no degree	associate's degree	bachelor's degree or more				
							total	bachelor's degree	master's degree	professional degree	doctoral degree
	100.0%	100.0%	100.0%	100.0%	100.0%	100.0%	100.0%	100.0%	100.0%	100.0%	100.0%
Without earnings	24.4	56.3	44.7	29.9	21.2	16.4	15.5	15.8	14.1	18.1	11.8
With earnings	75.6	43.7	55.3	70.1	78.8	83.6	84.5	84.2	85.9	81.9	88.2
Under $10,000	14.3	18.7	20.7	16.9	17.1	13.4	8.9	9.1	9.4	7.0	0.8
$10,000 to $19,999	15.9	16.6	19.6	20.0	17.8	18.5	9.7	10.6	7.8	3.5	7.9
$20,000 to $29,999	16.1	6.4	10.0	18.7	19.6	20.9	13.5	14.9	9.7	9.7	7.9
$30,000 to $39,999	13.2	1.7	3.3	9.3	13.9	16.9	18.6	19.0	18.2	10.6	19.7
$40,000 to $49,999	7.4	0.0	0.6	3.1	5.8	7.5	14.2	13.1	17.9	13.2	14.2
$50,000 to $59,999	3.7	0.4	0.6	0.6	2.9	3.8	7.7	7.5	9.2	3.5	3.9
$60,000 to $69,999	2.0	0.0	0.1	0.6	0.6	1.2	4.7	4.4	5.6	4.0	7.1
$70,000 to $79,999	0.9	0.1	0.2	0.1	0.3	1.1	2.1	1.6	2.9	6.2	4.7
$80,000 to $89,999	0.7	0.0	0.1	0.2	0.6	0.2	1.7	1.4	1.9	4.0	4.7
$90,000 to $99,999	0.4	0.0	0.0	0.1	0.0	0.1	1.0	0.7	1.0	1.8	7.1
$100,000 or more	1.0	0.0	0.0	0.5	0.2	0.2	2.6	1.8	2.2	18.1	9.4

Source: Bureau of the Census, 2005 Current Population Survey Annual Social and Economic Supplement, Internet site http://pubdb3.census.gov/macro/032005/perinc/new03_000.htm; calculations by New Strategist

Table 4.26 Earnings of Women by Education, 2004: Aged 35 to 44

(number and percent distribution of women aged 35 to 44 by earnings and education, 2004; women in thousands as of 2005)

	total	less than 9th grade	9th to 12th grade, no degree	high school graduate, including GED	some college, no degree	associate's degree	bachelor's degree or more				
							total	bachelor's degree	master's degree	professional degree	doctoral degree
TOTAL WOMEN AGED 35 TO 44	21,882	847	1,423	6,455	3,932	2,485	6,739	4,618	1,573	324	223
Without earnings	4,965	399	588	1,530	793	413	1,242	910	254	50	28
With earnings	16,916	448	835	4,925	3,139	2,073	5,497	3,709	1,319	274	195
Under $10,000	2,610	139	228	858	520	280	584	430	120	24	10
$10,000 to $19,999	3,343	200	339	1,339	668	328	471	384	68	13	6
$20,000 to $29,999	3,458	81	173	1,346	699	490	671	526	110	20	14
$30,000 to $39,999	2,716	16	49	776	582	367	927	655	236	26	10
$40,000 to $49,999	1,752	9	18	335	333	255	803	538	208	22	35
$50,000 to $59,999	980	2	14	123	124	136	580	351	186	22	21
$60,000 to $69,999	720	0	2	66	91	106	457	267	150	19	20
$70,000 to $79,999	454	0	4	26	56	71	296	160	93	20	22
$80,000 to $89,999	232	0	5	12	21	15	180	110	38	18	14
$90,000 to $99,999	151	0	0	6	16	11	118	75	17	12	11
$100,000 or more	497	1	2	41	31	12	410	210	91	77	32
Median earnings of women with earnings	$26,523	$12,216	$14,748	$21,299	$25,664	$28,221	$40,636	$37,181	$45,453	$64,718	$60,356
Median earnings of full-time workers	32,274	16,657	19,094	25,740	31,179	34,077	48,002	44,486	51,989	79,239	62,386
Percent working full-time	51.2%	33.2%	36.1%	51.6%	52.6%	54.1%	54.4%	53.4%	55.5%	54.3%	66.4%

(continued)

	total	less than 9th grade	9th to 12th grade, no degree	high school graduate, including GED	some college, no degree	associate's degree	bachelor's degree or more				
							total	bachelor's degree	master's degree	professional degree	doctoral degree
TOTAL WOMEN AGED 35 TO 44	**100.0%**	**100.0%**	**100.0%**	**100.0%**	**100.0%**	**100.0%**	**100.0%**	**100.0%**	**100.0%**	**100.0%**	**100.0%**
Without earnings	**22.7**	**47.1**	**41.3**	**23.7**	**20.2**	**16.6**	**18.4**	**19.7**	**16.1**	**15.4**	**12.6**
With earnings	**77.3**	**52.9**	**58.7**	**76.3**	**79.8**	**83.4**	**81.6**	**80.3**	**83.9**	**84.6**	**87.4**
Under $10,000	11.9	16.4	16.0	13.3	13.2	11.3	8.7	9.3	7.6	7.4	4.5
$10,000 to $19,999	15.3	23.6	23.8	20.7	17.0	13.2	7.0	8.3	4.3	4.0	2.7
$20,000 to $29,999	15.8	9.6	12.2	20.9	17.8	19.7	10.0	11.4	7.0	6.2	6.3
$30,000 to $39,999	12.4	1.9	3.4	12.0	14.8	14.8	13.8	14.2	15.0	8.0	4.5
$40,000 to $49,999	8.0	1.1	1.3	5.2	8.5	10.3	11.9	11.7	13.2	6.8	15.7
$50,000 to $59,999	4.5	0.2	1.0	1.9	3.2	5.5	8.6	7.6	11.8	6.8	9.4
$60,000 to $69,999	3.3	0.0	0.1	1.0	2.3	4.3	6.8	5.8	9.5	5.9	9.0
$70,000 to $79,999	2.1	0.0	0.3	0.4	1.4	2.9	4.4	3.5	5.9	6.2	9.9
$80,000 to $89,999	1.1	0.0	0.4	0.2	0.5	0.6	2.7	2.4	2.4	5.6	6.3
$90,000 to $99,999	0.7	0.0	0.0	0.1	0.4	0.4	1.8	1.6	1.1	3.7	4.9
$100,000 or more	2.3	0.1	0.1	0.6	0.8	0.5	6.1	4.5	5.8	23.8	14.3

Source: Bureau of the Census, 2005 Current Population Survey Annual Social and Economic Supplement, Internet site http://pubdb3.census.gov/macro/032005/perinc/ new03_000.htm; calculations by New Strategist

Wage and Salary Income Is Most Important for Generation Xers

Interest income is second in importance.

Earnings from wages and salaries are the most common source of income for adults aged 25 to 44. The percentage of them who received wage or salary income in 2004 ranged from 88 to 91 percent among men and from 81 to 84 percent among women.

Interest is the second most common source of income for adults aged 25 to 44. From 37 to 52 percent of men and women in the age group receive interest income, but the amount is too small to have a significant impact on their lifestyle. The median amount of interest income received by 25-to-44-year-olds ranged from $1,300 to $1,368 in 2004.

One in ten women aged 25 to 44 receives child support income, the median amount ranging from $3,281 to $4,221 in 2004. Ten percent of men aged 35 to 44 receive income from self-employment. Those with self-employment income earned a median of $20,502 from self-employment in 2004.

■ The percentage of people receiving wage or salary income falls slightly with age as self-employment becomes a more-important source of income.

Most men and women aged 25 to 44 have wage or salary income

(percent of people aged 25 to 44 with wage or salary income, by sex, 2004)

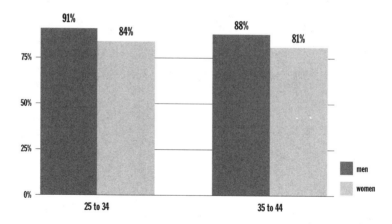

Table 4.27 Sources of Income for Men Aged 25 to 34, 2004

(number and percent distribution of men aged 25 to 34 with income and median income for those with income, by selected sources of income, 2004; men in thousands as of 2005; ranked by percentage receiving source)

	number	percent with income	median income
Total men aged 25 to 34 with income	**18,724**	**100.0%**	**$30,984**
Earnings	17,900	95.6	31,346
Wages and salary	17,061	91.1	31,415
Nonfarm self-employment	1,260	6.7	14,802
Farm self-employment	229	1.2	2,170
Property income	7,400	39.5	1,379
Interest	6,974	37.2	1304
Dividends	2,198	11.7	1,408
Rents, royalties, estates or trusts	492	2.6	1,935
Educational assistance	924	4.9	3,834
Unemployment compensation	864	4.6	2,615
SSI (Supplemental Security Income)	306	1.6	5,643
Social Security	301	1.6	7,303
Workers' compensation	203	1.1	2,615
Financial assistance from other household	168	0.9	4,110
Retirement income	134	0.7	7,350
Veterans' benefits	121	0.6	3,566
Disability benefits	78	0.4	7,572
Child support	51	0.3	–
Pension income	47	0.3	–
Public assistance	38	0.2	–
Survivor benefits	34	0.2	–
Alimony	1	0.0	–
Other income	24	0.1	–

Note: "–" means sample is too small to make a reliable estimate.
Source: Bureau of the Census, 2005 Current Population Survey Annual Social and Economic Supplement, Internet site http:// pubdb3.census.gov/macro/032005/perinc/new08_000.htm; calculations by New Strategist

Table 4.28 Sources of Income for Men Aged 35 to 44, 2004

(number and percent distribution of men aged 35 to 44 with income and median income for those with income, by selected sources of income, 2004; men in thousands as of 2005; ranked by percent receiving source)

	number	percent with income	median income
Total men aged 35 to 44 with income	**20,617**	**100.0%**	**$40,568**
Earnings	19,551	94.8	41,029
Wages and salary	18,069	87.6	41,446
Nonfarm self-employment	2,003	9.7	20,502
Farm self-employment	356	1.7	2,298
Property income	10,488	50.9	1,528
Interest	9,900	48.0	1,368
Dividends	3,971	19.3	1,529
Rents, royalties, estates or trusts	1,125	5.5	2,064
Unemployment compensation	927	4.5	2,867
Social Security	564	2.7	8,606
SSI (Supplemental Security Income)	431	2.1	6,156
Educational assistance	321	1.6	3,112
Retirement income	311	1.5	8,812
Workers' compensation	297	1.4	4,221
Veterans' benefits	175	0.8	4,214
Child support	161	0.8	2,696
Disability benefits	154	0.7	7,701
Pension income	138	0.7	11,627
Financial assistance from other household	106	0.5	4,274
Public assistance	78	0.4	2,379
Survivor benefits	70	0.3	–
Alimony	2	0.0	–
Other income	45	0.2	–

Note: "–" means sample is too small to make a reliable estimate.
Source: Bureau of the Census, 2005 Current Population Survey Annual Social and Economic Supplement, Internet site http:// pubdb3.census.gov/macro/032005/perinc/new08_000.htm; calculations by New Strategist

Table 4.29 Sources of Income for Women Aged 25 to 34, 2004

(number and percent distribution of women aged 25 to 34 with income and median income for those with income, by selected sources of income, 2004; women in thousands as of 2005; ranked by percentage receiving source)

	number	percent with income	median income
Total women aged 25 to 34 with income	**17,023**	**100.0%**	**$22,009**
Earnings	14,843	87.2	24,165
Wages and salary	14,353	84.3	24,514
Nonfarm self-employment	866	5.1	5,371
Farm self-employment	158	0.9	1,767
Property income	7,584	44.6	1357
Interest	7,205	42.3	1300
Dividends	1,924	11.3	1,415
Rents, royalties, estates or trusts	410	2.4	1,697
Child support	1,702	10.0	3,281
Educational assistance	1,306	7.7	3,494
Unemployment compensation	670	3.9	2,426
Public assistance	551	3.2	2,614
SSI (Supplemental Security Income)	404	2.4	5,994
Social Security	377	2.2	6,281
Financial assistance from other household	237	1.4	2,751
Retirement income	164	1.0	4,522
Workers' compensation	139	0.8	2,115
Disability benefits	89	0.5	3,551
Pension income	57	0.3	–
Survivor benefits	37	0.2	–
Veterans' benefits	36	0.2	–
Alimony	24	0.1	–
Other income	53	0.3	–

Note: "–" means sample is too small to make a reliable estimate.
Source: Bureau of the Census, 2005 Current Population Survey Annual Social and Economic Supplement, Internet site http:// pubdb3.census.gov/macro/032005/perinc/new08_000.htm; calculations by New Strategist

Table 4.30 Sources of Income for Women Aged 35 to 44, 2004

(number and percent distribution of women aged 35 to 44 with income and median income for those with income, by selected sources of income, 2004; women in thousands as of 2005; ranked by percent receiving source)

	number	percent with income	median income
Total women aged 35 to 44 with income	**19,734**	**100.0%**	**$24,332**
Earnings	16,916	85.7	26,523
Wages and salary	16,012	81.1	26,852
Nonfarm self-employment	1,303	6.6	8,242
Farm self-employment	194	1.0	1,935
Property income	10,814	54.8	1,476
Interest	10,212	51.7	1,358
Dividends	3,712	18.8	1,526
Rents, royalties, estates or trusts	951	4.8	1,847
Child support	2,089	10.6	4,221
Unemployment compensation	736	3.7	2,583
Social Security	691	3.5	8,421
Educational assistance	530	2.7	2,221
SSI (Supplemental Security Income)	438	2.2	5,995
Public assistance	368	1.9	2,478
Retirement income	220	1.1	5,728
Workers' compensation	212	1.1	2,196
Financial assistance from other household	179	0.9	2,672
Disability benefits	118	0.6	5,695
Alimony	101	0.5	4,533
Survivor benefits	87	0.4	6,988
Pension income	64	0.3	–
Veterans' benefits	31	0.2	–
Other income	81	0.4	2,072

Note: "–" means sample is too small to make a reliable estimate.
Source: Bureau of the Census, 2005 Current Population Survey Annual Social and Economic Supplement, Internet site http:// pubdb3.census.gov/macro/032005/perinc/new08_000.htm; calculations by New Strategist

The Poverty Rate Is below Average for Generation Xers

Poverty falls below average in the 30-to-34 age group.

Generation Xers (aged 28 to 39 in 2004) are slightly less likely to be poor than the average American. Overall, 12.7 percent of Americans lived in poverty in 2004. Among people aged 28 to 39, however, a smaller 11.5 percent are poor. People under age 25 are more likely than average to be poor, with a poverty rate of 17.9 percent. Among people aged 25 to 29, an above-average 13.1 percent are poor. In the 30-to-34 age group, the poverty rate falls to 11.9 percent. Among people aged 35 to 39, 10.5 percent are poor.

Black and Hispanic Gen Xers are more than twice as likely as Asian or non-Hispanic white Gen Xers to be poor. Twenty percent of blacks and Hispanics aged 28 to 39 live below the poverty level versus 7 to 8 percent of Asians and non-Hispanic whites. Blacks and Hispanics, together, account for the majority of poor Gen Xers, while non-Hispanic whites account for the 42 percent minority.

■ Blacks are more likely to be poor than Asians or non-Hispanic whites because they are less likely to live in married-couple families, the most-affluent household type.

The young are most likely to be poor

(percent of people with incomes below poverty level, by age, 2004)

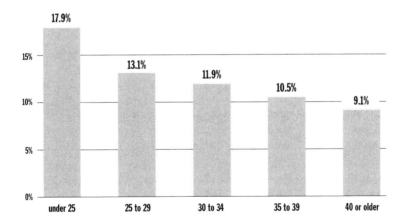

Table 4.31 People below Poverty Level by Age, Race, and Hispanic Origin, 2004

(number, percent, and percent distribution of people below poverty level by age, race, and Hispanic origin, 2004; people in thousands as of 2005)

	total	Asian	black	Hispanic	non-Hispanic white
NUMBER IN POVERTY					
Total people	**36,997**	**1,303**	**9,393**	**9,132**	**16,870**
Under age 25	18,094	546	5,204	5,222	7,028
Generation X (28 to 39)	5,525	217	1,237	1,686	2,345
Aged 25 to 29	2,558	103	642	744	1,058
Aged 30 to 34	2,366	91	514	748	995
Aged 35 to 39	2,171	97	493	603	963
Aged 40 or older	11,811	466	2,540	1,818	6,826
PERCENT IN POVERTY					
Total people	**12.7%**	**9.9%**	**24.7%**	**21.9%**	**8.6%**
Under age 25	17.9	11.7	31.9	27.3	11.6
Generation X (28 to 39)	11.5	7.2	19.9	19.6	7.8
Aged 25 to 29	13.1	9.2	23.8	18.8	9.1
Aged 30 to 34	11.9	7.1	19.8	20.3	8.3
Aged 35 to 39	10.5	7.9	18.7	18.3	7.2
Aged 40 or older	9.1	9.2	18.5	15.7	7.0
PERCENT DISTRIBUTION OF POOR BY AGE					
Total people	**100.0%**	**100.0%**	**100.0%**	**100.0%**	**100.0%**
Under age 25	48.9	41.9	55.4	57.2	41.7
Generation X (28 to 39)	14.9	16.7	13.2	18.5	13.9
Aged 25 to 29	6.9	7.9	6.8	8.1	6.3
Aged 30 to 34	6.4	7.0	5.5	8.2	5.9
Aged 35 to 39	5.9	7.4	5.2	6.6	5.7
Aged 40 or older	31.9	35.8	27.0	19.9	40.5
PERCENT DISTRIBUTION OF POOR BY RACE AND HISPANIC ORIGIN					
Total people	**100.0%**	**3.5%**	**25.4%**	**24.7%**	**45.6%**
Under age 25	100.0	3.0	28.8	28.9	38.8
Generation X (28 to 39)	100.0	3.9	22.4	30.5	42.4
Aged 25 to 29	100.0	4.0	25.1	29.1	41.4
Aged 30 to 34	100.0	3.8	21.7	31.6	42.1
Aged 35 to 39	100.0	4.5	22.7	27.8	44.4
Aged 40 or older	100.0	3.9	21.5	15.4	57.8

Note: Numbers will not add to total because Asians and blacks include those identifying themselves as being of the race alone and those identifying themselves as being of the race in combination with one or more other races, because Hispanics may be of any race, and because not all races are shown. Non-Hispanic whites include only those identifying themselves as being white alone and not Hispanic.

Source: Bureau of the Census, 2005 Current Population Survey Annual Social and Economic Supplement, Internet site http:// pubdb3.census.gov/macro/032005/pov/new34_100.htm; calculations by New Strategist

5

Labor Force

■ Generation Xers are at the career-building stage of their lives. But their labor force participation rate has declined, thanks to the weak economy of the past few years.

■ Eighty-three percent of people aged 25 to 39 were in the labor force in 2005 (Generation Xers were aged 29 to 40 in that year). Among men in the age group, from 91 to 93 percent are in the labor force. Among women, the figure stands at 74 to 75 percent.

■ Among Asian men aged 25 to 39, only 3.1 percent were unemployed in 2005. Among their black counterparts, unemployment stood at 9.0 percent.

■ The 66 percent majority of couples aged 25 to 39 are dual earners, while the husband is the only one in the labor force in another 29 percent.

■ Only 7 percent of all workers are self-employed. The figure is an even smaller 5 percent among those aged 25 to 34, rising to the 7 percent average in the 35-to-44 age group.

■ Among men aged 35 to 39, the percentage who had been with their current employer for 10 or more years fell from 36 to 25 percent between 1991 and 2004.

■ Between 2005 and 2014, the small Generation X will fill the 40-to-49 age group (Gen Xers will be aged 38 to 49 in 2014). The number of workers in the age group will decline by nearly 3 million.

Fewer Gen Xers Are Working

Labor force participation rate has declined for both men and women.

Generation Xers are at the career-building stage of their lives. But their labor force participation rate has shrunk, thanks to the weak economy of the past few years.

Men in their thirties typically have a higher labor force participation rate than men in any other age group. But fewer men in their thirties are in the labor force today. Among men aged 30 to 34 (Gen Xers were aged 29 to 40 in 2005), the labor force participation rate fell from 94.2 percent in 2000 to 92.7 percent in 2005. Among those aged 35 to 39, the rate fell from 93.2 to 92.6 percent. The same pattern holds true for women in the age group. Those aged 30 to 34 saw their labor force participation rate fall from 75.5 to 73.9 percent. Those aged 35 to 39 saw their participation decline from 75.7 to 74.6 percent.

While some women (and men) may be opting to stay home with young children for a few years, it is more likely that the decline in labor force participation is a consequence of industry layoffs and a lackluster economy. If jobs become plentiful again, labor force participation in the age group will rise.

■ Although the labor force participation rate is down for Generation Xers, the great majority of both men and women are still in the labor force.

The labor force participation rate of men aged 30 to 39 has declined

(percent of men aged 30 to 39 in the labor force, 2000 and 2005)

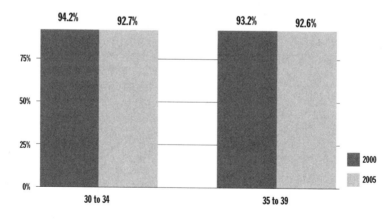

Table 5.1 Labor Force Participation Rate by Sex and Age, 1990 to 2005

(civilian labor force participation rate of people aged 16 or older, by sex and age, 1990 to 2005; percentage point change, 2000–2005 and 1990–2005)

	2005	2000	1990	percentage point change 2000–05	percentage point change 1990–2005
Men aged 16 or older	**73.3%**	**74.8%**	**76.4%**	**–1.5**	**–3.1**
Aged 16 to 17	30.5	40.9	43.5	–10.4	–13.0
Aged 18 to 19	57.9	65.0	67.1	–7.1	–9.2
Aged 20 to 24	79.1	82.6	84.4	–3.5	–5.3
Aged 25 to 29	90.8	92.5	93.7	–1.7	–2.9
Aged 30 to 34	92.7	94.2	94.5	–1.5	–1.8
Aged 35 to 39	92.6	93.2	94.8	–0.6	–2.2
Aged 40 to 44	91.6	92.1	93.9	–0.5	–2.3
Aged 45 to 49	89.3	90.2	92.2	–0.9	–2.9
Aged 50 to 54	85.9	86.8	88.8	–0.9	–2.9
Aged 55 to 59	77.6	77.0	79.9	0.6	–2.3
Aged 60 to 64	58.0	54.9	55.5	3.1	2.5
Aged 65 or older	19.8	17.7	16.3	2.1	3.5
Women aged 16 or older	**59.3**	**59.9**	**57.5**	**–0.6**	**1.8**
Aged 16 to 17	33.9	40.8	41.7	–6.9	–7.8
Aged 18 to 19	55.9	61.3	60.3	–5.4	–4.4
Aged 20 to 24	70.1	73.1	71.3	–3.0	–1.2
Aged 25 to 29	74.0	76.7	73.6	–2.7	0.4
Aged 30 to 34	73.9	75.5	73.3	–1.6	0.6
Aged 35 to 39	74.6	75.7	75.5	–1.1	–0.9
Aged 40 to 44	76.8	78.7	77.5	–1.9	–0.7
Aged 45 to 49	77.7	79.1	74.7	–1.4	3.0
Aged 50 to 54	74.0	74.1	66.9	–0.1	7.1
Aged 55 to 59	65.6	61.4	55.3	4.2	10.3
Aged 60 to 64	45.8	40.2	35.5	5.6	10.3
Aged 65 or older	11.5	9.4	8.6	2.1	2.9

Source: Bureau of Labor Statistics, Public Query Data Tool, Internet site http://www.bls.gov/data; and 2005 Current Population Survey, Internet site http://www.bls.gov/cps/home.htm; calculations by New Strategist

More than 80 Percent of Generation Xers Are in the Labor Force

Among men, labor force participation is over 90 percent.

Eighty-three percent of people aged 25 to 39 were in the labor force in 2005 (Generation Xers were aged 29 to 40 in that year). Labor force participation variees little within the age group. Among men, from 91 to 93 percent of those aged 25 to 39 are in the labor force. Among women, the figure stands at 74 to 75 percent throughout the age group.

Generation X men are slightly less likely to be unemployed than the average male worker—4.4 percent of men aged 25 to 39 versus 5.1 percent of all male workers. The unemployment rate among Gen X women is slightly above the average for all women, at 5.2 percent. Gen Xers are less likely to be unemployed than workers under age 25, but more likely to be job hunting than those aged 40 or older.

■ The labor force participation of men and women in their twenties and thirties would rise if jobs became more plentiful.

Most men and women of Generation X are in the labor force

(percent of people aged 25 to 39 in the labor force, by sex, 2005)

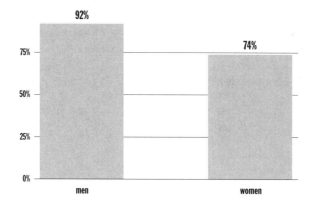

Table 5.2 Employment Status by Sex and Age, 2005

(number and percent of people aged 16 or older in the civilian labor force by sex and age, 2005; numbers in thousands)

| | | civilian labor force | | | | |
| | | | | | unemployed | |
	civilian noninstitutional population	total	percent of population	employed	number	percent of labor force
Total aged 16 or older	**226,082**	**149,320**	**66.0%**	**141,730**	**7,591**	**5.1%**
Under age 25	36,674	22,291	60.8	19,770	2,521	11.3
Aged 25 to 39	59,575	49,465	83.0	47,110	2,356	4.8
Aged 25 to 29	19,484	16,049	82.4	15,116	933	5.8
Aged 30 to 34	19,580	16,291	83.2	15,564	728	4.5
Aged 35 to 39	20,511	17,125	83.5	16,430	695	4.1
Aged 40 to 64	94,766	72,286	76.3	69,756	2,530	3.5
Aged 65 or older	35,068	5,278	15.1	5,094	184	3.5
Men aged 16 or older	**109,151**	**80,033**	**73.3**	**75,973**	**4,059**	**5.1**
Under age 25	18,498	11,644	62.9	10,202	1,442	12.4
Aged 25 to 39	29,569	27,211	92.0	26,003	1,208	4.4
Aged 25 to 29	9,744	8,843	90.8	8,363	480	5.4
Aged 30 to 34	9,701	8,994	92.7	8,630	364	4.0
Aged 35 to 39	10,124	9,374	92.6	9,010	364	3.9
Aged 40 to 64	46,140	38,219	82.8	36,913	1,306	3.4
Aged 65 or older	14,944	2,959	19.8	2,857	102	3.4
Women aged 16 or older	**116,931**	**69,288**	**59.3**	**65,757**	**3,531**	**5.1**
Under age 25	18,176	10,647	58.6	9,568	1,079	10.1
Aged 25 to 39	30,005	22,253	74.2	21,106	1,147	5.2
Aged 25 to 29	9,740	7,206	74.0	6,753	453	6.3
Aged 30 to 34	9,878	7,297	73.9	6,933	364	5.0
Aged 35 to 39	10,387	7,750	74.6	7,420	330	4.3
Aged 40 to 64	48,625	34,067	70.1	32,844	1,224	3.6
Aged 65 or older	20,125	2,319	11.5	2,238	82	3.5

Source: Bureau of Labor Statistics, 2005 Current Population Survey, Internet site http://www.bls.gov/cps/home.htm; calculations by New Strategist

Asians Are Least Likely to Be Unemployed

Nine percent of black men aged 25 to 39 are looking for work.

Most men of Generation X are in the labor force, but there are differences in labor force participation and unemployment by race and Hispanic origin. Among Hispanic and white men aged 25 to 39, fully 93 percent are in the labor force. Among Asian men in the age group, 90 percent are in the labor force, and among black men the figure is 86 percent.

Asian men aged 25 to 39 are less likely to be unemployed than others. In 2005, only 3.1 percent were unemployed, lower than the 4.0 percent average for all Asian men and less than the 3.9 percent rate among white men in the age group. A larger 4.2 percent of Hispanic men aged 25 to 39 were unemployed. Among blacks in the age group, 9.0 percent were unemployed in 2005.

■ Higher unemployment among black men contributes to their lower labor force participation rate. Discouraged by the prospects for work in their communities, some black men give up looking for jobs.

Unemployment rates differ by race and Hispanic origin

(percent of men aged 25 to 39 who are unemployed, by race and Hispanic origin, 2005)

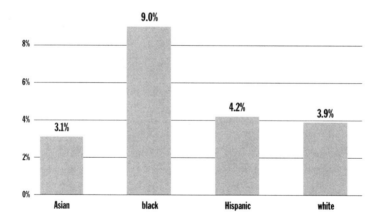

Table 5.3 Employment Status of Men by Race, Hispanic Origin, and Age, 2005

(number and percent of men aged 16 or older in the civilian labor force by race, Hispanic origin, and age, 2005; numbers in thousands)

	civilian noninstitutional population	civilian labor force total	percent of population	employed	unemployed number	percent of labor force
ASIAN MEN						
Total aged 16 or older	**4,679**	**3,500**	**74.8%**	**3,359**	**141**	**4.0%**
Under age 25	745	360	48.3	321	39	10.8
Aged 25 to 39	1,641	1,470	89.6	1,426	45	3.1
Aged 25 to 29	518	438	84.6	416	23	5.3
Aged 30 to 34	594	543	91.4	531	12	2.2
Aged 35 to 39	529	489	92.4	479	10	2.0
Aged 40 to 64	1,818	1,577	86.7	1,522	55	3.5
Aged 65 or older	474	94	19.8	91	3	3.2
BLACK MEN						
Total aged 16 or older	**11,882**	**7,998**	**67.3**	**7,155**	**844**	**10.6**
Under age 25	2,564	1,339	52.2	1,002	337	25.2
Aged 25 to 39	3,409	2,941	86.3	2,676	264	9.0
Aged 25 to 29	1,175	987	84.0	871	116	11.8
Aged 30 to 34	1,102	961	87.2	887	73	7.6
Aged 35 to 39	1,132	993	87.7	918	75	7.6
Aged 40 to 64	4,760	3,524	74.0	3,295	229	6.5
Aged 65 or older	1,148	196	17.1	182	14	7.1
HISPANIC MEN						
Total aged 16 or older	**14,962**	**11,985**	**80.1**	**11,337**	**647**	**5.4**
Under age 25	3,332	2,222	66.7	1,976	246	11.1
Aged 25 to 39	5,908	5,519	93.4	5,287	231	4.2
Aged 25 to 29	2,167	2,015	93.0	1,923	92	4.6
Aged 30 to 34	1,988	1,865	93.8	1,788	76	4.1
Aged 35 to 39	1,753	1,639	93.5	1,576	63	3.8
Aged 40 to 64	4,768	4,053	85.0	3,892	161	4.0
Aged 65 or older	953	192	20.1	183	9	4.7
WHITE MEN						
Total aged 16 or older	**90,027**	**66,694**	**74.1**	**63,763**	**2,931**	**4.4**
Under age 25	14,528	9,550	65.7	8,549	1,002	10.5
Aged 25 to 39	23,716	22,089	93.1	21,233	856	3.9
Aged 25 to 29	7,765	7,165	92.3	6,844	322	4.5
Aged 30 to 34	7,742	7,260	93.8	6,996	264	3.6
Aged 35 to 39	8,209	7,664	93.4	7,393	270	3.5
Aged 40 to 64	38,661	32,423	83.9	31,431	992	3.1
Aged 65 or older	13,123	2,631	20.0	2,550	81	3.1

Note: People who selected more than one race are not included. Hispanics may be of any race.
Source: Bureau of Labor Statistics, 2005 Current Population Survey, Internet site http://www.bls.gov/cps/home.htm; calculations by New Strategist

Labor Force Participation of Gen X Women Varies by Race and Ethnicity

Asian and Hispanic women are least likely to be in the labor force.

Black women aged 25 to 39 are more likely than Asian, Hispanic, or white women to be in the labor force. Seventy-nine percent of black women in the age group were working or looking for work in 2005. This figure compares with 74 percent of white women, 68 percent of Asian women, and just 64 percent of Hispanic women in the age group.

Unemployment is greater among black and Hispanic women than among Asian or white women. More than 9 percent of black women aged 25 to 39 were unemployed in 2005. Among their Hispanic counterparts, the figure was 6.6 percent. For white women aged 25 to 39, unemployment stood at 4.3 percent, while for Asian women it was 3.7 percent.

■ Among young adults, Hispanic women are less likely to work than black or white women because a larger proportion of them are married and caring for young children.

Labor force participation rate is highest for black women

(labor force participation rate of women aged 25 to 39, by race and Hispanic origin, 2005)

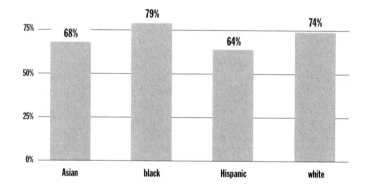

Table 5.4 Employment Status of Women by Race, Hispanic Origin, and Age, 2005

(number and percent of women aged 16 or older in the civilian labor force by race, Hispanic origin, and age, 2005; numbers in thousands)

	civilian noninstitutional population	civilian labor force			unemployed	
		total	percent of population	employed	number	percent of labor force
ASIAN WOMEN						
Total aged 16 or older	**5,163**	**3,002**	**58.1%**	**2,885**	**118**	**3.9%**
Under age 25	738	339	45.9	323	16	4.7
Aged 25 to 39	1,742	1,180	67.7	1,136	44	3.7
Aged 25 to 29	560	362	64.6	343	19	5.2
Aged 30 to 34	612	419	68.5	404	15	3.6
Aged 35 to 39	570	399	70.0	389	10	2.5
Aged 40 to 64	2,064	1,407	68.2	1,353	55	3.9
Aged 65 or older	619	76	12.3	74	2	2.6
BLACK WOMEN						
Total aged 16 or older	**14,635**	**9,014**	**61.6**	**8,158**	**856**	**9.5**
Under age 25	2,752	1,422	51.7	1,134	289	20.3
Aged 25 to 39	4,214	3,318	78.7	3,004	314	9.5
Aged 25 to 29	1,414	1,087	76.9	958	129	11.9
Aged 30 to 34	1,383	1,110	80.3	1,006	104	9.4
Aged 35 to 39	1,417	1,121	79.1	1,040	81	7.2
Aged 40 to 64	5,849	4,066	69.5	3,827	240	5.9
Aged 65 or older	1,819	207	11.4	193	14	6.8
HISPANIC WOMEN						
Total aged 16 or older	**14,172**	**7,839**	**55.3**	**7,295**	**544**	**6.9**
Under age 25	3,005	1,467	48.8	1,294	173	11.8
Aged 25 to 39	5,105	3,257	63.8	3,043	215	6.6
Aged 25 to 29	1,787	1,094	61.2	1,011	83	7.6
Aged 30 to 34	1,742	1,107	63.5	1,035	73	6.6
Aged 35 to 39	1,576	1,056	67.0	997	59	5.6
Aged 40 to 64	4,773	2,996	62.8	2,844	152	5.1
Aged 65 or older	1,289	119	9.2	113	6	5.0
WHITE WOMEN						
Total aged 16 or older	**94,419**	**55,605**	**58.9**	**53,186**	**2,419**	**4.4**
Under age 25	14,033	8,508	60.6	7,787	721	8.5
Aged 25 to 39	23,226	17,166	73.9	16,421	745	4.3
Aged 25 to 29	7,490	5,559	74.2	5,272	287	5.2
Aged 30 to 34	7,595	5,564	73.3	5,331	233	4.2
Aged 35 to 39	8,141	6,043	74.2	5,818	225	3.7
Aged 40 to 64	39,727	27,940	70.3	27,048	891	3.2
Aged 65 or older	17,433	1,993	11.4	1,930	63	3.2

Note: People who selected more than one race are not included. Hispanics may be of any race.
Source: Bureau of Labor Statistics, 2005 Current Population Survey, Internet site http://www.bls.gov/cps/home.htm; calculations by New Strategist

Most Generation X Couples Are Dual Earners

The husband is the sole support for fewer than one in three couples.

Dual incomes are the norm among married couples. Both husband and wife are in the labor force in 55 percent of the nation's couples. In another 23 percent, the husband is the only worker. Not far behind are the 17 percent of couples in which neither spouse is in the labor force. The wife is the sole worker among 6 percent of couples.

Sixty-six percent of couples aged 25 to 39 are dual earners, while the husband is the only one in the labor force in another 29 percent. The dual-earner lifestyle accounts for an even larger share of couples aged 40 to 54 because their children are grown and wives are more likely to work. The dual-earner share falls to just 47 percent among couples aged 55 to 64, in part because of early retirement.

■ The dual-earner share of married couples will rise in the older age groups as early retirement becomes less common.

Few Generation X couples are supported solely by the husband

(percent distribution of married couples aged 25 to 39, by labor force status of husband and wife, 2004)

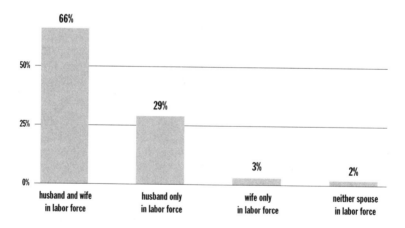

Table 5.5 Labor Force Status of Married-Couple Family Groups by Age of Reference Person, 2004

(number and percent distribution of married-couple family groups by age of reference person and labor force status of husband and wife, 2004; numbers in thousands)

	total	husband and/or wife in labor force			neither husband nor wife in labor force
		husband and wife	husband only	wife only	
Total married-couple family groups	**59,064**	**32,199**	**13,328**	**3,771**	**9,766**
Under age 25	1,595	902	582	55	58
Aged 25 to 39	16,354	10,863	4,754	447	292
Aged 25 to 29	3,931	2,561	1,156	123	92
Aged 30 to 34	5,918	3,904	1,780	140	94
Aged 35 to 39	6,505	4,398	1,818	184	106
Aged 40 to 44	7,339	5,141	1,800	267	132
Aged 45 to 54	13,793	9,701	2,847	795	451
Aged 55 to 64	10,013	4,741	2,274	1,257	1,741
Aged 65 or older	9,970	853	1,073	953	7,092
PERCENT DISTRIBUTION					
Total married-couple family groups	**100.0%**	**54.5%**	**22.6%**	**6.4%**	**16.5%**
Under age 25	100.0	56.6	36.5	3.4	3.6
Aged 25 to 39	100.0	66.4	29.1	2.7	1.8
Aged 25 to 29	100.0	65.1	29.4	3.1	2.3
Aged 30 to 34	100.0	66.0	30.1	2.4	1.6
Aged 35 to 39	100.0	67.6	27.9	2.8	1.6
Aged 40 to 44	100.0	70.1	24.5	3.6	1.8
Aged 45 to 54	100.0	70.3	20.6	5.8	3.3
Aged 55 to 64	100.0	47.3	22.7	12.6	17.4
Aged 65 or older	100.0	8.6	10.8	9.6	71.1

Source: Bureau of the Census, 2004 Current Population Survey Annual Demographic Supplement, Internet site http://www .census.gov/population/www/socdemo/hh-fam/cps2004.html; calculations by New Strategist

Generation Xers Are Overrepresented in Technical Jobs

They are also overrepresented in jobs requiring physical stamina.

Nearly half of American workers (46 percent) were aged 25 to 44 in 2005 (Generation X was aged 29 to 40 in that year), but the share varies widely by occupation. Workers in the 25-to-44 age group tend to be underrepresented in leadership positions and overrepresented in jobs requiring technical skills. The 25-to-44 age group accounts for only 18 percent of legislators and 35 percent of chief executives. But fully 66 percent of computer software engineers and 71 percent of medical scientists are aged 25 to 44.

Generation Xers make up a large share of employees in jobs requiring physical stamina. Sixty-nine percent of firefighters and police are in the 25-to-44 age group. The age group accounts for 64 percent of physical therapists and the majority of construction laborers.

■ Generation X was raised on computers, which explains their disproportionate presence in high-tech jobs.

Many computer workers are aged 25 to 44

(percent of workers in the 25-to-44 age group, by occupation, 2005)

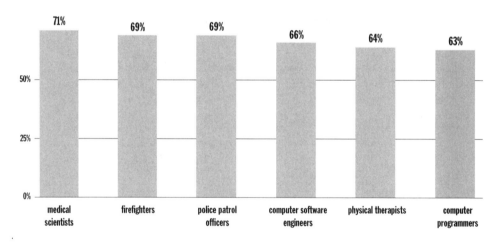

Table 5.6 Occupations of Workers Aged 25 to 44, 2005

(number of employed workers aged 16 or older, median age of workers, and number of workers aged 25 to 44, by occupation, 2005; numbers in thousands)

	total	median age	aged 25 to 44 total	25 to 34	35 to 44
TOTAL WORKERS	**141,730**	**40.7**	**65,310**	**30,680**	**34,630**
Management and professional occupations	**49,245**	**43.1**	**23,901**	**10,890**	**13,011**
Management, business and financial operations	20,450	44.3	9,539	3,959	5,580
Management	14,685	45.1	6,586	2,520	4,066
Business and financial operations	5,765	42.1	2,953	1,439	1,514
Professional and related occupations	28,795	42.2	14,361	6,931	7,430
Computer and mathematical	3,246	39.4	2,044	1,061	983
Architecture and engineering	2,793	42.3	1,411	637	774
Life, physical, and social sciences	1,406	41.6	718	364	354
Community and social services	2,138	44.0	983	482	501
Legal	1,614	43.9	803	354	449
Education, training, and library	8,114	43.0	3,757	1,837	1,920
Arts, design, entertainment, sports, and media	2,736	40.5	1,335	674	661
Health care practitioner and technician	6,748	42.9	3,310	1,522	1,788
Service occupations	**23,133**	**36.9**	**9,882**	**4,904**	**4,978**
Health care support	3,092	38.4	1,482	739	743
Protective service	2,894	40.6	1,502	714	788
Food preparation and serving	7,374	28.6	2,686	1,507	1,179
Building and grounds cleaning and maintenance	5,241	41.5	2,281	978	1,303
Personal care and service	4,531	38.6	1,931	966	965
Sales and office occupations	**35,962**	**39.9**	**15,238**	**7,211**	**8,027**
Sales and related occupations	16,433	39.1	6,717	3,167	3,550
Office and administrative support	19,529	40.5	8,521	4,044	4,477
Natural resources, construction, and maintenance occupations	**15,348**	**38.9**	**7,857**	**3,878**	**3,979**
Farming, fishing, and forestry	976	36.8	431	215	216
Construction and extraction	9,145	38.0	4,837	2,482	2,355
Installation, maintenance, and repair	5,226	40.8	2,590	1,181	1,409
Production, transportation, and material-moving occupations	**18,041**	**41.0**	**8,431**	**3,796**	**4,635**
Production	9,378	41.5	4,467	1,976	2,491
Transportation and material moving	8,664	40.5	3,964	1,820	2,144

Source: Bureau of Labor Statistics, unpublished data from the 2005 Current Population Survey; calculations by New Strategist

Table 5.7   Distribution of Workers Aged 25 to 44 by Occupation, 2005

(percent distribution of employed people aged 16 or older and aged 25 to 44 by occupation, 2005)

	total	aged 25 to 44 total	aged 25 to 44 25 to 34	aged 25 to 44 35 to 44
TOTAL WORKERS	**100.0%**	**46.1%**	**21.6%**	**24.4%**
Management and professional occupations	**100.0**	**48.5**	**22.1**	**26.4**
Management, business and financial operations	100.0	46.6	19.4	27.3
Management	100.0	44.8	17.2	27.7
Business and financial operations	100.0	51.2	25.0	26.3
Professional and related occupations	100.0	49.9	24.1	25.8
Computer and mathematical	100.0	63.0	32.7	30.3
Architecture and engineering	100.0	50.5	22.8	27.7
Life, physical, and social sciences	100.0	51.1	25.9	25.2
Community and social services	100.0	46.0	22.5	23.4
Legal	100.0	49.8	21.9	27.8
Education, training, and library	100.0	46.3	22.6	23.7
Arts, design, entertainment, sports, and media	100.0	48.8	24.6	24.2
Health care practitioner and technician	100.0	49.1	22.6	26.5
Service occupations	**100.0**	**42.7**	**21.2**	**21.5**
Health care support	100.0	47.9	23.9	24.0
Protective service	100.0	51.9	24.7	27.2
Food preparation and serving	100.0	36.4	20.4	16.0
Building and grounds cleaning and maintenance	100.0	43.5	18.7	24.9
Personal care and service	100.0	42.6	21.3	21.3
Sales and office occupations	**100.0**	**42.4**	**20.1**	**22.3**
Sales and related occupations	100.0	40.9	19.3	21.6
Office and administrative support	100.0	43.6	20.7	22.9
Natural resources, construction, maintenance occupations	**100.0**	**51.2**	**25.3**	**25.9**
Farming, fishing, and forestry	100.0	44.2	22.0	22.1
Construction and extraction	100.0	52.9	27.1	25.8
Installation, maintenance, and repair	100.0	49.6	22.6	27.0
Production, transportation, material-moving occupations	**100.0**	**46.7**	**21.0**	**25.7**
Production	100.0	47.6	21.1	26.6
Transportation and material moving	100.0	45.8	21.0	24.7

Source: Calculations by New Strategist based on Bureau of Labor Statistics' unpublished 2005 Current Population Survey data

Table 5.8 Share of Workers Aged 25 to 44 by Occupation, 2005

(percent distribution of total employed and employed aged 25 to 44, by occupation, 2005)

| | | aged 25 to 44 | | |
	total	total	25 to 34	35 to 44
TOTAL WORKERS	**100.0%**	**100.0%**	**100.0%**	**100.0%**
Management and professional occupations	**34.7**	**36.6**	**35.5**	**37.6**
Management, business and financial operations	14.4	14.6	12.9	16.1
Management	10.4	10.1	8.2	11.7
Business and financial operations	4.1	4.5	4.7	4.4
Professional and related occupations	20.3	22.0	22.6	21.5
Computer and mathematical	2.3	3.1	3.5	2.8
Architecture and engineering	2.0	2.2	2.1	2.2
Life, physical, and social sciences	1.0	1.1	1.2	1.0
Community and social services	1.5	1.5	1.6	1.4
Legal	1.1	1.2	1.2	1.3
Education, training, and library	5.7	5.8	6.0	5.5
Arts, design, entertainment, sports, and media	1.9	2.0	2.2	1.9
Health care practitioner and technician	4.8	5.1	5.0	5.2
Service occupations	**16.3**	**15.1**	**16.0**	**14.4**
Health care support	2.2	2.3	2.4	2.1
Protective service	2.0	2.3	2.3	2.3
Food preparation and serving	5.2	4.1	4.9	3.4
Building and grounds cleaning and maintenance	3.7	3.5	3.2	3.8
Personal care and service	3.2	3.0	3.1	2.8
Sales and office occupations	**25.4**	**23.3**	**23.5**	**23.2**
Sales and related occupations	11.6	10.3	10.3	10.3
Office and administrative support	13.8	13.0	13.2	12.9
Natural resources, construction, maintenance occupations	**10.8**	**12.0**	**12.6**	**11.5**
Farming, fishing, and forestry	0.7	0.7	0.7	0.6
Construction and extraction	6.5	7.4	8.1	6.8
Installation, maintenance, and repair	3.7	4.0	3.8	4.1
Production, transportation, material-moving occupations	**12.7**	**12.9**	**12.4**	**13.4**
Production	6.6	6.8	6.4	7.2
Transportation and material moving	6.1	6.1	5.9	6.2

Source: Calculations by New Strategist based on Bureau of Labor Statistics' unpublished 2005 Current Population Survey data

Table 5.9   Workers Aged 25 to 44 by Detailed Occupation, 2005

(number of employed workers aged 16 or older, median age, and number and percent aged 25 to 44, by selected detailed occupation, 2005; numbers in thousands)

	total workers	median age	total aged 25 to 44		aged 25 to 34		aged 35 to 44	
			number	percent of total	number	percent of total	number	percent of total
Total workers	**141,730**	**40.7**	**65,310**	**46.1%**	**30,680**	**21.6%**	**34,630**	**24.4%**
Chief executives	1,644	49.3	573	34.9	138	8.4	435	26.5
Legislators	17	54.2	3	17.6	1	5.9	2	11.8
Marketing and sales managers	798	41.2	467	58.5	198	24.8	269	33.7
Computer and information systems managers	351	42.5	197	56.1	68	19.4	129	36.8
Financial managers	1,045	42.2	554	53.0	241	23.1	313	30.0
Human resources managers	272	43.6	142	52.2	58	21.3	84	30.9
Farmers and ranchers	827	56.4	178	21.5	55	6.7	123	14.9
Education administrators	805	47.3	325	40.4	119	14.8	206	25.6
Food service managers	929	39.9	496	53.4	232	25.0	264	28.4
Medical and health services managers	470	47.8	187	39.8	65	13.8	122	26.0
Accountants and auditors	1,683	41.7	904	53.7	440	26.1	464	27.6
Computer scientists and systems analysts	745	40.6	444	59.6	222	29.8	222	29.8
Computer programmers	581	39.6	367	63.2	179	30.8	188	32.4
Computer software engineers	832	39.3	552	66.3	272	32.7	280	33.7
Architects	235	45.3	111	47.2	57	24.3	54	23.0
Civil engineers	319	43.3	158	49.5	72	22.6	86	27.0
Electrical engineers	352	42.1	197	56.0	75	21.3	122	34.7
Mechanical engineers	318	42.2	168	52.8	76	23.9	92	28.9
Medical scientists	125	37.6	89	71.2	46	36.8	43	34.4
Psychologists	188	50.7	63	33.5	27	14.4	36	19.1
Social workers	670	42.9	339	50.6	183	27.3	156	23.3
Clergy	435	48.2	160	36.8	53	12.2	107	24.6
Lawyers	961	45.4	466	48.5	183	19.0	283	29.4
Postsecondary teachers	1,185	45.1	508	42.9	254	21.4	254	21.4
Preschool and kindergarten teachers	719	38.2	362	50.3	206	28.7	156	21.7
Elementary and middle school teachers	2,616	43.1	1,321	50.5	674	25.8	647	24.7
Secondary school teachers	1,136	44.1	553	48.7	295	26.0	258	22.7
Librarians	214	50.3	61	28.5	26	12.1	35	16.4
Teacher assistants	947	42.6	413	43.6	131	13.8	282	29.8
Artists	234	44.0	111	47.4	54	23.1	57	24.4
Actors	41	34.7	19	46.3	10	24.4	9	22.0
Athletes	273	31.0	116	42.5	59	21.6	57	20.9
Editors	150	41.8	81	54.0	38	25.3	43	28.7
Writers and authors	178	47.5	67	37.6	32	18.0	35	19.7
Dentists	164	48.2	63	38.4	29	17.7	34	20.7
Pharmacists	248	42.6	126	50.8	71	28.6	55	22.2
Physicians and surgeons	830	44.9	415	50.0	164	19.8	251	30.2
Registered nurses	2,416	44.6	1,100	45.5	462	19.1	638	26.4
Physical therapists	177	39.9	114	64.4	57	32.2	57	32.2
Licensed practical nurses	510	43.8	245	48.0	107	21.0	138	27.1
Nursing, psychiatric, and home health aides	1,900	39.4	862	45.4	423	22.3	439	23.1

(continued)

	total workers	median age	total aged 25 to 44		aged 25 to 34		aged 35 to 44	
			number	percent of total	number	percent of total	number	percent of total
Firefighters	243	38.2	167	68.7%	85	35.0%	82	33.7%
Police and sheriff's patrol officers	677	39.2	467	69.0	233	34.4	234	34.6
Security guards and gaming surveillance officers	814	42.5	335	41.2	175	21.5	160	19.7
Chefs and head cooks	317	37.5	176	55.5	93	29.3	83	26.2
Cooks	1,838	32.9	766	41.7	407	22.1	359	19.5
Food preparation workers	664	27.6	216	32.5	119	17.9	97	14.6
Waiters and waitresses	1,927	24.4	643	33.4	407	21.1	236	12.2
Janitors and building cleaners	2,074	43.2	800	38.6	320	15.4	480	23.1
Maids and housekeeping cleaners	1,382	42.2	650	47.0	255	18.5	395	28.6
Grounds maintenance workers	1,187	36.1	544	45.8	290	24.4	254	21.4
Hairdressers, hair stylists, and cosmetologists	738	39.5	378	51.2	179	24.3	199	27.0
Child care workers	1,329	36.8	539	40.6	277	20.8	262	19.7
Cashiers	3,075	25.8	862	28.0	482	15.7	380	12.4
Retail salespersons	3,248	34.5	1,096	33.7	591	18.2	505	15.5
Insurance sales agents	531	44.7	231	43.5	113	21.3	118	22.2
Securities, commodities, and financial services sales agents	392	39.7	223	56.9	110	28.1	113	28.8
Sales representatives, wholesale and manufacturing	1,379	42.7	691	50.1	291	21.1	400	29.0
Real estate brokers and sales agents	995	47.5	378	38.0	147	14.8	231	23.2
Bookkeeping, accounting, and auditing clerks	1,456	45.0	627	43.1	254	17.4	373	25.6
Customer service representatives	1,833	35.8	895	48.8	502	27.4	393	21.4
Receptionists and information clerks	1,376	36.9	509	37.0	273	19.8	236	17.2
Stock clerks and order fillers	1,461	32.4	544	37.2	289	19.8	255	17.5
Secretaries and administrative assistants	3,499	44.0	1,499	42.8	619	17.7	880	25.2
Miscellaneous agricultural workers	698	34.5	315	45.1	163	23.4	152	21.8
Carpenters	1,797	37.4	769	42.8	317	17.6	452	25.2
Construction laborers	1,491	34.6	777	52.1	422	28.3	355	23.8
Automotive service technicians, mechanics	954	38.8	498	52.2	223	23.4	275	28.8
Miscellaneous assemblers and fabricators	1,107	39.8	550	49.7	265	23.9	285	25.7
Machinists	420	44.7	181	43.1	76	18.1	105	25.0
Aircraft pilots and flight engineers	121	44.9	54	44.6	21	17.4	33	27.3
Driver/sales workers and truck drivers	3,409	42.4	1,641	48.1	726	21.3	915	26.8
Freight, stock, material movers, hand laborers	1,806	33.1	804	44.5	429	23.8	375	20.8

Source: Bureau of Labor Statistics, unpublished tables from the 2005 Current Population Survey; calculations by New Strategist

Few Generation Xers Work Part-Time

Among workers aged 25 to 44, full-time work is the norm.

The majority of workers aged 25 to 44 had full-time jobs in 2005 (Generation X was aged 29 to 40 in that year). Among working men in the age groups, 94 to 96 percent work full-time. Among working women, the figure is 80 to 81 percent. Only 4 to 6 percent of working men and 19 to 20 percent of working women in the age group have part-time jobs.

Men and women aged 25 to 44 account for almost half of the nation's full-time workers—slightly more than their share of the total labor force. They account for a much smaller share of part-time workers. Men aged 25 to 44 who work part-time account for only 21 percent of all men who work part-time. Among women, the figure is 35 percent.

■ Although part-time work might appeal to many Gen Xers with young children at home, most cannot afford to live on a part-time income.

Most Generation Xers work full-time

(percent of workers aged 25 to 44 who work full-time, by sex, 2005)

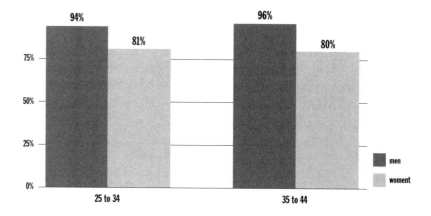

Table 5.10 Full- and Part-Time Workers by Age and Sex, 2005

(number and percent distribution of employed people aged 16 or older in the civilian labor force by age, sex, and employment status, 2005; numbers in thousands)

	men			women		
	total	full-time	part-time	total	full-time	part-time
Total employed	**80,033**	**71,302**	**8,731**	**69,288**	**51,890**	**17,398**
Under age 25	11,644	7,704	3,940	10,647	5,671	4,976
Aged 25 to 34	17,837	16,785	1,052	14,503	11,695	2,808
Aged 35 to 44	19,495	18,714	781	16,535	13,196	3,339
Aged 45 to 64	28,098	26,314	1,784	25,283	20,260	5,023
Aged 65 or older	2,959	1,785	1,174	2,319	1,068	1,251
PERCENT DISTRIBUTION BY AGE						
Total employed	**100.0%**	**100.0%**	**100.0%**	**100.0%**	**100.0%**	**100.0%**
Under age 25	14.5	10.8	45.1	15.4	10.9	28.6
Aged 25 to 34	22.3	23.5	12.0	20.9	22.5	16.1
Aged 35 to 44	24.4	26.2	8.9	23.9	25.4	19.2
Aged 45 to 64	35.1	36.9	20.4	36.5	39.0	28.9
Aged 65 or older	3.7	2.5	13.4	3.3	2.1	7.2
PERCENT DISTRIBUTION BY EMPLOYMENT STATUS						
Total employed	**100.0%**	**89.1%**	**10.9%**	**100.0%**	**74.9%**	**25.1%**
Under age 25	100.0	66.2	33.8	100.0	53.3	46.7
Aged 25 to 34	100.0	94.1	5.9	100.0	80.6	19.4
Aged 35 to 44	100.0	96.0	4.0	100.0	79.8	20.2
Aged 45 to 64	100.0	93.7	6.3	100.0	80.1	19.9
Aged 65 or older	100.0	60.3	39.7	100.0	46.1	53.9

Source: Unpublished data from the 2005 Current Population Survey, Bureau of Labor Statistics; calculations by New Strategist

Self-Employment Is Uncommon among Gen Xers

Self-employment requires experience, which is why few young adults work for themselves.

Although many people may prefer self-employment, few have the skills until they are older to strike out on their own. Only 7 percent of all workers are self-employed. The figure is an even smaller 5 percent among those aged 25 to 34, rising to the 7 percent average in the 35-to-44 age group. In contrast, fully 20 percent of workers aged 65 or older are self-employed.

At every age, men are more likely than women to be self-employed. Among 25-to-34-year-olds, 5.8 percent of men and a smaller 4.5 percent of women are self-employed. Among 35-to-44-year-olds, 8.4 percent of men and 6.2 percent of women work for themselves.

■ Self-employment is becoming a more difficult proposition for Americans because the cost of buying private health insurance can be prohibitive, especially for those starting businesses.

Few Generation Xers are self-employed

(percent of workers who are self-employed, by age, 2005)

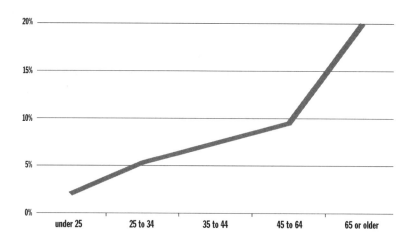

Table 5.11 Self-Employed Workers by Sex and Age, 2005

(number of employed workers aged 16 or older, number and percent who are self-employed, and percent distribution of self-employed, by age, 2005; numbers in thousands)

	total	self-employed number	self-employed percent	percent distribution
Total, aged 16 or older	**141,729**	**10,464**	**7.4%**	**100.0%**
Under age 25	19,769	389	2.0	3.7
Aged 25 to 34	30,680	1,612	5.3	15.4
Aged 35 to 44	34,630	2,554	7.4	24.4
Aged 45 to 64	51,557	4,890	9.5	46.7
Aged 65 or older	5,095	1,019	20.0	9.7
Total men aged 16 or older	**75,973**	**6,632**	**8.7**	**100.0**
Under age 25	10,200	275	2.7	4.1
Aged 25 to 34	16,993	991	5.8	14.9
Aged 35 to 44	18,780	1,570	8.4	23.7
Aged 45 to 64	27,143	3,094	11.4	46.7
Aged 65 or older	2,857	703	24.6	10.6
Total women aged 16 or older	**65,757**	**3,832**	**5.8**	**100.0**
Under age 25	9,568	115	1.2	3.0
Aged 25 to 34	13,687	622	4.5	16.2
Aged 35 to 44	15,850	986	6.2	25.7
Aged 45 to 64	24,413	1,795	7.4	46.8
Aged 65 or older	2,238	315	14.1	8.2

Source: Bureau of Labor Statistics, 2005 Current Population Survey, Internet site http://www.bls.gov/cps/home.htm; calculations by New Strategist

Job Tenure Has Changed Little for Men Aged 25 to 44

Long-term employment is much less common, however.

Job tenure (the number of years a worker has been with his current employer) has been declining among men for many years. Among men aged 25 to 34, however, job tenure has changed little—down only 0.1 years between 1991 and 2004 and up slightly since 2000. The numbers are similar for women in the age group.

Long-term employment has fallen among young and middle-aged workers, however. The percentage of 30-to-44-year-olds who have been with their current employer for ten or more years fell steeply between 1991 and 2004 for both men and women. The percentage of men aged 35 to 39 who had been with their current employer for 10 or more years fell from 36 to 25 percent between 1991 and 2004.

■ The decline in long-term employment is due to massive job cuts in many sectors.

Fewer men aged 30 to 39 have long-term jobs

(percent of men aged 30 to 39 who have worked for their current employer for ten or more years, 1991 and 2004)

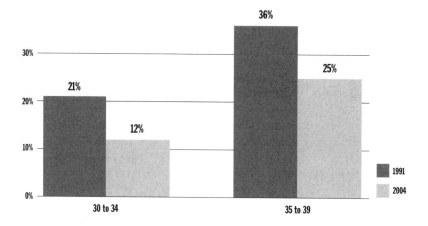

Table 5.12 Job Tenure by Sex and Age, 1991 to 2004

(median number of years employed wage and salary workers aged 25 or older have been with their current employer, by sex and age, 1991 to 2004; change in years, 2000–2004 and 1991–2004)

	2004	2000	1991	change 2000–04	change 1991–2004
Total workers aged 25 or older	**4.9**	**4.7**	**4.8**	**0.2**	**0.1**
Aged 25 to 34	2.9	2.6	2.9	0.3	0.0
Aged 35 to 44	4.9	4.8	5.4	0.1	–0.5
Aged 45 to 54	7.7	8.2	8.9	–0.5	–1.2
Aged 55 to 64	9.6	10.0	11.1	–0.4	–1.5
Aged 65 or older	9.0	9.4	8.1	–0.4	0.9
Total men aged 25 or older	**5.1**	**4.9**	**5.4**	**0.2**	**–0.3**
Aged 25 to 34	3.0	2.7	3.1	0.3	–0.1
Aged 35 to 44	5.2	5.3	6.5	–0.1	–1.3
Aged 45 to 54	9.6	9.5	11.2	0.1	–1.6
Aged 55 to 64	9.8	10.2	13.4	–0.4	–3.6
Aged 65 or older	8.2	9.0	7.0	–0.8	1.2
Total women aged 25 or older	**4.7**	**4.4**	**4.3**	**0.3**	**0.4**
Aged 25 to 34	2.8	2.5	2.7	0.3	0.1
Aged 35 to 44	4.5	4.3	4.5	0.2	0.0
Aged 45 to 54	6.4	7.3	6.7	–0.9	–0.3
Aged 55 to 64	9.2	9.9	9.9	–0.7	–0.7
Aged 65 or older	9.6	9.7	9.5	–0.1	0.1

Source: Bureau of Labor Statistics, Employee Tenure, Internet site http://www.bls.gov/news.release/tenure.t01.htm; calculations by New Strategist

Table 5.13 Long-Term Employment by Sex and Age, 1991 to 2004

(percent of employed wage and salary workers aged 25 or older who have been with their current employer for ten or more years, by sex and age, 1991 to 2004; percentage point change in share, 2000–2004 and 1991–2004)

	2004	2000	1991	percentage point change 2000–04	percentage point change 1991–2004
Total workers aged 25 or older	**30.6%**	**31.5%**	**32.2%**	**–0.9**	**–1.6**
Aged 25 to 29	2.4	2.5	5.1	–0.1	–2.7
Aged 30 to 34	10.9	13.9	19.3	–3.0	–8.4
Aged 35 to 39	23.2	26.1	31.1	–2.9	–7.9
Aged 40 to 44	32.4	35.9	39.3	–3.5	–6.9
Aged 45 to 49	42.1	45.3	46.5	–3.2	–4.4
Aged 50 to 54	48.5	48.6	51.4	–0.1	–2.9
Aged 55 to 59	50.9	53.1	56.7	–2.2	–5.8
Aged 60 to 64	49.7	53.2	55.4	–3.5	–5.7
Aged 65 or older	48.7	50.0	46.3	–1.3	2.4
Men aged 25 or older	**32.4**	**33.4**	**35.9**	**–1.0**	**–3.5**
Aged 25 to 29	2.7	3.0	5.7	–0.3	–3.0
Aged 30 to 34	11.9	15.1	21.1	–3.2	–9.2
Aged 35 to 39	24.9	29.4	35.6	–4.5	–10.7
Aged 40 to 44	36.2	40.4	46.3	–4.2	–10.1
Aged 45 to 49	48.1	49.0	53.5	–0.9	–5.4
Aged 50 to 54	53.0	51.6	58.5	1.4	–5.5
Aged 55 to 59	53.4	53.7	61.0	–0.3	–7.6
Aged 60 to 64	48.5	52.5	57.5	–4.0	–9.0
Aged 65 or older	46.8	48.9	42.6	–2.1	4.2
Women aged 25 or older	**28.6**	**29.5**	**28.2**	**–0.9**	**0.4**
Aged 25 to 29	1.9	1.9	4.4	0.0	–2.5
Aged 30 to 34	9.8	12.5	17.3	–2.7	–7.5
Aged 35 to 39	21.3	22.3	26.1	–1.0	–4.8
Aged 40 to 44	28.5	31.4	32.0	–2.9	–3.5
Aged 45 to 49	36.2	41.5	39.3	–5.3	–3.1
Aged 50 to 54	44.1	45.6	43.4	–1.5	0.7
Aged 55 to 59	48.4	52.5	51.4	–4.1	–3.0
Aged 60 to 64	51.0	54.0	53.1	–3.0	0.9
Aged 65 or older	50.7	51.2	49.9	–0.5	1.3

Source: Bureau of Labor Statistics, Employee Tenure, Internet site http://www.bls.gov/news.release/tenure.t02.htm; calculations by New Strategist

Some Generation Xers Have Alternative Work Arrangements

Less than 10 percent are independent contractors.

Among the nation's 15 million alternative workers, only 6 million (43 percent) are aged 25 to 44. The Bureau of Labor Statistics defines alternative workers as independent contractors, on-call workers (such as substitute teachers), temporary-help agency workers, and people who work for contract firms (such as lawn or janitorial service companies).

The most popular alternative work arrangement is independent contracting—which includes most of the self-employed. Among the 15 million alternative workers, 10 million are independent contractors. Among alternative workers aged 25 to 44, independent contractors account for the 67 percent majority.

The percentage of workers with alternative work arrangements rises with age as independent contracting becomes more popular. Ten percent of workers aged 45 or older are independent contractors.

■ Older workers have more skills and experience, which makes it easier for them to earn a living by self-employment.

The percentage of workers who are independent contractors rises with age

(percent of employed workers who are independent contractors, by age, 2004)

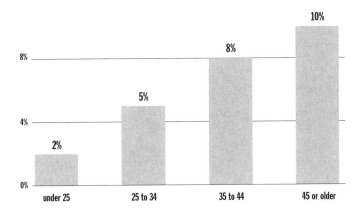

Table 5.14 Alternative Work Arrangements by Age, 2005

(number and percent distribution of employed people aged 16 or older by age and work arrangement, 2005; numbers in thousands)

			alternative workers				
	total employed	total in traditional arrangements	total	independent contractors	on-call workers	temporary-help agency workers	workers provided by contract firms
Total people	**138,952**	**123,843**	**14,826**	**10,342**	**2,454**	**1,217**	**813**
Under age 25	18,624	17,249	1,262	445	488	235	94
Aged 25 to 34	30,103	27,427	2,622	1,520	535	362	205
Aged 35 to 44	34,481	30,646	3,774	2,754	571	253	196
Aged 45 or older	55,744	48,521	7,168	5,623	859	368	318
PERCENT DISTRIBUTION BY ALTERNATIVE WORK STATUS							
Total people	**100.0%**	**89.1%**	**10.7%**	**7.4%**	**1.8%**	**0.9%**	**0.6%**
Under age 25	100.0	92.6	6.8	2.4	2.6	1.3	0.5
Aged 25 to 34	100.0	91.1	8.7	5.0	1.8	1.2	0.7
Aged 35 to 44	100.0	88.9	10.9	8.0	1.7	0.7	0.6
Aged 45 or older	100.0	87.0	12.9	10.1	1.5	0.7	0.6
PERCENT DISTRIBUTION BY AGE							
Total people	**100.0%**	**100.0%**	**100.0%**	**100.0%**	**100.0%**	**100.0%**	**100.0%**
Under age 25	13.4	13.9	8.5	4.3	19.9	19.3	11.6
Aged 25 to 34	21.7	22.1	17.7	14.7	21.8	29.7	25.2
Aged 35 to 44	24.8	24.7	25.5	26.6	23.3	20.8	24.1
Aged 45 or older	40.1	39.2	48.3	54.4	35.0	30.2	39.1

Note: Numbers may not add to total because the total employed include day laborers, an alternative arrangement not shown separately, and a small number of workers were both "on call" and "provided by contract firms." Independent contractors are workers who obtain customers on their own to provide a product or service, including the self-employed. On-call workers are in a pool of workers who are called to work only as needed, such as substitute teachers and construction workers supplied by a union hiring hall. Temporary-help agency workers are those who said they are paid by a temporary0help agency. Workers provided by contract firms are those employed by a company that provides employees or their services under contract, such as security, landscaping, and computer programming.
Source: Bureau of Labor Statistics, Contingent and Alternative Employment Arrangements, February 2005, Internet site http:// www.bls.gov/news.release/conemp.t05.htm; calculations by New Strategist

Many Workers Have Flexible Schedules

Men are more likely than women to have flexible schedules.

Twenty-seven percent of the nation's wage and salary workers have flexible schedules—meaning they can vary the time they begin or end work, according to the Bureau of Labor Statistics. Men are slightly more likely than women to have flexible schedules—28 versus 27 percent in 2004. The percentage of full-time wage and salary workers with flexible schedules varies little by age.

Fifteen percent of wage and salary workers do not work a regular daytime schedule. The youngest workers are most likely to work shifts—22 percent of those aged 16 to 24 work the evening, night, or other shifts. The figure falls to 15 percent in the 25-to-34 age group and is an even lower 14 percent among those aged 35 to 44.

■ Younger workers are less likely to work a regular daytime shift because many are students in school during the day.

More than one in four 35-to-44-year-olds has a flexible work schedule

(percent of full-time wage and salary workers aged 35 to 44 who have flexible work schedules, by sex, 2004)

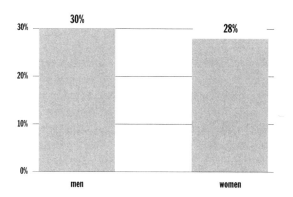

Table 5.15 Workers with Flexible Work Schedules by Sex and Age, 2004

(total number of full-time wage and salary workers aged 16 or older and number and percent with flexible work schedules, by sex and age, 2004; numbers in thousands)

		with flexible schedules	
	total	number	percent
Total full-time wage and salary workers	**99,778**	**27,411**	**27.5%**
Under age 25	10,431	2,394	23.0
Aged 25 to 34	24,640	6,902	28.0
Aged 35 to 44	26,766	7,807	29.2
Aged 45 or older	37,941	10,307	27.2
Total men	**56,412**	**15,853**	**28.1**
Under age 25	6,050	1,250	20.7
Aged 25 to 34	14,358	4,051	28.2
Aged 35 to 44	15,424	4,605	29.9
Aged 45 or older	20,580	5,948	28.9
Total women	**43,366**	**11,558**	**26.7**
Under age 25	4,380	1,144	26.1
Aged 25 to 34	10,283	2,851	27.7
Aged 35 to 44	11,342	3,202	28.2
Aged 45 or older	17,361	4,359	25.1

Note: Flexible schedules are those that allow workers to vary the time they begin or end work.
Source: Bureau of Labor Statistics, Workers on Flexible and Shift Schedules, Internet site http://www.bls.gov/news.release/flex
.t01.htm

Table 5.16 Workers by Age and Shift Usually Worked, 2004

(total number of full-time wage and salary workers aged 20 or older and percent distribution by age and shift usually worked, 2004; numbers in thousands)

				shift schedule					
	total workers		regular daytime schedule		evening shift	night shift	rotating shift	employer-arranged irregular shift	split or other shift
	number	percent		total					
Total aged 20 or older	**98,351**	**100.0%**	**84.9%**	**14.6%**	**4.6%**	**3.2%**	**2.5%**	**3.0%**	**1.2%**
Aged 20 to 24	9,004	100.0	76.8	22.3	8.8	3.7	3.3	4.6	1.8
Aged 25 to 34	24,640	100.0	84.1	15.2	5.0	3.4	2.7	2.8	1.3
Aged 35 to 44	26,766	100.0	85.4	14.1	4.1	3.2	2.5	3.1	1.1
Aged 45 to 54	24,855	100.0	86.8	12.8	3.6	3.2	2.3	2.5	1.2
Aged 55 to 64	11,745	100.0	87.1	12.5	3.8	2.6	2.0	3.0	1.1
Aged 65 or older	1,341	100.0	88.8	10.3	3.5	1.8	1.4	2.9	0.7

Source: Bureau of Labor Statistics, Workers on Flexible and Shift Schedules, Internet site http://www.bls.gov/news.release/flex
.t04.htm

Few Gen Xers Work for Minimum Wage

Only 2 percent of workers aged 25 to 39 make minimum wage or less.

Among the nation's 74 million workers who are paid hourly rates, only 2 million (3 percent) make minimum wage or less, according to the Bureau of Labor Statistics. Among those making minimum wage or less, the 74 percent majority makes even less than minimum wage, which stood at $5.15 per hour in 2004.

Fully 51 percent of minimum-wage workers are under age 25. Only 25 percent are between the ages of 25 and 39. Among hourly workers in the 25-to-39 age group, only 500,000 make minimum wage or less.

■ Younger workers are most likely to earn minimum wage or less because many are in entry-level jobs.

Most minimum wage workers are under age 25

(percent distribution of workers making minimum wage or less, by age, 2004)

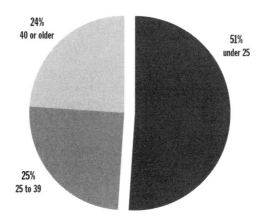

24%
40 or older

51%
under 25

25%
25 to 39

Table 5.17 Workers Earning Minimum Wage by Age, 2004

(number and percent distribution of workers paid hourly rates at or below minimum wage, by age, 2004; numbers in thousands)

	total paid hourly rates	at or below minimum wage		
		total	at $5.15/hour	below $5.15/hour
Total aged 16 or older	**73,939**	**2,003**	**520**	**1,483**
Under age 25	16,174	1,022	272	750
Aged 25 to 39	24,581	500	89	411
Aged 25 to 29	8,449	226	34	192
Aged 30 to 34	8,125	157	30	127
Aged 35 to 39	8,007	117	25	92
Aged 40 or older	15,766	481	158	323
PERCENT DISTRIBUTION BY AGE				
Total aged 16 or older	**100.0%**	**100.0%**	**100.0%**	**100.0%**
Under age 25	21.9	51.0	52.3	50.6
Aged 25 to 39	11.4	25.0	17.1	27.7
Aged 25 to 29	11.0	11.3	6.5	12.9
Aged 30 to 34	11.0	7.8	5.8	8.6
Aged 35 to 39	10.8	5.8	4.8	6.2
Aged 40 or older	33.2	24.0	30.4	21.8
PERCENT DISTRIBUTION BY WAGE STATUS				
Total aged 16 or older	**100.0%**	**2.7%**	**0.7%**	**2.0%**
Under age 25	100.0	6.3	1.7	4.6
Aged 25 to 39	100.0	2.0	0.4	1.7
Aged 25 to 29	100.0	2.7	0.4	2.3
Aged 30 to 34	100.0	1.9	0.4	1.6
Aged 35 to 39	100.0	1.5	0.3	1.1
Aged 40 or older	100.0	3.1	1.0	2.0

Source: Bureau of Labor Statistics, Characteristics of Minimum Wage Workers, 2004, Internet site http://www.bls.gov/cps/minwage2004.htm; calculations by New Strategist

Few 25-to-44-Year-Olds Are Represented by Unions

Men are more likely than women to be represented by a union.

Union representation has fallen sharply over the past few decades. In 2005, only 14 percent of employed wage and salary workers were represented by a union.

The percentage of male workers who are represented by a union peaks in the 45-to-54 age group at 20 percent. For women the peak is in the 55-to-64 age group at 17 percent. A larger percentage of men is represented by a union because men are more likely to work in manufacturing jobs—the traditional strongholds of labor unions. In fact, the decline of labor unions is partly the result of the shift in jobs from manufacturing to services. Among 25-to-34-year-olds, only 12 percent of men and 11 percent of women are represented by a union. In the 35-to-44 age group the figures are 16 and 14 percent, respectively.

■ Union representation may rise along with workers' concerns about the cost of health care coverage.

Few workers are represented by a union

(percent of employed wage and salary workers who are represented by unions, by age, 2005)

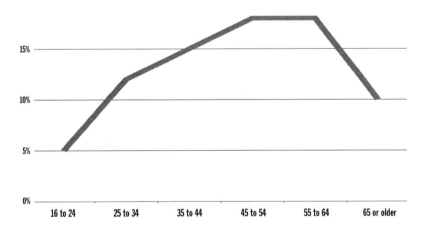

Table 5.18 Union Representation by Sex and Age, 2005

(number and percent of employed wage and salary workers aged 16 or older by union representation status, sex, and age, 2005; numbers in thousands)

	total employed	represented by unions	
		number	percent
Total aged 16 or older	**125,889**	**17,223**	**13.7%**
Aged 16 to 24	19,283	1,019	5.3
Aged 25 to 34	28,450	3,368	11.8
Aged 35 to 44	30,654	4,579	14.9
Aged 45 to 54	28,714	5,158	18.0
Aged 55 to 64	15,158	2,732	18.0
Aged 65 or older	3,631	366	10.1
Men aged 16 or older	**65,466**	**9,597**	**14.7**
Aged 16 to 24	9,860	603	6.1
Aged 25 to 34	15,559	1,915	12.3
Aged 35 to 44	16,196	2,582	15.9
Aged 45 to 54	14,421	2,849	19.8
Aged 55 to 64	7,606	1,458	19.2
Aged 65 or older	1,824	190	10.4
Women aged 16 or older	**60,423**	**7,626**	**12.6**
Aged 16 to 24	9,423	417	4.4
Aged 25 to 34	12,891	1,454	11.3
Aged 35 to 44	14,457	1,997	13.8
Aged 45 to 54	14,293	2,309	16.2
Aged 55 to 64	7,552	1,274	16.9
Aged 65 or older	1,806	176	9.8

Note: Workers represented by unions are either members of a labor union or similar employee association or workers who report no union affiliation but whose jobs are covered by a union or an employee association contract.
Source: Bureau of Labor Statistics, 2005 Current Population Survey, Internet site http://www.bls.gov/cps/home.htm

Number of Workers Aged 35 to 49 Will Decline

The number of workers aged 25 to 34 will grow.

Between 2005 and 2014, the small Generation X will fill the 40-to-49 age group (Gen Xers will be aged 38 to 49 in 2014). The number of workers in the age group will decline by nearly 3 million. The 25-to-34 age group, in contrast, will be filling with the larger Millennial generation. Consequently the number of workers aged 25 to 34 will expand by more than 4 million during those years. The labor force participation rates of Gen X men and women are projected to remain relatively stable through the coming decade.

The number of older workers is projected to soar between 2005 and 2014. The Bureau of Labor Statistics projects a 59 percent increase in the number of workers aged 60 or older during those years. In contrast, the number of workers under age 60 is projected to grow by just 3.5 percent.

■ Generation X may find it difficult to advance on the job as Boomers, working well into their sixties, clog the ranks of upper management.

The number of workers aged 35 to 49 will decline

(percent change in number of workers aged 25 to 49, by sex, 2005–14)

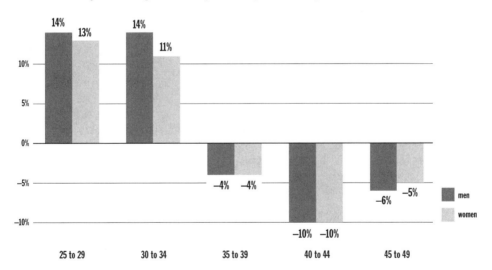

Table 5.19 Projections of the Labor Force by Sex and Age, 2005 and 2014

(number and percent of people aged 16 or older in the civilian labor force by sex and age, 2005 and 2014; percent change in number and percentage point change in participation rate 2005–14; numbers in thousands)

	number			participation rate		
	2005	2014	percent change	2005	2014	percentage point change
Total labor force	**149,132**	**162,100**	**8.7%**	**66.0%**	**65.6%**	**–0.4**
Total men in labor force	**80,040**	**86,194**	**7.7**	**73.3**	**71.8**	**–1.5**
Aged 16 to 24	11,678	11,389	–2.5	63.0	60.5	–2.5
Aged 25 to 29	8,968	10,200	13.7	91.7	94.1	2.4
Aged 30 to 34	9,122	10,365	13.6	93.7	96.5	2.8
Aged 35 to 39	9,401	9,027	–4.0	92.7	92.0	–0.7
Aged 40 to 44	10,043	9,040	–10.0	91.0	89.5	–1.5
Aged 45 to 49	9,714	9,156	–5.7	89.1	89.4	0.3
Aged 50 to 54	8,241	9,199	11.6	85.3	83.9	–1.4
Aged 55 to 59	6,451	7,849	21.7	77.5	76.6	–0.9
Aged 60 to 61	1,701	2,412	41.8	65.1	65.7	0.6
Aged 62 to 64	1,823	2,761	51.5	51.2	54.7	3.5
Aged 65 or older	2,898	4,795	65.5	19.4	24.6	5.2
Total women in labor force	**69,092**	**75,906**	**9.9**	**59.1**	**59.7**	**0.6**
Aged 16 to 24	10,666	10,769	1.0	58.4	57.8	–0.6
Aged 25 to 29	7,140	8,073	13.1	73.5	75.2	1.7
Aged 30 to 34	7,295	8,116	11.3	74.1	75.6	1.5
Aged 35 to 39	7,730	7,395	–4.3	74.4	74.2	–0.2
Aged 40 to 44	8,741	7,882	–9.8	76.7	76.6	–0.1
Aged 45 to 49	8,897	8,456	–5.0	78.4	80.2	1.8
Aged 50 to 54	7,380	8,716	18.1	72.6	76.2	3.6
Aged 55 to 59	5,806	7,654	31.8	65.6	70.7	5.1
Aged 60 to 61	1,582	2,490	57.4	54.7	61.4	6.7
Aged 62 to 64	1,547	2,463	59.2	39.3	44.8	5.5
Aged 65 or older	2,307	3,892	68.7	11.5	15.9	4.4

Note: Figures for 2005 are slightly different from those shown elsewhere in this chapter because they are projections rather than estimates.
Source: Bureau of Labor Statistics, Projected Labor Force Data, Internet site http://www.bls.gov/emp/emplab1.htm; calculations by New Strategist

6

Living Arrangements

■ Among householders aged 25 to 29, a 43 percent minority are married couples. The figure rises to the 56 percent majority in the 30-to-34 age group and climbs to 58 percent among householders aged 35 to 39.

■ In the 25-to-39 age group, non-Hispanic whites head the 68 percent majority of married couples but only a 44 percent minority of female-headed families.

■ The average American household is home to 2.57 people. Household size peaks at 3.28 people among householders aged 35 to 39.

■ More than half of households headed by people aged 25 to 39 include children under age 18. The proportion rises from a 46 percent minority among householders aged 25 to 29 to the 66 percent majority among householders aged 35 to 39.

■ The proportion of men and women who live with their spouse rises from a minority among 25-to-29-year-olds (35 percent of men and 47 percent of women) to the majority among 30-to-34-year-olds (55 and 61 percent, respectively).

Married Couples Become the Norm among 30-to-34-Year-Olds

Female-headed families account for a large share of householders aged 25 to 39.

As people age from their mid-twenties through their thirties, life gets serious. Most embark on a career, marry for the first time, have children, and buy a home.

Among householders aged 25 to 29, a 43 percent minority are married couples. The figure rises to the 56 percent majority in the 30-to-34 age group and climbs to 58 percent among householders aged 35 to 39. More than one-third of households headed by 25-to-29-year-olds are people who live alone or with nonrelatives (nonfamily households). As more people marry, the proportion of young adults living in nonfamily households falls to 22 percent by the 35-to-39 age group.

Fifteen percent of householders in the 25-to-39 age group are women heading families without a spouse, making it the second-most-common household type. Men who live alone rank third, accounting for 10 to 12 percent of householders aged 25 to 39. Women who live alone account for only 7 to 10 percent of householders in the age group, and men heading families without a spouse are just 5 to 7 percent.

■ People in their twenties and thirties are undergoing many changes, making these years exciting and stressful.

Most householders in their thirties are married

(married couples as a percent of householders aged 25 to 39, by age, 2005)

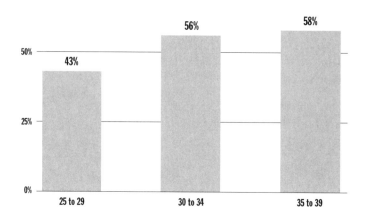

Table 6.1 Households Headed by People Aged 25 to 39 by Household Type, 2005: Total Households

(number and percent distribution of total households and households headed by people aged 25 to 39, by household type, 2005; numbers in thousands)

	total	aged 25 to 39			
		total	25 to 29	30 to 34	35 to 39
TOTAL HOUSEHOLDS	**113,146**	**30,272**	**9,145**	**10,110**	**11,017**
Family households	**77,010**	**22,296**	**5,991**	**7,704**	**8,601**
Married couples	58,109	15,945	3,930	5,647	6,368
Female householder, no spouse present	14,009	4,691	1,435	1,539	1,717
Male householder, no spouse present	4,893	1,660	626	519	515
Nonfamily households	**36,136**	**7,976**	**3,154**	**2,405**	**2,417**
Female householder	19,792	3,177	1,302	932	943
Living alone	17,207	2,399	899	727	773
Male householder	16,344	4,799	1,852	1,473	1,474
Living alone	12,652	3,281	1,113	1,033	1,135
PERCENT DISTRIBUTION BY TYPE					
TOTAL HOUSEHOLDS	**100.0%**	**100.0%**	**100.0%**	**100.0%**	**100.0%**
Family households	**68.1**	**73.7**	**65.5**	**76.2**	**78.1**
Married couples	51.4	52.7	43.0	55.9	57.8
Female householder, no spouse present	12.4	15.5	15.7	15.2	15.6
Male householder, no spouse present	4.3	5.5	6.8	5.1	4.7
Nonfamily households	**31.9**	**26.3**	**34.5**	**23.8**	**21.9**
Female householder	17.5	10.5	14.2	9.2	8.6
Living alone	15.2	7.9	9.8	7.2	7.0
Male householder	14.4	15.9	20.3	14.6	13.4
Living alone	11.2	10.8	12.2	10.2	10.3
PERCENT DISTRIBUTION BY AGE					
TOTAL HOUSEHOLDS	**100.0%**	**26.8%**	**8.1%**	**8.9%**	**9.7%**
Family households	**100.0**	**29.0**	**7.8**	**10.0**	**11.2**
Married couples	100.0	27.4	6.8	9.7	11.0
Female householder, no spouse present	100.0	33.5	10.2	11.0	12.3
Male householder, no spouse present	100.0	33.9	12.8	10.6	10.5
Nonfamily households	**100.0**	**22.1**	**8.7**	**6.7**	**6.7**
Female householder	100.0	16.1	6.6	4.7	4.8
Living alone	100.0	13.9	5.2	4.2	4.5
Male householder	100.0	29.4	11.3	9.0	9.0
Living alone	100.0	25.9	8.8	8.2	9.0

Source: Bureau of the Census, 2005 Current Population Survey, Annual Social and Economic Supplement, Internet site http://pubdb3.census.gov/macro/032005/hhinc/new02_000.htm; calculations by New Strategist

Hispanics and Blacks Head Many Generation X Households

Non-Hispanic whites head fewer than half of female-headed families.

Among all households headed by people aged 25 to 39, non-Hispanic whites head the 63 percent majority. But the figure varies greatly by type of household. Non-Hispanic whites head only 44 percent of female-headed families in the 25-to-39 age group, for example, but they head 68 percent of married-couple households. Blacks account for 34 percent of female family householders aged 25 to 39.

Although blacks and Hispanics are nearly equal in number in the U.S. population, Hispanic married couples greatly outnumber black couples. Among couples aged 25 to 39, 17 percent are Hispanic, 8 percent are black, and 6 percent are Asian.

■ As the even more diverse Millennial generation enters its late twenties and thirties, the non-Hispanic white share of households will continue to shrink.

Hispanics account for a large share of Generation X couples

(percent distribution of married couples aged 25 to 39 by race and Hispanic origin, 2005)

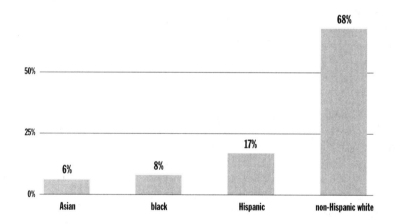

Table 6.2 Households Headed by People Aged 25 to 39 by Household Type, Race, and Hispanic Origin, 2005

(number and percent distribution of households headed by people aged 25 to 39, by household type, race, and Hispanic origin, 2005; numbers in thousands)

	total	Asian	black	Hispanic	non-Hispanic white
TOTAL HOUSEHOLDERS AGED 25 TO 39	**30,272**	**1,661**	**4,312**	**4,926**	**19,149**
Family households	**22,296**	**1,238**	**3,068**	**4,052**	**13,782**
Married couples	15,945	1,022	1,233	2,743	10,828
Female householder, no spouse present	4,691	115	1,583	935	2,050
Male householder, no spouse present	1,660	101	252	374	904
Nonfamily households	**7,976**	**423**	**1,246**	**873**	**5,368**
Female householder	3,177	172	631	229	2,127
Living alone	2,399	133	535	162	1,550
Male householder	4,799	251	615	644	3,241
Living alone	3,281	178	488	368	2,217
PERCENT DISTRIBUTION BY RACE AND HISPANIC ORIGIN					
TOTAL HOUSEHOLDERS AGED 25 TO 39	**100.0%**	**5.5%**	**14.2%**	**16.3%**	**63.3%**
Family households	**100.0**	**5.6**	**13.8**	**18.2**	**61.8**
Married couples	100.0	6.4	7.7	17.2	67.9
Female householder, no spouse present	100.0	2.5	33.7	19.9	43.7
Male householder, no spouse present	100.0	6.1	15.2	22.5	54.5
Nonfamily households	**100.0**	**5.3**	**15.6**	**10.9**	**67.3**
Female householder	100.0	5.4	19.9	7.2	66.9
Living alone	100.0	5.5	22.3	6.8	64.6
Male householder	100.0	5.2	12.8	13.4	67.5
Living alone	100.0	5.4	14.9	11.2	67.6

Note: Numbers will not add to total because Asians and blacks include those identifying themselves as being of the respective race alone and those identifying themselves as being of the race in combination with other races. Non-Hispanic whites include only those identifying themselves as being white alone and not Hispanic. Hispanics may be of any race.
Source: Bureau of the Census, 2005 Current Population Survey, Annual Social and Economic Supplement, Internet site http://pubdb3. census.gov/macro/032005/hhinc/new02_000.htm; calculations by New Strategist

Asian Generation Xers Are in Transition

Single in their twenties, they are married by their thirties.

Although married couples accounted for the majority of Asian households headed by 25-to-39-year-olds in 2005 (Generation Xers were aged 29 to 40 in that year), there are stark differences in living arrangements within the age group. Among Asian householders aged 25 to 29, only 38 percent are married couples. A much larger 43 percent head nonfamily households, with 28 percent living alone. The figures change dramatically among 30-to-34-year-olds. Married couples head the 64 percent majority of households in the age group, and the percentage who live alone drops to 20 percent. The trend continues in the 35-to-39 age group, with couples heading 74 percent of households and people living alone only 12 percent.

Single parents head few Asian households. Female-headed families account for only 7 percent of households headed by 25-to-39-year-olds. Male-headed families account for an even smaller 6 percent.

■ Asians are by far the best-educated segment of the American population. Many live alone or with nonrelatives during their twenties because they are attending school.

Many Asian Gen Xers live alone or with nonrelatives

(percent distribution of households headed by Asians aged 25 to 39, by household type, 2005)

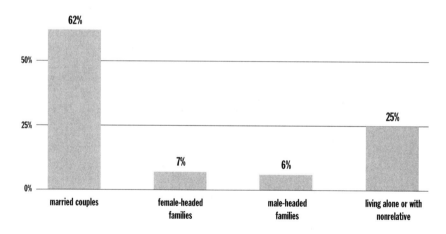

Table 6.3. Households Headed by People Aged 25 to 39 by Household Type, 2005: Asian Households

(number and percent distribution of total households headed by Asians and households headed by Asians aged 25 to 39, by household type, 2005; numbers in thousands)

	total	aged 25 to 39 total	25 to 29	30 to 34	35 to 39
TOTAL ASIAN HOUSEHOLDS	**4,360**	**1,661**	**427**	**591**	**643**
Family households	**3,295**	**1,238**	**244**	**446**	**548**
Married couples	2,649	1,022	163	380	479
Female householder, no spouse present	385	115	36	35	44
Male householder, no spouse present	261	101	45	31	25
Nonfamily households	**1,065**	**423**	**183**	**145**	**95**
Female householder	558	172	81	53	38
Living alone	463	133	56	44	33
Male householder	507	251	102	92	57
Living alone	372	178	62	72	44
PERCENT DISTRIBUTION BY TYPE					
TOTAL ASIAN HOUSEHOLDS	**100.0%**	**100.0%**	**100.0%**	**100.0%**	**100.0%**
Family households	**75.6**	**74.5**	**57.1**	**75.5**	**85.2**
Married couples	60.8	61.5	38.2	64.3	74.5
Female householder, no spouse present	8.8	6.9	8.4	5.9	6.8
Male householder, no spouse present	6.0	6.1	10.5	5.2	3.9
Nonfamily households	**24.4**	**25.5**	**42.9**	**24.5**	**14.8**
Female householder	12.8	10.4	19.0	9.0	5.9
Living alone	10.6	8.0	13.1	7.4	5.1
Male householder	11.6	15.1	23.9	15.6	8.9
Living alone	8.5	10.7	14.5	12.2	6.8
PERCENT DISTRIBUTION BY AGE					
TOTAL ASIAN HOUSEHOLDS	**100.0%**	**38.1%**	**9.8%**	**13.6%**	**14.7%**
Family households	**100.0**	**37.6**	**7.4**	**13.5**	**16.6**
Married couples	100.0	38.6	6.2	14.3	18.1
Female householder, no spouse present	100.0	29.9	9.4	9.1	11.4
Male householder, no spouse present	100.0	38.7	17.2	11.9	9.6
Nonfamily households	**100.0**	**39.7**	**17.2**	**13.6**	**8.9**
Female householder	100.0	30.8	14.5	9.5	6.8
Living alone	100.0	28.7	12.1	9.5	7.1
Male householder	100.0	49.5	20.1	18.1	11.2
Living alone	100.0	47.8	16.7	19.4	11.8

Note: Asians include those identifying themselves as being of the race alone and those identifying themselves as being of the race in combination with other races.
Source: Bureau of the Census, 2005 Current Population Survey, Annual Social and Economic Supplement, Internet site http://pubdb3.census.gov/macro/032005/hhinc/new02_000.htm; calculations by New Strategist

Female-Headed Families Are Common among Generation X Blacks

Married couples head a minority of black households.

The majority of black householders aged 25 to 39 were family heads in 2005 (Generation Xers were aged 29 to 40 in that year), but female-headed families outnumbered married couples by a considerable margin. Female-headed families account for 37 percent of households headed by blacks aged 25 to 39, while married couples head a smaller 29 percent. Male-headed families account for only 6 percent of black households in the 25-to-39 age group.

A substantial 29 percent of black householders aged 25 to 39 head nonfamily households, which means they live alone or with nonrelatives. Nearly one in four black householders in the age group lives alone.

■ During the past few decades, female-headed families have grown steadily as a proportion of black households. Today, black children are more likely to be raised by a single parent than by two parents.

Married couples head few black households

(percent distribution of black households headed by people aged 25 to 39, by household type, 2005)

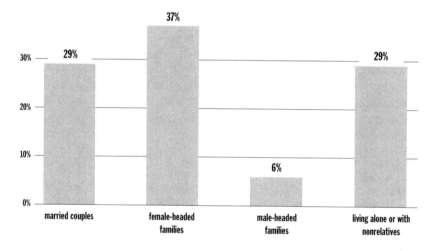

Table 6.4 Households Headed by People Aged 25 to 39 by Household Type, 2005: Black Households

(number and percent distribution of total households headed by blacks and households headed by blacks aged 25 to 39, by household type, 2005; numbers in thousands)

		aged 25 to 39			
	total	total	25 to 29	30 to 34	35 to 39
TOTAL BLACK HOUSEHOLDS	**14,127**	**4,312**	**1,338**	**1,489**	**1,485**
Family households	**9,109**	**3,068**	**880**	**1,094**	**1,094**
Married couples	4,272	1,233	288	470	475
Female householder, no spouse present	4,084	1,583	493	558	532
Male householder, no spouse present	754	252	99	66	87
Nonfamily households	**5,018**	**1,246**	**458**	**396**	**392**
Female householder	2,863	631	264	165	202
Living alone	2,599	535	219	140	176
Male householder	2,155	615	194	231	190
Living alone	1,833	488	158	172	158
PERCENT DISTRIBUTION BY AGE					
TOTAL BLACK HOUSEHOLDS	**100.0%**	**100.0%**	**100.0%**	**100.0%**	**100.0%**
Family households	**64.5**	**71.2**	**65.8**	**73.5**	**73.7**
Married couples	30.2	28.6	21.5	31.6	32.0
Female householder, no spouse present	28.9	36.7	36.8	37.5	35.8
Male householder, no spouse present	5.3	5.8	7.4	4.4	5.9
Nonfamily households	**35.5**	**28.9**	**34.2**	**26.6**	**26.4**
Female householder	20.3	14.6	19.7	11.1	13.6
Living alone	18.4	12.4	16.4	9.4	11.9
Male householder	15.3	14.3	14.5	15.5	12.8
Living alone	13.0	11.3	11.8	11.6	10.6
PERCENT DISTRIBUTION BY TYPE					
TOTAL BLACK HOUSEHOLDS	**100.0%**	**30.5%**	**9.5%**	**10.5%**	**10.5%**
Family households	**100.0**	**33.7**	**9.7**	**12.0**	**12.0**
Married couples	100.0	28.9	6.7	11.0	11.1
Female householder, no spouse present	100.0	38.8	12.1	13.7	13.0
Male householder, no spouse present	100.0	33.4	13.1	8.8	11.5
Nonfamily households	**100.0**	**24.8**	**9.1**	**7.9**	**7.8**
Female householder	100.0	22.0	9.2	5.8	7.1
Living alone	100.0	20.6	8.4	5.4	6.8
Male householder	100.0	28.5	9.0	10.7	8.8
Living alone	100.0	26.6	8.6	9.4	8.6

Note: Blacks include those identifying themselves as being of the race alone and those identifying themselves as being of the race in combination with other races.
Source: Bureau of the Census, 2005 Current Population Survey, Annual Social and Economic Supplement, Internet site http://pubdb3.census.gov/macro/032005/hhinc/new02_000.htm; calculations by New Strategist

Married Life Is Popular among Hispanic Generation Xers

Few Hispanic Gen Xers live alone.

Married couples accounted for the 56 percent majority of Hispanic households headed by 25-to-39-year-olds in 2005 (Generation Xers were aged 29 to 40 in that year). Female-headed families account for 19 percent, and male-headed families are an even smaller 8 percent.

Nonfamily households are much less common among Hispanic Gen Xers than among their non-Hispanic white counterparts. Only 18 percent of Hispanic households headed by 25-to-39-year-olds are nonfamilies (meaning they live alone or with nonrelatives) versus a much larger 28 percent of non-Hispanic white households in the age group. Only 11 percent of Hispanic householders aged 25 to 39 live alone versus 20 percent of non-Hispanic whites.

■ The Hispanic population is more traditional than the non-Hispanic white population because many are immigrants from Mexico.

Among Hispanic Gen Xers, most households are headed by married couples

(percent distribution of households headed by Hispanics aged 25 to 39, by household type, 2005)

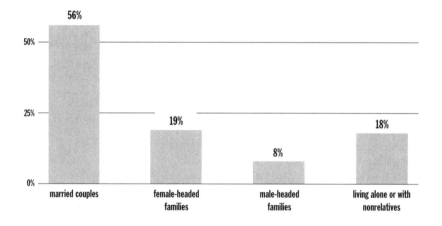

Table 6.5 Households Headed by People Aged 25 to 39 by Household Type, 2005: Hispanic Households

(number and percent distribution of total households headed by Hispanics and households headed by Hispanics aged 25 to 39, by household type, 2005; numbers in thousands)

	total	aged 25 to 39 total	25 to 29	30 to 34	35 to 39
TOTAL HISPANIC HOUSEHOLDS	**12,181**	**4,926**	**1,596**	**1,715**	**1,615**
Family households	**9,537**	**4,052**	**1,237**	**1,462**	**1,353**
Married couples	6,367	2,743	787	1,037	919
Female householder, no spouse present	2,240	935	303	304	328
Male householder, no spouse present	930	374	147	121	106
Nonfamily households	**2,644**	**873**	**359**	**252**	**262**
Female householder	1,177	229	96	76	57
Living alone	981	162	74	50	38
Male householder	1,467	644	263	176	205
Living alone	941	368	122	120	126
PERCENT DISTRIBUTION BY AGE					
TOTAL HISPANIC HOUSEHOLDS	**100.0%**	**100.0%**	**100.0%**	**100.0%**	**100.0%**
Family households	**78.3**	**82.3**	**77.5**	**85.2**	**83.8**
Married couples	52.3	55.7	49.3	60.5	56.9
Female householder, no spouse present	18.4	19.0	19.0	17.7	20.3
Male householder, no spouse present	7.6	7.6	9.2	7.1	6.6
Nonfamily households	**21.7**	**17.7**	**22.5**	**14.7**	**16.2**
Female householder	9.7	4.6	6.0	4.4	3.5
Living alone	8.1	3.3	4.6	2.9	2.4
Male householder	12.0	13.1	16.5	10.3	12.7
Living alone	7.7	7.5	7.6	7.0	7.8
PERCENT DISTRIBUTION BY TYPE					
TOTAL HISPANIC HOUSEHOLDS	**100.0%**	**40.4%**	**13.1%**	**14.1%**	**13.3%**
Family households	**100.0**	**42.5**	**13.0**	**15.3**	**14.2**
Married couples	100.0	43.1	12.4	16.3	14.4
Female householder, no spouse present	100.0	41.7	13.5	13.6	14.6
Male householder, no spouse present	100.0	40.2	15.8	13.0	11.4
Nonfamily households	**100.0**	**33.0**	**13.6**	**9.5**	**9.9**
Female householder	100.0	19.5	8.2	6.5	4.8
Living alone	100.0	16.5	7.5	5.1	3.9
Male householder	100.0	43.9	17.9	12.0	14.0
Living alone	100.0	39.1	13.0	12.8	13.4

Source: Bureau of the Census, 2005 Current Population Survey, Annual Social and Economic Supplement, Internet site http:// pubdb3.census.gov/macro/032005/hhinc/new02_000.htm; calculations by New Strategist

Many Non-Hispanic White Generation Xers Live Alone

Married couples account for the majority of their households, however.

Married couples accounted for the 57 percent majority of non-Hispanic white householders aged 25 to 39 in 2005 (Generation Xers were aged 29 to 40 in that year). But many in the age group live alone—especially among those still in their twenties. Nearly one in four non-Hispanic white householders aged 25 to 29 lives by him- or herself. The proportion drops with age, but even among 35-to-39-year-olds a substantial 18 percent live alone.

Female-headed families accounted for only 11 percent of households headed by non-Hispanic whites in the 25-to-39 age group. This figure is far below the 37 percent female-headed family share among blacks and the 19 percent share among Hispanics in the age group. It exceeds the 7 percent share among Asians, however.

■ Married couples account for the 47 percent minority of non-Hispanic white householders aged 25-to-29. The figure rises to the 62 percent majority among 35-to-39-year-olds as marriage and family become priorities.

Female-headed families account for few Gen X households

(percent distribution of households headed by non-Hispanic whites aged 25 to 39, by household type, 2005)

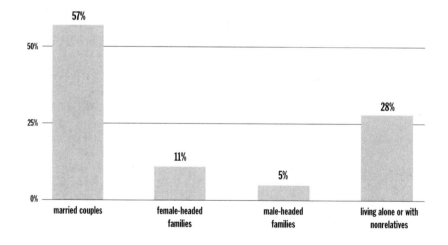

Table 6.6 Households Headed by People Aged 25 to 39 by Household Type, 2005: Non-Hispanic White Households

(number and percent distribution of total households headed by non-Hispanic whites and households headed by non-Hispanic whites aged 25 to 39, by household type, 2005; numbers in thousands)

	total	aged 25 to 39			
		total	25 to 29	30 to 34	35 to 39
TOTAL NON-HISPANIC					
WHITE HOUSEHOLDS	**81,445**	**19,149**	**5,710**	**6,233**	**7,206**
Family households	**54,383**	**13,782**	**3,594**	**4,637**	**5,551**
Married couples	44,296	10,828	2,671	3,717	4,440
Female householder, no spouse present	7,200	2,050	598	636	816
Male householder, no spouse present	2,888	904	325	284	295
Nonfamily households	**27,062**	**5,368**	**2,116**	**1,596**	**1,656**
Female householder	15,052	2,127	850	636	641
Living alone	13,053	1,550	537	491	522
Male householder	12,009	3,241	1,266	960	1,015
Living alone	9,349	2,217	755	664	798
PERCENT DISTRIBUTION BY AGE					
TOTAL NON-HISPANIC					
WHITE HOUSEHOLDS	**100.0%**	**100.0%**	**100.0%**	**100.0%**	**100.0%**
Family households	**66.8**	**72.0**	**62.9**	**74.4**	**77.0**
Married couples	54.4	56.5	46.8	59.6	61.6
Female householder, no spouse present	8.8	10.7	10.5	10.2	11.3
Male householder, no spouse present	3.5	4.7	5.7	4.6	4.1
Nonfamily households	**33.2**	**28.0**	**37.1**	**25.6**	**23.0**
Female householder	18.5	11.1	14.9	10.2	8.9
Living alone	16.0	8.1	9.4	7.9	7.2
Male householder	14.7	16.9	22.2	15.4	14.1
Living alone	11.5	11.6	13.2	10.7	11.1
PERCENT DISTRIBUTION BY TYPE					
TOTAL NON-HISPANIC					
WHITE HOUSEHOLDS	**100.0%**	**23.5%**	**7.0%**	**7.7%**	**8.8%**
Family households	**100.0**	**25.3**	**6.6**	**8.5**	**10.2**
Married couples	100.0	24.4	6.0	8.4	10.0
Female householder, no spouse present	100.0	28.5	8.3	8.8	11.3
Male householder, no spouse present	100.0	31.3	11.3	9.8	10.2
Nonfamily households	**100.0**	**19.8**	**7.8**	**5.9**	**6.1**
Female householder	100.0	14.1	5.6	4.2	4.3
Living alone	100.0	11.9	4.1	3.8	4.0
Male householder	100.0	27.0	10.5	8.0	8.5
Living alone	100.0	23.7	8.1	7.1	8.5

Note: Non-Hispanic whites include only those identifying themselves as being white alone and not Hispanic.
Source: Bureau of the Census, 2005 Current Population Survey, Annual Social and Economic Supplement, Internet site http://pubdb3.census.gov/macro/032005/hhinc/new02_000.htm; calculations by New Strategist

Generation X Households Are Growing

Household size peaks in the 35-to-39 age group.

The average American household was home to 2.57 people in 2004. Household size grows as householders age through their twenties and into their thirties. It peaks among house-holders aged 35 to 39—at 3.28 people—because this age group is most likely to have at least one child at home. As householders age into their forties and fifties, the nest empties and household size shrinks.

Households headed by Gen Xers (aged 28 to 39 in 2004) are growing as they marry and have children. The average household headed by a 25-to-29-year-old has fewer than one child in the home. But the average household headed by a 30-to-34-year-old has more than one child as they enter the crowded-nest stage of life. Householders aged 35 to 39 have an average of 1.42 children in the home.

■ Generation Xers are marrying, having children, buying houses, and taking on the re-sponsibilities of home and family.

The nest is filling for householders in their thirties

(average household size by age of householder, 2004)

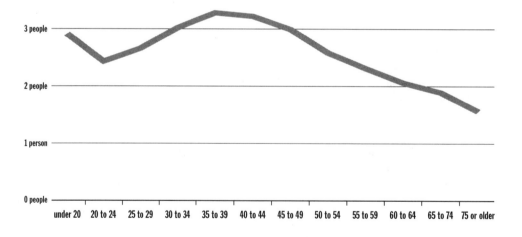

Table 6.7 Average Size of Household by Age of Householder, 2004

(number of households, average number of people per household, and average number of people under age 18 per household, by age of householder, 2004; number of households in thousands)

	number	average number of people	average number of people under age 18
Total households	**112,000**	**2.57**	**0.66**
Under age 20	837	2.91	0.84
Aged 20 to 24	5,772	2.43	0.55
Aged 25 to 29	8,738	2.66	0.85
Aged 30 to 34	10,421	3.02	1.21
Aged 35 to 39	10,997	3.28	1.42
Aged 40 to 44	12,224	3.22	1.22
Aged 45 to 49	12,360	2.99	0.82
Aged 50 to 54	10,778	2.58	0.41
Aged 55 to 59	9,504	2.31	0.23
Aged 60 to 64	7,320	2.06	0.14
Aged 65 to 74	11,499	1.89	0.08
Aged 75 or older	11,550	1.56	0.03

Source: Bureau of the Census, Current Population Survey Annual Social and Economic Supplement, America's Families and Living Arrangements: 2004, detailed tables, Internet site http://www.census.gov/population/www/socdemo/hh-fam/cps2004.html

The Majority of Generation Xers Have Children at Home

Female-headed families are most likely to have children.

More than half the households headed by people aged 25 to 39 (Generation X was aged 28 to 39 in 2004) include children under age 18. The proportion of householders with children rises from the 46 percent minority of those aged 25 to 29 to the 66 percent majority of those aged 35 to 39.

Seventy-seven percent of married couples aged 25 to 39 have children at home. Families headed by women in the age group are even more likely to have children, at 90 percent. Among families headed by men, a smaller 59 percent include children under age 18.

■ The presence of children drives the spending of households headed by 25-to-39-year-olds,

Male-headed families are least likely to have children at home

(percent of households headed by people aged 25 to 39 with children under age 18 at home, by household type, 2004)

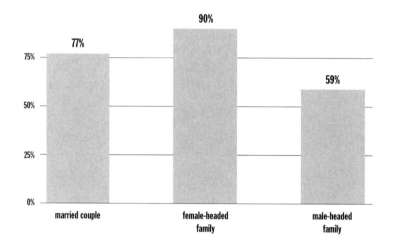

Table 6.8 Households by Type, Age of Householder, and Presence of Children, 2004: Total Households

(total number of households and number and percent with own children under age 18 at home, by household type and age of householder, 2004; numbers in thousands)

		with own children under age 18	
	total	number	percent
Total households	**112,000**	**35,944**	**32.1%**
Under age 25	6,609	1,980	30.0
Aged 25 to 39	30,156	17,463	57.9
Aged 25 to 29	8,738	4,023	46.0
Aged 30 to 34	10,421	6,223	59.7
Aged 35 to 39	10,997	7,217	65.6
Aged 40 to or older	75,235	16,503	21.9
Married couples	**57,719**	**25,793**	**44.7**
Under age 25	1,416	829	58.5
Aged 25 to 39	15,956	12,297	77.1
Aged 25 to 29	3,779	2,523	66.8
Aged 30 to 34	5,794	4,469	77.1
Aged 35 to 39	6,383	5,305	83.1
Aged 40 to or older	40,347	12,668	31.4
Female family householder, no spouse present	**13,781**	**8,221**	**59.7**
Under age 25	1,398	979	70.0
Aged 25 to 39	4,708	4,255	90.4
Aged 25 to 29	1,399	1,247	89.1
Aged 30 to 34	1,560	1,441	92.4
Aged 35 to 39	1,749	1,567	89.6
Aged 40 to or older	7,675	2,987	38.9
Male family householder, no spouse present	**4,716**	**1,931**	**40.9**
Under age 25	774	174	22.5
Aged 25 to 39	1,533	911	59.4
Aged 25 to 29	533	252	47.3
Aged 30 to 34	492	313	63.6
Aged 35 to 39	508	346	68.1
Aged 40 to or older	2,407	846	35.1

Source: Bureau of the Census, Current Population Survey Annual Social and Economic Supplement, America's Families and Living Arrangements: 2004, detailed tables, Internet site http://www.census.gov/population/www/socdemo/hh-fam/cps2004.html; calculations by New Strategist

Hispanic Generation Xers Are Most Likely to Have Children

Households headed by Asian Gen Xers are least likely to include children.

Seventy percent of Hispanic households headed by 25-to-39-year-olds include children under age 18. The proportion is a smaller 62 percent among black households in the age group. For non-Hispanic whites, the 55 percent majority of households headed by 25-to-39-year-olds include children. Among Asian householders in the age group, just 51 percent have children in their home. Hispanics and blacks become parents at a younger age than non-Hispanic whites or Asians, in part because non-Hispanic whites and Asians are more likely to go to college and postpone childbearing.

Regardless of race, the majority of households headed by married couples aged 25 to 39 include children under age 18, the proportion ranging from 73 percent among Asians to 86 percent among Hispanics. The same is true for families headed by women, in which group the proportion with children ranges from 78 percent among Asians to fully 92 percent among blacks.

■ Because blacks and Hispanics have children at a younger age than non-Hispanic whites or Asians, there are important lifestyle differences by race and Hispanic origin among adults in their twenties and thirties.

Asians are most likely to delay childbearing

(percent of households headed by people aged 25 to 39 with children under age 18 at home, by race and Hispanic origin, 2004)

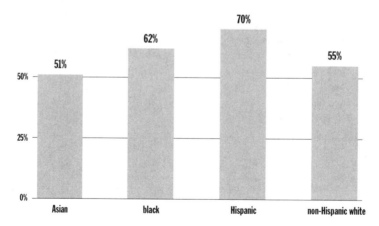

Table 6.9 Households by Type, Age of Householder, and Presence of Children, 2004: Asian Households

(total number of Asian households and number and percent with own children under age 18 at home, by household type and age of householder, 2004; numbers in thousands)

	total	with own children under age 18	
		number	percent
Total Asian households	**4,235**	**1,711**	**40.4%**
Under age 25	286	29	10.1
Aged 25 to 39	1,560	791	50.7
Aged 25 to 29	410	117	28.5
Aged 30 to 34	602	308	51.2
Aged 35 to 39	548	366	66.8
Aged 40 to or older	2,389	889	37.2
Married couples	**2,574**	**1,462**	**56.8**
Under age 25	37	19	51.4
Aged 25 to 39	899	655	72.9
Aged 25 to 29	169	86	50.9
Aged 30 to 34	370	256	69.2
Aged 35 to 39	360	313	86.9
Aged 40 to or older	1,637	787	48.1
Female family householder, no spouse present	**378**	**196**	**51.9**
Under age 25	51	5	9.8
Aged 25 to 39	136	106	77.9
Aged 25 to 29	32	24	75.0
Aged 30 to 34	48	38	79.2
Aged 35 to 39	56	44	78.6
Aged 40 to or older	192	85	44.3
Male family householder, no spouse present	**241**	**53**	**22.0**
Under age 25	69	5	7.2
Aged 25 to 39	91	31	34.1
Aged 25 to 29	36	7	19.4
Aged 30 to 34	35	15	42.9
Aged 35 to 39	20	9	45.0
Aged 40 to or older	81	18	22.2

Note: Asians include those identifying themselves as being of the race alone and those identifying themselves as being of the race in combination with other races.
Source: Bureau of the Census, Current Population Survey Annual Social and Economic Supplement, America's Families and Living Arrangements: 2004, detailed tables, Internet site http://www.census.gov/population/www/socdemo/hh-fam/cps2004.html; calculations by New Strategist

Table 6.10 Households by Type, Age of Householder, and Presence of Children, 2004: Black Households

(total number of black households and number and percent with own children under age 18 at home, by household type and age of householder, 2004; numbers in thousands)

	total	with own children under age 18	
		number	percent
Total black households	**13,969**	**5,104**	**36.5%**
Under age 25	1,133	521	46.0
Aged 25 to 39	4,310	2,657	61.6
Aged 25 to 29	1,299	745	57.4
Aged 30 to 34	1,526	966	63.3
Aged 35 to 39	1,485	946	63.7
Aged 40 to or older	8,527	1,926	22.6
Married couples	**4,259**	**2,102**	**49.4**
Under age 25	119	85	71.4
Aged 25 to 39	1,271	1,023	80.5
Aged 25 to 29	289	224	77.5
Aged 30 to 34	481	387	80.5
Aged 35 to 39	501	412	82.2
Aged 40 to or older	2,868	993	34.6
Female family householder, no spouse present	**4,067**	**2,640**	**64.9**
Under age 25	491	391	79.6
Aged 25 to 39	1,598	1,470	92.0
Aged 25 to 29	496	463	93.3
Aged 30 to 34	563	529	94.0
Aged 35 to 39	539	478	88.7
Aged 40 to or older	1,978	779	39.4
Male family householder, no spouse present	**804**	**362**	**45.0**
Under age 25	138	43	31.2
Aged 25 to 39	273	164	60.1
Aged 25 to 29	109	59	54.1
Aged 30 to 34	80	49	61.3
Aged 35 to 39	84	56	66.7
Aged 40 to or older	392	155	39.5

Note: Blacks include those identifying themselves as being of the race alone and those identifying themselves as being of the race in combination with other races.
Source: Bureau of the Census, Current Population Survey Annual Social and Economic Supplement, America's Families and Living Arrangements: 2004, detailed tables, Internet site http://www.census.gov/population/www/socdemo/hh-fam/cps2004.html; calculations by New Strategist

Table 6.11 Households by Type, Age of Householder, and Presence of Children, 2004: Hispanic Households

(total number of Hispanic households and number and percent with own children under age 18 at home, by household type and age of householder, 2004; numbers in thousands)

	total	with own children under age 18	
		number	percent
Total Hispanic households	**11,692**	**5,837**	**49.9%**
Under age 25	1,162	484	41.7
Aged 25 to 39	4,751	3,316	69.8
Aged 25 to 29	1,479	934	63.2
Aged 30 to 34	1,702	1,226	72.0
Aged 35 to 39	1,570	1,156	73.6
Aged 40 to or older	5,780	2,038	35.3
Married couples	**6,227**	**4,086**	**65.6**
Under age 25	364	272	74.7
Aged 25 to 39	2,697	2,327	86.3
Aged 25 to 29	743	619	83.3
Aged 30 to 34	1,011	884	87.4
Aged 35 to 39	943	824	87.4
Aged 40 to or older	3,165	1,487	47.0
Female family householder, no spouse present	**2,138**	**1,422**	**66.5**
Under age 25	264	167	63.3
Aged 25 to 39	870	795	91.4
Aged 25 to 29	285	251	88.1
Aged 30 to 34	287	269	93.7
Aged 35 to 39	298	275	92.3
Aged 40 to or older	1,003	461	46.0
Male family householder, no spouse present	**908**	**329**	**36.2**
Under age 25	221	44	19.9
Aged 25 to 39	396	195	49.2
Aged 25 to 29	145	65	44.8
Aged 30 to 34	142	74	52.1
Aged 35 to 39	109	56	51.4
Aged 40 to or older	291	90	30.9

Source: Bureau of the Census, Current Population Survey Annual Social and Economic Supplement, America's Families and Living Arrangements: 2004, detailed tables, Internet site http://www.census.gov/population/www/socdemo/hh-fam/cps2004.html; calculations by New Strategist

Table 6.12 Households by Type, Age of Householder, and Presence of Children, 2004: Non-Hispanic White Households

(total number of non-Hispanic white households and number and percent with own children under age 18 at home, by household type and age of householder, 2004; numbers in thousands)

	total	with own children under age 18	
		number	percent
Total non-Hispanic white households	**81,149**	**23,040**	**28.4%**
Under age 25	3,979	927	23.3
Aged 25 to 39	19,323	10,577	54.7
Aged 25 to 29	5,480	2,183	39.8
Aged 30 to 34	6,508	3,679	56.5
Aged 35 to 39	7,335	4,715	64.3
Aged 40 to or older	57,846	11,535	19.9
Married couples	**44,197**	**17,961**	**40.6**
Under age 25	905	458	50.6
Aged 25 to 39	10,977	8,196	74.7
Aged 25 to 29	2,544	1,568	61.6
Aged 30 to 34	3,887	2,905	74.7
Aged 35 to 39	4,546	3,723	81.9
Aged 40 to or older	32,314	9,307	28.8
Female family householder, no spouse present	**7,115**	**3,927**	**55.2**
Under age 25	570	395	69.3
Aged 25 to 39	2,097	1,876	89.5
Aged 25 to 29	583	505	86.6
Aged 30 to 34	656	600	91.5
Aged 35 to 39	858	771	89.9
Aged 40 to or older	4,447	1,656	37.2
Male family householder, no spouse present	**2,711**	**1,152**	**42.5**
Under age 25	340	74	21.8
Aged 25 to 39	752	503	66.9
Aged 25 to 29	228	110	48.2
Aged 30 to 34	233	173	74.2
Aged 35 to 39	291	220	75.6
Aged 40 to or older	1,620	575	35.5

Note: Non-Hispanic whites include only those identifying themselves as being white alone and not Hispanic.
Source: Bureau of the Census, Current Population Survey Annual Social and Economic Supplement, America's Families and Living Arrangements: 2004, detailed tables, Internet site http://www.census.gov/population/www/socdemo/hh-fam/cps2004.html; calculations by New Strategist

Many Households Headed by Generation Xers include Preschoolers

Gen Xers head more than 70 percent of all households with infants.

During their twenties and early thirties, most people become parents. Only 30 percent of householders under age 25 have children under age 18 at home. The proportion rises to the 60 percent majority in the 30-to-34 age group.

Thirty-six percent of householders aged 25 to 39 have preschoolers (children under age 6) at home. This age group accounts for the 70 percent majority of all households with preschoolers. The proportion of households with preschoolers peaks at 40 percent in the 30-to-34 age group. Only 17 percent of householders aged 25 to 39 have teenagers in their home, although the figure is a much larger 31 percent among householders aged 35 to 39.

■ As people have children, their priorities shift from pursuing their own wants and needs to meeting the needs of their children.

Children are the norm for householders aged 25 to 39

(percent of households headed by people aged 25 to 39 with children at home, by age of child, 2004)

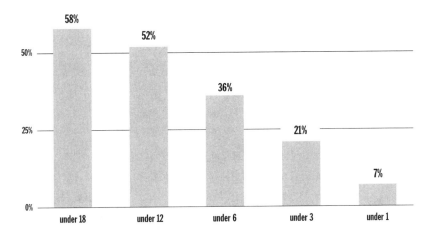

Table 6.13 Households by Presence and Age of Children and Age of Householder, 2004

(number and percent distribution of households by presence and age of own children at home, by age of children and age of householder, 2004; numbers in thousands)

	total	under 25	aged 25 to 39 total	25 to 29	30 to 34	35 to 39	40 or older
Total households	**112,000**	**6,609**	**30,156**	**8,738**	**10,421**	**10,997**	**75,235**
With children of any age	46,253	2,000	17,693	4,043	6,256	7,394	26,561
Under age 25	41,544	2,000	17,661	4,035	6,242	7,384	21,883
Under age 18	35,944	1,980	17,463	4,023	6,223	7,217	16,503
Under age 12	26,118	1,964	15,667	3,974	5,854	5,839	8,487
Under age 6	15,614	1,830	10,899	3,384	4,194	3,321	2,886
Under age 3	8,954	1,412	6,395	2,158	2,564	1,673	1,149
Under age 1	3,057	603	2,167	795	834	538	287
Aged 12 to 17	16,960	43	5,134	226	1,509	3,399	11,783

PERCENT DISTRIBUTION BY AGE OF CHILD

	total	under 25	aged 25 to 39 total	25 to 29	30 to 34	35 to 39	40 or older
Total households	**100.0%**	**100.0%**	**100.0%**	**100.0%**	**100.0%**	**100.0%**	**100.0%**
With children of any age	41.3	30.3	58.7	46.3	60.0	67.2	35.3
Under age 25	37.1	30.3	58.6	46.2	59.9	67.1	29.1
Under age 18	32.1	30.0	57.9	46.0	59.7	65.6	21.9
Under age 12	23.3	29.7	52.0	45.5	56.2	53.1	11.3
Under age 6	13.9	27.7	36.1	38.7	40.2	30.2	3.8
Under age 3	8.0	21.4	21.2	24.7	24.6	15.2	1.5
Under age 1	2.7	9.1	7.2	9.1	8.0	4.9	0.4
Aged 12 to 17	15.1	0.7	17.0	2.6	14.5	30.9	15.7

PERCENT DISTRIBUTION BY AGE OF HOUSEHOLDER

	total	under 25	aged 25 to 39 total	25 to 29	30 to 34	35 to 39	40 or older
Total households	**100.0%**	**5.9%**	**26.9%**	**7.8%**	**9.3%**	**9.8%**	**67.2%**
With children of any age	100.0	4.3	38.3	8.7	13.5	16.0	57.4
Under age 25	100.0	4.8	42.5	9.7	15.0	17.8	52.7
Under age 18	100.0	5.5	48.6	11.2	17.3	20.1	45.9
Under age 12	100.0	7.5	60.0	15.2	22.4	22.4	32.5
Under age 6	100.0	11.7	69.8	21.7	26.9	21.3	18.5
Under age 3	100.0	15.8	71.4	24.1	28.6	18.7	12.8
Under age 1	100.0	19.7	70.9	26.0	27.3	17.6	9.4
Aged 12 to 17	100.0	0.3	30.3	1.3	8.9	20.0	69.5

Source: Bureau of the Census, Current Population Survey Annual Social and Economic Supplement, America's Families and Living Arrangements: 2004, detailed tables, Internet site http://www.census.gov/population/www/socdemo/hh-fam/cps2004.html; calculations by New Strategist

Two-Child Families Are Most Common

Many Generation X couples have more than two children, however.

Smaller families have been growing in popularity for decades. Most Americans now consider two children the ideal number. But many Gen X couples have three or more children.

Among couples aged 25 to 29, the largest share (33 percent) do not yet have children. Twenty-eight percent have one child under age 18 at home and another 28 percent have two. Only 11 percent have three or more. Among couples aged 30 to 34, the largest share of couples (34 percent) have two children under age 18 at home. Among couples aged 35 to 39, an even larger 37 percent have two children, and a substantial 26 percent have three or more.

■ Only 17 percent of couples aged 35 to 39 do not have children under age 18 at home.

Most Gen X couples have one or two children

(percent distribution of married couples aged 25 to 39, by number of children under age 18 at home, 2004)

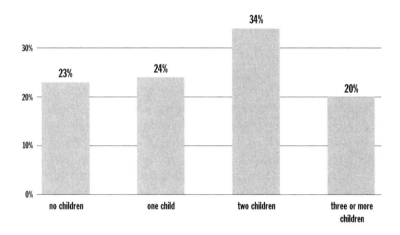

Table 6.14 Married Couples by Presence and Number of Children and Age of Householder, 2004

(number and percent distribution of married couples by presence and number of own children under age 18 at home, by age of householder, 2004; numbers in thousands)

	total	under 25	aged 25 to 39 total	25 to 29	30 to 34	35 to 39	40 to 44	45 or older
Total married couples	**57,719**	**1,416**	**15,956**	**3,779**	**5,794**	**6,383**	**7,201**	**33,146**
Without children under 18	31,926	589	3,660	1,256	1,325	1,079	1,639	26,039
With children under 18	25,792	829	12,298	2,524	4,470	5,304	5,561	7,106
One child	9,763	419	3,767	1,054	1,419	1,294	1,796	3,781
Two children	10,481	303	5,378	1,044	1,954	2,380	2,410	2,391
Three children	4,073	84	2,265	293	780	1,192	1,015	709
Four or more children	1,475	23	888	133	317	438	340	225

PERCENT DISTRIBUTION BY NUMBER OF CHILDREN

	total	under 25	aged 25 to 39 total	25 to 29	30 to 34	35 to 39	40 to 44	45 or older
Total married couples	**100.0%**	**100.0%**	**100.0%**	**100.0%**	**100.0%**	**100.0%**	**100.0%**	**100.0%**
Without children under 18	55.3	41.6	22.9	33.2	22.9	16.9	22.8	78.6
With children under 18	44.7	58.5	77.1	66.8	77.1	83.1	77.2	21.4
One child	16.9	29.6	23.6	27.9	24.5	20.3	24.9	11.4
Two children	18.2	21.4	33.7	27.6	33.7	37.3	33.5	7.2
Three children	7.1	5.9	14.2	7.8	13.5	18.7	14.1	2.1
Four or more children	2.6	1.6	5.6	3.5	5.5	6.9	4.7	0.7

Source: Bureau of the Census, Current Population Survey Annual Social and Economic Supplement, America's Families and Living Arrangements: 2004, detailed tables, Internet site http://www.census.gov/population/www/socdemo/hh-fam/cps2004.html; calculations by New Strategist

Most Female-Headed Families include Children

Male-headed families are much less likely to include children.

Most Gen X women who head families without a spouse are single mothers. Among female family householders aged 25 to 39, fully 90 percent head families with children under age 18. Among male family heads aged 25 to 39, a much smaller 59 percent have children under age 18 at home. Family heads without children under age 18 in the household live with grown children or with other relatives, such as siblings or parents.

Among women aged 25 to 39 who head families, the largest share (34 percent) has one child living with them, 33 percent have two, and a substantial 23 percent have three or more. Among their male counterparts, 33 percent have one child, 18 percent have two, and just 8 percent have three or more.

■ Single-parent families have less flexibility in choosing jobs since they need work that meshes with their children's schedules.

Many female-headed Gen X families include three or more children

(percent distribution of female-headed families headed by women aged 25 to 39, by number of children under age 18 at home, 2004)

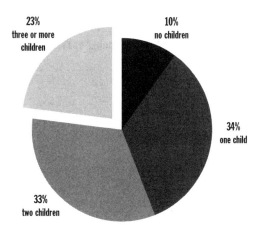

Table 6.15 Female-Headed Families by Presence and Number of Children and Age of Householder, 2004

(number and percent distribution of female-headed families by presence and number of own children under age 18 at home, by age of householder, 2004; numbers in thousands)

	total	under 25	aged 25 to 39 total	25 to 29	30 to 34	35 to 39	40 to 44	45 or older
Total female-headed families	**13,781**	**1,398**	**4,708**	**1,399**	**1,560**	**1,749**	**1,893**	**5,782**
Without children under 18	5,560	419	454	151	120	183	385	4,302
With children under 18	8,221	979	4,255	1,247	1,441	1,567	1,508	1,480
One child	4,055	571	1,615	502	511	602	795	1,075
Two children	2,665	287	1,556	444	489	623	516	307
Three children	1,046	87	739	194	280	265	140	79
Four or more children	455	34	345	107	161	77	57	19
PERCENT DISTRIBUTION								
Total female-headed families	**100.0%**	**100.0%**	**100.0%**	**100.0%**	**100.0%**	**100.0%**	**100.0%**	**100.0%**
Without children under18	40.3	30.0	9.6	10.8	7.7	10.5	20.3	74.4
With children under 18	59.7	70.0	90.4	89.1	92.4	89.6	79.7	25.6
One child	29.4	40.8	34.3	35.9	32.8	34.4	42.0	18.6
Two children	19.3	20.5	33.1	31.7	31.3	35.6	27.3	5.3
Three children	7.6	6.2	15.7	13.9	17.9	15.2	7.4	1.4
Four or more children	3.3	2.4	7.3	7.6	10.3	4.4	3.0	0.3

Source: Bureau of the Census, Current Population Survey Annual Social and Economic Supplement, America's Families and Living Arrangements: 2004, detailed tables, Internet site http://www.census.gov/population/www/socdemo/hh-fam/cps2004.html; calculations by New Strategist

Table 6.16 Male-Headed Families by Presence and Number of Children and Age of Householder, 2004

(number and percent distribution of male-headed families by presence and number of own children under age 18 at home, by age of householder, 2004; numbers in thousands)

	total	under 25	aged 25 to 39 total	25 to 29	30 to 34	35 to 39	40 to 44	45 or older
Total male-headed families	**4,716**	**774**	**1,533**	**533**	**492**	**508**	**588**	**1,819**
Without children under 18	2,786	602	624	282	179	163	218	1,342
With children under 18	1,931	173	910	251	313	346	370	476
One child	1,146	110	511	164	181	166	200	325
Two children	550	46	278	50	99	129	115	110
Three children	180	13	99	35	26	38	40	27
Four or more children	55	4	22	2	7	13	15	14
PERCENT DISTRIBUTION								
Total male-headed families	**100.0%**	**100.0%**	**100.0%**	**100.0%**	**100.0%**	**100.0%**	**100.0%**	**100.0%**
Without children under 18	59.1	77.8	40.7	52.9	36.4	32.1	37.1	73.8
With children under 18	40.9	22.4	59.4	47.1	63.6	68.1	62.9	26.2
One child	24.3	14.2	33.3	30.8	36.8	32.7	34.0	17.9
Two children	11.7	5.9	18.1	9.4	20.1	25.4	19.6	6.0
Three children	3.8	1.7	6.5	6.6	5.3	7.5	6.8	1.5
Four or more children	1.2	0.5	1.4	0.4	1.4	2.6	2.6	0.8

Source: Bureau of the Census, Current Population Survey Annual Social and Economic Supplement, America's Families and Living Arrangements: 2004, detailed tables, Internet site http://www.census.gov/population/www/socdemo/hh-fam/cps2004.html; calculations by New Strategist

The Living Arrangements of Generation Xers Are Changing

Most men and women live with their spouse by their early thirties.

The majority of men and women aged 25 to 39 were living with a spouse in 2004 (Generation Xers were aged 28 to 39 in that year). But there are dramatic differences in living arrangements within the age group. Among 25-to-29-year-olds, only 35 percent of men and 47 percent of women live with their spouse. In the 30-to-34 age group, the proportions rise to the 55 and 61 percent majorities, respectively.

A large share of men and women aged 25 to 29 live alone or with nonrelatives—33 percent of men and 23 percent of women. These figures fall to 22 and 13 percent, respectively, among 35-to-39-year-olds. Fully 19 percent of men and 11 percent of women aged 25 to 29 still live with their parents. By the 35-to-39 age group, only 8 percent of men and 4 percent of women still live with mom and dad.

■ Women establish their own household sooner than men because they marry at a younger age.

Some Gen Xers still live with their parents

(percent of people aged 25 to 39 who live with their parents, by sex and age, 2004)

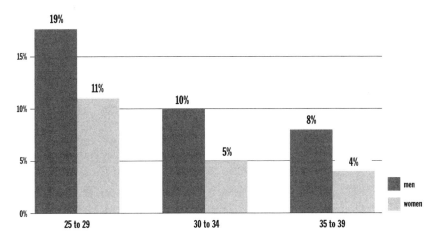

Table 6.17 Living Arrangements of Men by Age, 2004

(number and percent distribution of men aged 15 or older by living arrangement and age, 2004; numbers in thousands)

	total	under 25	aged 25 to 39 total	25 to 29	30 to 34	35 to 39	40 or older
NUMBER							
Total men	**110,048**	**20,569**	**29,860**	**9,535**	**10,018**	**10,307**	**59,621**
Married-couple householder or spouse	57,719	1,121	15,208	3,362	5,545	6,301	41,390
Other householder	20,852	2,296	6,377	2,315	2,042	2,020	12,178
Male family householder	4,716	774	1,533	533	492	508	2,407
Living alone	12,562	769	3,326	1,104	1,125	1,097	8,467
Living with nonrelatives	3,574	753	1,518	678	425	415	1,304
Nonhouseholder	31,477	17,152	8,275	3,858	2,431	1,986	6,049
Child of householder	18,936	13,695	3,499	1,764	956	779	1,742
Other relative of householder	5,575	1,647	1,658	723	482	453	2,271
Living with nonrelatives	6,965	1,810	3,118	1,371	993	754	2,036
PERCENT DISTRIBUTION BY LIVING ARRANGEMENT							
Total men	**100.0%**	**100.0%**	**100.0%**	**100.0%**	**100.0%**	**100.0%**	**100.0%**
Married-couple householder or spouse	52.4	5.4	50.9	35.3	55.4	61.1	69.4
Other householder	18.9	11.2	21.4	24.3	20.4	19.6	20.4
Male family householder	4.3	3.8	5.1	5.6	4.9	4.9	4.0
Living alone	11.4	3.7	11.1	11.6	11.2	10.6	14.2
Living with nonrelatives	3.2	3.7	5.1	7.1	4.2	4.0	2.2
Nonhouseholder	28.6	83.4	27.7	40.5	24.3	19.3	10.1
Child of householder	17.2	66.6	11.7	18.5	9.5	7.6	2.9
Other relative of householder	5.1	8.0	5.6	7.6	4.8	4.4	3.8
Living with nonrelatives	6.3	8.8	10.4	14.4	9.9	7.3	3.4
PERCENT DISTRIBUTION BY AGE							
Total men	**100.0%**	**18.7%**	**27.1%**	**8.7%**	**9.1%**	**9.4%**	**54.2%**
Married-couple householder or spouse	100.0	1.9	26.3	5.8	9.6	10.9	71.7
Other householder	100.0	11.0	30.6	11.1	9.8	9.7	58.4
Male family householder	100.0	16.4	32.5	11.3	10.4	10.8	51.0
Living alone	100.0	6.1	26.5	8.8	9.0	8.7	67.4
Living with nonrelatives	100.0	21.1	42.5	19.0	11.9	11.6	36.5
Nonhouseholder	100.0	54.5	26.3	12.3	7.7	6.3	19.2
Child of householder	100.0	72.3	18.5	9.3	5.0	4.1	9.2
Other relative of householder	100.0	29.5	29.7	13.0	8.6	8.1	40.7
Living with nonrelatives	100.0	26.0	44.8	19.7	14.3	10.8	29.2

Source: Bureau of the Census, Current Population Survey Annual Social and Economic Supplement, America's Families and Living Arrangements: 2004, detailed tables, Internet site http://www.census.gov/population/www/socdemo/hh-fam/cps2004.html; calculations by New Strategist

Table 6.18 Living Arrangements of Women by Age, 2004

(number and percent distribution of women aged 15 or older by living arrangement and age, 2004; numbers in thousands)

	total	under 25	aged 25 to 39 total	25 to 29	30 to 34	35 to 39	40 or older
NUMBER							
Total women	**117,295**	**20,028**	**30,064**	**9,460**	**10,127**	**10,477**	**67,204**
Married-couple householder or spouse	57,719	2,024	17,405	4,454	6,192	6,759	38,291
Other householder	33,428	2,896	7,823	2,643	2,586	2,594	22,709
Female family householder	13,781	1,398	4,708	1,399	1,560	1,749	7,675
Living alone	17,024	762	2,357	845	815	697	13,905
Living with nonrelatives	2,623	736	758	399	211	148	1,129
Nonhouseholder	26,147	15,108	4,836	2,364	1,349	1,123	6,205
Child of householder	14,863	11,976	1,928	1,054	505	369	962
Other relative of householder	5,926	1,330	923	374	272	277	3,673
Living with nonrelatives	5,358	1,802	1,985	936	572	477	1,570
PERCENT DISTRIBUTION BY LIVING ARRANGEMENT							
Total women	**100.0%**	**100.0%**	**100.0%**	**100.0%**	**100.0%**	**100.0%**	**100.0%**
Married-couple householder or spouse	49.2	10.1	57.9	47.1	61.1	64.5	57.0
Other householder	28.5	14.5	26.0	27.9	25.5	24.8	33.8
Female family householder	11.7	7.0	15.7	14.8	15.4	16.7	11.4
Living alone	14.5	3.8	7.8	8.9	8.0	6.7	20.7
Living with nonrelatives	2.2	3.7	2.5	4.2	2.1	1.4	1.7
Nonhouseholder	22.3	75.4	16.1	25.0	13.3	10.7	9.2
Child of householder	12.7	59.8	6.4	11.1	5.0	3.5	1.4
Other relative of householder	5.1	6.6	3.1	4.0	2.7	2.6	5.5
Living with nonrelatives	4.6	9.0	6.6	9.9	5.6	4.6	2.3
PERCENT DISTRIBUTION BY AGE							
Total women	**100.0%**	**17.1%**	**25.6%**	**8.1%**	**8.6%**	**8.9%**	**57.3%**
Married-couple householder or spouse	100.0	3.5	30.2	7.7	10.7	11.7	66.3
Other householder	100.0	8.7	23.4	7.9	7.7	7.8	67.9
Female family householder	100.0	10.1	34.2	10.2	11.3	12.7	55.7
Living alone	100.0	4.5	13.8	5.0	4.8	4.1	81.7
Living with nonrelatives	100.0	28.1	28.9	15.2	8.0	5.6	43.0
Nonhouseholder	100.0	57.8	18.5	9.0	5.2	4.3	23.7
Child of householder	100.0	80.6	13.0	7.1	3.4	2.5	6.5
Other relative of householder	100.0	22.4	15.6	6.3	4.6	4.7	62.0
Living with nonrelatives	100.0	33.6	37.0	17.5	10.7	8.9	29.3

Source: Bureau of the Census, Current Population Survey Annual Social and Economic Supplement, America's Families and Living Arrangements: 2004, detailed tables, Internet site http://www.census.gov/population/www/socdemo/hh-fam/cps2004.html; calculations by New Strategist

Generation Xers Are at the Age of Marriage

Most 30-to-34-year-olds are currently married.

Women marry at a younger age than men. Consequently, among 25-to-39-year-olds, men are less likely than women to be currently married—54 percent of men versus 61 percent of women in 2004 (Generation Xers were aged 28 to 39 in that year). Among men, only 39 percent of 25-to-29-year-olds are currently married. Fifty percent of their female counterparts are married. In the 30-to-34 age group, 59 percent of men and 64 percent of women are married. But a substantial 32 percent of men and 24 percent of women aged 30 to 34 have never married. The never-married share falls to 23 percent among men and 15 percent among women in the 35-to-39 age group.

With most Gen Xers just reaching the age of first marriage, few are divorced. Only 9 percent of men and 13 percent of women aged 25 to 39 are currently divorced or separated.

■ The median age at first marriage is rising because today's young adults are more likely to attend college and start a career before committing to family life.

Most people marry by their early thirties

(percent of people aged 25 to 39 who are currently married, by age and sex, 2004)

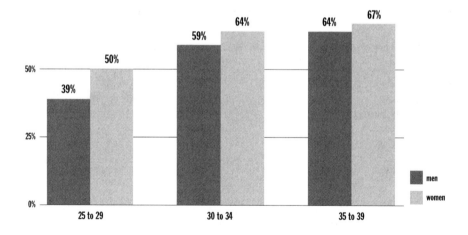

Table 6.19 Marital Status by Sex and Age, 2004: Total People

(number and percent distribution of people aged 15 or older by sex, age, and current marital status, 2004; numbers in thousands)

	total	never married	married	separated or divorced	widowed
NUMBER					
Total men	**110,048**	**35,885**	**60,724**	**10,791**	**2,648**
Under age 25	20,569	19,042	1,319	199	7
Aged 25 to 39	29,860	11,028	16,185	2,588	58
Aged 25 to 29	9,535	5,395	3,684	448	8
Aged 30 to 34	10,018	3,223	5,866	909	20
Aged 35 to 39	10,307	2,410	6,635	1,231	30
Aged 40 or older	59,621	5,815	43,218	8,004	2,581
Total women	**117,295**	**29,975**	**60,616**	**15,558**	**11,146**
Under age 25	20,028	17,292	2,340	378	18
Aged 25 to 39	30,064	7,789	18,225	3,806	244
Aged 25 to 29	9,460	3,855	4,746	817	42
Aged 30 to 34	10,127	2,400	6,462	1,198	67
Aged 35 to 39	10,477	1,534	7,017	1,791	135
Aged 40 or older	67,204	4,894	40,052	11,375	10,886
PERCENT DISTRIBUTION					
Total men	**100.0%**	**32.6%**	**55.2%**	**9.8%**	**2.4%**
Under age 25	100.0	92.6	6.4	1.0	0.0
Aged 25 to 39	100.0	36.9	54.2	8.7	0.2
Aged 25 to 29	100.0	56.6	38.6	4.7	0.1
Aged 30 to 34	100.0	32.2	58.6	9.1	0.2
Aged 35 to 39	100.0	23.4	64.4	11.9	0.3
Aged 40 or older	100.0	9.8	72.5	13.4	4.3
Total women	**100.0**	**25.6**	**51.7**	**13.3**	**9.5**
Under age 25	100.0	86.3	11.7	1.9	0.1
Aged 25 to 39	100.0	25.9	60.6	12.7	0.8
Aged 25 to 29	100.0	40.8	50.2	8.6	0.4
Aged 30 to 34	100.0	23.7	63.8	11.8	0.7
Aged 35 to 39	100.0	14.6	67.0	17.1	1.3
Aged 40 or older	100.0	7.3	59.6	16.9	16.2

Source: Bureau of the Census, Current Population Survey Annual Social and Economic Supplement, America's Families and Living Arrangements: 2004, detailed tables, Internet site http://www.census.gov/population/www/socdemo/hh-fam/cps2004.html; calculations by New Strategist

Black Generation Xers Are Least Likely to Be Married

Singles outnumber marrieds among blacks aged 25 to 39.

Among Asians, Hispanics, and non-Hispanic whites aged 25 to 39, the percentages of those who are currently married are similar—ranging from 53 to 57 percent among men and from 63 to 69 percent among women. Blacks in the age group are far less likely to be currently married—only 35 percent of women and 38 percent of men are married. Fifty-two percent of black men and 49 percent of black women in the age group have not yet married.

Asian Gen Xers are least likely to be currently divorced or separated. Only 4 percent of Asian men aged 25 to 39 are currently divorced versus 9 percent of black and non-Hispanic white men in the age group. Among Asian women aged 25 to 39, only 7 percent are currently divorced or separated compared with 13 percent of non-Hispanic white women and 15 percent of black women in the age group.

■ As the nation has become more diverse racially and ethnically, it has also become more diverse in its living arrangements.

Among 25-to-39-year-olds, Asian women are most likely to be married

(percent of people aged 25 to 39 who are currently married, by race, Hispanic origin, and sex, 2004)

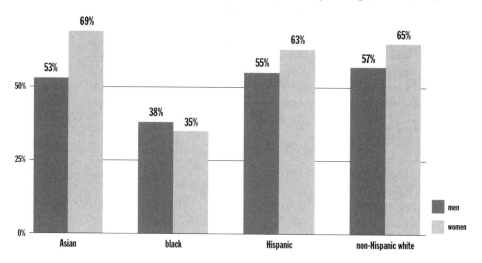

Table 6.20 Marital Status by Sex and Age, 2004: Asians

(number and percent distribution of Asians aged 15 or older by sex, age, and current marital status, 2004; numbers in thousands)

	total	never married	married	separated or divorced	widowed
NUMBER					
Total Asian men	**4,874**	**1,752**	**2,842**	**213**	**68**
Under age 25	938	893	38	7	0
Aged 25 to 39	1,680	727	883	66	4
Aged 25 to 29	539	355	179	5	–
Aged 30 to 34	603	238	343	20	2
Aged 35 to 39	538	134	361	41	2
Aged 40 or older	2,257	132	1,920	139	64
Total Asian women	**5,247**	**1,327**	**3,197**	**377**	**346**
Under age 25	881	769	104	5	2
Aged 25 to 39	1,784	422	1,235	118	10
Aged 25 to 29	551	219	314	12	6
Aged 30 to 34	644	132	482	28	2
Aged 35 to 39	589	71	439	78	2
Aged 40 or older	2,583	137	1,858	253	334
PERCENT DISTRIBUTION					
Total Asian men	**100.0%**	**35.9%**	**58.3%**	**4.4%**	**1.4%**
Under age 25	100.0	95.2	4.1	0.7	0.0
Aged 25 to 39	100.0	43.3	52.6	3.9	0.2
Aged 25 to 29	100.0	65.9	33.2	0.9	–
Aged 30 to 34	100.0	39.5	56.9	3.3	0.3
Aged 35 to 39	100.0	24.9	67.1	7.6	0.4
Aged 40 or older	100.0	5.8	85.1	6.2	2.8
Total Asian women	**100.0**	**25.3**	**60.9**	**7.2**	**6.6**
Under age 25	100.0	87.3	11.8	0.6	0.2
Aged 25 to 39	100.0	23.7	69.2	6.6	0.6
Aged 25 to 29	100.0	39.7	57.0	2.2	1.1
Aged 30 to 34	100.0	20.5	74.8	4.3	0.3
Aged 35 to 39	100.0	12.1	74.5	13.2	0.3
Aged 40 or older	100.0	5.3	71.9	9.8	12.9

Note: Asians include those identifying themselves as being of the race alone and those identifying themselves as being of the race in combination with other races. "–" means number is less than 500 or sample is too small to make a reliable estimate.
Source: Bureau of the Census, Current Population Survey Annual Social and Economic Supplement, America's Families and Living Arrangements: 2004, detailed tables, Internet site http://www.census.gov/population/www/socdemo/hh-fam/cps2004.html; calculations by New Strategist

Table 6.21 Marital Status by Sex and Age, 2004: Blacks

(number and percent distribution of blacks aged 15 or older by sex, age, and current marital status, 2004; numbers in thousands)

	total	never married	married	separated or divorced	widowed
NUMBER					
Total black men	**12,330**	**5,795**	**4,689**	**1,535**	**312**
Under age 25	2,983	2,825	128	28	0
Aged 25 to 39	3,521	1,848	1,337	329	9
Aged 25 to 29	1,148	836	257	55	0
Aged 30 to 34	1,170	543	491	135	2
Aged 35 to 39	1,203	469	589	139	7
Aged 40 or older	5,827	1,123	3,225	1,176	304
Total black women	**15,110**	**6,417**	**4,587**	**2,715**	**1,390**
Under age 25	3,189	2,936	181	69	2
Aged 25 to 39	4,333	2,107	1,519	658	50
Aged 25 to 29	1,421	899	423	94	5
Aged 30 to 34	1,443	699	513	220	12
Aged 35 to 39	1,469	509	583	344	33
Aged 40 or older	7,587	1,375	2,885	1,989	1,338
PERCENT DISTRIBUTION					
Total black men	**100.0%**	**47.0%**	**38.0%**	**12.4%**	**2.5%**
Under age 25	100.0	94.7	4.3	0.9	0.0
Aged 25 to 39	100.0	52.5	38.0	9.3	0.3
Aged 25 to 29	100.0	72.8	22.4	4.8	0.0
Aged 30 to 34	100.0	46.4	42.0	11.5	0.2
Aged 35 to 39	100.0	39.0	49.0	11.6	0.6
Aged 40 or older	100.0	19.3	55.3	20.2	5.2
Total black women	**100.0**	**42.5**	**30.4**	**18.0**	**9.2**
Under age 25	100.0	92.1	5.7	2.2	0.1
Aged 25 to 39	100.0	48.6	35.1	15.2	1.2
Aged 25 to 29	100.0	63.3	29.8	6.6	0.4
Aged 30 to 34	100.0	48.4	35.6	15.2	0.8
Aged 35 to 39	100.0	34.6	39.7	23.4	2.2
Aged 40 or older	100.0	18.1	38.0	26.2	17.6

Note: Blacks include those identifying themselves as being of the race alone and those identifying themselves as being of the race in combination with other races.
Source: Bureau of the Census, Current Population Survey Annual Social and Economic Supplement, America's Families and Living Arrangements: 2004, detailed tables, Internet site http://www.census.gov/population/www/socdemo/hh-fam/cps2004.html; calculations by New Strategist

Table 6.22 Marital Status by Sex and Age, 2004: Hispanics

(number and percent distribution of Hispanics aged 15 or older by sex, age, and current marital status, 2004; numbers in thousands)

	total	never married	married	separated or divorced	widowed
NUMBER					
Total Hispanic men	**14,640**	**6,003**	**7,248**	**1,199**	**190**
Under age 25	3,662	3,248	378	35	–
Aged 25 to 39	5,676	2,133	3,109	429	7
Aged 25 to 29	2,087	1,137	865	84	1
Aged 30 to 34	1,907	617	1,139	149	2
Aged 35 to 39	1,682	379	1,105	196	4
Aged 40 or older	5,302	623	3,761	734	183
Total Hispanic women	**13,878**	**4,306**	**6,987**	**1,825**	**761**
Under age 25	3,272	2,626	570	74	1
Aged 25 to 39	4,933	1,200	3,120	581	31
Aged 25 to 29	1,730	622	961	143	4
Aged 30 to 34	1,688	358	1,124	203	3
Aged 35 to 39	1,515	220	1,035	235	24
Aged 40 or older	5,672	480	3,297	1,169	728
PERCENT DISTRIBUTION					
Total Hispanic men	**100.0%**	**41.0%**	**49.5%**	**8.2%**	**1.3%**
Under age 25	100.0	88.7	10.3	1.0	–
Aged 25 to 39	100.0	37.6	54.8	7.6	0.1
Aged 25 to 29	100.0	54.5	41.4	4.0	0.0
Aged 30 to 34	100.0	32.4	59.7	7.8	0.1
Aged 35 to 39	100.0	22.5	65.7	11.7	0.2
Aged 40 or older	100.0	11.8	70.9	13.8	3.5
Total Hispanic women	**100.0**	**31.0**	**50.3**	**13.2**	**5.5**
Under age 25	100.0	80.3	17.4	2.3	0.0
Aged 25 to 39	100.0	24.3	63.2	11.8	0.6
Aged 25 to 29	100.0	36.0	55.5	8.3	0.2
Aged 30 to 34	100.0	21.2	66.6	12.0	0.2
Aged 35 to 39	100.0	14.5	68.3	15.5	1.6
Aged 40 or older	100.0	8.5	58.1	20.6	12.8

Note: "–" means number is less than 500 or sample is too small to make a reliable estimate.
Source: Bureau of the Census, Current Population Survey Annual Social and Economic Supplement, America's Families and Living Arrangements: 2004, detailed tables, Internet site http://www.census.gov/population/www/socdemo/hh-fam/cps2004.html; calculations by New Strategist

Table 6.23 Marital Status by Sex and Age, 2004: Non-Hispanic Whites

(number and percent distribution of non-Hispanic whites aged 15 or older by sex, age, and current marital status, 2004; numbers in thousands)

	total	never married	married	separated or divorced	widowed
NUMBER					
Total non-Hispanic white men	**77,192**	**22,000**	**45,438**	**7,710**	**2,045**
Under age 25	12,842	11,929	780	124	7
Aged 25 to 39	18,686	6,202	10,714	1,732	38
Aged 25 to 29	5,672	3,011	2,355	299	7
Aged 30 to 34	6,213	1,788	3,825	586	15
Aged 35 to 39	6,801	1,403	4,534	847	16
Aged 40 or older	45,664	3,869	33,942	5,855	2,000
Total non-Hispanic white women	**82,115**	**17,683**	**45,380**	**10,484**	**8,567**
Under age 25	12,489	10,784	1,466	224	13
Aged 25 to 39	18,821	4,025	12,246	2,398	155
Aged 25 to 29	5,700	2,096	3,030	549	26
Aged 30 to 34	6,281	1,205	4,299	727	51
Aged 35 to 39	6,840	724	4,917	1,122	78
Aged 40 or older	50,805	2,873	31,666	7,864	8,401
PERCENT DISTRIBUTION					
Total non-Hispanic white men	**100.0%**	**28.5%**	**58.9%**	**10.0%**	**2.6%**
Under age 25	100.0	92.9	6.1	1.0	0.1
Aged 25 to 39	100.0	33.2	57.3	9.3	0.2
Aged 25 to 29	100.0	53.1	41.5	5.3	0.1
Aged 30 to 34	100.0	28.8	61.6	9.4	0.2
Aged 35 to 39	100.0	20.6	66.7	12.5	0.2
Aged 40 or older	100.0	8.5	74.3	12.8	4.4
Total non-Hispanic white women	**100.0**	**21.5**	**55.3**	**12.8**	**10.4**
Under age 25	100.0	86.3	11.7	1.8	0.1
Aged 25 to 39	100.0	21.4	65.1	12.7	0.8
Aged 25 to 29	100.0	36.8	53.2	9.6	0.5
Aged 30 to 34	100.0	19.2	68.4	11.6	0.8
Aged 35 to 39	100.0	10.6	71.9	16.4	1.1
Aged 40 or older	100.0	5.7	62.3	15.5	16.5

Note: Non-Hispanic whites include only those identifying themselves as being white alone and not Hispanic.
Source: Bureau of the Census, Current Population Survey Annual Social and Economic Supplement, America's Families and Living Arrangements: 2004, detailed tables, Internet site http://www.census.gov/population/www/socdemo/hh-fam/cps2004.html; calculations by New Strategist

7

Population

■ Generation X numbers 49 million, a figure that includes all those born between 1965 and 1976 (aged 29 to 40 in 2005). Generation Xers account for 17 percent of the population.

■ In the 15 years between 2005 and 2020, the number of people aged 45 to 54 (Generation Xers will be aged 44 to 55 in 2020) will shrink by 4 percent—a decrease of more than 1 million people.

■ Sixty-three percent of Generation Xers are non-Hispanic white, according to 2005 projections by the Census Bureau. Within Generation X, Hispanics outnumber blacks. Seventeen percent of Gen Xers are Hispanic, 13 percent are black, and 6 percent are Asian.

■ A substantial 12 percent of all Americans in 2004 were foreign-born, but the proportion is an even higher 19 percent among 25-to-39-year-olds (Gen Xers were aged 28 to 39 in 2004).

■ The diversity of Generation X varies greatly by state of residence. In Maine, North Dakota, and Vermont, at least 95 percent of Generation Xers are non-Hispanic white. But in California, the most populous state, the figure is just 39 percent.

Generation X Is Sandwiched between Larger Generations

Age groups shrink when Generation X moves in.

Generation X numbers 49 million, a figure that includes all those born between 1965 and 1976 (aged 29 to 40 in 2005). Generation Xers account for 17 percent of the total population. They are surrounded by the two largest generations: the 78 million Boomers (26 percent of the population) and the 75 million Millennials (25 percent).

As Generation X moves through the age structure, age groups shrink. Between 2000 and 2005, the number of 35-to-39-year-olds fell 8 percent as Generation Xers replaced Boomers in the age group. The number of 30-to-34-year-olds fell 3 percent during those years.

In the 15 years between 2005 and 2020, the number of people aged 45 to 54 (Generation Xers will be aged 44 to 55 in 2020) will shrink by 4 percent—a decrease of more than 1 million people. In 2020, Generation X will account for 15 percent of the population, outnumbering only the generations preceding the Baby Boom.

■ Because Generation X is small, the nation focuses more of its attention on Boomers and Millennials. But Generation X is about to enter the peak earning and spending years and should not be ignored.

The middle-aged population will shrink during the next 15 years

(percent change in number of people by age, 2005–20)

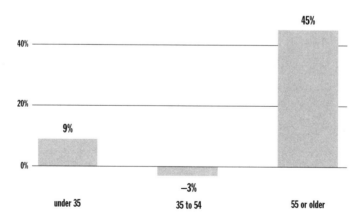

Table 7.1 Population by Age and Generation, 2005

(number and percent distribution of people by age and generation, 2005; numbers in thousands)

	number	percent distribution
Total people	**295,507**	**100.0%**
Under age 5	20,495	6.9
Aged 5 to 9	19,467	6.6
Aged 10 to 14	20,838	7.1
Aged 15 to 19	21,172	7.2
Aged 20 to 24	20,823	7.0
Aged 25 to 39	60,469	20.5
Aged 25 to 29	19,753	6.7
Aged 30 to 34	19,847	6.7
Aged 35 to 39	20,869	7.1
Aged 40 to 44	22,735	7.7
Aged 45 to 49	22,453	7.6
Aged 50 to 54	19,983	6.8
Aged 55 to 59	17,359	5.9
Aged 60 to 64	13,017	4.4
Aged 65 to 69	10,123	3.4
Aged 70 to 74	8,500	2.9
Aged 75 to 79	7,376	2.5
Aged 80 to 84	5,576	1.9
Aged 85 or older	5,120	1.7
Total people	**295,507**	**100.0**
Post-Millennial (under age 11)	43,978	14.9
Millennial (aged 11 to 28)	74,775	25.3
Generation X (aged 29 to 40)	48,985	16.6
Baby Boom (aged 41 to 59)	78,056	26.4
Older Americans (aged 60 or older)	49,713	16.8

Source: Bureau of the Census, State Interim Population Projections by Age and Sex: 2004–2030, Internet site http://www.census .gov/population/www/projections/projectionsagesex.html; calculations by New Strategist

Table 7.2 Population by Age and Sex, 2005

(number of people by age and sex, and sex ratio by age, 2005; numbers in thousands)

	total	female	male	sex ratio
Total people	**295,507**	**150,394**	**145,113**	**96**
Under age 5	20,495	10,024	10,471	104
Aged 5 to 9	19,467	9,512	9,954	105
Aged 10 to 14	20,838	10,167	10,670	105
Aged 15 to 19	21,172	10,310	10,862	105
Aged 20 to 24	20,823	10,166	10,657	105
Aged 25 to 39	60,469	30,016	30,453	101
Aged 25 to 29	19,753	9,737	10,016	103
Aged 30 to 34	19,847	9,860	9,987	101
Aged 35 to 39	20,869	10,420	10,449	100
Aged 40 to 44	22,735	11,452	11,282	99
Aged 45 to 49	22,453	11,377	11,076	97
Aged 50 to 54	19,983	10,212	9,771	96
Aged 55 to 59	17,359	8,944	8,415	94
Aged 60 to 64	13,017	6,814	6,203	91
Aged 65 to 69	10,123	5,412	4,712	87
Aged 70 to 74	8,500	4,697	3,804	81
Aged 75 to 79	7,376	4,282	3,094	72
Aged 80 to 84	5,576	3,459	2,117	61
Aged 85 or older	5,120	3,548	1,572	44

Note: The sex ratio is the number of males per 100 females.
Source: Bureau of the Census, State Interim Population Projections by Age and Sex: 2004–2030, Internet site http://www.census
.gov/population/www/projections/projectionsagesex.html; calculations by New Strategist

Table 7.3 Population by Age, 2000 and 2005

(number of people by age, April 1, 2000, and July 1, 2005; percent change 2000–05; numbers in thousands)

	2000	2005	percent change
Total people	**281,422**	**295,507**	**5.0%**
Under age 5	19,176	20,495	6.9
Aged 5 to 9	20,550	19,467	–5.3
Aged 10 to 14	20,528	20,838	1.5
Aged 15 to 19	20,220	21,172	4.7
Aged 20 to 24	18,964	20,823	9.8
Aged 25 to 29	19,381	19,753	1.9
Aged 30 to 34	20,510	19,847	–3.2
Aged 35 to 39	22,707	20,869	–8.1
Aged 40 to 44	22,442	22,735	1.3
Aged 45 to 49	20,092	22,453	11.7
Aged 50 to 54	17,586	19,983	13.6
Aged 55 to 59	13,469	17,359	28.9
Aged 60 to 64	10,805	13,017	20.5
Aged 65 to 69	9,534	10,123	6.2
Aged 70 to 74	8,857	8,500	–4.0
Aged 75 to 79	7,416	7,376	–0.5
Aged 80 to 84	4,945	5,576	12.7
Aged 85 or older	4,240	5,120	20.8

Source: Bureau of the Census, State Interim Population Projections by Age and Sex: 2004–2030, Internet site http://www.census .gov/population/www/projections/projectionsagesex.html; calculations by New Strategist

Table 7.4 Population by Age, 2005 to 2020

(number of people by age, 2005 to 2020; percent change, 2005–20; numbers in thousands)

	2005	2010	2015	2020	percent change 2005–20
Total people	**295,507**	**308,936**	**322,366**	**335,805**	**13.6%**
Under age 5	20,495	21,426	22,358	22,932	11.9
Aged 5 to 9	19,467	20,706	21,623	22,564	15.9
Aged 10 to 14	20,838	19,767	20,984	21,914	5.2
Aged 15 to 19	21,172	21,336	20,243	21,478	1.4
Aged 20 to 24	20,823	21,676	21,810	20,751	–0.3
Aged 25 to 29	19,753	21,375	22,195	22,361	13.2
Aged 30 to 34	19,847	20,271	21,858	22,704	14.4
Aged 35 to 39	20,869	20,137	20,543	22,143	6.1
Aged 40 to 44	22,735	20,984	20,250	20,673	–9.1
Aged 45 to 49	22,453	22,654	20,926	20,219	–9.9
Aged 50 to 54	19,983	22,173	22,376	20,702	3.6
Aged 55 to 59	17,359	19,507	21,649	21,876	26.0
Aged 60 to 64	13,017	16,679	18,761	20,856	60.2
Aged 65 to 69	10,123	12,172	15,621	17,618	74.0
Aged 70 to 74	8,500	9,097	10,987	14,161	66.6
Aged 75 to 79	7,376	7,186	7,761	9,450	28.1
Aged 80 to 84	5,576	5,665	5,600	6,134	10.0
Aged 85 or older	5,120	6,123	6,822	7,269	42.0

Source: Bureau of the Census, State Interim Population Projections by Age and Sex: 2004–2030, Internet site http://www.census .gov/population/www/projections/projectionsagesex.html; calculations by New Strategist

Table 7.5 Population by Generation, 2005 and 2020

(number and percent distribution of people by generation, 2005 and 2020; percent change in number, 2005–20; numbers in thousands)

	2005			2020		percent change 2005–20
	number	percent distribution		number	percent distribution	
Total people	**295,507**	**100.0%**	**Total people**	**335,805**	**100.0%**	**13.6%**
Post-Millennial (under 11)	43,978	14.9	Post-Millennial (under 26)	113,942	33.9	159.1
Millennial (11 to 28)	74,775	25.3	Millennial (26 to 43)	79,639	23.7	6.5
Generation X (29 to 40)	48,985	16.6	Generation X (44 to 55)	49,219	14.7	0.5
Baby Boom (41 to 59)	78,056	26.4	Baby Boom (56 to 74)	70,151	20.9	–10.1
Older Americans (60+)	49,713	16.8	Older Americans (75+)	22,853	6.8	–54.0

Source: Bureau of the Census, State Interim Population Projections by Age and Sex: 2004–2030, Internet site http://www.census .gov/population/www/projections/projectionsagesex.html; calculations by New Strategist

Generation X Is More Diverse than Average

The generation is less diverse than children and young adults, however.

Sixty-three percent of Generation Xers are non-Hispanic white, according to 2005 projections by the Census Bureau. This figure is smaller than the 67 percent share of the population as a whole, but larger than the share among the youngest Americans—only 56 percent of children under age 5 are non-Hispanic white. Older generations of Americans are much less diverse than Generation X. Among Boomers, 73 percent are non-Hispanic white. Among Americans aged 60 or older, the proportion is 81 percent.

Within Generation X, Hispanics outnumber blacks. Seventeen percent of Gen Xers are Hispanic, 13 percent are black, and 6 percent are Asian. Generation Xers account for only 16 percent of the non-Hispanic white population. They account for a larger 17 percent of blacks, 20 percent of Hispanics, and 22 percent of Asians. Among Hispanics, Generation Xers outnumber Boomers.

■ The differing racial and ethnic makeup of older versus younger generations of Americans may create political tension in the years ahead.

Fewer than two-thirds of Generation Xers are non-Hispanic white

(non-Hispanic white share of population by generation, 2005)

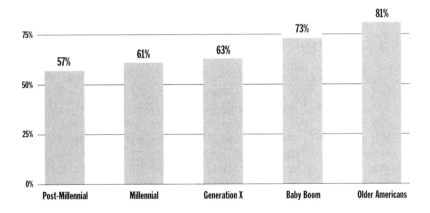

Table 7.6 Population by Age, Race, and Hispanic Origin, 2005

(number and percent distribution of people by age, race, and Hispanic origin, 2005; numbers in thousands)

	total	Asian	black	Hispanic	non-Hispanic white
Total people	**295,507**	**12,419**	**38,056**	**41,801**	**198,451**
Under age 5	20,495	833	3,113	4,397	11,528
Aged 5 to 9	19,467	763	2,941	3,892	11,330
Aged 10 to 14	20,838	787	3,332	3,853	12,370
Aged 15 to 19	21,172	815	3,306	3,576	13,013
Aged 20 to 24	20,823	898	3,078	3,604	12,836
Aged 25 to 39	60,469	3,291	8,217	10,745	37,421
Aged 25 to 29	19,753	985	2,807	3,781	11,881
Aged 30 to 34	19,847	1,190	2,678	3,666	12,060
Aged 35 to 39	20,869	1,117	2,732	3,297	13,480
Aged 40 to 44	22,735	1,033	2,892	2,926	15,606
Aged 45 to 49	22,453	948	2,736	2,375	16,113
Aged 50 to 54	19,983	828	2,276	1,823	14,812
Aged 55 to 59	17,359	685	1,788	1,393	13,289
Aged 60 to 64	13,017	480	1,250	978	10,161
Aged 65 to 69	10,123	370	972	745	7,931
Aged 70 to 74	8,500	275	767	571	6,811
Aged 75 to 79	7,376	200	591	433	6,097
Aged 80 to 84	5,576	125	407	275	4,733
Aged 85 or older	5,120	87	390	216	4,398

PERCENT DISTRIBUTION BY RACE AND HISPANIC ORIGIN

Total people	**100.0%**	**4.2%**	**12.9%**	**14.1%**	**67.2%**
Under age 5	100.0	4.1	15.2	21.5	56.2
Aged 5 to 9	100.0	3.9	15.1	20.0	58.2
Aged 10 to 14	100.0	3.8	16.0	18.5	59.4
Aged 15 to 19	100.0	3.8	15.6	16.9	61.5
Aged 20 to 24	100.0	4.3	14.8	17.3	61.6
Aged 25 to 39	100.0	5.4	13.6	17.8	61.9
Aged 25 to 29	100.0	5.0	14.2	19.1	60.1
Aged 30 to 34	100.0	6.0	13.5	18.5	60.8
Aged 35 to 39	100.0	5.4	13.1	15.8	64.6
Aged 40 to 44	100.0	4.5	12.7	12.9	68.6
Aged 45 to 49	100.0	4.2	12.2	10.6	71.8
Aged 50 to 54	100.0	4.1	11.4	9.1	74.1
Aged 55 to 59	100.0	3.9	10.3	8.0	76.6
Aged 60 to 64	100.0	3.7	9.6	7.5	78.1
Aged 65 to 69	100.0	3.7	9.6	7.4	78.3
Aged 70 to 74	100.0	3.2	9.0	6.7	80.1
Aged 75 to 79	100.0	2.7	8.0	5.9	82.7
Aged 80 to 84	100.0	2.2	7.3	4.9	84.9
Aged 85 or older	100.0	1.7	7.6	4.2	85.9

Note: Numbers will not add to total because Asians and blacks include those who identified themselves as being of the respective race alone and those who identified themselves as being of the race in combination with one or more other races, and because Hispanics may be of any race. Non-Hispanic whites include only those who identified themselves as being white alone and not Hispanic.
Source: Bureau of the Census, U.S. Interim Projections by Age, Sex, Race, and Hispanic Origin, Internet site http://www.census .gov/ipc/www/usinterimproj/; calculations by New Strategist

Table 7.7 Population by Generation, Race, and Hispanic Origin, 2005

(number and percent distribution of people by generation, race, and Hispanic origin, 2005; numbers in thousands)

	total	Asian	black	Hispanic	non-Hispanic white
Total people	**295,507**	**12,419**	**38,056**	**41,801**	**198,451**
Post-Millennial (under age 11)	43,978	1,751	6,680	9,058	25,223
Millennial (aged 11 to 28)	74,775	3,114	11,375	13,287	45,488
Generation X (aged 29 to 40)	48,985	2,735	6,522	8,353	30,772
Baby Boom (aged 41 to 59)	78,056	3,280	9,101	7,885	56,836
Older Americans (aged 60 or older)	49,713	1,538	4,377	3,218	40,132
PERCENT DISTRIBUTION BY RACE AND HISPANIC ORIGIN					
Total people	**100.0%**	**4.2%**	**12.9%**	**14.1%**	**67.2%**
Post-Millennial (under age 11)	100.0	4.0	15.2	20.6	57.4
Millennial (aged 11 to 28)	100.0	4.2	15.2	17.8	60.8
Generation X (aged 29 to 40)	100.0	5.6	13.3	17.1	62.8
Baby Boom (aged 41 to 59)	100.0	4.2	11.7	10.1	72.8
Older Americans (aged 60 or older)	100.0	3.1	8.8	6.5	80.7
PERCENT DISTRIBUTION BY GENERATION					
Total people	**100.0%**	**100.0%**	**100.0%**	**100.0%**	**100.0%**
Post-Millennial (under age 11)	14.9	14.1	17.6	21.7	12.7
Millennial (aged 11 to 28)	25.3	25.1	29.9	31.8	22.9
Generation X (aged 29 to 40)	16.6	22.0	17.1	20.0	15.5
Baby Boom (aged 41 to 59)	26.4	26.4	23.9	18.9	28.6
Older Americans (aged 60 or older)	16.8	12.4	11.5	7.7	20.2

Note: Numbers will not add to total because Asians and blacks include those who identified themselves as being of the respective race alone and those who identified themselves as being of the race in combination with one or more other races, and because Hispanics may be of any race. Non-Hispanic whites include only those who identified themselves as being white alone and not Hispanic.
Source: Bureau of the Census, U.S. Interim Projections by Age, Sex, Race, and Hispanic Origin, Internet site http://www.census .gov/ipc/www/usinterimproj/; calculations by New Strategist

Nearly One in Five Generation Xers Is Foreign-Born

Immigrants are making Generation X more diverse.

A substantial 12 percent of all Americans were foreign-born in 2004, but the proportion is an even higher 19 percent among 25-to-39-year-olds (Gen Xers were aged 28 to 39 in 2004). Among the 12 million 25-to-39-year-olds who were born in a foreign country, only 26 percent are naturalized citizens. The 25-to-39 age group accounts for 34 percent of the nation's foreign-born.

Among the foreign-born in the 25-to-39 age group, 47 percent are from Central America (a region that includes Mexico in these statistics). Twenty-five percent were born in Asia, and only 9 percent are from Europe. These figures differ greatly from those for the older foreign-born population. A smaller 26 percent of the foreign-born aged 40 or older are from Central America and a larger 19 percent are from Europe.

■ The foreign-born population adds to the multicultural mix, which is becoming a significant factor in American business and politics.

Nearly half of foreign-born 25-to-39-year-olds are from Central America

(percent distribution of foreign-born aged 25 to 39 by region of birth, 2004)

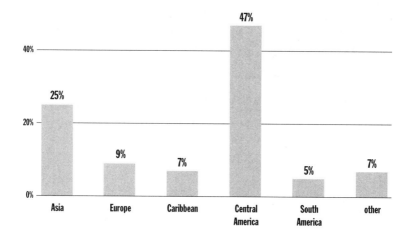

Table 7.8 Population by Age and Citizenship Status, 2004

(number and percent distribution of people by age and citizenship status, 2004; numbers in thousands)

	total	native born	foreign-born total	naturalized citizen	not a citizen
Total people	**288,280**	**254,037**	**34,244**	**13,128**	**21,116**
Under age 25	101,404	94,687	6,717	1,125	5,592
Aged 25 to 39	59,992	48,336	11,657	3,012	8,645
Aged 25 to 29	19,008	15,257	3,751	711	3,040
Aged 30 to 34	20,193	16,160	4,033	994	3,039
Aged 35 to 39	20,791	16,919	3,873	1,307	2,566
Aged 40 or older	126,887	111,014	15,870	8,990	6,880
PERCENT DISTRIBUTION BY CITIZENSHIP STATUS					
Total people	**100.0%**	**88.1%**	**11.9%**	**4.6%**	**7.3%**
Under age 25	100.0	93.4	6.6	1.1	5.5
Aged 25 to 39	100.0	80.6	19.4	5.0	14.4
Aged 25 to 29	100.0	80.3	19.7	3.7	16.0
Aged 30 to 34	100.0	80.0	20.0	4.9	15.0
Aged 35 to 39	100.0	81.4	18.6	6.3	12.3
Aged 40 or older	100.0	87.5	12.5	7.1	5.4
PERCENT DISTRIBUTION BY AGE					
Total people	**100.0%**	**100.0%**	**100.0%**	**100.0%**	**100.0%**
Under age 25	35.2	37.3	19.6	8.6	26.5
Aged 25 to 39	20.8	19.0	34.0	22.9	40.9
Aged 25 to 29	6.6	6.0	11.0	5.4	14.4
Aged 30 to 34	7.0	6.4	11.8	7.6	14.4
Aged 35 to 39	7.2	6.7	11.3	10.0	12.2
Aged 40 or older	44.0	43.7	46.3	68.5	32.6

Source: Bureau of the Census, Foreign Born Population of the United States, Current Population Survey, March 2004, Internet site http://www.census.gov/population/www/socdemo/foreign/ppl-176.html#cit; calculations by New Strategist

Table 7.9 Foreign-Born Population by Age and World Region of Birth, 2004

(number and percent distribution of people by age, foreign-born status, and region of birth, 2004; numbers in thousands)

		foreign-born							
		total	Asia	Europe	Latin America				
					total	Caribbean	Central America	South America	other
	total	total	Asia	Europe	total	Caribbean	Central America	South America	other
Total people	**288,280**	**34,244**	**8,685**	**4,661**	**18,314**	**3,323**	**12,924**	**2,066**	**2,584**
Under age 25	101,404	6,717	1,319	634	4,225	515	3,263	448	541
Aged 25 to 39	59,992	11,657	2,900	998	6,932	835	5,473	623	827
Aged 25 to 29	19,008	3,751	804	294	2,390	249	1,915	226	263
Aged 30 to 34	20,193	4,033	1,039	320	2,405	272	1,927	205	269
Aged 35 to 39	20,791	3,873	1,057	384	2,137	314	1,631	192	295
Aged 40 or older	126,887	15,870	4,466	3,030	7,157	1,974	4,187	995	1,218

PERCENT DISTRIBUTION OF FOREIGN-BORN BY REGION OF BIRTH

Total people	–	**100.0%**	**25.4%**	**13.6%**	**53.5%**	**9.7%**	**37.7%**	**6.0%**	**7.5%**
Under age 25	–	100.0	19.6	9.4	62.9	7.7	48.6	6.7	8.1
Aged 25 to 39	–	100.0	24.9	8.6	59.5	7.2	47.0	5.3	7.1
Aged 25 to 29	–	100.0	21.4	7.8	63.7	6.6	51.1	6.0	7.0
Aged 30 to 34	–	100.0	25.8	7.9	59.6	6.7	47.8	5.1	6.7
Aged 35 to 39	–	100.0	27.3	9.9	55.2	8.1	42.1	5.0	7.6
Aged 40 or older	–	100.0	28.1	19.1	45.1	12.4	26.4	6.3	7.7

PERCENT DISTRIBUTION BY AGE

Total people	**100.0%**	**100.0%**	**100.0%**	**100.0%**	**100.0%**	**100.0%**	**100.0%**	**100.0%**	**100.0%**
Under age 25	35.2	19.6	15.2	13.6	23.1	15.5	25.2	21.7	20.9
Aged 25 to 39	20.8	34.0	33.4	21.4	37.9	25.1	42.3	30.2	32.0
Aged 25 to 29	6.6	11.0	9.3	6.3	13.1	7.5	14.8	10.9	10.2
Aged 30 to 34	7.0	11.8	12.0	6.9	13.1	8.2	14.9	9.9	10.4
Aged 35 to 39	7.2	11.3	12.2	8.2	11.7	9.4	12.6	9.3	11.4
Aged 40 or older	44.0	46.3	51.4	65.0	39.1	59.4	32.4	48.2	47.1

Note: Central America includes Mexico in these statistics. "–" means not applicable.
Source: Bureau of the Census, Foreign Born Population of the United States, Current Population Survey, March 2004, Internet site http://www.census.gov/population/www/socdemo/foreign/ppl-176.html#cit; calculations by New Strategist

Many Recent Immigrants Are Generation Xers

Nearly four out of ten immigrants in 2004 were aged 25 to 39.

The number of legal immigrants admitted to the U.S. numbered over 900,000 in 2004. More than 375,000 were aged 25 to 39, accounting for 40 percent of the total. In fact, the 25-to-29, 30-to-34, and 35-to-39 age groups are the top three in their share of immigrants admitted to the U.S. each year as eager foreign workers seek better opportunities for themselves and their families.

Thirteen percent of immigrants to the U.S. in 2004 were aged 25 to 29. An even larger 15 percent were aged 30 to 34—the largest share of any five-year age group. Another 11 percent of immigrants were aged 35 to 39. The figure declines with age. Just 5 percent of new immigrants were aged 65 or older.

■ Because most immigrants are children and young adults, immigration has a much greater impact on the diversity of younger Americans than on the middle-aged or older population.

Immigrants aged 25 to 39 accounted for 40 percent of the 2004 total

(percent distribution of immigrants by age, 2004)

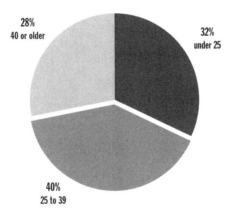

28%
40 or older

32%
under 25

40%
25 to 39

Table 7.10 Immigrants by Age, 2004

(number and percent distribution of immigrants by age, 2004)

	number	percent distribution
Total immigrants	**946,142**	**100.0%**
Under age 1	7,807	0.8
Aged 1 to 4	22,932	2.4
Aged 5 to 9	48,181	5.1
Aged 10 to 14	58,821	6.2
Aged 15 to 19	78,069	8.3
Aged 20 to 24	86,278	9.1
Aged 25 to 39	375,578	39.7
Aged 25 to 29	124,406	13.1
Aged 30 to 34	143,921	15.2
Aged 35 to 39	107,251	11.3
Aged 40 to 44	76,404	8.1
Aged 45 to 49	55,223	5.8
Aged 50 to 54	39,661	4.2
Aged 55 to 59	30,037	3.2
Aged 60 to 64	23,829	2.5
Aged 65 to 74	32,346	3.4
Aged 75 or older	10,936	1.2

Note: Numbers may not sum to total because "age not stated" is not shown.
Source: Office of Immigration Statistics, 2004 Yearbook of Immigration Statistics, Internet site http://uscis.gov/graphics/shared/statistics/yearbook/YrBk04Im.htm; calculations by New Strategist

Many Americans Do Not Speak English at Home

Most are Spanish speakers, but many also speak English.

Nearly 50 million Americans speak a language other than English at home, according to the Census Bureau's 2004 American Community Survey—19 percent of the population aged 5 or older. Among those who do not speak English at home, 61 percent speak Spanish.

The percentage of Americans who do not speak English at home does not vary much by age—19 percent of school children, 20 percent of working-age adults, and 13 percent of the elderly. But the languages spoken by each age group at home do vary by age. Fully 71 percent of children aged 5 to 17 who do not speak English at home are Spanish speakers. The proportion is a smaller 61 percent among adults aged 18 to 64, and falls to just 43 percent among people aged 65 or older. Thirty-seven percent of the elderly who do not speak English at home speak another Indo-European language, and 17 percent speak an Asian language.

Among school children, most of those who do not speak English at home are able to speak English "very well." Only 29 percent of the Spanish speakers aged 5 to 17, for example, cannot speak English very well. Among working-age adults, a much larger 53 percent of the Spanish speakers cannot speak English very well. Among people aged 65 or older, most of those who speak Spanish or an Asian language at home cannot speak English very well.

■ The language barrier is a bigger problem for adults than for school children.

Few children who speak Spanish at home cannot speak English "very well"

(percent of people aged 5 or older who speak Spanish at home and do not speak English "very well," by age, 2004)

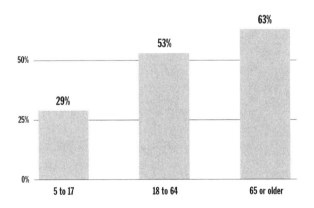

Table 7.11 Language Spoken at Home by Age, 2004

(number and percent distribution of people aged 5 or older who speak a language other than English at home by language spoken at home and ability to speak English "very well," by age, 2004; numbers in thousands)

	total		aged 5 to 17		aged 18 to 64		aged 65 or older	
	number	percent distribution	number	percent distribution	number	percent distribution	number	percent distribution
Total, aged 5 or older	**265,683**	**100.0%**	**52,916**	**100.0%**	**178,562**	**100.0%**	**34,205**	**100.0%**
Speak only English at home	216,050	81.3	42,939	81.1	143,420	80.3	29,691	86.8
Speak a language other than English at home	49,633	18.7	9,977	18.9	35,142	19.7	4,514	13.2
Speak English less than "very well"	22,305	8.4	2,774	5.2	16,944	9.5	2,587	7.6
Total who speak a language other than English at home	**49,633**	**100.0**	**9,977**	**100.0**	**35,142**	**100.0**	**4,514**	**100.0**
Speak Spanish at home	30,522	61.5	7,103	71.2	21,498	61.2	1,921	42.6
Speak other Indo-European language at home	9,634	19.4	1,440	14.4	6,530	18.6	1,664	36.9
Speak Asian or Pacific Island language at home	7,614	15.3	1,116	11.2	5,730	16.3	769	17.0
Speak other language at home	1,863	3.8	318	3.2	1,384	3.9	161	3.6
Speak Spanish at home	**30,522**	**100.0**	**7,103**	**100.0**	**21,498**	**100.0**	**1,921**	**100.0**
Speak English less than "very well"	14,637	48.0	2,075	29.2	11,358	52.8	1,203	62.6
Speak other Indo-European language at home	**9,634**	**100.0**	**1,440**	**100.0**	**6,530**	**100.0**	**1,664**	**100.0**
Speak English less than "very well"	3,317	34.4	341	23.6	2,237	34.3	740	44.4
Speak Asian or Pacific Island language at home	**7,614**	**100.0**	**1,116**	**100.0**	**5,730**	**100.0**	**769**	**100.0**
Speak English less than "very well"	3,807	50.0	306	27.4	2,932	51.2	569	74.0
Speak other language at home	**1,863**	**100.0**	**318**	**100.0**	**1,384**	**100.0**	**161**	**100.0**
Speak English less than "very well"	545	29.3	53	16.6	417	30.1	75	46.7

Source: Bureau of the Census, 2004 American Community Survey Data Profile, Internet site http://factfinder.census.gov/servlet/ DatasetMainPageServlet?_program=ACS&_submenuId=datasets_2&_lang=en&_ts=; calculations by New Strategist

The Largest Share of Generation Xers Lives in the South

Generation X accounts for only 14 percent of the population of Montana, but for 21 percent of the population of the District of Columbia.

The South is home to the largest share of the population and, consequently, to the largest share of Generation X. The Census Bureau's 2004 American Community Survey found 36 percent of Gen Xers living in the South, where they accounted for 17 percent of the population.

The diversity of Generation X varies greatly by state of residence. In Maine, North Dakota, and Vermont, at least 95 percent of people aged 28 to 39 are non-Hispanic white. But in California, the most populous state, the figure is just 39 percent. In Texas, only 46 percent of 28-to-39-year-olds are non-Hispanic white. Hawaii, New Mexico, and the District of Columbia also have minority majorities in the 28-to-39 age group.

Because of immigration and higher fertility rates, Hispanics outnumber blacks within Generation X in many states. In California, 38 percent of 28-to-39-year-olds are Hispanic—almost equal to the 39 percent non-Hispanic white share. Fourteen percent of Gen Xers in California are Asian, and 6 percent are black. In other states with large Hispanic populations, such as Texas and Florida, Hispanic Gen Xers also greatly outnumber blacks. Even in states such as Illinois, Hispanics have the edge, 17 versus 13 percent. In most southern states, however, black Gen Xers still greatly outnumber Hispanics.

■ Although Gen Xers are more diverse in some states than others, the nation's growing racial and ethnic diversity is influencing young adults everywhere.

In California, diversity is the rule among Generation Xers

(percent distribution of people aged 28 to 39 in California by race and Hispanic origin, 2004)

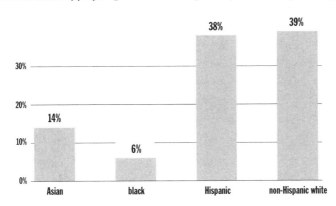

Table 7.12 Population by Age and Region, 2004

(number and percent distribution of people by age and region of residence, 2004; numbers in thousands)

	total	Northeast	Midwest	South	West
Total people	**285,692**	**52,865**	**63,910**	**103,021**	**65,896**
Under age 25	99,157	17,147	22,111	35,931	23,968
Aged 25 to 39	59,386	10,814	12,933	21,447	14,192
Aged 25 to 29	18,771	3,175	4,148	6,856	4,593
Aged 30 to 34	19,921	3,552	4,282	7,257	4,830
Aged 35 to 39	20,693	4,086	4,503	7,334	4,770
Aged 40 or older	127,148	24,904	28,866	45,643	27,735
PERCENT DISTRIBUTION BY AGE					
Total people	**100.0%**	**100.0%**	**100.0%**	**100.0%**	**100.0%**
Under age 25	34.7	32.4	34.6	34.9	36.4
Aged 25 to 39	20.8	20.5	20.2	20.8	21.5
Aged 25 to 29	6.6	6.0	6.5	6.7	7.0
Aged 30 to 34	7.0	6.7	6.7	7.0	7.3
Aged 35 to 39	7.2	7.7	7.0	7.1	7.2
Aged 40 or older	44.5	47.1	45.2	44.3	42.1
PERCENT DISTRIBUTION BY REGION					
Total people	**100.0%**	**18.5%**	**22.4%**	**36.1%**	**23.1%**
Under age 25	100.0	17.3	22.3	36.2	24.2
Aged 25 to 39	100.0	18.2	21.8	36.1	23.9
Aged 25 to 29	100.0	16.9	22.1	36.5	24.5
Aged 30 to 34	100.0	17.8	21.5	36.4	24.2
Aged 35 to 39	100.0	19.7	21.8	35.4	23.0
Aged 40 or older	100.0	19.6	22.7	35.9	21.8

Source: Bureau of the Census, 2004 American Community Survey, Internet site http://factfinder.census.gov/servlet/ DatasetMainPageServlet?_program=ACS&_lang=en&_ts=143547961449; calculations by New Strategist

Table 7.13 **Population by Generation and Region, 2004**

(number and percent distribution of people by generation and region of residence, 2004; numbers in thousands)

	total	Northeast	Midwest	South	West
Total people	**285,692**	**52,865**	**63,910**	**103,021**	**65,896**
Post-Millennial (under age 10)	39,667	6,778	8,693	14,542	9,655
Millennial (aged 10 to 27)	70,753	12,274	15,907	25,503	17,069
Generation X (aged 28 to 39)	48,123	8,908	10,445	17,334	11,437
Baby Boom (aged 40 to 58)	77,079	14,885	17,457	27,503	17,235
Older Americans (aged 59 or older)	50,069	10,020	11,409	18,140	10,500
PERCENT DISTRIBUTION BY GENERATION					
Total people	**100.0%**	**100.0%**	**100.0%**	**100.0%**	**100.0%**
Post-Millennial (under age 10)	13.9	12.8	13.6	14.1	14.7
Millennial (aged 10 to 27)	24.8	23.2	24.9	24.8	25.9
Generation X (aged 28 to 39)	16.8	16.9	16.3	16.8	17.4
Baby Boom (aged 40 to 58)	27.0	28.2	27.3	26.7	26.2
Older Americans (aged 59 or older)	17.5	19.0	17.9	17.6	15.9
PERCENT DISTRIBUTION BY REGION					
Total people	**100.0%**	**18.5%**	**22.4%**	**36.1%**	**23.1%**
Post-Millennial (under age 10)	100.0	17.1	21.9	36.7	24.3
Millennial (aged 10 to 27)	100.0	17.3	22.5	36.0	24.1
Generation X (aged 28 to 39)	100.0	18.5	21.7	36.0	23.8
Baby Boom (aged 40 to 58)	100.0	19.3	22.6	35.7	22.4
Older Americans (aged 59 or older)	100.0	20.0	22.8	36.2	21.0

Source: Bureau of the Census, 2004 American Community Survey, Internet site http://factfinder.census.gov/servlet/ DatasetMainPageServlet?_program=ACS&_lang=en&_ts=143547961449; calculations by New Strategist

Table 7.14 Generation X by Region, Race, and Hispanic Origin, 2004

(number and percent distribution of people aged 28 to 39 by region of residence, race, and Hispanic origin, 2004; numbers in thousands)

	total aged 28 to 39	Asian	black	Hispanic	non-Hispanic white
United States	**48,123**	**2,657**	**5,860**	**7,959**	**30,769**
Northeast	8,908	590	1,024	1,139	6,019
Midwest	10,445	344	1,063	728	8,227
South	17,334	562	3,253	2,740	10,571
West	11,437	1,161	521	3,352	5,952
PERCENT DISTRIBUTION BY RACE AND HISPANIC ORIGIN					
United States	**100.0%**	**5.5%**	**12.2%**	**16.5%**	**63.9%**
Northeast	100.0	6.6	11.5	12.8	67.6
Midwest	100.0	3.3	10.2	7.0	78.8
South	100.0	3.2	18.8	15.8	61.0
West	100.0	10.1	4.6	29.3	52.0
PERCENT DISTRIBUTION BY REGION					
United States	**100.0%**	**100.0%**	**100.0%**	**100.0%**	**100.0%**
Northeast	18.5	22.2	17.5	14.3	19.6
Midwest	21.7	12.9	18.1	9.1	26.7
South	36.0	21.1	55.5	34.4	34.4
West	23.8	43.7	8.9	42.1	19.3

Note: Blacks and Asians are those who identify themselves as being of the respective race alone. Non-Hispanic whites are those who identify themselves as being white alone and not Hispanic. Numbers will not sum to total because Hispanics may be of any race and not all races are shown.
Source: Bureau of the Census, 2004 American Community Survey, Internet site http://factfinder.census.gov/servlet/ DatasetMainPageServlet?_program=ACS&_lang=en&_ts=143547961449; calculations by New Strategist

Table 7.15 State Populations by Age, 2004

(number of people aged 25 to 39 by state of residence, 2004; numbers in thousands)

| | total population | aged 25 to 39 | | | |
		total	25 to 29	30 to 34	35 to 39
United States	**285,692**	**59,386**	**18,771**	**19,921**	**20,693**
Alabama	4,415	894	291	291	311
Alaska	636	121	36	42	44
Arizona	5,634	1,176	396	400	380
Arkansas	2,676	530	179	175	177
California	35,055	7,720	2,435	2,638	2,646
Colorado	4,499	1,010	330	355	324
Connecticut	3,389	668	181	216	271
Delaware	805	167	51	56	59
District of Columbia	518	146	57	49	41
Florida	16,990	3,216	971	1,072	1,172
Georgia	8,581	1,991	608	700	683
Hawaii	1,227	242	77	82	83
Idaho	1,360	263	90	86	87
Illinois	12,391	2,660	848	901	911
Indiana	6,059	1,224	399	409	416
Iowa	2,851	548	181	179	188
Kansas	2,653	536	182	169	185
Kentucky	4,031	837	274	279	284
Louisiana	4,381	858	285	278	295
Maine	1,279	234	65	75	94
Maryland	5,422	1,095	315	373	408
Massachusetts	6,201	1,349	402	443	504
Michigan	9,859	1,981	604	660	717
Minnesota	4,959	1,025	329	335	361
Mississippi	2,805	562	190	186	186
Missouri	5,586	1,104	356	364	384
Montana	902	160	54	49	56
Nebraska	1,697	335	114	110	110
Nevada	2,301	520	165	182	173
New Hampshire	1,262	244	65	81	98
New Jersey	8,503	1,717	462	578	676
New Mexico	1,863	360	119	117	124
New York	18,634	3,994	1,221	1,319	1,454
North Carolina	8,270	1,799	580	633	586
North Dakota	610	114	45	35	35
Ohio	11,154	2,202	692	737	773
Oklahoma	3,412	671	236	222	212
Oregon	3,514	740	235	253	252
Pennsylvania	11,958	2,279	676	741	862
Rhode Island	1,037	216	70	66	81

(continued)

	total population	aged 25 to 39			
		total	25 to 29	30 to 34	35 to 39
South Carolina	4,060	822	269	274	279
South Dakota	741	139	49	43	47
Tennessee	5,748	1,221	389	419	413
Texas	21,912	4,772	1,588	1,630	1,554
Utah	2,349	523	226	164	133
Vermont	601	113	33	34	45
Virginia	7,224	1,525	466	509	550
Washington	6,063	1,270	399	433	438
West Virginia	1,770	341	107	110	124
Wisconsin	5,351	1,066	349	340	377
Wyoming	493	88	30	29	29

Source: Bureau of the Census, 2004 American Community Survey, Internet site http://factfinder.census.gov/servlet/ DatasetMainPageServlet?_program=ACS&_lang=en&_ts=143547961449; calculations by New Strategist

Table 7.16 Distribution of State Populations by Age, 2004

(percent distribution of people by state of residence and age, 2004)

	total population	aged 25 to 39			
		total	25 to 29	30 to 34	35 to 39
United States	**100.0%**	**20.8%**	**6.6%**	**7.0%**	**7.2%**
Alabama	100.0	20.2	6.6	6.6	7.0
Alaska	100.0	19.0	5.6	6.6	6.9
Arizona	100.0	20.9	7.0	7.1	6.7
Arkansas	100.0	19.8	6.7	6.5	6.6
California	100.0	22.0	6.9	7.5	7.5
Colorado	100.0	22.5	7.3	7.9	7.2
Connecticut	100.0	19.7	5.3	6.4	8.0
Delaware	100.0	20.7	6.4	7.0	7.3
District of Columbia	100.0	28.3	11.0	9.5	7.8
Florida	100.0	18.9	5.7	6.3	6.9
Georgia	100.0	23.2	7.1	8.2	8.0
Hawaii	100.0	19.7	6.3	6.7	6.8
Idaho	100.0	19.4	6.6	6.3	6.4
Illinois	100.0	21.5	6.8	7.3	7.3
Indiana	100.0	20.2	6.6	6.7	6.9
Iowa	100.0	19.2	6.3	6.3	6.6
Kansas	100.0	20.2	6.8	6.4	7.0
Kentucky	100.0	20.8	6.8	6.9	7.0
Louisiana	100.0	19.6	6.5	6.3	6.7
Maine	100.0	18.3	5.1	5.8	7.4
Maryland	100.0	20.2	5.8	6.9	7.5
Massachusetts	100.0	21.8	6.5	7.1	8.1
Michigan	100.0	20.1	6.1	6.7	7.3
Minnesota	100.0	20.7	6.6	6.8	7.3
Mississippi	100.0	20.0	6.8	6.6	6.6
Missouri	100.0	19.8	6.4	6.5	6.9
Montana	100.0	17.7	6.0	5.4	6.3
Nebraska	100.0	19.8	6.7	6.5	6.5
Nevada	100.0	22.6	7.2	7.9	7.5
New Hampshire	100.0	19.3	5.2	6.4	7.8
New Jersey	100.0	20.2	5.4	6.8	8.0
New Mexico	100.0	19.3	6.4	6.3	6.7
New York	100.0	21.4	6.6	7.1	7.8
North Carolina	100.0	21.8	7.0	7.7	7.1
North Dakota	100.0	18.7	7.4	5.7	5.7
Ohio	100.0	19.7	6.2	6.6	6.9
Oklahoma	100.0	19.7	6.9	6.5	6.2
Oregon	100.0	21.1	6.7	7.2	7.2
Pennsylvania	100.0	19.1	5.7	6.2	7.2
Rhode Island	100.0	20.9	6.7	6.4	7.8

(continued)

	total population	aged 25 to 39			
		total	25 to 29	30 to 34	35 to 39
South Carolina	100.0%	20.2%	6.6%	6.8%	6.9%
South Dakota	100.0	18.8	6.6	5.8	6.4
Tennessee	100.0	21.2	6.8	7.3	7.2
Texas	100.0	21.8	7.2	7.4	7.1
Utah	100.0	22.3	9.6	7.0	5.6
Vermont	100.0	18.8	5.6	5.7	7.5
Virginia	100.0	21.1	6.5	7.0	7.6
Washington	100.0	21.0	6.6	7.1	7.2
West Virginia	100.0	19.3	6.1	6.2	7.0
Wisconsin	100.0	19.9	6.5	6.3	7.1
Wyoming	100.0	17.8	6.1	5.8	5.9

Source: Bureau of the Census, 2004 American Community Survey, Internet site http://factfinder.census.gov/servlet/ DatasetMainPageServlet?_program=ACS&_lang=en&_ts=143547961449; calculations by New Strategist

Table 7.17 State Populations by Generation, 2004

(number of people by state of residence and generation, 2004; numbers in thousands)

	total population	post-Millennial (under age 10)	Millennial (10 to 27)	Generation X (28 to 39)	Baby Boom (40 to 58)	Older Americans (59 or older)
United States	**285,692**	**39,667**	**70,753**	**48,123**	**77,079**	**50,069**
Alabama	4,415	573	1,110	719	1,186	827
Alaska	636	96	179	100	192	69
Arizona	5,634	877	1,447	938	1,358	1,014
Arkansas	2,676	353	680	423	702	518
California	35,055	5,239	9,111	6,258	9,068	5,379
Colorado	4,499	640	1,162	812	1,229	655
Connecticut	3,389	434	766	559	986	644
Delaware	805	104	193	136	222	151
District of Columbia	518	64	116	112	132	94
Florida	16,990	2,140	3,874	2,633	4,479	3,865
Georgia	8,581	1,315	2,180	1,627	2,228	1,232
Hawaii	1,227	163	288	196	337	243
Idaho	1,360	204	367	209	357	223
Illinois	12,391	1,774	3,112	2,151	3,262	2,091
Indiana	6,059	864	1,535	984	1,614	1,062
Iowa	2,851	364	697	439	791	561
Kansas	2,653	375	672	427	709	470
Kentucky	4,031	535	968	672	1,122	734
Louisiana	4,381	630	1,159	687	1,172	733
Maine	1,279	140	290	195	399	255
Maryland	5,422	764	1,289	906	1,545	917
Massachusetts	6,201	789	1,399	1,108	1,777	1,128
Michigan	9,859	1,353	2,438	1,618	2,714	1,735
Minnesota	4,959	655	1,244	827	1,394	838
Mississippi	2,805	406	739	448	728	485
Missouri	5,586	739	1,386	891	1,528	1,043
Montana	902	106	222	127	269	177
Nebraska	1,697	235	433	267	457	305
Nevada	2,301	338	562	421	597	384
New Hampshire	1,262	154	293	205	389	221
New Jersey	8,503	1,146	1,975	1,440	2,398	1,545
New Mexico	1,863	267	480	288	500	328
New York	18,634	2,451	4,413	3,262	5,083	3,426
North Carolina	8,270	1,170	1,978	1,451	2,233	1,438
North Dakota	610	71	156	87	175	120
Ohio	11,154	1,483	2,705	1,787	3,104	2,075
Oklahoma	3,412	474	854	529	923	632
Oregon	3,514	456	858	600	957	643
Pennsylvania	11,958	1,472	2,754	1,873	3,371	2,487
Rhode Island	1,037	124	249	174	291	198

(continued)

	total population	post-Millennial (under age 10)	Millennial (10 to 27)	Generation X (28 to 39)	Baby Boom (40 to 58)	Older Americans (59 or older)
South Carolina	4,060	549	996	660	1,120	734
South Dakota	741	101	191	110	199	141
Tennessee	5,748	767	1,366	988	1,582	1,046
Texas	21,912	3,529	5,856	3,820	5,576	3,132
Utah	2,349	436	736	387	507	284
Vermont	601	68	135	93	189	115
Virginia	7,224	976	1,737	1,245	2,044	1,221
Washington	6,063	772	1,530	1,031	1,716	1,014
West Virginia	1,770	193	409	277	508	384
Wisconsin	5,351	680	1,336	857	1,510	968
Wyoming	493	60	126	70	149	88

Source: Bureau of the Census, 2004 American Community Survey, Internet site http://factfinder.census.gov/servlet/DatasetMainPageServlet?_program=ACS&_lang=en&_ts=143547961449; calculations by New Strategist

Table 7.18 Distribution of State Populations by Generation, 2004

(percent distribution of people by state of residence and generation, 2004)

	total population	post-Millennial (under age 10)	Millennial (10 to 27)	Generation X (28 to 39)	Baby Boom (40 to 58)	Older Americans (59 or older)
United States	**100.0%**	**13.9%**	**24.8%**	**16.8%**	**27.0%**	**17.5%**
Alabama	100.0	13.0	25.1	16.3	26.9	18.7
Alaska	100.0	15.2	28.2	15.7	30.2	10.8
Arizona	100.0	15.6	25.7	16.7	24.1	18.0
Arkansas	100.0	13.2	25.4	15.8	26.2	19.4
California	100.0	14.9	26.0	17.9	25.9	15.3
Colorado	100.0	14.2	25.8	18.0	27.3	14.6
Connecticut	100.0	12.8	22.6	16.5	29.1	19.0
Delaware	100.0	12.9	23.9	16.8	27.6	18.8
District of Columbia	100.0	12.3	22.4	21.7	25.6	18.1
Florida	100.0	12.6	22.8	15.5	26.4	22.7
Georgia	100.0	15.3	25.4	19.0	26.0	14.4
Hawaii	100.0	13.3	23.5	16.0	27.5	19.8
Idaho	100.0	15.0	27.0	15.4	26.3	16.4
Illinois	100.0	14.3	25.1	17.4	26.3	16.9
Indiana	100.0	14.3	25.3	16.2	26.6	17.5
Iowa	100.0	12.8	24.4	15.4	27.7	19.7
Kansas	100.0	14.1	25.3	16.1	26.7	17.7
Kentucky	100.0	13.3	24.0	16.7	27.8	18.2
Louisiana	100.0	14.4	26.5	15.7	26.8	16.7
Maine	100.0	11.0	22.6	15.2	31.2	19.9
Maryland	100.0	14.1	23.8	16.7	28.5	16.9
Massachusetts	100.0	12.7	22.6	17.9	28.7	18.2
Michigan	100.0	13.7	24.7	16.4	27.5	17.6
Minnesota	100.0	13.2	25.1	16.7	28.1	16.9
Mississippi	100.0	14.5	26.3	16.0	25.9	17.3
Missouri	100.0	13.2	24.8	15.9	27.3	18.7
Montana	100.0	11.8	24.6	14.1	29.8	19.6
Nebraska	100.0	13.8	25.5	15.7	26.9	18.0
Nevada	100.0	14.7	24.4	18.3	25.9	16.7
New Hampshire	100.0	12.2	23.2	16.3	30.8	17.5
New Jersey	100.0	13.5	23.2	16.9	28.2	18.2
New Mexico	100.0	14.3	25.8	15.5	26.8	17.6
New York	100.0	13.2	23.7	17.5	27.3	18.4
North Carolina	100.0	14.1	23.9	17.5	27.0	17.4
North Dakota	100.0	11.6	25.6	14.3	28.8	19.6
Ohio	100.0	13.3	24.3	16.0	27.8	18.6
Oklahoma	100.0	13.9	25.0	15.5	27.0	18.5
Oregon	100.0	13.0	24.4	17.1	27.2	18.3
Pennsylvania	100.0	12.3	23.0	15.7	28.2	20.8
Rhode Island	100.0	12.0	24.0	16.8	28.0	19.1

(continued)

	total population	post-Millennial (under age 10)	Millennial (10 to 27)	Generation X (28 to 39)	Baby Boom (40 to 58)	Older Americans (59 or older)
South Carolina	100.0%	13.5%	24.5%	16.3%	27.6%	18.1%
South Dakota	100.0	13.6	25.7	14.8	26.8	19.1
Tennessee	100.0	13.3	23.8	17.2	27.5	18.2
Texas	100.0	16.1	26.7	17.4	25.4	14.3
Utah	100.0	18.6	31.3	16.5	21.6	12.1
Vermont	100.0	11.3	22.5	15.4	31.5	19.1
Virginia	100.0	13.5	24.0	17.2	28.3	16.9
Washington	100.0	12.7	25.2	17.0	28.3	16.7
West Virginia	100.0	10.9	23.1	15.7	28.7	21.7
Wisconsin	100.0	12.7	25.0	16.0	28.2	18.1
Wyoming	100.0	12.2	25.6	14.1	30.2	17.8

Source: Bureau of the Census, 2004 American Community Survey, Internet site http://factfinder.census.gov/servlet/ DatasetMainPageServlet?_program=ACS&_lang=en&_ts=143547961449; calculations by New Strategist

Table 7.19 Generation X by State, Race, and Hispanic Origin, 2004

(number and percent distribution of people aged 28 to 39 by state of residence, race, and Hispanic origin, 2004; numbers in thousands)

| | number | | | | | percent distribution | | | | |
	total 28 to 39	Asian	black	Hispanic	non-Hispanic white	total	Asian	black	Hispanic	non-Hispanic white
United States	**48,123**	**2,657**	**5,860**	**7,959**	**30,769**	**100.0%**	**5.5%**	**12.2%**	**16.5%**	**63.9%**
Alabama	719	9	185	21	490	100.0	1.3	25.7	3.0	68.2
Alaska	100	5	4	5	70	100.0	5.3	4.0	5.5	70.6
Arizona	938	30	31	298	530	100.0	3.2	3.3	31.7	56.5
Arkansas	423	6	65	26	322	100.0	1.5	15.3	6.2	76.2
California	6,258	857	359	2,357	2,467	100.0	13.7	5.7	37.7	39.4
Colorado	812	27	31	170	580	100.0	3.3	3.8	21.0	71.5
Connecticut	559	29	56	70	394	100.0	5.2	10.0	12.5	70.6
Delaware	136	6	28	10	90	100.0	4.4	21.0	7.6	66.7
District of Columbia	112	5	49	12	41	100.0	4.4	43.9	10.6	36.9
Florida	2,633	80	421	625	1,501	100.0	3.0	16.0	23.7	57.0
Georgia	1,627	63	449	149	913	100.0	3.9	27.6	9.2	56.1
Hawaii	196	80	6	16	47	100.0	41.0	3.1	8.4	23.8
Idaho	209	2	–	20	180	100.0	1.1	–	9.6	86.3
Illinois	2,151	116	289	365	1,343	100.0	5.4	13.4	17.0	62.5
Indiana	984	17	83	57	825	100.0	1.7	8.4	5.8	83.8
Iowa	439	11	13	21	399	100.0	2.5	3.0	4.7	90.7
Kansas	427	15	24	34	342	100.0	3.4	5.7	7.9	80.0
Kentucky	672	9	48	15	601	100.0	1.3	7.2	2.2	89.3
Louisiana	687	12	215	23	433	100.0	1.7	31.3	3.4	63.0
Maine	195	2	2	1	189	100.0	1.1	1.0	0.8	97.0
Maryland	906	56	275	66	511	100.0	6.1	30.3	7.3	56.4
Massachusetts	1,108	73	67	99	843	100.0	6.6	6.0	9.0	76.1
Michigan	1,618	57	229	66	1,227	100.0	3.5	14.2	4.1	75.8
Minnesota	827	39	41	36	710	100.0	4.8	5.0	4.3	85.8
Mississippi	448	3	166	10	267	100.0	0.7	37.0	2.3	59.5
Missouri	891	21	103	27	741	100.0	2.3	11.6	3.0	83.2
Montana	127	–	–	3	117	100.0	–	–	2.1	91.9
Nebraska	267	7	12	23	225	100.0	2.7	4.4	8.7	84.5
Nevada	421	27	29	115	235	100.0	6.5	6.8	27.4	55.9
New Hampshire	205	6	2	5	193	100.0	2.9	1.1	2.5	94.1
New Jersey	1,440	140	190	259	832	100.0	9.8	13.2	18.0	57.8
New Mexico	288	7	7	134	113	100.0	2.5	2.3	46.5	39.0
New York	3,262	272	503	596	1,829	100.0	8.3	15.4	18.3	56.1
North Carolina	1,451	34	302	134	972	100.0	2.4	20.8	9.3	67.0
North Dakota	87	1	–	1	84	100.0	1.1	–	1.2	96.4
Ohio	1,787	38	213	48	1,489	100.0	2.1	11.9	2.7	83.3
Oklahoma	529	13	38	43	383	100.0	2.5	7.2	8.2	72.3
Oregon	600	30	12	73	456	100.0	5.0	1.9	12.2	76.1
Pennsylvania	1,873	59	193	86	1,515	100.0	3.2	10.3	4.6	80.9
Rhode Island	174	7	9	21	134	100.0	3.9	5.4	11.9	77.0

(continued)

	number					percent distribution				
	total 28 to 39	Asian	black	Hispanic	non-Hispanic white	total	Asian	black	Hispanic	non-Hispanic white
South Carolina	660	9	184	29	438	100.0%	1.3%	27.9%	4.4%	66.4%
South Dakota	110	1	2	3	104	100.0	0.8	1.4	2.6	94.8
Tennessee	988	18	166	39	760	100.0	1.8	16.8	4.0	76.9
Texas	3,820	158	414	1,436	1,772	100.0	4.1	10.8	37.6	46.4
Utah	387	10	4	50	320	100.0	2.5	0.9	13.0	82.6
Vermont	93	1	–	1	89	100.0	1.6	–	0.9	96.1
Virginia	1,245	79	237	97	822	100.0	6.4	19.1	7.8	66.0
Washington	1,031	84	38	105	773	100.0	8.2	3.7	10.1	75.0
West Virginia	277	2	11	2	255	100.0	0.8	3.9	0.8	92.1
Wisconsin	857	21	54	48	738	100.0	2.5	6.3	5.6	86.2
Wyoming	70	–	1	5	64	100.0	–	0.7	6.9	91.8

Note: Blacks and Asians are those who identify themselves as being of the respective race alone. Non-Hispanic whites are those who identify themselves as being white alone and not Hispanic. Numbers will not sum to total because Hispanics may be of any race and not all races are shown. "–" means number is less than 500 or sample is too small to make a reliable estimate.
Source: Bureau of the Census, 2004 American Community Survey, Internet site http://factfinder.census.gov/servlet/ DatasetMainPageServlet?_program=ACS&_lang=en&_ts=143547961449; calculations by New Strategist

8

Spending

■ The average household boosted its spending by 4 percent between 2000 and 2004, after adjusting for inflation. In contrast, the spending of householders aged 25 to 34 did not grow at all during those years, while the spending of householders aged 35 to 44 grew by a small 1.8 percent. (Generation X was aged 28 to 39 in 2004.)

■ The spending of households headed by people aged 25 to 34 almost matches spending by the average household. In 2004, householders aged 25 to 34 spent $42,701, slightly less than the $43,395 spent by the average household.

■ Households headed by people aged 35 to 44 spent 20 percent more than the average household in 2004—or $50,402. Householders aged 35 to 44 spend significantly more than average on items commonly purchased by parents with children under age 18.

Spending Is Unchanged for Householders Aged 25 to 34

Householders aged 35 to 44 increased their spending by less than 2 percent between 2000 and 2004.

The members of Generation X are cautious spenders. While the average household boosted its spending by 4 percent between 2000 and 2004, after adjusting for inflation, the spending of householders aged 25 to 34 did not increase at all and the spending of householders aged 35 to 44 increased by a below-average 1.8 percent. (Generation X was aged 28 to 39 in 2004.)

Householders aged 25 to 34 spent $42,701 in 2004—almost unchanged from their spending in 2000 and slightly less than the $43,395 spent by the average household in 2004. The 2000 to 2004 spending trends for this age group are mixed, with significant declines in spending on a variety of items such as new and used cars and trucks, fees and admissions to entertainment events, and reading material. They boosted their spending on alcoholic beverages, health care, and education.

Householders aged 35 to 44—the age group now filling with Generation X—spent $50,402 in 2004, only 1.8 percent more than they spent in 2000 after adjusting for inflation. Although the spending of this age group grew slightly between 2000 and 2004, householders aged 35 to 44 either cut or checked their spending on many discretionary items such as food away from home, furniture, and entertainment. That may be because the cost of necessities is rising. Out-of-pocket health insurance expenses for the age group increased 29 percent. Spending on electricity rose 9 percent, property tax spending climbed 14 percent, and vehicle insurance saw a 10 percent increase.

■ The economic slowdown of the past few years has forced many young adults to devote more of their household budget to necessities.

Generation Xers have cut back on many, but not all, discretionary items

(percent change in spending by householders aged 25 to 34 on selected items, 2000 to 2004; in 2004 dollars)

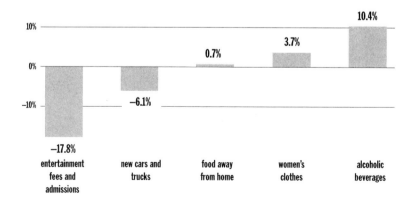

Table 8.1 Average Spending of Householders Aged 25 to 34, 2000 and 2004

(average annual spending of total consumer units and consumer units headed by people aged 25 to 34, 2000 and 2004; percent change, 2000–04; in 2004 dollars)

	total consumer units			aged 25 to 34		
	2004	2000	percent change 2000–04	2004	2000	percent change 2000–04
Number of consumer units (in 000s)	116,282	109,367	6.3%	19,439	18,887	2.9%
Average before-tax income	$54,453	$48,975	11.2	$52,484	$49,906	5.2
Average annual spending	43,395	41,731	4.0	42,701	42,718	0.0
FOOD	**5,781**	**5,658**	**2.2**	**5,705**	**5,770**	**–1.1**
Food at home	**3,347**	**3,314**	**1.0**	**3,155**	**3,237**	**–2.5**
Cereals and bakery products	461	497	–7.2	432	471	–8.2
Cereals and cereal products	154	171	–10.0	152	183	–17.0
Bakery products	307	326	–5.8	280	288	–2.9
Meats, poultry, fish, and eggs	880	872	0.9	812	845	–3.9
Beef	265	261	1.5	250	262	–4.6
Pork	181	183	–1.2	161	170	–5.3
Other meats	108	111	–2.5	97	107	–9.8
Poultry	156	159	–1.9	154	159	–3.2
Fish and seafood	128	121	6.1	112	112	0.1
Eggs	42	37	12.6	38	33	15.5
Dairy products	371	356	4.1	346	348	–0.5
Fresh milk and cream	144	144	0.2	147	147	0.0
Other dairy products	226	212	6.8	199	201	–0.9
Fruits and vegetables	561	571	–1.8	521	535	–2.7
Fresh fruits	187	179	4.6	168	160	4.9
Fresh vegetables	183	174	4.9	166	162	2.3
Processed fruits	110	126	–12.8	110	124	–11.3
Processed vegetables	82	92	–11.0	77	90	–14.4
Other food at home	1,075	1,017	5.7	1,043	1,038	0.5
Sugar and other sweets	128	128	–0.3	113	115	–1.9
Fats and oils	89	91	–2.2	78	84	–7.6
Miscellaneous foods	527	479	9.9	545	532	2.4
Nonalcoholic beverages	290	274	5.8	281	271	3.7
Food prepared by household on trips	41	44	–6.6	26	34	–23.5
Food away from home	**2,434**	**2,344**	**3.8**	**2,550**	**2,533**	**0.7**
ALCOHOLIC BEVERAGES	**459**	**408**	**12.5**	**522**	**473**	**10.4**
HOUSING	**13,918**	**13,513**	**3.0**	**14,379**	**14,314**	**0.5**
Shelter	**7,998**	**7,803**	**2.5**	**8,729**	**8,671**	**0.7**
Owned dwellings	5,324	5,048	5.5	4,700	4,543	3.4
Mortgage interest and charges	2,936	2,895	1.4	3,190	3,168	0.7
Property taxes	1,391	1,249	11.3	909	828	9.8
Maintenance, repairs, insurance, other expenses	997	905	10.2	601	547	9.8

	total consumer units			aged 25 to 34		
	2004	2000	percent change 2000–04	2004	2000	percent change 2000–04
Rented dwellings	$2,201	$2,231	–1.3%	$3,802	$3,854	–1.4%
Other lodging	473	524	–9.8	227	272	–16.6
Utilities, fuels, public services	**2,927**	**2,730**	**7.2**	**2,687**	**2,568**	**4.6**
Natural gas	424	337	25.9	366	299	22.2
Electricity	1,064	999	6.5	957	906	5.6
Fuel oil and other fuels	121	106	13.7	61	64	–4.1
Telephone services	990	962	2.9	1,028	1,042	–1.3
Water and other public services	327	325	0.7	275	257	7.1
Household services	**753**	**750**	**0.4**	**915**	**955**	**–4.2**
Personal services	300	358	–16.1	584	703	–16.9
Other household services	453	393	15.4	331	252	31.2
Housekeeping supplies	**594**	**529**	**12.4**	**499**	**479**	**4.1**
Laundry and cleaning supplies	149	144	3.7	142	137	3.6
Other household products	290	248	17.0	223	220	1.1
Postage and stationery	155	138	12.1	134	123	9.1
Household furnishings and equipment	**1,646**	**1,699**	**–3.1**	**1,548**	**1,640**	**–5.6**
Household textiles	158	116	35.9	104	132	–21.0
Furniture	417	429	–2.8	464	501	–7.4
Floor coverings	52	48	7.7	36	46	–21.9
Major appliances	204	207	–1.6	184	199	–7.3
Small appliances, misc. housewares	105	95	10.0	104	86	21.6
Miscellaneous household equipment	711	802	–11.3	657	677	–2.9
APPAREL AND SERVICES	**1,816**	**2,036**	**–10.8**	**2,134**	**2,258**	**–5.5**
Men and boys	**406**	**483**	**–15.9**	**456**	**561**	**–18.6**
Men, aged 16 or older	317	377	–16.0	336	404	–16.8
Boys, aged 2 to 15	89	105	–15.5	120	157	–23.5
Women and girls	**739**	**795**	**–7.1**	**755**	**772**	**–2.2**
Women, aged 16 or older	631	666	–5.2	638	615	3.7
Girls, aged 2 to 15	108	129	–16.6	118	158	–25.3
Children under age 2	**79**	**90**	**–12.2**	**182**	**181**	**0.6**
Footwear	**329**	**376**	**–12.6**	**398**	**432**	**–7.9**
Other apparel products and services	**264**	**292**	**–9.5**	**342**	**313**	**9.4**
TRANSPORTATION	**7,801**	**8,136**	**–4.1**	**8,485**	**9,167**	**–7.4**
Vehicle purchases	**3,397**	**3,749**	**–9.4**	**4,033**	**4,540**	**–11.2**
Cars and trucks, new	1,748	1,761	–0.7	1,901	2,024	–6.1
Cars and trucks, used	1,582	1,941	–18.5	2,086	2,432	–14.2
Gasoline and motor oil	**1,598**	**1,416**	**12.8**	**1,679**	**1,471**	**14.1**
Other vehicle expenses	**2,365**	**2,502**	**–5.5**	**2,407**	**2,722**	**–11.6**
Vehicle finance charges	323	360	–10.2	408	478	–14.7
Maintenance and repairs	652	684	–4.7	602	625	–3.7
Vehicle insurance	964	853	13.0	944	849	11.2
Vehicle rental, leases, licenses, other charges	426	604	–29.5	453	769	–41.1
Public transportation	**441**	**468**	**–5.8**	**366**	**433**	**–15.5**

	total consumer units			aged 25 to 34		
	2004	**2000**	**percent change 2000–04**	**2004**	**2000**	**percent change 2000–04**
HEALTH CARE	**$2,574**	**$2,266**	**13.6%**	**$1,519**	**$1,378**	**10.3%**
Health insurance	1,332	1,078	23.5	842	702	19.9
Medical services	648	623	4.0	403	403	0.1
Drugs	480	456	5.2	212	199	6.8
Medical supplies	114	109	5.0	62	76	−18.1
ENTERTAINMENT	**2,218**	**2,044**	**8.5**	**2,122**	**2,058**	**3.1**
Fees and admissions	528	565	−6.5	415	505	−17.8
Television, radio, sound equipment	788	682	15.5	843	746	13.0
Pets, toys, and playground equipment	381	366	4.0	404	385	4.9
Other entertainment supplies, services	522	431	21.1	460	422	8.9
PERSONAL CARE PRODUCTS AND SERVICES	**581**	**619**	**−6.1**	**552**	**632**	**−12.6**
READING	**130**	**160**	**−18.8**	**94**	**129**	**−27.4**
EDUCATION	**905**	**693**	**30.5**	**726**	**642**	**13.1**
TOBACCO PRODUCTS AND SMOKING SUPPLIES	**288**	**350**	**−17.7**	**283**	**340**	**−16.8**
MISCELLANEOUS	**690**	**851**	**−18.9**	**600**	**882**	**−32.0**
CASH CONTRIBUTIONS	**1,408**	**1,307**	**7.7**	**815**	**711**	**14.7**
PERSONAL INSURANCE AND PENSIONS	**4,823**	**3,691**	**30.7**	**4,765**	**3,964**	**20.2**
Life and other personal insurance	390	438	−10.9	235	265	−11.5
Pensions and Social Security	4,433	3,253	36.3	4,529	3,700	22.4
PERSONAL TAXES	**2,166**	**3,419**	**−36.6**	**1,665**	**3,107**	**−46.4**
Federal income taxes	1,519	2,642	−42.5	1,098	2,419	−54.6
State and local income taxes	472	616	−23.4	473	625	−24.3
Other taxes	175	160	9.3	94	64	47.8
GIFTS FOR NONHOUSEHOLD MEMBERS	**1,215**	**1,188**	**2.3**	**711**	**785**	**−9.5**

Note: The Bureau of Labor Statistics uses consumer unit rather than household as the sampling unit in the Consumer Expenditure Survey. For the definition of consumer unit, see the glossary. Spending on gifts is also included in the preceding product and service categories.
Source: Bureau of Labor Statistics, 2000 and 2004 Consumer Expenditure Surveys, Internet site http://www.bls.gov/cex/; calculations by New Strategist

Table 8.2 Average Spending of Householders Aged 35 to 44, 2000 and 2004

(average annual spending of total consumer units and consumer units headed by people aged 35 to 44, 2000 and 2004; percent change, 2000–04; in 2004 dollars)

	total consumer units			aged 35 to 44		
	2004	2000	percent change 2000–04	2004	2000	percent change 2000–04
Number of consumer units (in 000s)	116,282	109,367	6.3%	24,070	23,983	0.4%
Average before-tax income	$54,453	$48,975	11.2	$65,515	$61,974	5.7
Average annual spending	43,395	41,731	4.0	50,402	49,523	1.8
FOOD	**5,781**	**5,658**	**2.2**	**6,752**	**6,682**	**1.0**
Food at home	**3,347**	**3,314**	**1.0**	**3,897**	**3,822**	**2.0**
Cereals and bakery products	461	497	–7.2	552	582	–5.2
Cereals and cereal products	154	171	–10.0	194	208	–6.9
Bakery products	307	326	–5.8	357	374	–4.6
Meats, poultry, fish, and eggs	880	872	0.9	1,019	1,007	1.2
Beef	265	261	1.5	313	296	5.7
Pork	181	183	–1.2	204	204	0.0
Other meats	108	111	–2.5	125	132	–5.0
Poultry	156	159	–1.9	182	195	–6.8
Fish and seafood	128	121	6.1	151	138	9.3
Eggs	42	37	12.6	45	41	10.9
Dairy products	371	356	4.1	440	420	4.7
Fresh milk and cream	144	144	0.2	177	172	2.8
Other dairy products	226	212	6.8	263	248	6.1
Fruits and vegetables	561	571	–1.8	615	605	1.6
Fresh fruits	187	179	4.6	199	185	7.4
Fresh vegetables	183	174	4.9	200	180	11.2
Processed fruits	110	126	–12.8	122	137	–11.0
Processed vegetables	82	92	–11.0	94	101	–6.9
Other food at home	1,075	1,017	5.7	1,271	1,208	5.2
Sugar and other sweets	128	128	–0.3	146	161	–9.5
Fats and oils	89	91	–2.2	97	99	–1.7
Miscellaneous foods	527	479	9.9	643	568	13.2
Nonalcoholic beverages	290	274	5.8	340	329	3.3
Food prepared by household on trips	41	44	–6.6	44	50	–12.8
Food away from home	**2,434**	**2,344**	**3.8**	**2,855**	**2,860**	**–0.2**
ALCOHOLIC BEVERAGES	**459**	**408**	**12.5**	**535**	**461**	**16.1**
HOUSING	**13,918**	**13,513**	**3.0**	**16,794**	**16,575**	**1.3**
Shelter	**7,998**	**7,803**	**2.5**	**9,856**	**9,795**	**0.6**
Owned dwellings	5,324	5,048	5.5	7,025	7,056	–0.4
Mortgage interest and charges	2,936	2,895	1.4	4,575	4,719	–3.0
Property taxes	1,391	1,249	11.3	1,562	1,367	14.3
Maintenance, repairs, insurance, other expenses	997	905	10.2	888	970	–8.4

	total consumer units			aged 35 to 44		
	2004	**2000**	**percent change 2000–04**	**2004**	**2000**	**percent change 2000–04**
Rented dwellings	$2,201	$2,231	–1.3%	$2,450	$2,267	8.1%
Other lodging	473	524	–9.8	381	472	–19.2
Utilities, fuels, public services	**2,927**	**2,730**	**7.2**	**3,309**	**3,082**	**7.4**
Natural gas	424	337	25.9	474	384	23.5
Electricity	1,064	999	6.5	1,211	1,107	9.4
Fuel oil and other fuels	121	106	13.7	104	106	–2.3
Telephone services	990	962	2.9	1,145	1,117	2.5
Water and other public services	327	325	0.7	375	369	1.7
Household services	**753**	**750**	**0.4**	**992**	**983**	**0.9**
Personal services	300	358	–16.1	568	595	–4.5
Other household services	453	393	15.4	424	388	9.2
Housekeeping supplies	**594**	**529**	**12.4**	**677**	**625**	**8.3**
Laundry and cleaning supplies	149	144	3.7	170	172	–1.3
Other household products	290	248	17.0	339	307	10.4
Postage and stationery	155	138	12.1	169	146	15.8
Household furnishings and equipment	**1,646**	**1,699**	**–3.1**	**1,960**	**2,091**	**–6.3**
Household textiles	158	116	35.9	187	136	37.5
Furniture	417	429	–2.8	546	547	–0.2
Floor coverings	52	48	7.7	51	58	–12.3
Major appliances	204	207	–1.6	237	233	1.9
Small appliances, misc. housewares	105	95	10.0	97	102	–4.9
Miscellaneous household equipment	711	802	–11.3	841	1,016	–17.2
APPAREL AND SERVICES	**1,816**	**2,036**	**–10.8**	**2,142**	**2,548**	**–15.9**
Men and boys	**406**	**483**	**–15.9**	**532**	**604**	**–12.0**
Men, aged 16 or older	317	377	–16.0	356	403	–11.6
Boys, aged 2 to 15	89	105	–15.5	176	202	–12.8
Women and girls	**739**	**795**	**–7.1**	**801**	**1,026**	**–21.9**
Women, aged 16 or older	631	666	–5.2	580	759	–23.6
Girls, aged 2 to 15	108	129	–16.6	222	265	–16.4
Children under age 2	**79**	**90**	**–12.2**	**86**	**115**	**–25.3**
Footwear	**329**	**376**	**–12.6**	**416**	**440**	**–5.4**
Other apparel products and services	**264**	**292**	**–9.5**	**306**	**363**	**–15.7**
TRANSPORTATION	**7,801**	**8,136**	**–4.1**	**9,183**	**9,545**	**–3.8**
Vehicle purchases	**3,397**	**3,749**	**–9.4**	**4,190**	**4,383**	**–4.4**
Cars and trucks, new	1,748	1,761	–0.7	2,204	1,891	16.5
Cars and trucks, used	1,582	1,941	–18.5	1,907	2,411	–20.9
Gasoline and motor oil	**1,598**	**1,416**	**12.8**	**1,877**	**1,730**	**8.5**
Other vehicle expenses	**2,365**	**2,502**	**–5.5**	**2,681**	**2,936**	**–8.7**
Vehicle finance charges	323	360	–10.2	434	445	–2.5
Maintenance and repairs	652	684	–4.7	687	777	–11.5
Vehicle insurance	964	853	13.0	1,068	970	10.1
Vehicle rental, leases, licenses, other charges	426	604	–29.5	491	746	–34.2
Public transportation	**441**	**468**	**–5.8**	**435**	**495**	**–12.1**

	total consumer units			aged 35 to 44		
	2004	2000	percent change 2000–04	2004	2000	percent change 2000–04
HEALTH CARE	**$2,574**	**$2,266**	**13.6%**	**$2,263**	**$1,946**	**16.3%**
Health insurance	1,332	1,078	23.5	1,199	932	28.6
Medical services	648	623	4.0	654	609	7.4
Drugs	480	456	5.2	318	312	2.1
Medical supplies	114	109	5.0	92	93	−1.3
ENTERTAINMENT	**2,218**	**2,044**	**8.5**	**2,504**	**2,703**	**−7.4**
Fees and admissions	528	565	−6.5	666	784	−15.1
Television, radio, sound equipment	788	682	15.5	921	865	6.4
Pets, toys, and playground equipment	381	366	4.0	460	495	−7.0
Other entertainment supplies, services	522	431	21.1	457	558	−18.1
PERSONAL CARE PRODUCTS AND SERVICES	**581**	**619**	**−6.1**	**660**	**706**	**−6.6**
READING	**130**	**160**	**−18.8**	**123**	**166**	**−25.7**
EDUCATION	**905**	**693**	**30.5**	**786**	**675**	**16.5**
TOBACCO PRODUCTS AND SMOKING SUPPLIES	**288**	**350**	**−17.7**	**350**	**468**	**−25.3**
MISCELLANEOUS	**690**	**851**	**−18.9**	**773**	**935**	**−17.3**
CASH CONTRIBUTIONS	**1,408**	**1,307**	**7.7**	**1,265**	**1,100**	**15.0**
PERSONAL INSURANCE AND PENSIONS	**4,823**	**3,691**	**30.7**	**6,273**	**5,013**	**25.1**
Life and other personal insurance	390	438	−10.9	391	452	−13.5
Pensions and Social Security	4,433	3,253	36.3	5,881	4,561	28.9
PERSONAL TAXES	**2,166**	**3,419**	**−36.6**	**2,313**	**4,249**	**−45.6**
Federal income taxes	1,519	2,642	−42.5	1,557	3,306	−52.9
State and local income taxes	472	616	−23.4	598	805	−25.7
Other taxes	175	160	9.3	158	138	14.3
GIFTS FOR NONHOUSEHOLD MEMBERS	**1,215**	**1,188**	**2.3**	**1,096**	**1,098**	**−0.2**

Note: The Bureau of Labor Statistics uses consumer unit rather than household as the sampling unit in the Consumer Expenditure Survey. For the definition of consumer unit, see the glossary. Spending on gifts is also included in the preceding product and service categories.
Source: Bureau of Labor Statistics, 2000 and 2004 Consumer Expenditure Surveys, Internet site http://www.bls.gov/cex/; calculations by New Strategist

Householders Aged 25 to 34 Are Average Spenders

They spend more than average on the products and services typical of young adults.

The spending of households headed by people aged 25 to 34 almost matches spending by the average household. In 2004, householders aged 25 to 34 spent $42,701, slightly less than the $43,395 spent by the average household.

The lifestyle of young adults is readily discernable in the spending statistics. In 2004, householders aged 25 to 34 spent 32 percent more than average on used cars and trucks and 26 percent more than average on vehicle finance charges. Among age groups, 25-to-34-year-olds are second only to those aged 35 to 44 in the amount spent on alcoholic beverages, devoting an average of $522 to alcohol in 2004—or 14 percent more than the average household. Most in the age group cannot yet afford to buy a home. Consequently, their spending on rent is 73 percent more than average.

What is most clearly reflected in the spending data for 25-to-34-year-olds is their status as parents. The spending of these households far exceeds the average for products and services needed by young children. They spend more than twice as much as the average household on clothing for infants and 95 percent more than average on household personal services (mostly day care).

■ The incomes of young adults do not leave much room for extravagance, and the need to buy for children limits them further.

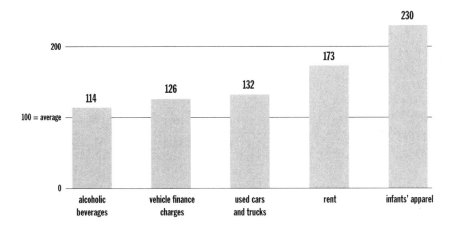

Young adults spend 14 percent more than average on alcoholic beverages

(indexed spending of householders aged 25 to 34 on selected items, 2004)

(average annual spending of total consumer units and average annual, indexed, and market share of spending by consumer units headed by 25-to-34-year-olds, 2004)

	total consumer units	consumer units headed by 25-to-34-year-olds		
		average spending	indexed spending	market share
Number of consumer units (in 000s)	116,282	19,439	–	16.7%
Average before-tax income	$54,453	$52,484	96	16.1
Average annual spending	43,395	42,701	98	16.4
FOOD	**5,781**	**5,705**	**99**	**16.5**
Food at home	**3,347**	**3,155**	**94**	**15.8**
Cereals and bakery products	461	432	94	15.7
Cereals and cereal products	154	152	99	16.5
Bakery products	307	280	91	15.2
Meats, poultry, fish, and eggs	880	812	92	15.4
Beef	265	250	94	15.8
Pork	181	161	89	14.9
Other meats	108	97	90	15.0
Poultry	156	154	99	16.5
Fish and seafood	128	112	88	14.6
Eggs	42	38	90	15.1
Dairy products	371	346	93	15.6
Fresh milk and cream	144	147	102	17.1
Other dairy products	226	199	88	14.7
Fruits and vegetables	561	521	93	15.5
Fresh fruits	187	168	90	15.0
Fresh vegetables	183	166	91	15.2
Processed fruits	110	110	100	16.7
Processed vegetables	82	77	94	15.7
Other food at home	1,075	1,043	97	16.2
Sugar and other sweets	128	113	88	14.8
Fats and oils	89	78	88	14.7
Miscellaneous foods	527	545	103	17.3
Nonalcoholic beverages	290	281	97	16.2
Food prepared by household on trips	41	26	63	10.6
Food away from home	**2,434**	**2,550**	**105**	**17.5**
ALCOHOLIC BEVERAGES	**459**	**522**	**114**	**19.0**
HOUSING	**13,918**	**14,379**	**103**	**17.3**
Shelter	**7,998**	**8,729**	**109**	**18.2**
Owned dwellings	5,324	4,700	88	14.8
Mortgage interest and charges	2,936	3,190	109	18.2
Property taxes	1,391	909	65	10.9
Maintenance, repairs, insurance, other expenses	997	601	60	10.1

	total consumer units	consumer units headed by 25-to-34-year-olds		
		average spending	indexed spending	market share
Rented dwellings	$2,201	$3,802	173	28.9%
Other lodging	473	227	48	8.0
Utilities, fuels, public services	**2,927**	**2,687**	**92**	**15.3**
Natural gas	424	366	86	14.4
Electricity	1,064	957	90	15.0
Fuel oil and other fuels	121	61	50	8.4
Telephone services	990	1,028	104	17.4
Water and other public services	327	275	84	14.1
Household services	**753**	**915**	**122**	**20.3**
Personal services	300	584	195	32.5
Other household services	453	331	73	12.2
Housekeeping supplies	**594**	**499**	**84**	**14.0**
Laundry and cleaning supplies	149	142	95	15.9
Other household products	290	223	77	12.9
Postage and stationery	155	134	86	14.5
Household furnishings and equipment	**1,646**	**1,548**	**94**	**15.7**
Household textiles	158	104	66	11.0
Furniture	417	464	111	18.6
Floor coverings	52	36	69	11.6
Major appliances	204	184	90	15.1
Small appliances, misc. housewares	105	104	99	16.6
Miscellaneous household equipment	711	657	92	15.4
APPAREL AND SERVICES	**1,816**	**2,134**	**118**	**19.6**
Men and boys	**406**	**456**	**112**	**18.8**
Men, aged 16 or older	317	336	106	17.7
Boys, aged 2 to 15	89	120	135	22.5
Women and girls	**739**	**755**	**102**	**17.1**
Women, aged 16 or older	631	638	101	16.9
Girls, aged 2 to 15	108	118	109	18.3
Children under age 2	**79**	**182**	**230**	**38.5**
Footwear	**329**	**398**	**121**	**20.2**
Other apparel products and services	**264**	**342**	**130**	**21.7**
TRANSPORTATION	**7,801**	**8,485**	**109**	**18.2**
Vehicle purchases	**3,397**	**4,033**	**119**	**19.8**
Cars and trucks, new	1,748	1,901	109	18.2
Cars and trucks, used	1,582	2,086	132	22.0
Gasoline and motor oil	**1,598**	**1,679**	**105**	**17.6**
Other vehicle expenses	**2,365**	**2,407**	**102**	**17.0**
Vehicle finance charges	323	408	126	21.1
Maintenance and repairs	652	602	92	15.4
Vehicle insurance	964	944	98	16.4
Vehicle rental, leases, licenses, other charges	426	453	106	17.8
Public transportation	**441**	**366**	**83**	**13.9**

	total consumer units	consumer units headed by 25-to-34-year-olds		
		average spending	indexed spending	market share
HEALTH CARE	**$2,574**	**$1,519**	**59**	**9.9%**
Health insurance	1,332	842	63	10.6
Medical services	648	403	62	10.4
Drugs	480	212	44	7.4
Medical supplies	114	62	54	9.1
ENTERTAINMENT	**2,218**	**2,122**	**96**	**16.0**
Fees and admissions	528	415	79	13.1
Television, radio, sound equipment	788	843	107	17.9
Pets, toys, and playground equipment	381	404	106	17.7
Other entertainment supplies, services	522	460	88	14.7
PERSONAL CARE PRODUCTS AND SERVICES	**581**	**552**	**95**	**15.9**
READING	**130**	**94**	**72**	**12.1**
EDUCATION	**905**	**726**	**80**	**13.4**
TOBACCO PRODUCTS AND SMOKING SUPPLIES	**288**	**283**	**98**	**16.4**
MISCELLANEOUS	**690**	**600**	**87**	**14.5**
CASH CONTRIBUTIONS	**1,408**	**815**	**58**	**9.7**
PERSONAL INSURANCE AND PENSIONS	**4,823**	**4,765**	**99**	**16.5**
Life and other personal insurance	390	235	60	10.1
Pensions and Social Security	4,433	4,529	102	17.1
PERSONAL TAXES	**2,166**	**1,665**	**77**	**12.9**
Federal income taxes	1,519	1,098	72	12.1
State and local income taxes	472	473	100	16.8
Other taxes	175	94	54	9.0
GIFTS FOR NONHOUSEHOLD MEMBERS	**1,215**	**711**	**59**	**9.8**

Note: The Bureau of Labor Statistics uses consumer unit rather than household as the sampling unit in the Consumer Expenditure Survey. For the definition of consumer unit, see the glossary. Spending on gifts is also included in the preceding product and service categories; "–" means not applicable.
Source: Bureau of Labor Statistics, 2004 Consumer Expenditure Survey, Internet site http://www.bls.gov/cex/; calculations by New Strategist

Householders Aged 35 to 44 Spend More than Average

Most households in the age group include children, which accounts for their above-average spending.

Households headed by people aged 35 to 44 spend 20 percent more than the average household—$50,402 versus $43,395 in 2004. The age group controls 24 percent of household spending. Householders aged 35 to 44 spend significantly more than average on items commonly purchased by parents with children under age 18. They spend 23 percent more than the average household on milk, 89 percent more on household personal services (mostly day care), and about twice the average on children's clothing.

Householders aged 35 to 44 spend less than average on some surprising items. They spend 8 percent less than average on women's clothing, 9 percent less on "other" lodging (mostly hotels and motels), 10 percent less on out-of-pocket health insurance expenses, and 10 percent less on gifts for nonhousehold members.

■ The spending of householders aged 35 to 44 is determined by children, boosting their spending on the products and services needed by children and reducing their spending on other items.

Householders aged 35 to 44 spend 26 percent more than the average household on cereal

(indexed spending of householders aged 35 to 44 on selected items, 2004)

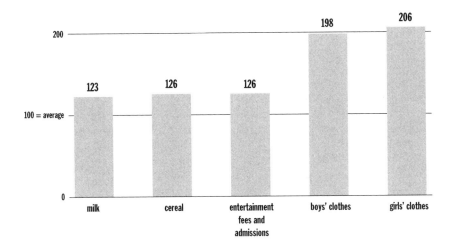

Table 8.4 Average, Indexed, and Market Share of Spending by Householders Aged 35 to 44, 2004

(average annual spending of total consumer units and average annual, indexed, and market share of spending by consumer units headed by 35-to-44-year-olds, 2004)

	total consumer units	consumer units headed by 35-to-44-year-olds		
		average spending	indexed spending	market share
Number of consumer units (in 000s)	116,282	24,070	–	20.7%
Average before-tax income	$54,453	$65,515	120	24.9
Average annual spending	43,395	50,402	116	24.0
FOOD	5,781	6,752	117	24.2
Food at home	3,347	3,897	116	24.1
Cereals and bakery products	461	552	120	24.8
Cereals and cereal products	154	194	126	26.1
Bakery products	307	357	116	24.1
Meats, poultry, fish, and eggs	880	1,019	116	24.0
Beef	265	313	118	24.4
Pork	181	204	113	23.3
Other meats	108	125	116	24.0
Poultry	156	182	117	24.1
Fish and seafood	128	151	118	24.4
Eggs	42	45	107	22.2
Dairy products	371	440	119	24.5
Fresh milk and cream	144	177	123	25.4
Other dairy products	226	263	116	24.1
Fruits and vegetables	561	615	110	22.7
Fresh fruits	187	199	106	22.0
Fresh vegetables	183	200	109	22.6
Processed fruits	110	122	111	23.0
Processed vegetables	82	94	115	23.7
Other food at home	1,075	1,271	118	24.5
Sugar and other sweets	128	146	114	23.6
Fats and oils	89	97	109	22.6
Miscellaneous foods	527	643	122	25.3
Nonalcoholic beverages	290	340	117	24.3
Food prepared by household on trips	41	44	107	22.2
Food away from home	2,434	2,855	117	24.3
ALCOHOLIC BEVERAGES	459	535	117	24.1
HOUSING	13,918	16,794	121	25.0
Shelter	7,998	9,856	123	25.5
Owned dwellings	5,324	7,025	132	27.3
Mortgage interest and charges	2,936	4,575	156	32.3
Property taxes	1,391	1,562	112	23.2
Maintenance, repairs, insurance, other expenses	997	888	89	18.4

	total consumer units	consumer units headed by 35-to-44-year-olds		
		average spending	indexed spending	market share
Rented dwellings	$2,201	$2,450	111	23.0%
Other lodging	473	381	81	16.7
Utilities, fuels, public services	**2,927**	**3,309**	**113**	**23.4**
Natural gas	424	474	112	23.1
Electricity	1,064	1,211	114	23.6
Fuel oil and other fuels	121	104	86	17.8
Telephone services	990	1,145	116	23.9
Water and other public services	327	375	115	23.7
Household services	**753**	**992**	**132**	**27.3**
Personal services	300	568	189	39.2
Other household services	453	424	94	19.4
Housekeeping supplies	**594**	**677**	**114**	**23.6**
Laundry and cleaning supplies	149	170	114	23.6
Other household products	290	339	117	24.2
Postage and stationery	155	169	109	22.6
Household furnishings and equipment	**1,646**	**1,960**	**119**	**24.6**
Household textiles	158	187	118	24.5
Furniture	417	546	131	27.1
Floor coverings	52	51	98	20.3
Major appliances	204	237	116	24.0
Small appliances, misc. housewares	105	97	92	19.1
Miscellaneous household equipment	711	841	118	24.5
APPAREL AND SERVICES	**1,816**	**2,142**	**118**	**24.4**
Men and boys	**406**	**532**	**131**	**27.1**
Men, aged 16 or older	317	356	112	23.2
Boys, aged 2 to 15	89	176	198	40.9
Women and girls	**739**	**801**	**108**	**22.4**
Women, aged 16 or older	631	580	92	19.0
Girls, aged 2 to 15	108	222	206	42.5
Children under age 2	**79**	**86**	**109**	**22.5**
Footwear	**329**	**416**	**126**	**26.2**
Other apparel products and services	**264**	**306**	**116**	**24.0**
TRANSPORTATION	**7,801**	**9,183**	**118**	**24.4**
Vehicle purchases	**3,397**	**4,190**	**123**	**25.5**
Cars and trucks, new	1,748	2,204	126	26.1
Cars and trucks, used	1,582	1,907	121	25.0
Gasoline and motor oil	**1,598**	**1,877**	**117**	**24.3**
Other vehicle expenses	**2,365**	**2,681**	**113**	**23.5**
Vehicle finance charges	323	434	134	27.8
Maintenance and repairs	652	687	105	21.8
Vehicle insurance	964	1,068	111	22.9
Vehicle rental, leases, licenses, other charges	426	491	115	23.9
Public transportation	**441**	**435**	**99**	**20.4**

	total consumer units	consumer units headed by 35-to-44-year-olds		
		average spending	indexed spending	market share
HEALTH CARE	**$2,574**	**$2,263**	**88**	**18.2%**
Health insurance	1,332	1,199	90	18.6
Medical services	648	654	101	20.9
Drugs	480	318	66	13.7
Medical supplies	114	92	81	16.7
ENTERTAINMENT	**2,218**	**2,504**	**113**	**23.4**
Fees and admissions	528	666	126	26.1
Television, radio, sound equipment	788	921	117	24.2
Pets, toys, and playground equipment	381	460	121	25.0
Other entertainment supplies, services	522	457	88	18.1
PERSONAL CARE PRODUCTS AND SERVICES	**581**	**660**	**114**	**23.5**
READING	**130**	**123**	**95**	**19.6**
EDUCATION	**905**	**786**	**87**	**18.0**
TOBACCO PRODUCTS AND SMOKING SUPPLIES	**288**	**350**	**122**	**25.2**
MISCELLANEOUS	**690**	**773**	**112**	**23.2**
CASH CONTRIBUTIONS	**1,408**	**1,265**	**90**	**18.6**
PERSONAL INSURANCE AND PENSIONS	**4,823**	**6,273**	**130**	**26.9**
Life and other personal insurance	390	391	100	20.8
Pensions and Social Security	4,433	5,881	133	27.5
PERSONAL TAXES	**2,166**	**2,313**	**107**	**22.1**
Federal income taxes	1,519	1,557	103	21.2
State and local income taxes	472	598	127	26.2
Other taxes	175	158	90	18.7
GIFTS FOR NONHOUSEHOLD MEMBERS	**1,215**	**1,096**	**90**	**18.7**

Note: The Bureau of Labor Statistics uses consumer unit rather than household as the sampling unit in the Consumer Expenditure Survey. For the definition of consumer unit, see the glossary. Spending on gifts is also included in the preceding product and service categories; "–" means not applicable.
Source: Bureau of Labor Statistics, 2004 Consumer Expenditure Survey, Internet site http://www.bls.gov/cex/; calculations by New Strategist

9

Time Use

■ Time use varies sharply by age. Not surprisingly, people aged 25 to 54 spend the most time working. Consequently, they have the least amount of leisure time.

■ Teenagers get the most sleep. People aged 15 to 19 sleep 9.46 hours a night. Men aged 45 to 54 get the least amount of sleep—just 8.08 hours.

■ People aged 65 or older spend the most time watching television—3.86 hours per day. Women aged 35 to 44 spend the least amount of time watching TV (1.91 hours per day).

■ Seventy-three percent of Americans aged 18 or older have children, the proportion rising from 39 percent in the 18-to-29 age group to 78 percent among 30-to-49-year-olds.

■ Fully 84 percent of 18-to-29-year-olds use the Internet, but those aged 30 to 49 are not far behind at 80 percent. The 30-to-49 age group is most likely to have been online yesterday (64 percent).

■ Gen Xers accounted for only 19 percent of voters in the 2004 presidential election, far behind the 40 percent share accounted for by Boomers.

■ Seventy-three percent of 25-to-34-year-olds attended at least one movie in the past year.

Americans Spend More Time in Leisure than at Work

Driving around ranks fifth in time use, ahead of eating and drinking.

The average person spends 9.33 hours a day in personal care activities, primarily sleeping. Socializing, relaxing, and leisure activities take up 4.62 hours a day, and work accounts for another 3.37 hours, according to the Bureau of Labor Statistics' American Time Use Survey. Household activities (i.e., housework) rank fourth in importance in the time use statistics, followed by traveling—a category that includes driving to work, to stores, to leisure activities, and to children's events.

Time use varies sharply by age. Not surprisingly, people aged 25 to 54 spend the most time working (29 to 36 percent more than the average person) and consequently they have the least amount of leisure time (12 to 20 percent less than average). People aged 25 to 44 spend the most time caring for and helping household members (mostly children). Older Americans have the most leisure time (49 percent more than average), but also spend the most time in household activities (44 percent more than average).

Time use also varies greatly by sex. Among 25-to-34-year-olds, for example, men spend more time than women working, eating and drinking, socializing, playing sports, and driving around. Women spend more time than men doing most other activities including household work, caring for household members, shopping, and making phone calls.

■ Gen Xers are entering the lifestage where leisure time is in increasingly short supply.

All but the oldest Americans spend more than one hour a day driving around

(average number of hours per day spent traveling, by age, 2004)

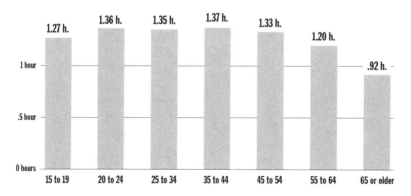

Table 9.1 Time Use by Primary Activity and Age, 2004

(average and indexed hours per day spent in primary activities, by age, 2004)

	total	15–19	20–24	25–34	35–44	45–54	55–64	65+
Total hours	**24.00**	**24.00**	**24.00**	**24.00**	**24.00**	**24.00**	**24.00**	**24.00**
Personal care activities	9.33	10.25	9.66	9.23	9.02	9.00	9.08	9.65
Household activities	1.82	0.69	1.02	1.53	1.89	2.07	2.18	2.62
Caring for and helping household members	0.48	0.10	0.44	1.01	0.88	0.32	0.14	0.09
Caring for and helping nonhousehold members	0.19	0.11	0.18	0.17	0.14	0.23	0.31	0.19
Work and related activities	3.37	1.14	3.49	4.35	4.60	4.50	3.49	0.65
Education	0.46	2.98	0.94	0.26	0.14	0.09	0.05	0.03
Consumer purchases	0.41	0.31	0.35	0.46	0.41	0.41	0.46	0.40
Professional and personal care services	0.09	0.05	0.03	0.07	0.08	0.11	0.09	0.16
Household services	0.02	–	–	0.01	0.01	0.02	0.02	0.03
Government services and civic obligations	0.01	–	0.01	0.01	0.01	–	0.01	–
Eating and drinking	1.11	0.86	0.97	1.05	1.06	1.12	1.23	1.38
Socializing, relaxing, and leisure	4.62	4.82	4.71	3.87	3.68	4.05	4.97	6.87
Sports, exercise, and recreation	0.33	0.71	0.44	0.30	0.28	0.25	0.26	0.25
Religious and spiritual activities	0.12	0.15	0.10	0.10	0.10	0.11	0.13	0.20
Volunteer activities	0.15	0.17	0.06	0.07	0.15	0.18	0.15	0.20
Telephone calls	0.12	0.26	0.14	0.08	0.08	0.11	0.10	0.14
Traveling	1.26	1.27	1.36	1.35	1.37	1.33	1.20	0.92
Unencodeable	0.12	0.14	0.09	0.07	0.09	0.10	0.13	0.22
Index of time use by age to total								
Personal care activities	100	110	104	99	97	96	97	103
Household activities	100	38	56	84	104	114	120	144
Caring for and helping household members	100	21	92	210	183	67	29	19
Caring for and helping nonhousehold members	100	58	95	89	74	121	163	100
Work and related activities	100	34	104	129	136	134	104	19
Education	100	648	204	57	30	20	11	7
Consumer purchases	100	76	85	112	100	100	112	98
Professional and personal care services	100	56	33	78	89	122	100	178
Household services	100	–	–	50	50	100	100	150
Government services and civic obligations	100	–	100	100	100	–	100	–
Eating and drinking	100	77	87	95	95	101	111	124
Socializing, relaxing, and leisure	100	104	102	84	80	88	108	149
Sports, exercise, and recreation	100	215	133	91	85	76	79	76
Religious and spiritual activities	100	125	83	83	83	92	108	167
Volunteer activities	100	113	40	47	100	120	100	133
Telephone calls	100	217	117	67	67	92	83	117
Traveling	100	101	108	107	109	106	95	73
Unencodeable	100	117	75	58	75	83	108	183

Note: "–" means number is less than .005 or sample is too small to make a reliable estimate.
Source: Bureau of Labor Statistics, unpublished tables from the American Time Use Survey, Internet site http://www.bls.gov/tus/home.htm; calculations by New Strategist

Table 9.2 Time Use by Age and Sex, 2004: Aged 25 to 34

(hours per day spent in primary activities by people aged 15 or older and aged 25 to 34 by sex; index of age group time use to total time use by sex, and index of time use by people aged 25 to 34 by sex, 2004)

| | | men aged 25 to 34 | | | women aged 25 to 34 | | aged 24 to 35 index of |
	total men	hours	index to total men	total women	hours	index to total women	women's time to men's
Total hours	**24.00**	**24.00**	**100**	**24.00**	**24.00**	**100**	**100**
Personal care activities	9.14	9.07	99	9.50	9.40	99	104
Household activities	1.33	1.01	76	2.28	2.06	90	204
Caring for/helping household members	0.29	0.45	155	0.65	1.57	242	349
Caring for/helping nonhousehold members	0.16	0.17	106	0.22	0.17	77	100
Work and related activities	4.03	5.29	131	2.76	3.42	124	65
Education	0.46	0.24	52	0.46	0.27	59	113
Consumer purchases	0.30	0.35	117	0.50	0.56	112	160
Professional and personal care services	0.07	0.05	71	0.11	0.09	82	180
Household services	0.01	0.01	100	0.02	0.01	50	100
Government services, civic obligations	–	0.01	–	0.01	0.01	100	–
Eating and drinking	1.17	1.13	97	1.06	0.98	92	87
Socializing, relaxing, and leisure	4.89	4.13	84	4.38	3.62	83	88
Sports, exercise, and recreation	0.43	0.42	98	0.23	0.19	83	45
Religious and spiritual activities	0.12	0.09	75	0.13	0.10	77	111
Volunteer activities	0.12	0.07	58	0.17	0.07	41	100
Telephone calls	0.07	0.05	71	0.17	0.11	65	220
Traveling	1.29	1.41	109	1.22	1.29	106	91
Unencodeable	0.11	0.06	55	0.13	0.08	62	133

Note: "–" means number is less than .005 or sample is too small to make a reliable estimate.
Source: Bureau of Labor Statistics, unpublished tables from the American Time Use Survey, Internet site http://www.bls.gov/tus/home.htm; calculations by New Strategist

Table 9.3 Time Use by Age and Sex, 2004: Aged 35 to 44

(hours per day spent in primary activities by people aged 15 or older and aged 35 to 44 by sex; index of age group time use to total time use by sex, and index of time use by people aged 35 to 44 by sex, 2004)

		men aged 35 to 44			women aged 35 to 44		aged 35 to 44 index of
	total men	hours	index to total men	total women	hours	index to total women	women's time to men's
Total hours	**24.00**	**24.00**	**100**	**24.00**	**24.00**	**100**	**100**
Personal care activities	9.14	8.92	98	9.50	9.12	96	102
Household activities	1.33	1.31	98	2.28	2.46	108	188
Caring for/helping household members	0.29	0.63	217	0.65	1.13	174	179
Caring for/helping nonhousehold members	0.16	0.16	100	0.22	0.13	59	81
Work and related activities	4.03	5.43	135	2.76	3.78	137	70
Education	0.46	0.09	20	0.46	0.18	39	200
Consumer purchases	0.30	0.30	100	0.50	0.52	104	173
Professional and personal care services	0.07	0.06	86	0.11	0.11	100	183
Household services	0.01	0.01	100	0.02	0.02	100	200
Government services, civic obligations	–	–	–	0.01	0.01	100	–
Eating and drinking	1.17	1.11	95	1.06	1.01	95	91
Socializing, relaxing, and leisure	4.89	3.92	80	4.38	3.44	79	88
Sports, exercise, and recreation	0.43	0.32	74	0.23	0.24	104	75
Religious and spiritual activities	0.12	0.11	92	0.13	0.09	69	82
Volunteer activities	0.12	0.13	108	0.17	0.17	100	131
Telephone calls	0.07	0.05	71	0.17	0.12	71	240
Traveling	1.29	1.37	106	1.22	1.37	112	100
Unencodeable	0.11	0.07	64	0.13	0.11	85	157

Note: "–" means number is less than .005 or sample is too small to make a reliable estimate.
Source: Bureau of Labor Statistics, unpublished tables from the American Time Use Survey, Internet site http://www.bls.gov/tus/ home.htm; calculations by New Strategist

Most Americans Get More than Eight Hours of Sleep

Sleep time shortens as people enter their thirties and forties.

On an average day, people aged 15 or older get 8.56 hours of sleep, according to the American Time Use Survey. Not surprisingly, teenagers get the most sleep. People aged 15 to 19 sleep 9.46 hours a night (or day), or 11 percent more than the average person. Men aged 45 to 54 get the least amount of sleep—just 8.08 hours a day, or 6 percent less than average. Typically, men in this age group are at the height of their career and sleep seems to be one of the sacrifices they make to achieve their goals.

The average person spends 0.67 hours (or 40 minutes) per day grooming—a category that includes bathing, hair care, dressing, and putting on make-up. Again, teens aged 15 to 19 spend the most time grooming, with teen girls devoting 39 percent more time than average to this task. In every age group, men spend less time than average grooming, with the oldest men spending 25 percent less time than average on grooming activities.

■ Gen Xers are in the busy lifestage where time spent grooming is at a minimum.

Teenagers sleep the most

(average number of hours per day spent sleeping, by age, 2004)

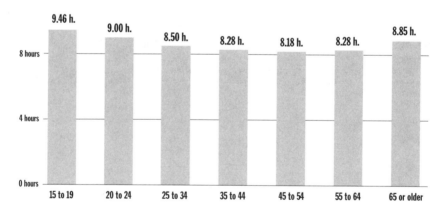

Table 9.4 Time Spent Sleeping by Age and Sex, 2004

(average hours per day spent sleeping as a primary activity and index of time to average, by age and sex, 2004)

	total	men	women
Aged 15 or older	**8.56**	**8.51**	**8.61**
Aged 15 to 19	9.46	9.44	9.49
Aged 20 to 24	9.00	8.83	9.16
Aged 25 to 34	8.50	8.47	8.54
Aged 35 to 44	8.28	8.26	8.29
Aged 45 to 54	8.18	8.08	8.27
Aged 55 to 64	8.28	8.29	8.27
Aged 65 or older	8.85	8.76	8.92
INDEX OF TIME TO AVERAGE			
Aged 15 or older	**100**	**99**	**101**
Aged 15 to 19	111	110	111
Aged 20 to 24	105	103	107
Aged 25 to 34	99	99	100
Aged 35 to 44	97	96	97
Aged 45 to 54	96	94	97
Aged 55 to 64	97	97	97
Aged 65 or older	103	102	104

Source: Bureau of Labor Statistics, unpublished tables from the American Time Use Survey, Internet site http://www.bls.gov/tus/home.htm; calculations by New Strategist

Table 9.5 Time Spent Grooming by Age and Sex, 2004

(average hours per day spent grooming as a primary activity and index of time to average, by age and sex, 2004)

	total	men	women
Aged 15 or older	**0.67**	**0.55**	**0.77**
Aged 15 to 19	0.74	0.56	0.93
Aged 20 to 24	0.66	0.58	0.73
Aged 25 to 34	0.65	0.57	0.73
Aged 35 to 44	0.66	0.55	0.76
Aged 45 to 54	0.69	0.57	0.80
Aged 55 to 64	0.68	0.54	0.80
Aged 65 or older	0.62	0.50	0.70
INDEX OF TIME TO AVERAGE			
Aged 15 or older	**100**	**82**	**115**
Aged 15 to 19	110	84	139
Aged 20 to 24	99	87	109
Aged 25 to 34	97	85	109
Aged 35 to 44	99	82	113
Aged 45 to 54	103	85	119
Aged 55 to 64	101	81	119
Aged 65 or older	93	75	104

Note: Time spent on this activity does not include travel time or professional grooming services.
Source: Bureau of Labor Statistics, unpublished tables from the American Time Use Survey, Internet site http://www.bls.gov/tus/home.htm; calculations by New Strategist

Women Aged 25 to 34 Spend the Most Time Caring for Household Children

Women devote much more time than men to child care.

The time spent caring for household children peaks in the 25-to-44 age group, when most families have children under age 18 at home. Women spend far more time on this activity than men. Women aged 25 to 34 spend 1.38 hours a day caring for household children as a primary activity. Their male counterparts spend only 0.40 hours (24 minutes) doing so. (These numbers seem low because they are averages based on both those with and without children at home.)

Among women aged 35 to 44, time spent caring for household children falls to 0.93 hours per day on average, less than the figure for women aged 25 to 34 because fewer have preschoolers at home. In contrast, men aged 35 to 44 spend more time caring for household children than their younger counterparts because men marry and become fathers at an older age than women.

■ Generation X is at the lifestage when childrearing responsibilities peak, cutting into their leisure time.

Time spent caring for household children is well above average among women aged 35 to 44

(index of time women spend caring for household children to the average, by age, 2004; 100 equals the average for all people aged 15 or older)

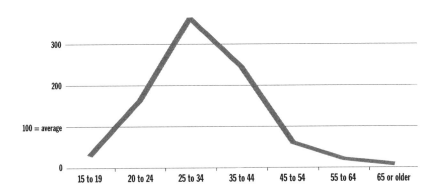

Table 9.6 Time Spent Caring for and Helping Household Children by Age and Sex, 2004

(average hours per day spent caring for and helping household children as a primary activity and index of time to average, by age and sex, 2004)

	total	men	women
Aged 15 or older	**0.38**	**0.23**	**0.52**
Aged 15 to 19	0.08	0.04	0.11
Aged 20 to 24	0.36	0.08	0.62
Aged 25 to 34	0.89	0.40	1.38
Aged 35 to 44	0.73	0.53	0.93
Aged 45 to 54	0.21	0.19	0.23
Aged 55 to 64	0.06	0.04	0.08
Aged 65 or older	0.02	–	0.03
INDEX OF TIME TO AVERAGE			
Aged 15 or older	**100**	**61**	**137**
Aged 15 to 19	21	11	29
Aged 20 to 24	95	21	163
Aged 25 to 34	234	105	363
Aged 35 to 44	192	139	245
Aged 45 to 54	55	50	61
Aged 55 to 64	16	11	21
Aged 65 or older	5	–	8

Note: Time spent on this activity does not include travel time. "–" means number is less than .005 or sample is too small to make a reliable estimate.
Source: Bureau of Labor Statistics, unpublished tables from the American Time Use Survey, Internet site http://www.bls.gov/tus/ home.htm; calculations by New Strategist

Women Still Do the Housework

The oldest women spend the most time cooking and cleaning.

Women spend 0.75 hours (45 minutes) a day preparing meals and 0.20 hours (12 minutes) cleaning up in the kitchen afterwards. Men spend much less time on these tasks—only 15 minutes cooking, on average, and 3 minutes cleaning up. These figures are low because they include those who participated in cooking and cleaning and those who did not. The many men who do not cook or clean on an average day drive the numbers to these low levels. Surprisingly, women aged 35 to 44—who have the largest households—spend only 0.59 hours (35 minutes) a day cooking as a primary activity. Women aged 65 or older spend the most time in the kitchen, despite their smaller household size.

The average woman spends 0.54 hours a day cleaning her house, or 32 minutes. Men spend only 9 minutes a day housecleaning. Women aged 65 or older devote the most time to housecleaning—97 percent more than average. They also spend 89 percent more time than average doing the laundry although they are most likely to live alone. Women aged 35 to 44 spend the most time doing the laundry (0.38 hours a day, or 23 minutes), but not much more than those aged 65 or older.

■ As leisure time expands in retirement, people fill some of it with household tasks such as cleaning and laundry.

Women aged 25 to 44 spend less time cleaning than those aged 65 or older

(index of time women spend housecleaning to the average, by age, 2004; 100 equals the average for all people aged 15 or older)

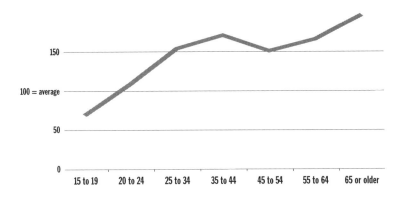

Table 9.7 Time Spent Preparing and Cleaning Up Meals by Age and Sex, 2004

(average hours per day spent on food and drink preparation and kitchen and food cleanup as primary activities, and index of time to average, by age and sex, 2004)

	food and drink preparation			kitchen and food cleanup		
	total	men	women	total	men	women
Aged 15 or older	**0.51**	**0.25**	**0.75**	**0.13**	**0.05**	**0.20**
Aged 15 to 19	0.10	0.05	0.15	0.03	0.01	0.05
Aged 20 to 24	0.23	0.11	0.34	0.05	0.02	0.08
Aged 25 to 34	0.37	0.16	0.58	0.11	0.04	0.18
Aged 35 to 44	0.42	0.24	0.59	0.15	0.05	0.24
Aged 45 to 54	0.43	0.23	0.61	0.15	0.06	0.22
Aged 55 to 64	0.43	0.22	0.63	0.15	0.06	0.23
Aged 65 or older	0.51	0.32	0.66	0.17	0.08	0.24
INDEX OF TIME TO AVERAGE						
Aged 15 or older	**100**	**49**	**147**	**100**	**38**	**154**
Aged 15 to 19	20	10	29	23	8	38
Aged 20 to 24	45	22	67	38	15	62
Aged 25 to 34	73	31	114	85	31	138
Aged 35 to 44	82	47	116	115	38	185
Aged 45 to 54	84	45	120	115	46	169
Aged 55 to 64	84	43	124	115	46	177
Aged 65 or older	100	63	129	131	62	185

Note: Time spent on these activities does not include travel time.
Source: Bureau of Labor Statistics, unpublished tables from the American Time Use Survey, Internet site http://www.bls.gov/tus/home.htm; calculations by New Strategist

Table 9.8 Time Spent Housecleaning and Doing Laundry by Age and Sex, 2004

(average hours per day spent on housecleaning and doing laundry as primary activities, and index of time to average, by age and sex, 2004)

	housecleaning			laundry		
	total	men	women	total	men	women
Aged 15 or older	**0.35**	**0.15**	**0.54**	**0.19**	**0.06**	**0.30**
Aged 15 to 19	0.15	0.08	0.24	0.05	0.03	0.07
Aged 20 to 24	0.23	0.08	0.38	0.09	0.05	0.11
Aged 25 to 34	0.34	0.15	0.54	0.18	0.06	0.29
Aged 35 to 44	0.38	0.15	0.60	0.23	0.07	0.38
Aged 45 to 54	0.35	0.16	0.53	0.23	0.08	0.37
Aged 55 to 64	0.38	0.16	0.58	0.20	0.05	0.33
Aged 65 or older	0.48	0.20	0.69	0.23	0.05	0.36
INDEX OF TIME TO AVERAGE						
Aged 15 or older	**100**	**43**	**154**	**100**	**32**	**158**
Aged 15 to 19	43	23	69	26	16	37
Aged 20 to 24	66	23	109	47	26	58
Aged 25 to 34	97	43	154	95	32	153
Aged 35 to 44	109	43	171	121	37	200
Aged 45 to 54	100	46	151	121	42	195
Aged 55 to 64	109	46	166	105	26	174
Aged 65 or older	137	57	197	121	26	189

Note: Time spent on these activities does not include travel time.
Source: Bureau of Labor Statistics, unpublished tables from the American Time Use Survey, Internet site http://www.bls.gov/tus/home.htm; calculations by New Strategist

Television Takes Up Time

Older Americans devote one-fourth of their waking hours to television.

Watching television is by far the most popular leisure time activity—so popular, in fact, that the average person spends more time watching TV as a primary activity than eating and drinking or doing household chores. People aged 65 or older spend the most time watching TV—3.86 hours per day, or one-fourth of the waking hours of people in the age group. Women aged 35 to 44 spend the least amount of time watching TV (1.91 hours per day).

Even among teenagers, television is more popular than playing on a computer. Teen boys aged 15 to 19 spend 1.24 hours per day on their computer versus 2.45 hours per day watching TV. Teen boys spend the most time playing on a computer, more than three times the average.

People aged 65 or older spend the most time reading, an average of about one hour a day—more than twice the average. Teens and young adults spend much more time on a computer than reading. For men, reading is more popular than leisure computer use only among those aged 45 or older. Among women, reading becomes more popular than computer use in the 25-to-34 age group.

■ As younger generations age, they may spend more time reading and less time on the computer.

People aged 35 to 44 spend the least amount of time watching TV

(average hours per day spent watching television as a primary activity, by age, 2004)

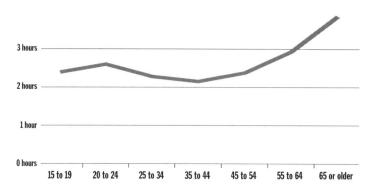

Table 9.9 Time Spent Watching TV, Reading, and Leisure Computer Use and Playing Games by Age and Sex, 2004

(average hours per day spent watching television, reading for personal interest, and leisure computer use and playing games as primary activities, and index of time to average, by age and sex, 2004)

	television			reading			computer use for leisure, games		
	total	men	women	total	men	women	total	men	women
Aged 15 or older	**2.64**	**2.85**	**2.43**	**0.38**	**0.32**	**0.44**	**0.34**	**0.44**	**0.26**
Aged 15 to 19	2.39	2.45	2.33	0.15	0.11	0.19	0.84	1.24	0.40
Aged 20 to 24	2.60	2.87	2.35	0.10	0.07	0.13	0.55	0.79	0.31
Aged 25 to 34	2.28	2.42	2.14	0.16	0.14	0.18	0.28	0.42	0.15
Aged 35 to 44	2.15	2.40	1.91	0.24	0.21	0.27	0.24	0.25	0.23
Aged 45 to 54	2.38	2.68	2.11	0.35	0.30	0.40	0.24	0.26	0.21
Aged 55 to 64	2.93	3.35	2.55	0.57	0.48	0.65	0.25	0.25	0.26
Aged 65 or older	3.86	4.16	3.64	0.99	0.94	1.03	0.35	0.35	0.36
INDEX OF TIME TO AVERAGE									
Aged 15 or older	**100**	**108**	**92**	**100**	**84**	**116**	**100**	**129**	**76**
Aged 15 to 19	91	93	88	39	29	50	247	365	118
Aged 20 to 24	98	109	89	26	18	34	162	232	91
Aged 25 to 34	86	92	81	42	37	47	82	124	44
Aged 35 to 44	81	91	72	63	55	71	71	74	68
Aged 45 to 54	90	102	80	92	79	105	71	76	62
Aged 55 to 64	111	127	97	150	126	171	74	74	76
Aged 65 or older	146	158	138	261	247	271	103	103	106

Note: Time spent on these activities does not include travel time.
Source: Bureau of Labor Statistics, unpublished tables from the American Time Use Survey, Internet site http://www.bls.gov/tus/home.htm; calculations by New Strategist

Many Parents and Adult Children Live Near One Another

Most adult children see their parents at least once a week.

Americans are known for their mobility, but despite the lure of distant places most parents and adult children live less than one hour's drive from each other, according to a survey by the Pew Research Center. Sixty-five percent of people aged 18 or older live less than an hour's drive from their parents. Conversely, 72 percent of parents live less than an hour away from an adult child.

The 54 percent majority of adults see a parent at least once a week. Adding telephone contact to the mix drives the proportion of Americans who see or talk to a parent on the phone on a weekly basis up to a near-universal 86 percent. Women talk to their parents on the phone much more frequently than men, with 42 percent doing so daily compared with 23 percent of men. Women are also more likely than men to stay in touch with an adult child, 47 percent talking on the phone to a child every day compared with 24 percent of men.

Seventy-three percent of Americans aged 18 or older have children, with the proportion rising from 39 percent in the 18-to-29 age group to 78 percent among 30-to-49-year-olds. Sixty-eight percent of adults have a living parent, but only 29 percent have a grandparent still living.

■ Ninety percent of American adults have a brother or sister, making it the most common family relationship.

Few adult children live far from their parents

(percent distribution of people aged 18 or older by distance from parents' home, 2005)

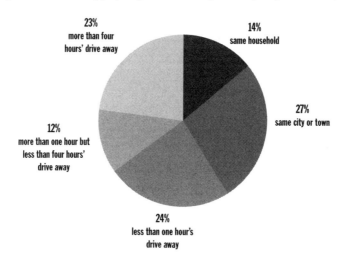

23%
more than four
hours' drive away

14%
same household

27%
same city or town

12%
more than one hour but
less than four hours'
drive away

24%
less than one hour's
drive away

Table 9.10 The Generations: Relationships and Contacts, 2005

(percent of people aged 18 or older with selected living relatives, by age; proximity of parents and adult children; frequency of contact with parents by type of contact; and telephone contact between parents and adult children by sex, 2005)

GENERATIONAL RELATIONSHIPS

	total	18 to 29	30 to 49	50 to 64	65 or older
Have grandchildren	32%	–	11%	56%	82%
Have children	73	39%	78	84	89
Have a brother or sister	90	92	94	91	78
Have at least one living parent	68	98	88	51	9
Have any living grandparents	29	79	31	2	–

PARENT/CHILD PROXIMITY

(among respondents with at least one living parent and among respondents with at least one financially independent adult child)

	parent(s)	adult child
Live in same household	14%	14%
Live in same city or town	27	30
Live less than an hour away	24	28
Live less than four hour's drive away	12	11
Live more than 4 hour's drive away	23	17

FREQUENCY OF CONTACT WITH PARENT(S)

(among respondents with at least one living parent)

	email	see	phone	see or phone
Every day	3%	24%	32%	42%
Once a week or more	10	30	47	44
Once a month or more	8	15	11	10
Several times a year	3	17	2	2
Once a year	–	7	1	1
Less often than once a year	–	7	5	1
Never	76	–	–	–
Don't know	–	–	2	–

TELEPHONE CONTACT WITH PARENT(S)

(among respondents with at least one living parent)

	total	men	women
Daily	32%	23%	42%
Weekly	47	52	41
Less often	19	23	15
Don't know	2	2	2

TELEPHONE CONTACT WITH ADULT CHILD

(among respondents with a financially independent adult child aged 18 or older)

	total	men	women
Daily	37%	24%	47%
Weekly	48	55	43
Less often	13	19	9
Don't know	2	2	1

Note: "–" means zero or sample too small to make a reliable estimate.
Source: Pew Research Center, Families Drawn Together by Communications Revolution, February 21, 2006; Internet site http://pewresearch.org/reports/?ReportID=9

More than Two-Thirds of Americans Are Online

Young adults are most likely to go online.

Sixty-eight percent of Americans aged 18 or older were Internet users in 2005, up substantially from the 46 percent of 2000, according to surveys by the Pew Internet & American Life Project. Fully 84 percent of young adults—those aged 18 to 29—use the Internet, but those aged 30 to 49 are not far behind at 80 percent. The 30-to-49 age group is most likely to have been online yesterday (64 percent).

Emailing is the most popular online activity, engaged in by 91 percent of Internet users. The oldest Internet users are just as likely to email as young adults. But young adults are far more likely to do instant messaging. The 62 percent majority of 18-to-29-year-olds uses instant messaging versus only 26 to 36 percent of older adults. Downloading music shows the biggest gap in Internet use by age, with 46 percent of young adults doing downloads compared with only 6 percent of people aged 65 or older.

■ The Internet is changing the way young and middle-aged adults interact with the world, affecting both government and business.

The oldest Americans are least likely to use the Internet

(percent of people using the Internet, by age, 2005)

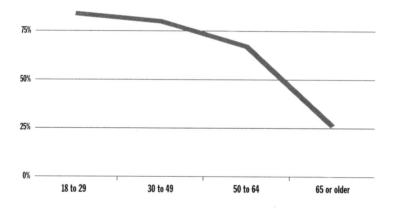

Table 9.11 Computer and Internet Use by Age, 2005

(percent of people aged 18 or older who use a computer, go online, and went online yesterday, by age, 2005)

	use a computer	go online	went online yesterday
Total people	**72%**	**68%**	**60%**
Aged 18 to 29	87	84	58
Aged 30 to 49	84	80	64
Aged 50 to 64	71	67	58
Aged 65 or older	29	26	49

Source: Pew Internet & American Life Project, Internet site http://www.pewinternet.org/trends.asp#demographics; calculations by New Strategist

Table 9.12 Online Activities Ever Done by Age, 2005

(percent of Internet users who have ever used the Internet for selected activities, by age, 2005)

	total	18 to 29	30 to 49	50 to 64	65 or older
Send or read email	91%	91%	91%	92%	91%
Research a product or service	78	79	82	78	65
Get news	72	75	75	71	56
Buy a product	67	68	69	66	48
Do research for job	51	44	59	51	17
Bank	41	40	48	35	27
Instant messaging	40	62	36	31	26
Download computer programs	39	46	40	32	26
Play a game	36	54	33	26	30
Use online classified ads to sell/buy/ find job, meet people	36	44	40	26	15
Read someone else's blog	27	32	27	24	17
Share files with others	27	39	24	22	14
Search for information about someone you know or might meet	27	32	27	23	29
Download music	25	46	22	12	6
Participate in an auction	24	27	27	19	12
Download screensavers	23	28	22	24	20
Download computer games	21	29	19	15	14
Download video files	18	28	18	8	3
Take part in chat rooms or discussions	17	34	15	7	5
View live remote images via a webcam	16	18	17	16	6
Visit an adult web site	13	18	13	9	2
Make a donation to charity	11	10	13	11	4
Create a blog	7	13	6	4	3

Source: Pew Internet & American Life Project, Internet site http://www.pewinternet.org/trends.asp#demographics

Voting Has Decreased among All but the Oldest Americans

Older Americans have considerable influence because so many vote.

The older people are, the more likely they are to vote. This has long been true, but the gap between young and old has widened over the years. In the 1972 presidential election (the first in which 18-to-20-year-olds could vote), 64 percent of people aged 65 or older voted compared with 50 percent of those aged 18 to 24—a gap of 14 percentage points. In the 2004 election, 69 percent of people aged 65 or older voted versus only 42 percent of people aged 18 to 24—a 27 percentage point difference.

A look at voting patterns in 2004 by generation reveals that voting rates rose from a low of 42 percent among Millennials to just over 50 percent among Gen Xers. Sixty-four percent of Boomers voted in 2004, as did 69 percent of Americans aged 59 or older. Because of their numbers, Boomers accounted for the largest share (40 percent) of voters in 2004. Older Americans were 28 percent of voters, while Gen Xers and Millennials were far behind at 19 and 13 percent, respectively.

■ The political power of Gen Xers will always be overshadowed by larger generations.

Generation Xers account for about one in five voters

(percent distribution of people voting in the 2004 presidential election, by generation)

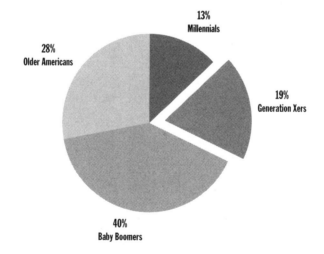

Table 9.13 Voting Rate by Age, 1964 to 2004

(percent of people who reported voting in presidential elections by age, and percentage point change, 1964 to 2004)

		presidential election years			
	total	18–24	25–44	45–64	65+
2004	58.3%	41.9%	52.2%	66.6%	68.9%
2000	54.7	32.3	49.8	64.1	67.6
1996	54.2	32.4	49.2	64.4	67.0
1992	61.3	42.8	58.3	70.0	70.1
1988	57.4	36.2	54.0	67.9	68.8
1984	59.9	40.8	58.4	69.8	67.7
1980	59.3	39.9	58.7	69.3	65.1
1976	59.2	42.2	58.7	68.7	62.2
1972	63.0	49.6	62.7	70.8	63.5
1968	67.8	50.4	66.6	74.9	65.8
1964	69.3	50.9	69.0	75.9	66.3
Percentage point change					
1964 to 2004	–11.0	–9.0	–16.8	–9.3	2.6

Note: Before 1972, data for 18-to-24-year-olds include only 21-to-24-year-olds.
Source: Bureau of the Census, Voting and Registration in the Election of November 2004, detailed tables, Internet site http://www.census.gov/population/www/socdemo/voting/cps2004.html; calculations by New Strategist

Table 9.14 Voting by Generation, 2004

(total number of people aged 18 or older, and number and percent who reported voting in the presidential election, by generation, 2004; numbers in thousands)

		voted		
	total	number	percent	percent distribution
Total people aged 18 or older	**215,694**	**125,736**	**58.3%**	**100.0%**
Millennials (aged 18 to 27)	39,335	16,636	42.3	13.2
Generation X (aged 28 to 39)	47,972	24,352	50.8	19.4
Baby Boom (aged 40 to 58)	78,253	50,060	64.0	39.8
Older Americans (aged 59 or older)	50,132	34,689	69.2	27.6

Source: Bureau of the Census, Voting and Registration in the Election of November 2004, detailed tables, Internet site http://

Young Adults Dominate Some Religious Groups

Presbyterians and Methodists are much older than Catholics or Baptists.

The religious affiliations of Americans are changing, in large part because younger adults adhere to different religious groups than older adults. The American Religious Identification Survey, taken in 2001 through the efforts of Egon Mayer, Barry A. Kosmin, and Ariela Keysar and sponsored by the Graduate Center of the City University of New York, reveals the differing age distributions of religious groups. In the nationally representative survey, respondents were asked to identify the religious group to which they belonged.

Catholics are by far the most numerous, with an estimated 51 million American adults identifying themselves as belonging to the Catholic Church.

Twenty-four percent of Catholics are aged 18 to 29, 62 percent are aged 30 to 64, and only 14 percent are aged 65 or older. Many religious groups are much older. Fully 35 percent of people who identify themselves as Congregational/UCC are aged 65 or older, as are 30 percent of self-identified Protestants, 29 percent of Presbyterians, and 27 percent of Methodists. At the other extreme, more than half of Muslims and Buddhists are aged 18 to 29. Typically, younger denominations have a greater potential for growth.

■ Twenty-nine million Americans do not identify with any religious group. Among those with no religion, only 8 percent are aged 65 or older.

Mormons are much younger than Methodists

(percent distribution of self-identified Methodists and Mormons, by age, 2001)

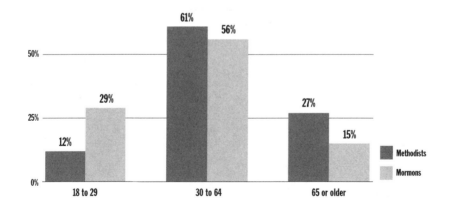

Table 9.15 Age Distribution of Religious Groups, 2001

(total number of adult members of selected religious groups and percent distribution by age, 2001; numbers in thousands)

	number	percent distribution			
		total	18–29	30–64	65 or older
Total U.S. adults	**208,000**	**100%**	**23%**	**61%**	**16%**
Catholic	50,873	100	24	62	14
Baptist	33,830	100	21	63	16
No religion	29,481	100	35	57	8
Christian	14,190	100	35	58	7
Methodist	14,140	100	12	61	27
Lutheran	9,580	100	15	63	22
Presbyterian	5,596	100	10	61	29
Protestant	4,647	100	13	57	30
Pentecostal	4,407	100	24	67	9
Episcopalian/Anglican	3,451	100	10	62	28
Jewish	2,831	100	14	58	28
Mormon	2,787	100	29	56	15
Churches of Christ	2,503	100	17	58	25
Nondenominational	2,489	100	23	65	12
Congregational/UCC	1,378	100	11	54	35
Jehovah's Witnesses	1,331	100	24	66	10
Assemblies of God	1,105	100	21	69	10
Muslim/Islamic	1,104	100	58	42	–
Buddhist	1,082	100	56	41	3
Evangelical/born again	1,032	100	19	72	9
Church of God	944	100	16	65	19
Seventh Day Adventist	724	100	10	64	26

Note: Religious group is self-identified; numbers will not add to total because not all groups are shown. "–" means sample is too small to make a reliable estimate.
Source: American Religious Indentification Survey 2001, Barry A. Kosmin, Egon Mayer, and Ariela Keysar. For further details see: Barry A. Kosmin and Ariela Keysar, Religion in a Free Market, Paramount Market Publishing, Inc. Ithaca, NY, 2006.

More than One in Four Volunteer

The middle aged are most likely to volunteer.

Among people aged 16 or older, 29 percent volunteered their time between September 2004 and September 2005, according to the Bureau of Labor Statistics, which defines volunteers as those who performed unpaid activities for an organization at least once during the time period. Volunteering peaks in middle age at 29 percent among men aged 35 to 54 and 40 percent among women aged 35 to 44. Many are volunteering at their children's school or for their children's extracurricular organizations.

Volunteers donate a median of 50 hours a year to the task, or an average of one hour a week. Among volunteers under age 45, the largest share donates time to educational and youth service organizations. Among volunteers aged 45 or older, the largest share works for a religious organization.

■ The most important reason people say they volunteer is because someone asked them to, cited by 43 percent. A slightly smaller share (40 percent) say they volunteered to volunteer.

Volunteering is lowest among young adults

(percent of people volunteering, by age, 2005)

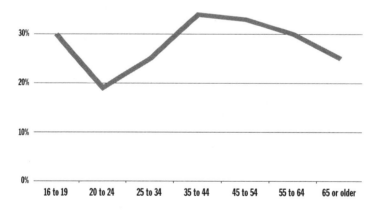

Table 9.16 Volunteering by Sex and Age, 2005

(number of people aged 16 or older, and number and percent who performed unpaid volunteer activities for an organization at any point during the past year, by sex and age, September 2005; numbers in thousands)

		volunteers	
	total	number	percent of total
Total people	**226,693**	**65,357**	**28.8%**
Aged 16 to 19	16,443	5,000	30.4
Aged 20 to 24	20,291	3,956	19.5
Aged 25 to 34	39,118	9,881	25.3
Aged 35 to 44	42,968	14,809	34.5
Aged 45 to 54	42,316	13,826	32.7
Aged 55 to 64	30,410	9,173	30.2
Aged 65 or older	35,146	8,712	24.8
Total men	**109,475**	**27,370**	**25.0**
Aged 16 to 19	8,339	2,282	27.4
Aged 20 to 24	10,193	1,576	15.5
Aged 25 to 34	19,479	3,949	20.3
Aged 35 to 44	21,165	6,105	28.8
Aged 45 to 54	20,701	5,999	29.0
Aged 55 to 64	14,622	3,999	27.3
Aged 65 or older	14,975	3,460	23.1
Total women	**117,218**	**37,987**	**32.4**
Aged 16 to 19	8,104	2,718	33.5
Aged 20 to 24	10,098	2,380	23.6
Aged 25 to 34	19,639	5,931	30.2
Aged 35 to 44	21,803	8,704	39.9
Aged 45 to 54	21,615	7,828	36.2
Aged 55 to 64	15,788	5,174	32.8
Aged 65 or older	20,170	5,252	26.0

Source: Bureau of Labor Statistics, Volunteering in the United States, 2005, Internet site http://www.bls.gov/news.release/volun .toc.htm

Table 9.17   Volunteering by Age and Type of Organization, 2005

(number of people aged 16 or older who performed unpaid volunteer activities for an organization at any point in the past year, median annual hours of volunteer work performed, and percent distribution by type of organization for which the volunteer worked the most hours, by age, September 2005)

	total	16 to 19	20 to 24	25 to 34	35 to 44	45 to 54	55 to 64	65 or older
Total volunteers (in 000s)	**65,357**	**5,000**	**3,956**	**9,881**	**14,809**	**13,826**	**9,173**	**8,712**
Median annual hours	50	36	40	36	48	50	56	96
TYPE OF ORGANIZATION								
Total volunteers	**100.0%**	**100.0%**	**100.0%**	**100.0%**	**100.0%**	**100.0%**	**100.0%**	**100.0%**
Civic, political, professional, or international	6.4	3.4	5.3	6.8	4.8	6.8	8.0	8.2
Educational or youth service	26.2	36.5	27.3	33.6	37.9	25.6	13.5	6.2
Environmental or animal care	1.8	2.1	2.9	2.1	1.3	2.1	2.1	0.9
Hospital or other health	7.7	7.6	9.0	6.6	5.8	7.7	8.9	10.1
Public safety	1.3	1.0	2.3	1.7	1.1	1.3	1.4	0.8
Religious	34.8	27.7	27.3	29.1	31.2	36.8	41.2	45.0
Social or community service	13.4	13.6	16.6	13.1	10.5	11.4	15.5	18.0
Sport, hobby, cultural, or arts	3.3	2.8	2.7	3.0	3.0	3.6	3.8	3.7
Other	3.5	2.9	4.5	3.1	3.1	3.1	4.0	4.7
Not determined	1.7	2.5	2.1	1.0	1.3	1.7	1.7	2.3

Source: Bureau of Labor Statistics, Volunteering in the United States, 2005, Internet site http://www.bls.gov/news.release/volun .toc.htm

Table 9.18 Volunteering by Age and Type of Work Performed, 2005

(number of people aged 16 or older who performed unpaid volunteer activities for an organization at any point in the past year, and percent distribution by type of work performed for the organization for which the volunteer worked the most hours, by age, September 2005)

	total	16 to 19	20 to 24	25 to 34	35 to 44	45 to 54	55 to 64	65 or older
Total volunteers (in 000s)	65,357	5,000	3,956	9,881	14,809	13,826	9,173	8,712

TYPE OF WORK PERFORMED FOR MAIN ORGANIZATION

	total	16 to 19	20 to 24	25 to 34	35 to 44	45 to 54	55 to 64	65 or older
Total volunteers	100.0%	100.0%	100.0%	100.0%	100.0%	100.0%	100.0%	100.0%
Coach, referee, or surpervise sports teams	8.9	12.0	11.1	11.6	13.0	9.1	3.4	1.5
Tutor or teach	21.3	21.4	22.8	24.0	24.6	21.4	19.4	13.6
Mentor youth	17.6	20.2	24.6	20.5	20.9	18.0	13.9	7.3
Be an usher, greeter, or minister	13.1	10.0	8.7	9.5	11.0	15.0	17.1	17.7
Collect, prepare, distribute, or serve food	26.3	25.2	21.4	23.4	25.5	27.3	28.5	29.9
Collect, make, distribute goods other than food	16.2	14.5	14.5	15.7	16.4	15.7	16.7	18.6
Fundraise or sell items to raise money	29.7	29.3	23.3	29.7	32.9	32.6	30.1	22.9
Provide counseling, medical care, fire/ EMS or protective services	7.4	3.9	9.1	7.9	6.6	8.3	8.7	6.8
Provide general office services	12.8	9.5	8.8	10.8	13.2	13.0	14.4	15.9
Provide professional or management assistance, including serving on a board or committee	17.7	4.4	8.1	12.8	18.9	21.6	23.8	20.6
Engage in music performance or other artistic activity	11.5	16.3	14.9	12.5	11.3	10.3	10.7	8.7
Engage in general labor, supply transportation	22.5	23.2	19.7	22.2	23.1	24.4	22.9	19.6
Other or not reported	15.3	14.9	15.8	15.4	14.0	14.5	14.3	19.9

Note: Percentages will sum to more than 100 because more than one type of activity may have been performed.
Source: Bureau of Labor Statistics, Volunteering in the United States, 2005, Internet site http://www.bls.gov/news.release/volun .toc.htm

Table 9.19 Volunteering by Method of Involvement and Age, 2005

(number of people aged 16 or older who performed unpaid volunteer activities for an organization at any point in the past year, and percent distribution by how they became involved with main organization for which they volunteered, by age, September, 2005)

	total	16 to 19	20 to 24	25 to 34	35 to 44	45 to 54	55 to 64	65 or older
Total volunteers (in 000s)	65,357	5,000	3,956	9,881	14,809	13,826	9,173	8,712

HOW VOLUNTEERS BECAME INVOLVED WITH MAIN ORGANIZATION

	total	16 to 19	20 to 24	25 to 34	35 to 44	45 to 54	55 to 64	65 or older
Total volunteers	100.0%	100.0%	100.0%	100.0%	100.0%	100.0%	100.0%	100.0%
Approached the organization	40.3	40.0	39.0	39.4	40.2	40.2	40.6	42.1
Were asked to volunteer	42.8	40.0	41.5	44.9	43.3	43.7	42.4	41.0
Asked by boss or employer	1.5	0.5	2.3	2.6	1.5	1.6	1.2	0.4
Asked by relative, friend, or co-worker	14.1	14.8	18.7	15.3	13.3	12.8	14.1	13.7
Asked by someone in organization/school	25.9	23.1	18.4	25.5	27.5	28.0	25.8	25.2
Asked by someone else	1.2	1.4	1.8	1.4	0.9	1.0	1.1	1.6
Other or not reported	16.9	20.0	19.6	15.7	16.5	16.0	17.1	16.9

Source: Bureau of Labor Statistics, Volunteering in the United States, 2005, Internet site http://www.bls.gov/news.release/volun .toc.htm

Vietnam Veterans Outnumber Others

One-third of veterans served in Vietnam.

Twenty-five million Americans are veterans, and 38 percent of them are aged 65 or older. Despite the older age of the nation's veterans, the largest share of vets served not in World War II, but in Vietnam. Seventeen percent served in the Gulf war, which includes anyone serving in the military from August 2, 1990, to the present.

World War II veterans, once most numerous, now number only 3.9 million and account for just 16 percent of the veteran population. The 8.1 million Vietnam vets account for a much larger 33 percent of the veteran population. Only 3.4 million veterans served during the Korean conflict, accounting for 14 percent of the total.

■ Women account for 7 percent of all veterans, but for 16 percent of Gulf war veterans.

Few living veterans served during World War II

(percent distribution of veterans by time of service, 2004)

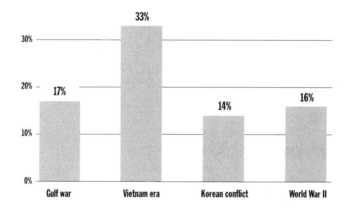

Table 9.20 Veterans by Age and Service, 2004

(number and percent distribution of living veterans by age and service, 2004; numbers in thousands)

	total veterans	wartime veterans total	Gulf war	Vietnam era	Korean conflict	World War II	peacetime veterans
Total veterans	**24,793**	**18,477**	**4,105**	**8,147**	**3,423**	**3,916**	**6,316**
Under age 35	2,007	1,946	1,946	0	0	0	61
Aged 35 to 39	1,332	768	768	0	0	0	564
Aged 40 to 44	1,732	520	520	0	0	0	1,212
Aged 45 to 49	1,906	738	383	393	0	0	1,168
Aged 50 to 54	2,172	1,858	267	1,731	0	0	314
Aged 55 to 59	3,572	3,448	151	3,409	0	0	124
Aged 60 to 64	2,553	1,762	48	1,755	0	0	791
Aged 65 or older	9,520	7,437	22	859	3,423	3,916	2,083
Female	1,692	1,130	647	262	80	178	562

PERCENT DISTRIBUTION BY AGE

	total veterans	wartime veterans total	Gulf war	Vietnam era	Korean conflict	World War II	peacetime veterans
Total veterans	**100.0%**	**100.0%**	**100.0%**	**100.0%**	**100.0%**	**100.0%**	**100.0%**
Under age 35	8.1	10.5	47.4	0.0	0.0	0.0	1.0
Aged 35 to 39	5.4	4.2	18.7	0.0	0.0	0.0	8.9
Aged 40 to 44	7.0	2.8	12.7	0.0	0.0	0.0	19.2
Aged 45 to 49	7.7	4.0	9.3	4.8	0.0	0.0	18.5
Aged 50 to 54	8.8	10.1	6.5	21.2	0.0	0.0	5.0
Aged 55 to 59	14.4	18.7	3.7	41.8	0.0	0.0	2.0
Aged 60 to 64	10.3	9.5	1.2	21.5	0.0	0.0	12.5
Aged 65 or older	38.4	40.3	0.5	10.5	100.0	100.0	33.0
Percent female	6.8	6.1	15.8	3.2	2.3	4.5	8.9

PERCENT DISTRIBUTION BY SERVICE

	total veterans	wartime veterans total	Gulf war	Vietnam era	Korean conflict	World War II	peacetime veterans
Total veterans	**100.0%**	**74.5%**	**16.6%**	**32.9%**	**13.8%**	**15.8%**	**25.5%**
Under age 35	100.0	97.0	97.0	0.0	0.0	0.0	3.0
Aged 35 to 39	100.0	57.7	57.7	0.0	0.0	0.0	42.3
Aged 40 to 44	100.0	30.0	30.0	0.0	0.0	0.0	70.0
Aged 45 to 49	100.0	38.7	20.1	20.6	0.0	0.0	61.3
Aged 50 to 54	100.0	85.5	12.3	79.7	0.0	0.0	14.5
Aged 55 to 59	100.0	96.5	4.2	95.4	0.0	0.0	3.5
Aged 60 to 64	100.0	69.0	1.9	68.7	0.0	0.0	31.0
Aged 65 or older	100.0	78.1	0.2	9.0	36.0	41.1	21.9
Female	100.0	66.8	38.2	15.5	4.7	10.5	33.2

Note: Veterans who served in more than one wartime period are counted only once in the wartime veterans total. Gulf war veterans are those serving from August 2, 1990, to present.
Source: Bureau of the Census, Statistical Abstract of the United States: 2006, Internet site http://www.census.gov/statab/www/; calculations by New Strategist

The Young Are Most Likely to Be Crime Victims

Victimization rate drops sharply with age.

Although older Americans are most fearful of crime, young people are more likely to become victims of crime. Among people aged 12 to 24, the violent-crime victimization rate stands at 43 to 50 crimes per 1,000 people in the age group. This is more than twice the rate for all Americans aged 12 or older. Among people aged 65 or older, the violent-crime victimization rate is just 2 per 1,000.

A variety of factors contribute to the higher victimization rate of young people, who are also more likely than their elders to commit crimes. Because older Americans are more fearful of crime, they take steps to protect themselves—such as avoiding going out at night or venturing into certain areas. Young people, on the other hand, are notorious for living on the edge, believing they are invulnerable to danger. As people enter middle age, they become increasingly aware of their vulnerability, which in turn reduces their chances of becoming a crime victim. People aged 35 or older are less likely than average to be victims of violent crime.

■ The crime rate has dropped over the past few years, but young adults are still most likely to be victims of crime.

The oldest Americans are least likely to be victims of crime

(number of crimes per 1,000 people in age group, by age of victim, 2004)

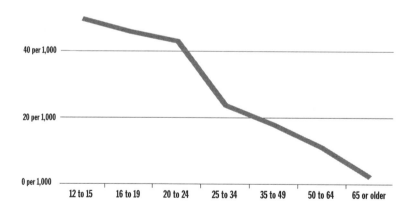

Table 9.21   Violent Crime and Personal Theft Victimization by Age, 2004

(population aged 12 or older, and number of victimizations per 1,000 people aged 12 or older, by age and type of crime, 2004)

		victimizations per 1,000 persons aged 12 or older						
		violent crime						
					assault			
	number (in 000s)	total	rape, sexual assault	robbery	total	aggravated	simple	personal theft
Total people	**241,704**	**21.4**	**0.9**	**2.1**	**18.5**	**4.3**	**14.2**	**0.9**
Aged 12 to 15	17,083	49.7	2.2	3.8	43.6	6.2	37.5	2.1
Aged 16 to 19	16,256	45.9	2.5	4.8	38.6	11.3	27.2	3.3
Aged 20 to 24	20,273	43.0	2.5	3.1	37.4	9.4	28.0	0.7
Aged 25 to 34	39,510	23.7	0.7	2.4	20.6	4.8	15.8	0.6
Aged 35 to 49	65,580	17.9	0.5	2.1	15.2	3.9	11.4	0.7
Aged 50 to 64	48,412	11.0	0.3	1.1	9.6	1.9	7.8	0.5
Aged 65 or older	34,590	2.1	0.1	0.3	1.8	0.5	1.3	0.8

Note: Violent crime as defined in the National Crime Victimization Survey includes rape/sexual assault, robbery, and assault. It does not include murder or manslaughter because it is based on interviews with victims. Personal theft includes pocket picking, purse snatching, and attempted purse snatching.
Source: Bureau of Justice Statistics, Criminal Victimization 2004, Internet site http://www.ojp.usdoj.gov/bjs/abstract/cv04.htm

Movies Lure Most People out of Their Home

Nearly three-quarters of Gen Xers have been to the movies.

Among the arts, movies attract the largest audience according to a study by the National Endowment for the Arts. Seventy-three percent of 25-to-34-year-olds (Generation X was aged 26 to 37 in 2002) attended at least one movie in the past year. Movie attendance drops below 50 percent in the 55-to-64 age group. But even among people aged 75 or older, about one in five went to a movie in the past year.

Literature also has a large audience. Forty-seven percent of people aged 18 or older read literature during the past year, with the figure peaking at 52 percent among people aged 45 to 54. Arts and crafts fairs or festivals attract about one-third of Americans each year, with attendance ranging from a low of 16 percent among people aged 75 or older to a high of 39 percent among those aged 45 to 54.

The most popular personal arts activity is purchasing original pieces of art—30 percent have done so in the past year. Among Gen Xers the figure is 39 percent. Sewing and needlework is especially popular among older Americans, with more than one in five 65-to-74-year-olds participating. Among Gen Xers the figure is 13 percent.

■ The arts audience is huge and diverse, spanning the age groups.

Movie attendance falls slowly with age

(percent of people aged 18 or older who went to the movies in the past year, by age, 2002)

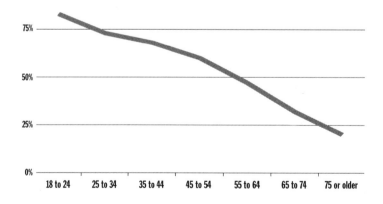

Table 9.22 Attendance at Arts Events by Age, 2002

(percent of people aged 18 or older who attended/visited/read selected arts during the past year, by age, 2002)

	total	18–24	25–34	35–44	45–54	55–64	65–74	75+
Read literature (novels, poetry, or plays)	46.7%	42.8%	47.7%	46.6%	51.6%	48.9%	45.3%	36.7%
Attended art fair/festival or craft fair/festival	33.4	29.2	33.5	37.2	38.8	35.1	31.1	15.7
Visited historic site	31.6	28.3	33.3	35.8	38.0	31.6	24.2	12.8
Visited art museum or gallery	26.5	23.7	26.7	27.4	32.9	27.8	23.4	13.4
Attended musical	17.1	14.8	15.4	19.1	19.3	19.7	16.6	10.1
Attended nonmusical play	12.3	11.4	10.7	13.0	15.2	13.8	13.0	5.4
Attended classical music performance	11.6	7.8	9.0	10.7	15.2	15.6	12.5	9.5
Attended jazz performance	10.8	10.5	10.8	13.0	13.9	8.8	7.6	3.9
Attended dance performance (except ballet)	6.3	6.2	5.9	7.0	8.0	6.0	5.4	3.0
Attended ballet	3.9	2.6	3.5	4.9	5.1	3.3	3.3	2.2
Attended opera	3.2	2.0	3.0	2.8	4.0	4.2	4.0	1.8

Source: National Endowment for the Arts, 2002 Survey of Public Participation in the Arts: Summary Report, Research Division Report No. 45, Internet site http://www.nea.gov/pub/ResearchReports_chrono.html

Table 9.23 Participation in the Arts through Media, 2002

(percent of people aged 18 or older who participated in the arts through media during the past year, by age, 2002)

	total	18–24	25–34	35–44	45–54	55–64	65–74	75+
Jazz								
TV	16.4%	10.7%	13.8%	17.7%	20.7%	17.0%	18.5%	15.1%
Radio	23.5	16.1	23.8	28.1	29.6	24.1	18.4	11.9
Recordings	17.2	13.1	17.5	21.1	21.8	16.8	11.8	7.7
Classical music								
TV	18.1	8.9	12.4	15.9	20.9	23.8	28.3	25.8
Radio	23.9	13.8	21.1	23.9	29.9	29.5	26.5	20.8
Recordings	19.3	14.1	18.1	19.3	23.1	22.9	20.8	14.2
Opera								
TV	5.8	3.0	3.7	4.5	5.7	8.1	10.5	9.7
Radio	5.7	2.0	4.5	4.3	6.4	8.7	9.4	7.7
Recordings	5.5	2.7	4.4	4.7	6.8	8.1	7.9	5.4
Musical play								
TV	11.7	7.2	9.8	11.8	13.3	12.3	16.2	14.1
Radio	2.4	1.9	1.7	2.5	2.6	2.8	3.2	2.6
Recordings	4.3	3.1	3.2	4.4	5.9	5.1	4.4	2.9
Non-musical play								
TV	9.4	7.0	7.3	8.5	9.7	12.3	13.6	11.1
Radio	2.1	1.3	2.1	2.3	2.8	1.6	2.4	1.4
Dance (on TV)	**12.6**	**8.7**	**10.0**	**13.0**	**13.8**	**15.0**	**15.1**	**14.4**
Artists, art work, or art museums (on TV)	**25.0**	**21.1**	**25.3**	**24.8**	**28.5**	**27.2**	**24.5**	**19.1**

Source: National Endowment for the Arts, 2002 Survey of Public Participation in the Arts: Summary Report, Research Division Report No. 45, Internet site http://www.nea.gov/pub/ResearchReports_chrono.html

Table 9.24 Personal Participation in the Arts, 2002

(percent of people aged 18 or older who personally participated in the arts during the past year, by age, 2002)

	total	18–24	25–34	35–44	45–54	55–64	65–74	75+
Purchased art in past year	29.5%	41.0%	39.1%	31.2%	27.9%	26.1%	23.7%	11.4%
Own original pieces of art	19.3	9.4	15.3	20.9	25.8	24.5	20.1	14.8
Sewing, weaving, crocheting, quilting, or needlepoint	16.0	10.4	13.0	15.3	18.6	19.1	20.5	18.0
Photography	11.5	12.9	12.3	14.1	12.1	10.5	8.1	3.8
Painting, drawing, sculpture, or printmaking	8.6	15.4	10.2	8.1	8.2	6.7	4.8	3.1
Writing	7.0	12.7	7.9	6.7	6.8	5.0	4.1	3.7
Pottery, jewelry, leatherwork, or metalwork	6.9	9.3	7.8	7.4	7.5	5.6	4.6	2.4
Choir/chorale	4.8	4.9	3.9	4.8	5.1	5.6	5.3	3.7
Dance (except ballet)	4.2	6.0	4.5	3.9	4.2	3.4	3.7	2.5
Musical play	2.4	2.5	2.1	2.1	2.7	2.6	2.1	2.2
Music composition	2.3	5.7	3.3	2.3	1.8	0.9	0.4	0.1
Classical music performance	1.8	2.5	1.4	1.8	2.5	1.5	1.4	0.7
Act in play	1.4	3.0	1.4	1.7	1.1	0.9	0.6	0.2
Jazz performance	1.3	1.9	1.2	1.5	2.0	0.8	0.5	0.4
Opera	0.7	0.7	0.6	0.6	0.9	0.9	0.8	0.7
Ballet	0.3	1.1	0.2	0.4	0.2	0.2	0.0	0.2

Source: National Endowment for the Arts, 2002 Survey of Public Participation in the Arts: Summary Report, Research Division Report No. 45, Internet site http://www.nea.gov/pub/ResearchReports_chrono.html

Table 9.25 Participation in Selected Leisure Activities, 2002

(percent of people aged 18 or older who participated in selected leisure activities during the past year, by age, 2002)

	total	18–24	25–34	35–44	45–54	55–64	65–74	75+
Go to the movies	60.0%	82.8%	73.3%	68.0%	60.4%	46.6%	32.2%	19.5%
Jog, lift weights, walk, or participate in any other exercise routine	55.1	61.3	60.2	59.5	58.6	48.4	47.0	31.3
Garden indoor or outdoor	47.3	20.7	41.4	51.0	55.4	56.6	57.2	47.9
Participate in home improvement or repair to own home	42.4	21.1	41.1	53.0	54.9	44.8	38.4	22.1
Go to an amusement park or carnival	41.7	57.6	56.2	53.3	37.1	27.1	18.4	9.6
Attend sports events (except youth sports)	35.0	46.0	41.8	42.2	35.8	25.5	19.7	11.1
Participate in outdoor activities such as camping, hiking, or canoeing	30.9	37.7	38.8	39.0	33.0	21.7	14.9	5.8
Participate in sports, such as golf, bowling, skiing, or basketball	30.4	49.4	39.6	36.6	28.6	16.0	13.7	6.0
Perform volunteer or charity work	29.0	25.3	26.0	33.2	33.4	28.1	28.8	21.3

Source: National Endowment for the Arts, 2002 Survey of Public Participation in the Arts: Summary Report, Research Division Report No. 45, Internet site http://www.nea.gov/pub/ResearchReports_chrono.html

10

Wealth

■ The median net worth of householders aged 35 to 44 (Generation X was aged 28 to 39 in 2004) fell 16 percent between 2001 and 2004, to $69,400, after adjusting for inflation.

■ The median value of the financial assets of households headed by 35-to-44-year-olds fell by an enormous 34 percent between 2001 and 2004, to $19,000, after adjusting for inflation. The value of their stock dropped 57 percent during those years—the biggest loss among age groups.

■ The median value of the nonfinancial assets owned by householders aged 35 to 44 rose by an average amount between 2001 and 2004—up by 21 percent to $151,300, after adjusting for inflation. The homes owned by householders aged 35 to 44 increased 20 percent in value, rising to a median of $160,000.

■ Householders aged 35 to 44 continue to be the biggest debtors, owing a median of $87,200 in 2004. Their debt increased by 33 percent between 2001 and 2004, after adjusting for inflation.

■ Only 42 percent of American workers were included in an employer's retirement plan in 2004. Among workers aged 35 to 44, a 48 percent minority participated in a retirement plan at work.

Net Worth Fell for Generation Xers

Net worth declined because they took on more debt.

Net worth is one of the most important measures of wealth. It is the amount remaining after a household's debts are subtracted from its assets. The median net worth of householders aged 35 to 44 (Generation X was aged 28 to 39 in 2004) fell a substantial 16 percent between 2001 and 2004, to $69,400. This was the only age group to experience a loss in net worth during those years.

One reason for the drop in the net worth of 35-to-44-year-olds is their late arrival to homeownership. Many delayed buying homes as home values rose. When they jumped into the housing market, prices were relatively high, forcing them to take on bigger mortgages. Householders aged 35 to 44 saw the median value of their primary residence climb 20 percent between 2001 and 2004 (to $160,000), but the value of their home-secured debt rose by an even larger 29 percent (to $110,000). To make matters worse, the median value of their financial assets fell 34 percent (to $19,000) because of stock market losses. With debt growing at a faster clip than assets, householders aged 35 to 44 lost ground.

■ The net worth of Gen Xers may always trail the net worth of Boomers and older Americans, who bought homes when prices were lower.

Householders aged 35 to 44 were the only ones who lost ground between 2001 and 2004

(percent change in net worth of households by age of householder, 2001 to 2004; in 2004 dollars)

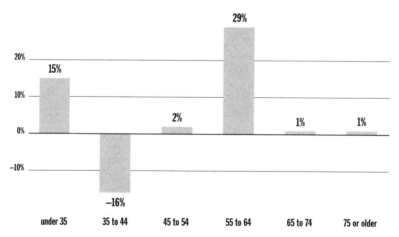

Table 10.1 Net Worth of Households by Age of Householder, 1995 to 2004

(median net worth of households by age of householder, 1995 to 2004; percent change, 1995–2004 and 2001–04; in 2004 dollars)

	2004	2001	1998	1995	percent change 2001–04	percent change 1995–2004
Total households	**$93,100**	**$91,700**	**$83,100**	**$70,800**	**1.5%**	**31.5%**
Under age 35	14,200	12,300	10,600	14,800	15.4	–4.1
Aged 35 to 44	69,400	82,600	73,500	64,200	–16.0	8.1
Aged 45 to 54	144,700	141,600	122,300	116,800	2.2	23.9
Aged 55 to 64	248,700	193,300	148,200	141,900	28.7	75.3
Aged 65 to 74	190,100	187,800	169,800	136,600	1.2	39.2
Aged 75 or older	163,100	161,200	145,600	114,500	1.2	42.4

Source: Federal Reserve Board, "Recent Changes in U.S. Family Finances: Evidence from the 2001 and 2004 Survey of Consumer Finances," Federal Reserve Bulletin, February 23, 2006, Internet site http://www.federalreserve.gov/pubs/bulletin/default.htm; calculations by New Strategist

Fewer Generation Xers Own Stock

The value of their financial assets has plunged.

Between 2001 and 2004, the financial assets of the average American household fell 23 percent after adjusting for inflation—to a median of $23,000, according to the Federal Reserve Board's Survey of Consumer Finances. The median value of the financial assets owned by house-holders aged 35 to 44 fell by an enormous 34 percent during those years (to $19,000).

Slightly fewer than half of households (48.6 percent) owned stock in 2004, down from the 51.9 percent majority in 2001. Stock ownership among householders aged 35 to 44 fell 7 percentage points between 2001 and 2004, to 52 percent. Householders aged 35 to 44 saw the value of their stock drop 57 percent during those years—the biggest drop among age groups.

Slightly fewer than half (49.7 percent) of households owned a retirement account in 2004, but among householders aged 35 to 44 the figure was 56 percent. The median value of the retirement accounts owned by the age group is a modest $27,900.

■ Nonfinancial assets have become increasingly important to household wealth because of declining stock values and rising housing prices.

The financial assets of Generation Xers are modest

(median value of financial assets of households by age of householder, 2004)

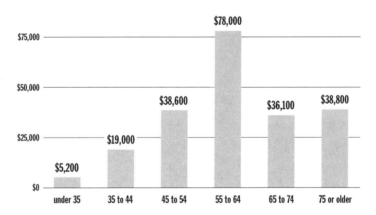

Table 10.2 Financial Assets of Households by Age of Householder, 2001 and 2004

(percentage of households owning financial assets and median value of assets for owners, by age of householder, 2001 and 2004; percentage point change in ownership and percent change in value of asset, 2001–04; in 2004 dollars)

	2004	2001	percentage point change
PERCENT OWNING ANY FINANCIAL ASSET			
Total households	**93.8%**	**93.4%**	**0.4**
Under age 35	90.1	89.7	0.4
Aged 35 to 44	93.6	93.5	0.1
Aged 45 to 54	93.6	94.7	–1.1
Aged 55 to 64	95.2	95.0	0.2
Aged 65 to 74	96.5	94.6	1.9
Aged 75 or older	97.6	95.1	2.5
	2004	**2001**	**percent change**
MEDIAN VALUE OF FINANCIAL ASSETS			
Total households	**$23,000**	**$29,800**	**–22.8%**
Under age 35	5,200	6,600	–21.2
Aged 35 to 44	19,000	28,600	–33.6
Aged 45 to 54	38,600	48,000	–19.6
Aged 55 to 64	78,000	59,800	30.4
Aged 65 to 74	36,100	54,700	–34.0
Aged 75 or older	38,800	42,600	–8.9

Source: Federal Reserve Board, "Recent Changes in U.S. Family Finances: Evidence from the 2001 and 2004 Survey of Consumer Finances," Federal Reserve Bulletin, February 23, 2006, Internet site http://www.federalreserve.gov/pubs/bulletin/default.htm; calculations by New Strategist

Table 10.3 Financial Assets of Households by Type of Asset and Age of Householder, 2004

(percentage of households owning financial assets, and median value of asset for owners, by type of asset and age of householder, 2004)

	total	under 35	35 to 44	45 to 54	55 to 64	65 to 74	75 or older
PERCENT OWNING ASSET							
Any financial asset	**93.8%**	**90.1%**	**93.6%**	**93.6%**	**95.2%**	**96.5%**	**97.6%**
Transaction accounts	91.3	86.4	90.8	91.8	93.2	93.9	96.4
Certificates of deposit	12.7	5.6	6.7	11.9	18.1	19.9	25.7
Savings bonds	17.6	15.3	23.3	21.0	15.2	14.9	11.0
Bonds	1.8	–	0.6	1.8	3.3	4.3	3.0
Stocks	20.7	13.3	18.5	23.2	29.1	25.4	18.4
Pooled investment funds	15.0	8.3	12.3	18.2	20.6	18.6	16.6
Retirement accounts	49.7	40.2	55.9	57.7	62.9	43.2	29.2
Cash value life insurance	24.2	11.0	20.1	26.0	32.1	34.8	34.0
Other managed assets	7.3	2.9	3.7	6.2	9.4	12.8	16.7
Other financial assets	10.0	11.6	10.0	12.1	7.2	8.1	8.1
MEDIAN VALUE OF ASSET							
Any financial asset	**$23,000**	**$5,200**	**$19,000**	**$38,600**	**$78,000**	**$36,100**	**$38,800**
Transaction accounts	3,800	1,800	3,000	4,800	6,700	5,500	6,500
Certificates of deposit	15,000	4,000	10,000	11,000	29,000	20,000	22,000
Savings bonds	1,000	500	500	1,000	2,500	3,000	5,000
Bonds	65,000	–	10,000	30,000	80,000	40,000	295,000
Stocks	15,000	4,400	10,000	14,500	25,000	42,000	50,000
Pooled investment funds	40,400	8,000	15,900	50,000	75,000	60,000	60,000
Retirement accounts	35,200	11,000	27,900	55,500	83,000	80,000	30,000
Cash value life insurance	6,000	3,000	5,000	8,000	10,000	8,000	5,000
Other managed assets	45,000	5,000	18,300	43,000	65,000	60,000	50,000
Other financial assets	4,000	1,000	3,500	5,000	7,000	10,000	22,000

Note: "–" means sample is too small to make a reliable estimate.
Source: Federal Reserve Board, "Recent Changes in U.S. Family Finances: Evidence from the 2001 and 2004 Survey of Consumer Finances," Federal Reserve Bulletin, February 23, 2006, Internet site http://www.federalreserve.gov/pubs/bulletin/default.htm; calculations by New Strategist

Table 10.4 Stock Ownership of Households by Age of Householder, 2001 and 2004

(percentage of householders owning stocks directly or indirectly, median value of stock for owners, and share of total household financial assets accounted for by stock holdings, by age of householder, 2001 and 2004; percent and percentage point change, 2001–04; in 2004 dollars)

	2004	2001	percentage point change
PERCENT OWNING STOCK			
Total households	**48.6%**	**51.9%**	**–3.3**
Under age 35	38.8	48.9	–10.1
Aged 35 to 44	52.3	59.5	–7.2
Aged 45 to 54	54.4	59.2	–4.8
Aged 55 to 64	61.6	57.1	4.5
Aged 65 to 74	45.8	39.2	6.6
Aged 75 or older	34.8	34.2	0.6

	2004	2001	percent change
MEDIAN VALUE OF STOCK			
Total households	**$24,300**	**$36,700**	**–33.8%**
Under age 35	5,200	7,500	–30.7
Aged 35 to 44	12,700	29,300	–56.7
Aged 45 to 54	30,600	53,300	–42.6
Aged 55 to 64	59,500	86,500	–31.2
Aged 65 to 74	75,000	159,800	–53.1
Aged 75 or older	85,900	127,800	–32.8

	2004	2001	percentage point change
STOCK AS SHARE OF FINANCIAL ASSETS			
Total households	**47.4%**	**56.0%**	**–8.6**
Under age 35	30.0	52.5	–22.5
Aged 35 to 44	47.7	57.3	–9.6
Aged 45 to 54	46.8	59.1	–12.3
Aged 55 to 64	51.1	56.2	–5.1
Aged 65 to 74	51.1	55.2	–4.1
Aged 75 or older	39.1	51.4	–12.3

Source: Federal Reserve Board, "Recent Changes in U.S. Family Finances: Evidence from the 2001 and 2004 Survey of Consumer Finances," Federal Reserve Bulletin, February 23, 2006, Internet site http://www.federalreserve.gov/pubs/bulletin/default.htm; calculations by New Strategist

The Nonfinancial Assets of Generation Xers Have Grown

Rising housing prices have helped and hurt.

The median value of the nonfinancial assets owned by the average American household stood at $147,800 in 2004, a gain of 22 percent since 2001, after adjusting for inflation. The value of the nonfinancial assets owned by householders aged 35 to 44 rose by 21 percent during those years. In 2004, the median value of the nonfinancial assets of householders aged 35 to 44 stood at $151,300.

Because housing equity accounts for the largest share of nonfinancial assets, the rise in home values is the biggest contributor to gains in this category. Among homeowners aged 35 to 44, median home value rose by 20 percent between 2001 and 2004, after adjusting for inflation. The homes of householders aged 35 to 44 had a median value of $160,000 in 2004. The value of home-secured debt also rose between 2001 and 2004, limiting gains in net worth.

■ Nonfinancial assets grew as a share of the average household's total assets between 2001 and 2004, rising from 58 to 64 percent.

The nonfinancial assets of Generation Xers are only slightly above average

(median value of nonfinancial assets of households by age of householder, 2004)

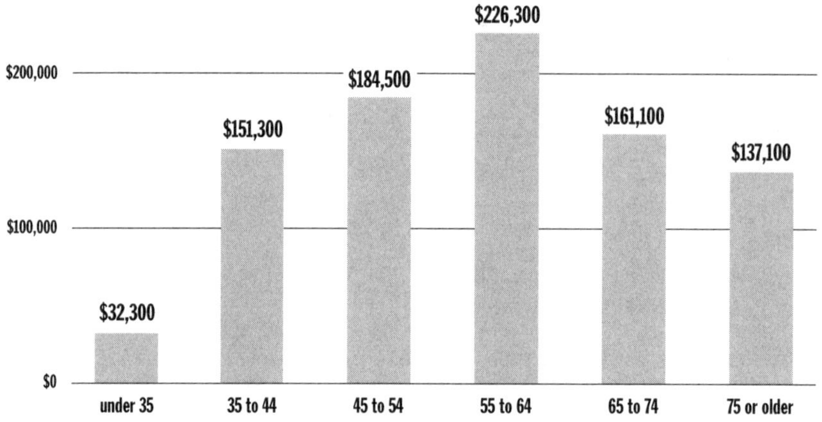
$200,000
$100,000
$0
$32,300
$151,300
$184,500
$226,300
$161,100
$137,100
under 35
35 to 44
45 to 54
55 to 64
65 to 74
75 or older

Table 10.5 Nonfinancial Assets of Households by Age of Householder, 2001 and 2004

(percentage of households owning nonfinancial assets and median value of assets for owners, by age of house-holder, 2001 and 2004; percentage point change in ownership and percent change in value of asset, 2001–04; in 2004 dollars)

	2004	2001	percentage point change
PERCENT OWNING ANY NONFINANCIAL ASSET			
Total households	**92.5%**	**90.7%**	**1.8**
Under age 35	88.6	83.0	5.6
Aged 35 to 44	93.0	93.2	–0.2
Aged 45 to 54	94.7	95.2	–0.5
Aged 55 to 64	92.6	95.4	–2.8
Aged 65 to 74	95.6	91.6	4.0
Aged 75 or older	92.5	86.4	6.1
	2004	**2001**	**percent change**
MEDIAN VALUE OF NONFINANCIAL ASSETS			
Total households	**$147,800**	**$120,900**	**22.2%**
Under age 35	32,300	31,700	1.9
Aged 35 to 44	151,300	125,500	20.6
Aged 45 to 54	184,500	150,800	22.3
Aged 55 to 64	226,300	157,500	43.7
Aged 65 to 74	161,100	158,900	1.4
Aged 75 or older	137,100	130,600	5.0

Source: Federal Reserve Board, "Recent Changes in U.S. Family Finances: Evidence from the 2001 and 2004 Survey of Consumer Finances," Federal Reserve Bulletin, February 23, 2006, Internet site http://www.federalreserve.gov/pubs/bulletin/default.htm; calculations by New Strategist

Table 10.6 Nonfinancial Assets of Households by Type of Asset and Age of Householder, 2004

(percentage of households owning nonfinancial assets, and median value of asset for owners, by type of asset and age of householder, 2004)

	total	under 35	35 to 44	45 to 54	55 to 64	65 to 74	75 or older
PERCENT OWNING ASSET							
Any nonfinancial asset	**92.5%**	**88.6%**	**93.0%**	**94.7%**	**92.6%**	**95.6%**	**92.5%**
Vehicles	86.3	82.9	89.4	88.8	88.6	89.1	76.9
Primary residence	69.1	41.6	68.3	77.3	79.1	81.3	85.2
Other residential property	12.5	5.1	9.4	16.3	19.5	19.9	9.7
Equity in nonresidential property	8.3	3.3	6.4	11.4	12.8	10.6	7.7
Business equity	11.5	6.9	13.9	15.7	15.8	8.0	5.3
Other nonfinancial assets	7.8	5.5	6.0	9.7	9.2	9.0	8.5
MEDIAN VALUE OF ASSET							
Total nonfinancial assets	**$147,800**	**$32,300**	**$151,300**	**$184,500**	**$226,300**	**$161,100**	**$137,100**
Vehicles	14,200	11,300	15,600	18,800	18,600	12,400	8,400
Primary residence	160,000	135,000	160,000	170,000	200,000	150,000	125,000
Other residential property	100,000	82,500	80,000	90,000	135,000	80,000	150,000
Equity in nonresidential property	60,000	55,000	42,200	43,000	75,000	78,000	85,800
Business equity	100,000	50,000	100,000	144,000	190,900	100,000	80,300
Other nonfinancial assets	15,000	5,000	10,000	20,000	25,000	30,000	11,000

Source: Federal Reserve Board, "Recent Changes in U.S. Family Finances: Evidence from the 2001 and 2004 Survey of Consumer Finances," Federal Reserve Bulletin, February 23, 2006, Internet site http://www.federalreserve.gov/pubs/bulletin/default.htm; calculations by New Strategist

Table 10.7 Household Ownership of Primary Residence by Age of Householder, 2001 and 2004

(percentage of households owning their primary residence, median value of asset for owners, and median value of home-secured debt for owners, by age of householder, 2001 and 2004; percentage point change in ownership and percent change in value of asset, 2001–04; in 2004 dollars)

	2004	2001	percentage point change
PERCENT OWNING PRIMARY RESIDENCE			
Total households	**69.1%**	**67.7%**	**1.4**
Under age 35	41.6	39.9	1.7
Aged 35 to 44	68.3	67.8	0.5
Aged 45 to 54	77.3	76.2	1.1
Aged 55 to 64	79.1	83.2	−4.1
Aged 65 to 74	81.3	82.5	−1.2
Aged 75 or older	85.2	76.2	9.0

	2004	2001	percent change
MEDIAN VALUE OF PRIMARY RESIDENCE			
Total households	**$160,000**	**$131,000**	**22.1%**
Under age 35	135,000	101,200	33.4
Aged 35 to 44	160,000	133,100	20.2
Aged 45 to 54	170,000	143,800	18.2
Aged 55 to 64	200,000	138,500	44.4
Aged 65 to 74	150,000	137,400	9.2
Aged 75 or older	125,000	118,200	5.8

	2004	2001	percent change
MEDIAN VALUE OF HOME-SECURED DEBT			
Total households	**$95,000**	**$74,600**	**27.3%**
Under age 35	107,000	82,000	30.5
Aged 35 to 44	110,000	85,200	29.1
Aged 45 to 54	97,000	79,900	21.4
Aged 55 to 64	83,000	58,600	41.6
Aged 65 to 74	51,000	41,500	22.9
Aged 75 or older	31,000	47,700	−35.0

Source: Federal Reserve Board, "Recent Changes in U.S. Family Finances: Evidence from the 2001 and 2004 Survey of Consumer Finances," Federal Reserve Bulletin, February 23, 2006, Internet site http://www.federalreserve.gov/pubs/bulletin/default.htm; calculations by New Strategist

Debt Increased for Generation Xers

The biggest debtors are householders aged 35 to 44.

The debt of the average American household grew by a substantial 34 percent between 2001 and 2004, to $55,300, after adjusting for inflation. Among householders aged 35 to 44, debt rose 33 percent during those years. Householders aged 35 to 44 continue to be the biggest debtors, owing a median of $87,200 in 2004.

Home-secured debt accounts for the largest share of debt by far. Forty-eight percent of households have home-secured debt, owing a median of $95,000. Householders aged 35 to 44 have the largest median amount of home-secured debt ($110,000). The 59 percent majority of householders aged 35 to 44 carry a credit card balance, owing a median of $2,500 on their credit cards in 2004. Fifty-six percent of householders aged 35 to 44 have an installment loan (primarily car loans), owing a median of $12,000.

■ Unless Gen Xers get serious about paying down their mortgage debt, they will not see much growth in their net worth.

Generation Xers owe the most

(median amount of debt owed by households by age of householder, 2004)

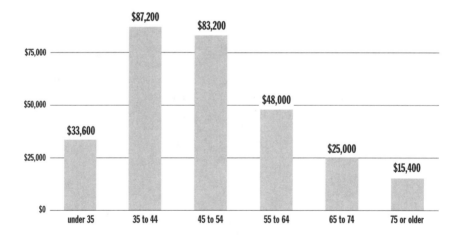

Table 10.8 Debt of Households by Age of Householder, 2001 and 2004

(percentage of households with debt and median amount of debt for debtors, by age of householder, 2001 and 2004; percentage point change in households with debt and percent change in amount of debt, 2001–04; in 2004 dollars)

	2004	2001	percentage point change
PERCENT WITH DEBT			
Total households	**76.4%**	**75.1%**	**1.3**
Under age 35	79.8	82.7	–2.9
Aged 35 to 44	88.6	88.6	0.0
Aged 45 to 54	88.4	84.6	3.8
Aged 55 to 64	76.3	75.4	0.9
Aged 65 to 74	58.8	56.8	2.0
Aged 75 or older	40.3	29.2	11.1

	2004	2001	percent change
MEDIAN AMOUNT OF DEBT			
Total households	**$55,300**	**$41,300**	**33.9%**
Under age 35	33,600	26,500	26.8
Aged 35 to 44	87,200	65,500	33.1
Aged 45 to 54	83,200	57,800	43.9
Aged 55 to 64	48,000	36,900	30.1
Aged 65 to 74	25,000	14,000	78.6
Aged 75 or older	15,400	5,300	190.6

Source: Federal Reserve Board, "Recent Changes in U.S. Family Finances: Evidence from the 2001 and 2004 Survey of Consumer Finances," Federal Reserve Bulletin, February 23, 2006, Internet site http://www.federalreserve.gov/pubs/bulletin/default.htm; calculations by New Strategist

Table 10.9 Debt of Households by Type of Debt and Age of Householder, 2004

(percentage of householders with debt, and median value of debt for those with debt, by type of debt and age of householder, 2004)

	total	under 35	35 to 44	45 to 54	55 to 64	65 to 74	75 or older
PERCENT WITH DEBT							
Any debt	**76.4%**	**79.8%**	**88.6%**	**88.4%**	**76.3%**	**58.8%**	**40.3%**
Secured by residential property							
Primary residence	47.9	37.7	62.8	64.6	51.0	32.1	18.7
Other	4.0	2.1	4.0	6.3	5.9	3.2	1.5
Lines of credit not secured by residential property	1.6	2.2	1.5	2.9	0.7	0.4	–
Installment loans	46.0	59.4	55.7	50.2	42.8	27.5	13.9
Credit card balances	46.2	47.5	58.8	54.0	42.1	31.9	23.6
Other debt	7.6	6.2	11.3	9.4	8.4	4.0	2.5
MEDIAN AMOUNT OF DEBT							
Any debt	**$55,300**	**$33,600**	**$87,200**	**$83,200**	**$48,000**	**$25,000**	**$15,400**
Secured by residential property							
Primary residence	95,000	107,000	110,000	97,000	83,000	51,000	31,000
Other	87,000	62,500	75,000	87,000	108,800	100,000	39,000
Lines of credit not secured by residential property	3,000	1,000	1,900	7,000	14,000	4,000	–
Installment loans	11,500	11,900	12,000	12,000	12,900	8,300	6,700
Credit card balances	2,200	1,500	2,500	2,900	2,200	2,200	1,000
Other debt	4,000	3,000	4,000	4,000	5,500	5,000	2,000

Note: "–" means sample is too small to make a reliable estimate.
Source: Federal Reserve Board, "Recent Changes in U.S. Family Finances: Evidence from the 2001 and 2004 Survey of Consumer Finances," Federal Reserve Bulletin, February 23, 2006, Internet site http://www.federalreserve.gov/pubs/bulletin/default.htm; calculations by New Strategist

Fewer than Half of Generation Xers Have a Retirement Plan

Many worry about their economic security in retirement.

Only 42 percent of American workers were included in an employer's retirement plan in 2004, according to an analysis of government statistics by the Employee Benefit Research Institute (EBRI). Retirement plan participation peaks among workers aged 45 to 64, at 53 to 54 percent. Among workers aged 35 to 44, only 48 percent participate in an employer's retirement plan. Those in the private sector are much less likely to participate than public sector workers, 47 versus 77 percent.

Another EBRI study shows only 43 percent of workers aged 35 to 44 own an IRA or participate in a 401(k)-type (defined-contribution) retirement plan. Among participants in 401(k)-type plans, the median balance was just $15,000.

Having minimal savings, it is no surprise that Gen Xers are worried about retirement. Only 25 percent of workers aged 35 to 44 are "very confident" they will have enough money to live comfortably throughout retirement. Just 20 percent have savings of $100,000 or more.

■ The substitution of defined-contribution for defined-benefit pension plans puts the burden of retirement savings on workers rather than employers. With Gen Xers finding it hard to save, their retirement lifestyle may be Spartan.

Among workers aged 35 to 44, fewer than half participate in an employer-sponsored retirement plan

(percent of workers participating in an employer-sponsored retirement plan, by age, 2004)

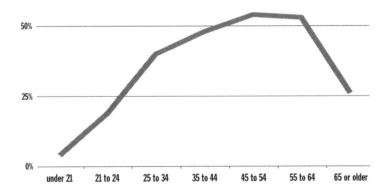

Table 10.10 Retirement-Plan Coverage by Age, 2004

(total number of workers, percent whose employer offers a retirement plan, and percent participating in plan, by type of employment and age of worker, 2004; numbers in thousands)

	number of workers	percent with an employer who sponsors a retirement plan	percent participating in employer's retirement plan
Total workers	**152,708**	**53.2%**	**41.9%**
Under age 21	10,824	24.9	4.1
Aged 21 to 24	12,602	41.0	19.4
Aged 25 to 34	32,468	52.8	39.7
Aged 35 to 44	36,214	57.3	48.3
Aged 45 to 54	34,585	61.2	53.9
Aged 55 to 64	19,654	60.3	53.0
Aged 65 or older	6,361	38.4	25.8
Private wage and salary workers aged 21 to 64			
Total workers	**105,703**	**54.5**	**43.0**
Aged 21 to 24	11,163	39.4	18.2
Aged 25 to 34	26,949	51.0	37.1
Aged 35 to 44	28,344	56.7	46.8
Aged 45 to 54	25,497	59.8	51.5
Aged 55 to 64	13,750	59.3	51.1
Public wage and salary workers aged 21 to 64			
Total workers	**20,529**	**85.1**	**75.8**
Aged 21 to 24	1,156	64.4	35.6
Aged 25 to 34	3,985	82.5	69.8
Aged 35 to 44	5,216	85.1	77.0
Aged 45 to 54	6,319	88.4	82.5
Aged 55 to 64	3,853	88.8	81.7

Source: Employee Benefit Research Institute, "Employment-Based Retirement Plan Participation: Geographic Differences and Trends, 2004," Issue Brief, No. 286, October 2005, Internet site http://www.ebri.org/publications/ib/index.cfm?fa=ibDisp&content_id=3590

Table 10.11 Ownership of IRAs and Participation in 401(k)s by Age, 2002

(percentage of workers aged 21 to 64 owning IRAs and/or participating in a 401(k)-type plan, by age, 2002)

	IRA and/or 401(k)-type plan	IRA only	401(k)-type plan only	both IRA and 401(k)-type plan	neither IRA nor 401(k)-type plan
Total workers	**40.4%**	**9.6%**	**21.7%**	**9.2%**	**59.6%**
Aged 21 to 24	10.6	1.5	8.4	0.7	89.4
Aged 25 to 34	34.3	5.7	22.9	5.7	65.7
Aged 35 to 44	43.0	9.1	24.4	9.6	57.0
Aged 45 to 54	48.3	12.0	23.9	12.4	51.7
Aged 55 to 64	50.6	18.3	18.5	13.8	49.4

Source: Employee Benefit Research Institute, "401(k)-Type Plan and IRA Ownership," by Craig Copeland, Notes, Vol. 26, No. 1, January 2005, Internet site http://www.ebri.org/

Table 10.12 Amount Saved in IRAs and 401(k)s by Age, 2002

(percentage of workers aged 21 to 64 owning an IRA or participating in a 401(k)-type plan, and average and median balance of IRA and 401(k), by age, 2002)

	percent owning IRA	IRA balance		percent participating in 401(k)	401(k) balance	
		average	median		average	median
Total workers	**18.7%**	**$26,951**	**$10,000**	**30.9%**	**$33,647**	**$14,000**
Aged 21 to 24	2.3	3,841	2,000	9.1	4,641	2,500
Aged 25 to 34	11.4	10,146	5,000	28.6	12,067	6,000
Aged 35 to 44	18.7	21,235	9,000	33.9	32,026	15,000
Aged 45 to 54	24.5	29,600	13,000	36.3	44,829	20,000
Aged 55 to 64	32.1	42,003	19,000	32.3	53,184	25,000

Source: Employee Benefit Research Institute, "401(k)-Type Plan and IRA Ownership," by Craig Copeland, Notes, Vol. 26, No. 1, January 2005, Internet site http://www.ebri.org/

Table 10.13 Retirement Planning by Age, 2005

(percentage of workers aged 25 or older responding by age, 2005)

	total	25 to 34	35 to 44	45 to 54	55 or older
Very confident in having enough money to live comfortably throughout retirement	25%	26%	25%	26%	20%
Very confident in having enough money to take care of medical expenses in retirement	20	21	19	20	19
Worker and/or spouse have saved for retirement	69	60	71	73	71
Worker and/or spouse are currently saving for retirement	62	53	67	65	66
Contribute to a workplace retirement savings plan	42	40	44	45	36
Have an IRA opened with money saved outside of an employer's retirement plan	31	25	27	38	38
Expected retirement age					
Less than 60	16	24	15	14	6
Aged 60 to 64	19	15	14	20	31
Aged 65	26	28	30	25	19
Aged 66 or older	24	19	28	26	24
Never retire	6	6	4	8	8
Don't know/refused	9	9	8	7	11
Expected sources of income in retirement					
Money from a workplace retirement savings plan	69	79	73	66	51
Money from a defined-benefit plan	33	34	37	29	33
Largest expected source of income in retirement					
A workplace retirement savings plan, such as a 401(k)	21	26	27	15	12
Other personal savings such as an IRA	18	22	17	19	15
Social Security	18	7	16	22	33
Employer-provided pension that pays a set amount each month for life	16	12	15	18	20
Employment	14	26	14	10	5
Sale or refinancing of your home	3	1	3	3	6
An inheritance	3	2	5	2	2
Other/don't know	6	4	4	11	7
Total savings and investments (not including value of primary residence)					
Less than $25,000	52	70	50	41	39
$25,000 to $49,999	13	12	15	14	12
$50,000 to $99,999	11	9	14	13	7
$100,000 to $249,999	12	5	10	17	23
$250,000 or more	11	4	10	16	19

Source: 2005 Retirement Confidence Survey, Employee Benefit Research Institute, American Savings Education Council, and Mathew Greenwald & Associates; Internet site http://www.ebri.org/surveys/rcs/

Glossary

adjusted for inflation Income or a change in income that has been adjusted for the rise in the cost of living, or the consumer price index (CPI-U-RS).

age Classification by age is based on the age of the person at his/her last birthday.

American Freshman Survey This is an annual survey taken each fall of students entering American colleges and universities as first-time, full-time freshmen. Initiated in Fall 1966, the survey is a project of the Cooperative Institutional Research Program sponsored by the American Council on Education and the Graduate School of Education & Information Studies at the University of California, Los Angeles. Survey results are based on the answers to the Student Information Form filled out by nearly 300,000 freshmen at more than 400 baccalaureate institutions during registration, freshman orientation, or the first few weeks of classes. Results are weighted to provide a normative picture of the American college freshman population.

American Housing Survey The AHS collects national and metropolitan-level data on the nation's housing, including apartments, single-family homes, and mobile homes. The nationally representative survey, with a sample of 55,000 homes, is conducted by the Census Bureau for the Department of Housing and Urban Development every other year.

American Indians In this book, American Indians include Alaska Natives (Eskimos and Aleuts) unless those groups are shown separately.

American Religious Identification Survey The 2001 ARIS, sponsored by the Graduate Center of the City University of New York, was based on a random telephone survey of 50,281 households in the continental U.S. Interviewers asked respondents aged 18 or older for their demographic characteristics and their religion. The 2001 ARIS updates the 1990 National Survey of Religious Identification.

American Time Use Survey Under contract with the Bureau of Labor Statistics, the Census Bureau collects ATUS information, revealing how people spend their time. The ATUS sample is drawn from U.S. households that have completed their final month of interviews for the Current Population Survey. One individual from each selected household is chosen to participate in the ATUS. Respondents are interviewed by telephone only once about their time use on the previous day. In 2003, the sample consisted of approximately 3,000 cases each month, which yielded about 1,700 completed interviews.

Asian The term "Asian" includes Native Hawaiians and other Pacific Islanders unless those groups are shown separately.

Baby Boom Americans born between 1946 and 1964.

Baby Bust Americans born between 1965 and 1976, also known as Generation X.

Behavioral Risk Factor Surveillance System The BRFSS is a collaborative project of the Centers for Disease Control and Prevention and U.S. states and territories. It is an ongoing data collection program designed to measure behavioral risk factors in the adult population aged 18 or older. All 50 states, three territories, and the District of Columbia take part in the survey, making the BRFSS the primary source of information on the health-related behaviors of Americans.

black The black racial category includes those who identified themselves as "black" or "African American."

central cities The largest city in a metropolitan area is called the central city. The balance of the metropolitan area outside the central city is regarded as the "suburbs."

Consumer Expenditure Survey The Consumer Expenditure Survey (CEX) is an ongoing study of the day-to-day spending of American households administered by the Bureau of Labor Statistics. The CEX includes an interview survey and a diary survey. The average spending figures shown in this book are the integrated data from both the diary and interview components of the survey. Two separate, nationally representative samples are used for the interview and diary surveys. For the interview survey, about 7,500 consumer units are interviewed on a rotating panel basis each quarter for five consecutive quarters. For the diary survey, 7,500 consumer units keep weekly diaries of spending for two consecutive weeks.

consumer unit *(on spending tables only)* For convenience, the term consumer unit and households are used interchangeably in the spending section of this book, although consumer units are somewhat different from the Census Bureau's households. Consumer units are all related members of a household, or financially independent members of a household. A household may include more than one consumer unit.

Current Population Survey The CPS is a nationally representative survey of the civilian noninstitutional population aged 15 or older. It is taken monthly by the Census Bureau for the Bureau of Labor Statistics, collecting information from more than 50,000 households on employment and unemployment. In March of each year, the survey includes the Annual Social and Economic Supplement (formerly called the Annual Demographic Survey), which is the source of most national data on the characteristics of Americans, such as educational attainment, living arrangements, and incomes.

disability As defined by the American Community Survey, respondents are asked whether they have a sensory, physical, mental, or self-care disability. Those who answer "yes" are classified as disabled.

disability As defined by the National Health Interview Survey, respondents aged 18 or older are asked whether they have difficulty in physical functioning, probing whether they can perform nine activities by themselves without using special equipment. The categories are walking a quarter mile; standing for two hours; sitting for two hours; walking up 10 steps without resting; stooping, bending, kneeling; reaching over one's head; grasping or handling small objects; carrying a 10-pound object; and pushing/pulling a large object. Adults who report that any of these activities is very difficult or they cannot do it at all are defined as having physical difficulties.

disability, work The Current Population Survey defines a work disability as a specific physical or mental condition that prevents an individual from working. The disability must be so severe that it completely incapacitates the individual and prevents him/her from doing any kind of work for at least the next six months.

dual-earner couple A married couple in which both the householder and the householder's spouse are in the labor force.

earnings A type of income, earnings is the amount of money a person receives from his or her job. *See also* Income.

employed All civilians who did any work as a paid employee or farmer/self-employed worker, or who worked 15 hours or more as an unpaid farm worker or in a family-owned business, during the reference period. All those who have jobs but who are temporarily absent from their jobs due to illness, bad weather, vacation, labor management dispute, or personal reasons are considered employed.

expenditure The transaction cost including excise and sales taxes of goods and services acquired during the survey period. The full cost of each purchase is recorded even though full payment may not have been made at the date of purchase. Average expenditure figures may be artificially low for infrequently purchased items such as cars because figures are calculated using all consumer units within a demographic segment rather than just purchasers. Expenditure estimates include money spent on gifts for others.

family A group of two or more people (one of whom is the householder) related by birth, marriage, or adoption and living in the same household.

family household A household maintained by a householder who lives with one or more people related to him or her by blood, marriage, or adoption.

female/male householder A woman or man who maintains a household without a spouse present. May head family or nonfamily households.

foreign-born population People who are not United States citizens at birth.

full-time employment Full-time is 35 or more hours of work per week during a majority of the weeks worked.

full-time, year-round Indicates 50 or more weeks of full-time employment during the previous calendar year.

Generation X Americans born between 1965 and 1976, also known as the baby-bust generation.

Hispanic Because Hispanic is an ethnic origin rather than a race, Hispanics may be of any race. While most Hispanics are white, there are black, Asian, and American Indian Hispanics.

household All the persons who occupy a housing unit. A household includes the related family members and all the unrelated persons, if any, such as lodgers, foster children, wards, or employees who share the housing unit. A person living alone is counted as a household. A group of unrelated people who share a housing unit as roommates or unmarried partners is also counted as a household. Households do not include group quarters such as college dormitories, prisons, or nursing homes.

household, race/ethnicity of Households are categorized according to the race or ethnicity of the householder only.

householder The householder is the person (or one of the persons) in whose name the housing unit is owned or rented or, if there is no such person, any adult member. With married couples, the householder may be either the husband or wife. The householder is the reference person for the household.

householder, age of The age of the householder is used to categorize households into age groups such as those used in this book. Married couples, for example, are classified according to the age of either the husband or wife, depending on which one identified him or herself as the householder.

housing unit A housing unit is a house, an apartment, a group of rooms, or a single room occupied or intended for occupancy as separate living quarters. Separate living quarters are those in which the occupants do not live and eat with any other persons in the structure and that have direct access from the outside of the building or through a common hall that is used or intended for use by the occupants of another unit or by the general public. The occupants may be a single family, one person living alone, two or more families living together, or any other group of related or unrelated persons who share living arrangements.

Housing Vacancy Survey The HVS is a supplement to the Current Population Survey, providing quarterly and annual data on rental and homeowner vacancy rates, characteristics of units available for occupancy, and homeownership rates by age, household type,

region, state, and metropolitan area. The Current Population Survey sample includes 51,000 occupied housing units and 9,000 vacant units.

housing value The respondent's estimate of how much his or her house and lot would sell for if it were for sale.

immigration The relatively permanent movement (change of residence) of people into the country of reference.

income Money received in the preceding calendar year by each person aged 15 or older from each of the following sources: (1) earnings from longest job (or self-employment); (2) earnings from jobs other than longest job; (3) unemployment compensation; (4) workers' compensation; (5) Social Security; (6) Supplemental Security income; (7) public assistance; (8) veterans' payments; (9) survivor benefits; (10) disability benefits; (11) retirement pensions; (12) interest; (13) dividends; (14) rents and royalties or estates and trusts; (15) educational assistance; (16) alimony; (17) child support; (18) financial assistance from outside the household, and other periodic income. Income is reported in several ways in this book. Household income is the combined income of all household members. Income of persons is all income accruing to a person from all sources. Earnings are the money a person receives from his or her job.

industry Refers to the industry in which a person worked longest in the preceding calendar year.

job tenure The length of time a person has been employed continuously by the same employer.

labor force The labor force tables in this book show the civilian labor force only. The labor force includes both the employed and the unemployed (people who are looking for work). People are counted as in the labor force if they were working or looking for work during the reference week in which the Census Bureau fields the Current Population Survey.

labor force participation rate The percent of the civilian noninstitutional population that is in the civilian labor force, which includes both the employed and the unemployed.

married couples with or without children under age 18 Refers to married couples with or without own children under age 18 living in the same household. Couples without children under age 18 may be parents of grown children who live elsewhere, or they could be childless couples.

median The median is the amount that divides the population or households into two equal portions: one below and one above the median. Medians can be calculated for income, age, and many other characteristics.

median income The amount that divides the income distribution into two equal groups, half having incomes above the median, half having incomes below the median. The medians for households or families are based on all households or families. The median for persons are based on all persons aged 15 or older with income.

Medical Expenditure Panel Survey MEPS is a nationally representative survey that collects detailed information on the health status, access to care, health care use and expenses and health insurance coverage of the civilian noninstitutionalized population of the U.S. and nursing home residents. MEPS comprises four component surveys: the Household Component, the Medical Provider Component, the Insurance Component, and the Nursing Home Component. The Household Component, which is the core survey, is conducted each year and includes 15,000 households and 37,000 people.

metropolitan statistical area To be defined as a metropolitan statistical area (or MSA), an area must include a city with 50,000 or more inhabitants, or a Census Bureau-defined urbanized area of at least 50,000 inhabitants and a total metropolitan population of at least 100,000 (75,000 in New England). The county (or counties) that contains the largest city becomes the "central county" (counties), along with any adjacent counties that have at least 50 percent of their population in the urbanized area surrounding the largest city. Additional "outlying counties" are included in the MSA if they meet specified requirements of commuting to the central counties and other selected requirements of metropolitan character (such as population density and percent urban). In New England, MSAs are defined in terms of cities and towns rather than counties. For this reason, the concept of NECMA is used to define metropolitan areas in the New England division.

Millennial generation Americans born between 1977 and 1994.

mobility status People are classified according to their mobility status on the basis of a comparison between their place of residence at the time of the March Current Population Survey and their place of residence in March of the previous year. Nonmovers are people living in the same house at the end of the period as at the beginning of the period. Movers are people living in a different house at the end of the period than at the beginning of the period. Movers from abroad are either citizens or aliens whose place of residence is outside the United States at the beginning of the period, that is, in an outlying area under the jurisdiction of the United States or in a foreign country. The mobility status for children is fully allocated from the mother if she is in the household; otherwise it is allocated from the householder.

Monitoring the Future Project The MTF survey is conducted by the University of Michigan Survey Research Center. The survey is administered to approximately 50,000 students in 420 public and private secondary schools every year. High school seniors have been surveyed annually since 1975. Students in 8th and 10th grade have been surveyed annually since 1991.

National Ambulatory Medical Care Survey The NAMCS is an annual survey of visits to nonfederally employed office-based physicians who are primarily engaged in direct patient care. Data are collected from physicians rather than patients, with each physician assigned a one-week reporting period. During that week, a systematic random sample of visit characteristics are recorded by the physician or office staff.

National Crime Victimization Survey The NCVS collects data each year on nonfatal crimes against people age 12 or older, reported and not reported to the police, from a nationally representative sample of 42,000 households and 76,000 persons in the United States. The NCVS provides information about victims, offenders, and criminal offenses.

National Health and Nutrition Examination Survey The NHANES is a continuous survey of a representative sample of the U.S. civilian noninstitutionalized population. Respondents are interviewed at home about their health and nutrition, and the interview is followed up by a physical examination that measures such things as height and weight in mobile examination centers.

National Health Interview Survey The NHIS is a continuing nationwide sample survey of the civilian noninstitutional population of the U.S. conducted by the Census Bureau for the National Center for Health Statistics. Each year, data are collected from more than 100,000 people about their illnesses, injuries, impairments, chronic and acute conditions, activity limitations, and the use of health services.

National Home and Hospice Care Survey These are a series of surveys of a nationally representative sample of home and hospice care agencies in the U.S., sponsored by the National Center for Health Statistics. Data on the characteristics of patients and services provided are collected through personal interviews with administrators and staff.

National Hospital Ambulatory Medical Care Survey The NHAMCS, sponsored by the National Center for Health Statistics, is an annual national probability sample survey of visits to emergency departments and outpatient departments at non-Federal, short stay and general hospitals. Data are collected by hospital staff from patient records.

National Hospital Discharge Survey This survey has been conducted annually since 1965, sponsored by the National Center for Health Statistics, to collect nationally representative information on the characteristics of inpatients discharged from nonfederal, short-stay hospitals in the U.S. The survey collects data from a sample of approximately 270,000 inpatient records acquired from a national sample of about 500 hospitals.

National Household Education Survey The NHES, sponsored by the National Center for Education Statistics, provides descriptive data on the educational activities of the U.S. population, including after-school care and adult education. The NHES is a system of telephone surveys of a representative sample of 45,000 to 60,000 households in the U.S. It has been conducted in 1991, 1993, 1995, 1996, 1999, 2001, and 2003.

National Nursing Home Survey This is a series of national sample surveys of nursing homes, their residents, and staff conducted at various intervals since 1973-74 and sponsored by the National Center for Health Statistics. The latest survey was taken in 1999. data for the survey are obtained through personal interviews with administrators and staff, and

occasionally with self-administered questionnaires, in a sample of about 1,500 facilities.

National Survey of Family Growth The 2002 NSFG, sponsored by the National Center for Health Statistics, is a nationally representative survey of the civilian noninstitutional population aged 15 to 44. In-person interviews were completed with 12,571 men and women, collecting data on marriage, divorce, contraception, and infertility. The 2002 survey updates previous NSFG surveys taken in 1973, 1976, 1988, and 1995.

National Survey on Drug Use and Health *(formerly called the National Household Survey on Drug Abuse)* This survey, sponsored by the Substance Abuse and Mental Health Services Administration, has been conducted since 1971. It is the primary source of information on the use of illegal drugs by the U.S. population. Each year, a nationally representative sample of about 70,000 individuals aged 12 or older are surveyed in the 50 states and the District of Columbia.

net worth The amount of money left over after a household's debts are subtracted from its assets.

nonfamily household A household maintained by a householder who lives alone or who lives with people to whom he or she is not related.

nonfamily householder A householder who lives alone or with nonrelatives.

non-Hispanic People who do not identify themselves as Hispanic are classified as non-Hispanic. Non-Hispanics may be of any race.

non-Hispanic white People who identify their race as white and who do not indicate a Hispanic origin.

nonmetropolitan area Counties that are not classified as metropolitan areas.

occupation Occupational classification is based on the kind of work a person did at his or her job during the previous calendar year. If a person changed jobs during the year, the data refer to the occupation of the job held the longest during that year.

occupied housing units A housing unit is classified as occupied if a person or group of people is living in it or if the occupants are only temporarily absent—on vacation, example. By definition, the count of occupied housing units is the same as the count of households.

outside central city The portion of a metropolitan county or counties that falls outside of the central city or cities; generally regarded as the suburbs.

own children Own children are sons and daughters, including stepchildren and adopted children, of the householder. The totals include never-married children living away from home in college dormitories.

owner occupied A housing unit is "owner occupied" if the owner lives in the unit, even if it is mortgaged or not fully paid for. A cooperative or condominium unit is "owner occupied" only if the owner lives in it. All other occupied units are classified as "renter occupied."

part-time employment Part-time is less than 35 hours of work per week in a majority of the weeks worked during the year.

percent change The change (either positive or negative) in a measure that is expressed as a proportion of the starting measure. When median income changes from $20,000 to $25,000, for example, this is a 25 percent increase.

percentage point change The change (either positive or negative) in a value which is already expressed as a percentage. When a labor force participation rate changes from 70 percent of 75 percent, for example, this is a 5 percentage point increase.

poverty level The official income threshold below which families and people are classified as living in poverty. The threshold rises each year with inflation and varies depending on family size and age of householder.

primary activity In the time use tables, primary activities are those that respondents identify as their main activity. Other activities done simultaneously are not included.

proportion or share The value of a part expressed as a percentage of the whole. If there are 4 million people aged 25 and 3 million of them are white, then the white proportion is 75 percent.

race Race is self-reported and can be defined in three ways. The "race alone" population comprises people who identify themselves as only one race. The "race in combination" population comprises people who identify themselves as more than one race, such as white and black. The "race, alone or in combination"

population includes both those who identify themselves as one race and those who identify themselves as more than one race.

regions The four major regions and nine census divisions of the United States are the state groupings as shown below:

Northeast:
—New England: Connecticut, Maine, Massachusetts, New Hampshire, Rhode Island, and Vermont
—Middle Atlantic: New Jersey, New York, and Pennsylvania

Midwest:
—East North Central: Illinois, Indiana, Michigan, Ohio, and Wisconsin
—West North Central: Iowa, Kansas, Minnesota, Missouri, Nebraska, North Dakota, and South Dakota

South:
—South Atlantic: Delaware, District of Columbia, Florida, Georgia, Maryland, North Carolina, South Carolina, Virginia, and West Virginia
—East South Central: Alabama, Kentucky, Mississippi, and Tennessee
—West South Central: Arkansas, Louisiana, Oklahoma, and Texas

West:
—Mountain: Arizona, Colorado, Idaho, Montana, Nevada, New Mexico, Utah, and Wyoming
—Pacific: Alaska, California, Hawaii, Oregon, and Washington

renter occupied *See* Owner occupied.

Retirement Confidence Survey The RCS, sponsored by the Employee Benefit Research Institute (EBRI), the American Savings Education Council (ASEC), and Mathew Greenwald & Associates (Greenwald), is an annual survey of a nationally representative sample of 1,000 people aged 25 or older. Respondents are asked a core set of questions that have been asked since 1996, measuring attitudes and behavior towards retirement. Additional questions are also asked about current retirement issues such as 401(k) participation.

rounding Percentages are rounded to the nearest tenth of a percent; therefore, the percentages in a distribution do not always add exactly to 100.0 percent. The totals, however, are always shown as

100.0. Moreover, individual figures are rounded to the nearest thousand without being adjusted to group totals, which are independently rounded; percentages are based on the unrounded numbers.

self-employment A person is categorized as self-employed if he or she was self-employed in the job held longest during the reference period. Persons who report self-employment from a second job are excluded, but those who report wage-and-salary income from a second job are included. Unpaid workers in family businesses are excluded. Self-employment statistics include only nonagricultural workers and exclude people who work for themselves in incorporated business.

sex ratio The number of men per 100 women.

suburbs See Outside central city.

Survey of Consumer Finances The Survey of Consumer Finances is a triennial survey taken by the Federal Reserve Board. It collects data on the assets, debts, and net worth of American households. For the 2004 survey, the Federal Reserve Board interviewed more than 4,000 households.

Survey of Public Participation in the Arts Initiated in 1982 by the National Endowment for the Arts, this survey examines the public's participation in the performing arts, visual arts, historic site visits, music, and literature. The 2002 survey is the fifth (earlier surveys were in 1982, 1985, 1992, and 1997) and was conducted as a supplement to the Current Population Survey. More than 17,000 respondents to the August 2002 Current Population Survey were asked about their arts participation and involvement.

unemployed Unemployed people are those who, during the survey period, had no employment but were available and looking for work. Those who were laid off from their jobs and were waiting to be recalled are also classified as unemployed.

white The "white" racial category includes many Hispanics (who may be of any race) unless the term "non-Hispanic white" is used.

Youth Risk Behavior Surveillance System The YRBSS was created by the Centers for Disease Control to monitor health risks being taken by young people at the national, state, and local level. The national survey is taken every two years based on a nationally representative sample of 16,000 students in 9th through 12th grade in public and private schools.

Bibliography

Agency for Healthcare Research and Quality
    Internet site http://www.ahrq.gov/
    —Medical Expenditure Panel Survey, Internet site http://www.meps.ahrq.gov/
    CompendiumTables/TC_TOC.htm

Bureau of Justice Statistics
    Internet site http://www.ojp.usdoj.gov/bjs/welcome.html
    —*Criminal Victimization 2004*, Internet site http://www.ojp.usdoj.gov/bjs/abstract/cv04.htm
    —Sourcebook of Criminal Justice Statistics Online, Internet site http://www.albany.edu/
    sourcebook

Bureau of Labor Statistics
    Internet site http://www.bls.gov
    —American Time Use Survey, Internet site http://www.bls.gov/tus/home.htm and unpub-
    lished data
    —Characteristics of Minimum Wage Workers, Internet site http://www.bls.gov/cps/
    minwage2004.htm
    —Consumer Expenditure Survey, Internet site http://www.bls.gov/cex/
    —Contingent and Alternative Employment Arrangements, Internet site http://www.bls
    .gov/news.release/conemp.toc.htm
    —Current Population Survey, Internet site http://www.bls.gov/cps/home.htm and unpub-
    lished data
    —Employee Tenure, Internet site http://www.bls.gov/news.release/tenure.toc.htm
    —Employment Characteristics of Families, Internet site http://www.bls.gov/news.release/
    famee.toc.htm
    —Labor force participation rates, historical, Public Query Data Tool, Internet site http://
    www.bls.gov/data
    —Labor force projections, 2004–2014, Internet site http://www.bls.gov/emp/emplab1.htm
    —Statistical Abstract of the United States: 2006, Internet site, http://www.census.gov/
    statab/www/
    —Volunteering in the United States, Internet site http://www.bls.gov/news.release/volun
    .toc.htm
    —Workers on Flexible and Shift Schedules, Internet site http://www.bls.gov/news.release/
    flex.toc.htm

Bureau of the Census
    Internet site http://www.census.gov
    —*Adopted Children and Stepchildren: 2000*, Census 2000 Special Reports, CENSR-GRV, 2003,
    Internet site http://www.census.gov/population/www/cen2000/phc-t21.html
    —American Community Survey, 2004 custom tables, Internet site http://factfinder.census
    .gov/servlet/DatasetMainPageServlet?_program=ACS&_lang=en
    —American Housing Survey National Tables: 2003, Internet site http://www.census.gov/
    hhes/www/housing/ahs/ahs03/ahs03.html
    —America's Families and Living Arrangements: 2004, Internet site http://www.census.gov/
    population/www/socdemo/hh-fam/cps2004.html

—Current Population Survey, Detailed Income Tabulations, 2005 Annual Social and Economic Supplement, Internet site http://www.census.gov/hhes/www/income/dinctabs.html

—Current Population Survey, Historical Income Tables, Internet site http://www.census.gov/hhes/income/histinc/histinctb.html

—Disability, 2003, Internet site http://www.census.gov/hhes/www/disability/data_title.html#2003

—Educational Attainment, Historical Tables, Internet site http://www.census.gov/population/www/socdemo/educ-attn.html

—Educational Attainment in the United States: 2004, Detailed Tables, Internet site http://www.census.gov/population/www/socdemo/education/cps2004.html

—Fertility of American Women, Current Population Survey—June 2004, Detailed Tables, Internet site http://www.census.gov/population/www/socdemo/fertility/cps2004.html

—Foreign Born Population of the United States, Current Population Survey—March 2004, Detailed Tables, (PPL-176), Internet site http://www.census.gov/population/www/socdemo/foreign/ppl-176.html

—Geographic Mobility: 2004, Detailed Tables, Internet site http://www.census.gov/population/www/socdemo/migrate/cps2004.html

—Health Insurance Coverage: 2004, Internet site http://pubdb3.census.gov/macro/032005/health/toc.htm

—Housing Vacancy Survey, Annual Statistics: 2005, Internet site http://www.census.gov/hhes/www/housing/hvs/annual05/ann05ind.html

—National and State Population Estimates, Internet site http://www.census.gov/popest/states/NST-ann-est.html

—Population Estimates by State, Internet site http://www.census.gov/popest/states/asrh/SC-est2004-02.html

—Poverty, Detailed Tables, Internet site http://pubdb3.census.gov/macro/032005/pov/toc.htm

—School Enrollment, Historical Tables, Internet site http://www.census.gov/population/www/socdemo/school.html

—School Enrollment—Social and Economic Characteristics of Students: October 2004, Internet site http://www.census.gov/population/www/socdemo/school/cps2004.html

—State Interim Population Projections by Age and Sex, Internet site http://www.census.gov/population/www/projections/projectionsagesex.html

—U.S. Interim Projections by Age, Sex, Race, and Hispanic Origin; Internet site http://www.census.gov/ipc/www/usinterimproj/

—Voting and Registration, Historical Time Series Tables, Internet site http://www.census.gov/population/www/socdemo/voting.html

—Voting and Registration in the Election of November 2004, Detailed Tables, Internet site http://www.census.gov/population/www/socdemo/voting/cps2004.html

Centers for Disease Control and Prevention
Internet site http://www.cdc.gov

—Behavioral Risk Factor Surveillance System Prevalence Data, Internet site http://apps.nccd.cdc.gov/brfss/index.asp

—"Youth Risk Behavior Surveillance–United States, 2003," *Mortality and Morbidity Weekly Report*, Vol. 53/SS-2, May 21, 2004; Internet site http://www.cdc.gov/mmwr/indss_2004.html

Employee Benefit Research Institute

    Internet site http://www.ebri.org/

    —"401(k)-Type Plan and IRA Ownership," Craig Copeland, *Notes*, Vol. 26, No. 1, January 2005

    —"Employment-Based Retirement Plan Participation: Geographic Differences and Trends, 2004," *Issue Brief*, No. 286, October 2005

    —"Income and the Elderly Population, Age 65 and Over, 2004," by Ken McDonnell, *Notes*, Vol. 27, No. 1, January 2006

Employee Benefit Research Institute, American Savings Education Council, and Mathew Greenwald & Associates

    Internet site http://www.ebri.org/

    —2005 Retirement Confidence Survey, Internet site http://www.ebri.org/surveys/rcs/2005/

Federal Interagency Forum on Child and Family Statistics

    Internet site http://www.childstats.gov/index.asp

    —America's Children: Key National Indicators of Well-Being, Internet site http://www.childstats.gov/americaschildren/index.asp

Federal Reserve Board

    Internet site http://www.federalreserve.gov/

    —"Recent Changes in U.S. Family Finances: Evidence from the 2001 and 2004 Survey of Consumer Finances," Federal Reserve Board, Internet site http://www.federalreserve.gov/pubs/oss/oss2/2004/scf2004home.html

Graduate Center of the City University of New York

    Internet site http://www.gc.cuny.edu/index.htm

    —American Religious Identification Survey 2001, Egon Mayer, Barry A. Kosmin, and Ariela Keysar, Internet site http://www.gc.cuny.edu/faculty/research_briefs/aris/aris_index.htm

Higher Education Research Institute

    Internet site http://www.gseis.ucla.edu/heri/whatis.html

    —*The American Freshman: National Norms for Fall 2005*, John H. Pryor, Sylvia Hurtado, Victor B. Saenz, Jennifer A. Lindholm, William S. Korn, and Kathryn M. Mahoney, Higher Education Research Institute, UCLA, 2005, Internet site http://www.gseis.ucla.edu/heri/american_freshman.html

Institute for Social Research, University of Michigan

    Internet site http://www.isr.umich.edu/

    —Monitoring the Future Survey, Internet site http://monitoringthefuture.org/index.html

National Center for Education Statistics

    Internet site http://nces.ed.gov

    —Digest of Education Statistics, 2004, Internet site http://nces.ed.gov/programs/digest/d04_tf.asp

National Center for Health Statistics

    Internet site http://www.cdc.gov/nchs

    —2003 *National Hospital Discharge Survey*, Advance Data, No. 359, 2005, Internet site http://www.cdc.gov/nchs/about/major/hdasd/listpubs.htm

—*1999 National Nursing Home Survey*, Internet site http://www.cdc.gov/nchs/nnhs.htm

—*Births: Final Data for 2003*, National Vital Statistics Reports, Vol. 54, No. 2, 2005, Internet site http://www.cdc.gov/nchs/products/pubs/pubd/nvsr/54/54-pre.htm

—*Births: Preliminary Data for 2004*, National Vital Statistics Reports, Vol. 54, No. 8, 2005, Internet site http://www.cdc.gov/nchs/products/pubs/pubd/nvsr/54/54-pre.htm

—*Characteristics of Hospice Care Discharges and Their Length of Service: United States, 2000*, Vital and Health Statistics, Series 13, No. 154, 2003; Internet site http://www.cdc.gov/nchs/pressroom/03facts/hospicecare.htm

—*Deaths: Final Data for 2002*, National Vital Statistics Reports, Vol. 53, No. 5, 2004, Internet site http://www.cdc.gov/nchs/about/major/dvs/mortdata.htm

—*Deaths: Preliminary Data for 2003*, National Vital Statistics Reports, Vol. 53, No. 15, 2005, Internet site http://www.cdc.gov/nchs/products/pubs/pubd/nvsr/53/53-21.htm

—*Fertility, Family Planning, and Reproductive Health of U.S. Women: Data from the 2002 National Survey of Family Growth*, Vital and Health Statistics, Series 23, No. 25, 2005; Internet site http://www.cdc.gov/nchs/nsfg.htm

—*Health, United States, 2005*, Internet site http://www.cdc.gov/nchs/hus.htm

—*Mean Body Weight, Height, and Body Mass Index, United States 1960–2002*, Advance Data, No. 347, 2004, Internet site http://www.cdc.gov/nchs/pressroom/04news/americans.htm

—*National Ambulatory Medical Care Survey: 2003 Summary*, Advance Data No. 365, 2005, Internet site http://www.cdc.gov/nchs/about/major/ahcd/adata.htm

—*National Hospital Ambulatory Medical Care Survey: 2003 Emergency Department Summary*, Advance Data No. 358, 2005, Internet site http://www.cdc.gov/nchs/about/major/ahcd/adata.htm

—*National Hospital Ambulatory Medical Care Survey: 2003 Outpatient Department Summary*, Advance Data, No. 366, 2005, Internet site http://www.cdc.gov/nchs/about/major/ahcd/adata.htm

—*Revised Birth and Fertility Rates for the 1990s and New Rates for the Hispanic Populations 2000 and 2001: United States*, National Vital Statistics Reports, Vol. 51, No. 12, 2003

—*Sexual Behavior and Selected Health Measures: Men and Women 15-44 Years of Age, United States, 2002*, Advance Data, No. 362, 2005; Internet site http://www.cdc.gov/nchs/nsfg.htm

—*Summary Health Statistics for U.S. Adults: National Health Interview Survey, 2003*, Vital and Health Statistics, Series 10, No. 225, 2005; Internet site http://www.cdc.gov/nchs/nhis.htm

—*Summary Health Statistics for U.S. Children: National Health Interview Survey, 2004*, Vital and Health Statistics, Series 10, No. 227, 2003; Internet site http://www.cdc.gov/nchs/nhis.htm

—*Teenagers in the United States: Sexual Activity, Contraceptive Use, and Childbearing, 2002*; Vital and Health Statistics, Series 23, No. 24, 2004; Internet site http://www.cdc.gov/nchs/nsfg.htm

National Endowment for the Arts
Internet site http://www.arts.endow.gov/
—*2002 Survey of Public Participation in the Arts: Summary Report*, Research Division Report No. 45, Internet site http://www.nea.gov/pub/ResearchReports_chrono.html

National Sporting Goods Association
Internet site http://www.nsga.org
—Sports Participation, Internet site http://www.nsga.org/public/pages/index.cfm?pageid=158

Office of Immigration Statistics
  —2004 Yearbook of Immigration Statistics, Internet site http://uscis.gov/graphics/shared/statistics/index.htm

Pew Internet & American Life Project
  Internet site http://www.pewinternet.org
  —Latest Trends, Internet site http://www.pewinternet.org/trends.asp#usage

Pew Research Center
  Internet site http://people-press.org/
  —"Families Drawn Together by Communications Revolution," February 21, 2006

Substance Abuse and Mental Health Services Administration
  Internet site http://www.samhsa.gov/
  —National Survey on Drug Use and Health, Internet site http://oas.samhsa.gov/nsduh.htm

Index

computer:
time spent playing on, 276–277
use, 280–281
congenital malformations, as cause of death, 77
contractors. *See* Independent contractors.
coronary, 61, 63, 65
credit card debt, 308, 310
crime, 292–293

death, causes of, 76–77
debt, household, 308–310
diabetes:
as cause of death, 77
health condition, 61, 63, 65
dieting, 30, 32
disability:
benefits, as source of income, 139–142
work, 60, 67
dividends, as source of income, 139–142
divorce, 210–216
doctor visits. *See* Physician visits.
drinking, alcoholic beverages, 50–51
drugs:
illicit, use of, 52–53
prescription, 69–71
spending on, 69, 71, 248–262
dual-income couples, 154–155

earnings: *See also* Income.
as source of income, 138–142
by educational attainment, 129–137
minimum wage, 173–174
of full-time workers, 129–137
eating, time spent, 264–267
education:
adult, 24–25
spending on, 248–262
time spent, 265–267
educational assistance, as source of income, 139–142
educational attainment:
by race and Hispanic origin, 16–19
by sex, 6–8, 10, 12–19
earnings by, 129–137
work disability status by, 60, 67
email, 280–281
emergency department visits, 72, 75
emphysema, 61, 63, 65

employment. *See* Labor force.
employment-based health insurance, 54, 56, 58
employment, long-term, 166, 168
English speakers, 231–232
entertainment, spending on, 248–262
exercise:
participation in, 30, 33
percent participating in, 296
time spent, 265–267

face pain, 61, 63, 65
families. *See* Households.
family, as a reason for moving, 96, 98
female-headed household. *See* Households, female-headed.
food:
preparation and cleanup, time spent, 273–274
spending on, 248–262
foreign-born:
by country of birth, 226, 228
citizenship status, 226–227
population, 226–228
women giving birth, 40, 42
full-time workers, 117–137, 162–163
furnishings and equipment, spending on, 248–262

gardening, percent participating in, 296
gasoline, spending on, 248–262
geographic mobility. *See* Mobility, geographic.
gifts, spending on, 248–262
government health insurance, 54–55, 57. *See also* Medicaid and Medicare.
grandchildren, percent with, 278–279
grandparents, percent with living, 278–279
grooming, time spent, 268, 270

hay fever, 61, 63, 65
headaches, 60–61, 63, 65
health care:
rating of, 72, 75
spending on, 54, 59, 69, 71, 248–262
health care visits. *See* Physician visits, Hospital outpatient visits, and Hospital emergency visits.
health conditions, 60–66, 68

health insurance:
    coverage, 54–58
    reason for no coverage, 54, 59
    spending on, 248–262
health status, 28–29
hearing impairments, 61, 63, 65
heart disease:
    as cause of death, 76–77
    health condition, 61, 63, 65
high blood pressure. *See* Hypertension.
Hispanic Americans:
    births to, 40, 42–44, 46–47
    by region, 236
    by state, 233, 245–246
    educational attainment, 16–19
    employment status, 150–153
    full-time workers, 117, 121, 123, 127
    homeownership of, 86–87
    household income, 104, 107
    household type, 182–183, 188–189, 196, 199
    households with children, 196, 199
    in poverty, 143–144
    marital status, 212, 215
    men's income, 117, 121
    population, 223–225, 233, 236, 245–246
    women's income, 123, 127
homeowners:
    by household type, 84–85
    by race and Hispanic origin, 86–87
    by value of home, 94–95, 298, 304, 306–307
    housing costs of, 92–93
    in new housing, 90–91
    number of, 82–83
    trends in, 80–81
homes, as nonfinancial assets, 298, 304, 306–307
home-secured debt, 298, 304, 307–308, 310
homicide, as a cause of death, 76–77
homosexuality, 34, 37
hospital emergency visits, 72, 74
hospital outpatient visits, 72, 75
housecleaning, time spent, 273, 275
household services, spending on, 248–262
households: *See also* Households, female-headed; Households, male-headed; Households, married-couple; and Households, single-person.
    assets of, 298–307
    by race and Hispanic origin, 182–191, 196–200

by type, 180–191, 194–206
    debt of, 298, 308–310
    income of, 109–113
    size, 192–193
    wealth of, 298–299
    with children, 194–206
households, female-headed:
    by race and Hispanic origin, 182–191, 196–200
    by value of home, 95
    homeownership of, 84–85
    housing costs of, 93
    income of, 109–113
    living alone, 180–181
    with children, 194–200, 205–206
households, male-headed:
    by race and Hispanic origin, 182–191, 196–200
    by value of home, 95
    homeownership of, 84–85
    housing costs of, 93
    income of, 109–113
    living alone, 180–181
    with children, 194–200, 205–206
households, married-couple:
    by race and Hispanic origin, 182–191, 196–200
    by value of home, 94–95
    dual-income, 154–155
    homeownership of, 84–85
    housing costs of, 92–93
    income of, 109–113
    with children, 194–200, 203–204
households, single-person:
    by race and Hispanic origin, 182–191
    by sex, 180–191
    by value of home, 95
    homeownership of, 84–85
    housing costs of, 93
    income of, 109–113
housekeeping supplies, spending on, 248–262
housing: *See also* Shelter, Homeowners, and Renters.
    as a reason for moving, 96, 98
    by type of structure, 88–89
    costs of, 92–93
    new, 90–91
    spending on, 248–262
    value of, 94–95, 298, 304, 306–307

human immunodeficiency disease (HIV):
    as cause of death, 76–77
    people with, 60, 68
hypertension, 61, 63, 65

immigrants, 229–230
income: *See also* Earnings.
    by household type, 109–113
    by race and Hispanic origin, 104–108, 117,
        119–123, 125–128
    household, 100–113
    men's, 114–115, 117–122, 138–140
    of full-time workers, 117–128
    source of, 138–142
    trends in, 100–101
    women's, 114, 116, 123–128, 138, 141–142
independent contractors, 169–170
inheritance, as source of income in retirement,
    314
installment debt, 308, 310
insurance, personal, spending on, 248–262.
        See also Life insurance, and Health
        insurance.
interest, as source of income, 138–142
Internet, 280–281
IRAs, 311, 313–314

job: *See also* Occupation.
    as a reason for moving, 96, 98
    long-term, 166, 168
    tenure, 166–167

kidney disease, 61, 63, 65

labor force: *See also* Workers.
    by occupation, 156–161
    by race and Hispanic origin, 150–153
    by sex, 146–153, 177–178
    full-time, 162–163
    participation, 146–153, 177–178
    part-time, 162–163
    projections, 177–178
    self-employed, 164–165
    trends, 146–147, 177–178
    unemployed, 148–153
language spoken at home, 231–232
laundry, time spent, 273, 275
leisure:
    activities, 294–296
    time, 264–267, 276–277

life expectancy, 76, 78
life insurance:
    as financial asset, 302
    consumer spending on, 248–262
liver disease:
    as cause of death, 77
    health condition, 61, 63, 65
living alone. *See* Households, single-person.
living arrangements, 207–209

male-headed households. *See* Households,
    male-headed.
marital status:
    births by, 46–47
    by race and Hispanic origin, 212–216
    by sex, 210–216
    change in, as reason for no health
        insurance, 58
married couples. *See* Households, married-
    couple.
media, percent participating in arts through,
    295
Medicaid, 54, 57–59, 71
Medicare, 54, 57, 59, 71
men:
    earnings by educational attainment,
        129–133
    educational attainment, 6–8, 10, 12–14,
        16–17
    employment, long-term, 166, 168
    exercise, participation in, 33
    full-time workers, 117–122, 129–133,
        162–163
    income, 114–115, 117–122, 138–140
    job tenure of, 166–167
    labor force participation, 146–151, 177–178
    labor force projections, 177–178
    life expectancy, 78
    living alone, 180–191, 208
    living arrangements, 207–208
    marital status, 210–216
    part-time workers, 162–163
    physician visits, 72–73
    population, 220
    prescription drug use, 69–70
    school enrollment, 20–21
    self-employed, 164–165
    sex partners, number of, 34–36
    sexual orientation, 34, 37

women:
    birth rate, 38–39
    births to, 40, 42–49
    children, number of, 40–41
    earnings by educational attainment, 129,
        134–137
    educational attainment, 6–8, 10, 14–15,
        18–19
    employment, long-term, 166, 168
    exercise, participation in, 33
    foreign born, 40, 42
    full-time workers, 123–129, 134–137,
        162–163
    income, 114, 116, 123–128, 138, 141–142
    job tenure of, 166–167
    labor force participation, 146–149, 152–153,
        177–178
    labor force projections, 177–178
    life expectancy, 78
    living alone, 180–191, 209
    living arrangements, 207, 209
    marital status, 210–216
    part-time workers, 162–163
    physician visits, 72–73
    population, 220
    prescription drug use, 69–70
    school enrollment, 20–21
    self-employed, 164–165
    sex partners, number of, 34–36
    sexual orientation, 34, 37
    source of income, 138, 141–142
    telephone contact with parents/children,
        278–279
    time use, 264–277
    unemployed, 148–149, 152–153
    union representation, 175–176
    veterans, 290–291
    volunteers, 265–267, 286–287
    weight, 30–32
    with flexible schedules, 171–172
work:
    arrangements, alternative, 169–170
    time spent at, 264–267

workers: *See also* Labor force and Occupation.
    alternative, 169–170
    compensation, as source of income, 139–142
    contract, 169–170
    disabled, 60, 67
    full-time, 117–137, 162–163
    in unions, 175–176
    independent contractors, 169–170
    minimum wage, 173–174
    on call, 169–170
    part-time, 162–163
    pension coverage of, 311–314
    self-employed, 164–165, 169–170
    shift, 171–172
    temporary, 169–170
    unemployed, 148–153
    with flexible schedules, 171–172